World Politics 13/14

Thirty-Fourth Edition

EDITOR

Robert Weiner

University of Massachusetts—Boston

Dr. Robert Weiner received his PhD in international relations from New York University. He is the Graduate Program Director of International Relations at the University of Massachusetts/Boston, a Center Associate at the Davis Center for Russian and Eurasian Studies at Harvard University, and a Fellow at the Center for Peace, Democracy, and Development at the University of Massachusetts/Boston. His research interests cover theories and concepts of international relations, Eastern Europe, comparative foreign policy, diplomacy and war, genocide, and the European Union and the emerging democracies. He is the author of *Romanian Foreign Policy at the United Nations* (Praeger, 1984) and *Change in Eastern Europe* (Praeger, 1994). He also is the author of a number of book chapters, and his articles have been published in such journals as *Orbis, Problems of Postcommunism, The International and Comparative Law Quarterly, Sudost Europa, Demokratizatsiya,* and *The International Studies Encyclopedia.*

ANNUAL EDITIONS: WORLD POLITICS, THIRTY-FOURTH EDITION

Published by McGraw-Hill, a business unit of The McGraw-Hill Companies, Inc., 1221 Avenue
of the Americas, New York, NY 10020. Copyright © 2014 by The McGraw-Hill Companies, Inc.
All rights reserved. Printed in the United States of America. Previous editions © 2013, 2012,
2011, and 2009. No part of this publication may be reproduced or distributed in any form or by
any means, or stored in a database or retrieval system, without the prior written consent of
The McGraw-Hill Companies, Inc., including, but not limited to, in any network or other electronic
storage or transmission, or broadcast for distance learning.

Some ancillaries, including electronic and print components, may not be available to customers
outside the United States.

This book is printed on acid-free paper.

Annual Editions® is a registered trademark of the McGraw-Hill Companies, Inc.
Annual Editions is published by the **Contemporary Learning Series** group within the
McGraw-Hill Higher Education division.

1 2 3 4 5 6 7 8 9 0 QDB/QDB 1 0 9 8 7 6 5 4 3

ISBN: 978-0-07-8135996
MHID: 0-07-81335990
ISSN: 1098-0300 (print)
ISSN: 2159-0990 (online)

Acquisitions Editor: *Joan L. McNamara*
Marketing Director: *Adam Kloza*
Marketing Manager: *Nathan Edwards*
Senior Developmental Editor: *Jade Benedict*
Senior Project Manager: *Joyce Watters*
Buyer: *Nichole Birkenholz*
Cover Designer: *Studio Montage, St. Louis, MO.*
Senior Content Licensing Specialist: *Shirley Lanners*
Media Project Manager: *Sridevi Palani*

Compositor: Laserwords Private Limited
Cover Image: © Alasdair Drysdale (inset), Nikada/Getty Images (background)

Editors/Academic Advisory Board

Members of the Academic Advisory Board are instrumental in the final selection of articles for each edition of ANNUAL EDITIONS. Their review of articles for content, level, and appropriateness provide critical direction to the editors and staff. We think that you will find their careful consideration well reflected in this volume.

ANNUAL EDITIONS: World Politics 13/14
34th Edition

EDITOR

Robert Weiner
University of Massachusetts–Boston

Preface

The International Political Science Association (IPSA) meeting in Madrid in July 2012 had as its theme the reordering of power and the shifting of boundaries taking place in a globalizing world in which new nonstate actors have engaged in challenging the traditional Westphalian notion of the primacy of the state as the major force in the international system. The concept of state sovereignty, although still an important factor in world politics, is being eroded by the increased salience of nonstate actors (as system affecting actors) in dealing with such problems as global governance, human security, and conflict resolution. The IPSA emphasized the growing importance of subnational governments, regional organizations, multinational corporations, international governmental organizations, and international non-governmental organizations interacting with states and new state configurations of power such as BRICS (Brazil, Russia, India, China, and South Africa) in a complex international system marked by a changing and reconfiguring multipolar structure. For example, the BRICS emerging power center comprises 40 percent of the world's population and has a combined GDP (gross domestic product) equal to 25 percent of the world's GDP, although even the BRICS may not be immune to a global economic slowdown in 2012.

Another example of the reconfiguration of power in the international system has been the significant increase of activities of subnational governments on a global scale. State sovereignty, in the age of globalization and the Internet, is still an objective and normative foundation of international order. But by the latter part of the 20th century, the international system was marked by an increase in the number of substate or subnational regional actors engaging in international activity. The phenomenon of the increased activity of substate governments in the world is reflective of the existence of a multilayered diplomacy in a globalized and complex world. For example, there are now about 200 substate actors that are represented in Brussels at the headquarters of the European Union. The diplomatic activity of substate actors has now become normalized in the international system, as they have mobilized internationally to assert and gain recognition of their (regional) identity.

The collection of articles in this book provides the student with information and analysis about some of the most important recent developments in the international system. The articles contain the best available analysis of the most important developments that occurred in the international system in 2012: the rise of China and the BRICS; the grand strategy of the Obama administration within the context of a declining power; the state of democratization in the Middle East as well as Burma, Nigeria, Russia, and North Korea; US–Chinese relations; the Chinese expansion of naval power in the region; the civil war that raged in Syria in 2012; Iran and the bomb; the UN and an arms trade treaty; the trial of Serbian General Ratko Mladic for genocide at Srebrenica, Bosnia; the state of the global economy; as of 2012, the continuing crisis in the Eurozone; the opening up of the resources of the Arctic as a result of global warming; the international energy conundrum; and the global population of 7 billion.

I would also like to express my thanks to the editorial team at McGraw-Hill, especially managing editor Larry Loeppke and development editor Jade Benedict for their direction and assistance in working on this book. I would also like to thank my graduate students who helped me during this project, especially Jeremy Lowe, who played a major role in helping to locate the articles that were used in this project. I also wish to thank Edwile Mbameg, Jacqueline Millette, Joshua Pritchard, Joseph Sarkisian, and Kyle Vale.

Robert Weiner
Editor

The Annual Editions Series

VOLUMES AVAILABLE

Adolescent Psychology

Aging

American Foreign Policy

American Government

Anthropology

Archaeology

Assessment and Evaluation

Business Ethics

Child Growth and Development

Comparative Politics

Criminal Justice

Developing World

Drugs, Society, and Behavior

Dying, Death, and Bereavement

Early Childhood Education

Economics

Educating Children with Exceptionalities

Education

Educational Psychology

Entrepreneurship

Environment

The Family

Gender

Geography

Global Issues

Health

Homeland Security

Human Development

Human Resources

Human Sexualities

International Business

Management

Marketing

Mass Media

Microbiology

Multicultural Education

Nursing

Nutrition

Physical Anthropology

Psychology

Race and Ethnic Relations

Social Problems

Sociology

State and Local Government

Sustainability

Technologies, Social Media, and Society

United States History, Volume 1

United States History, Volume 2

Urban Society

Violence and Terrorism

Western Civilization, Volume 1

World History, Volume 1

World History, Volume 2

World Politics

Contents

UNIT 1
The Multipolar International System

The concepts in bold italics are developed in the article. For further expansion, please refer to the Topic Guide.

UNIT 2
Democratization

The concepts in bold italics are developed in the article. For further expansion, please refer to the Topic Guide.

UNIT 3
Foreign Policy

UNIT 4
War, Arms Control, and Disarmament

The concepts in bold italics are developed in the article. For further expansion, please refer to the Topic Guide.

UNIT 5
International Organization, International Law, and Human Security

UNIT 6
International Political Economy

The concepts in bold italics are developed in the article. For further expansion, please refer to the Topic Guide.

UNIT 7
Global Environmental Issues

The concepts in bold italics are developed in the article. For further expansion, please refer to the Topic Guide.

Correlation Guide

The *Annual Editions* series provides students with convenient, inexpensive access to current, carefully selected articles from the public press. **Annual Editions: World Politics 12/13** is an easy-to-use reader that presents articles on important topics such as *democratization, human rights, political economy,* and many more. For more information on *Annual Editions* and other *McGraw-Hill Contemporary Learning Series* titles, visit www.mhhe.com/cls.

This convenient guide matches the units in **Annual Editions: World Politics 13/14** with the corresponding chapters in one of our best-selling McGraw-Hill Political Science textbooks by Rourke/Boyer.

Annual Editions: World Politics 13/14	International Politics on the World Stage, Brief, 8/e by Rourke/Boyer
Unit 1: The Multipolar International System	**Chapter 2:** The Evolution of World Politics **Chapter 5:** Globalization: The Alternative Orientation
Unit 2: Democratization	**Chapter 6:** Power, Statecraft, and the National State: The Traditional Structure
Unit 3: Foreign Policy and Terrorism	**Chapter 3:** Levels of Analysis and Foreign Policy **Chapter 9:** Pursuing Security
Unit 4: War, Arms Control, and Disarmament	**Chapter 9:** Pursuing Security
Unit 5: International Organization, International Law, and Human Security	**Chapter 6:** Power, Statecraft, and the National States: The Traditional Structure **Chapter 7:** Intergovernmental Organizations: Alternative Governance **Chapter 8:** International Law and Human Rights **Chapter 9:** Pursuing Security
Unit 6: International Political Economy	**Chapter 5:** Globalization: The Alternative Orientation **Chapter 10:** National Economic Competition: The Traditional Road **Chapter 11:** International Economics: The Alternative Road
Unit 7: Global Environmental Issues	**Chapter 12:** Preserving and Enhancing the Biosphere

Topic Guide

This topic guide suggests how the selections in this book relate to the subjects covered in your course. You may want to use the topics listed on these pages to search the web more easily.

On the following pages a number of websites have been gathered specifically for this book. They are arranged to reflect the units of this Annual Editions reader. You can link to these sites by going to www.mhhe.com/cls

All the articles that relate to each topic are listed below the bold-faced term.

Internet References

The following Internet sites have been selected to support the articles found in this reader. These sites were available at the time of publication. However, because websites often change their structure and content, the information listed may no longer be available. We invite you to visit www.mhhe.com/cls for easy access to these sites.

Annual Editions: World Politics 13/14

General Sources

Asean (Association of Southeast Asian Nations)
www.aseansec.org

This organization was created in 1967, to "promote economic growth, social progress and cultural development in the region". However, it has not been very successful in achieving its goal of integration.

Avalon Project at Yale Law School
avalon.law.yale.edu/default.asp

A vast source of data about international relations, especially important historical documents, ranging from ancient documents to the twenty-first century.

British International Studies Association
www.bisa.ac.uk

An academic organization designed to promote the study of international relations in the United kingdom and beyond. Organizes conferences and workshops on such themes as U.S. foreign policy and terrorism. It also provides links to the work of the English School of International relations.

Carnegie Endowment for International Peace
www.ceip.org

One of the goals of this organization is to stimulate discussion about learning among experts and the public on a wide range of international relations issues.

Central Intelligence Agency
www.cia.gov

Use this official home page to learn about many facets of the CIA and get connections to other sites and resources such as the CIA World Factbook, which provides extensive statistical information about every country in the world.

Chatham House
www.chathamhouse.org

A British–based organization that provides access to papers dealing with such themes as "Libya: Policy Options for Transitions" and various conferences such as the "Economics of the Arab Spring" mainly focuses on research dealing with energy, environment and resources governance, and international economics and regional security affairs. It publishes the journal *International Affairs* and the monthly magazine *the World Today*.

Columbia International Affairs Online (CIAO)
www.ciaonet.org

Contains a wide variety of information, including articles and journals, excerpts from books, working papers, and conference proceedings.

e-International Relations
www.e-IR.info

This is described as "the world's leading websites on international relations." Contains a wide variety of articles, essays, and blogs, a site which claims to experience 750,000 hits per year.

Fletcher-Ginn Multilaterals Project
fletcher.tufts.edu/multilaterals

It makes available the texts of major international multilateral conventions and other instruments, mostly after 1945, but also includes the Treaty of Westphalia and the Covenant of the League of Nations.

International Political Science Association
www.ipsa.org

This is the major international professional political cience organization, which sponsors world conferences, including the 2012 world congress in Madrid, focusing on the theme of "Reshaping Power, Sharing Boundaries." The IPSA has a major portal that provides links to the top 300 websites for political science. The aim of the portal is to "foster online research", and states that it is specifically concerned with making online access available to scholars from developing countries.

International Relations Security Networks
www.isn.ethz.ch

This site is maintained by the Swiss government and is a clearing house for extensive information about international relations and security policy.

The International Studies Association
www.isanet.org

This is a United States–based organization for professionals in the field. It provides information about conferences, jobs, journals, grants, and publishing opportunities. It is also a major portal to a variety of sources in international relations.

World Wide Virtual Library: International Affairs Resources
www.etown.edu/vl

Surf this site and learn about specific countries and regions, research think tanks and organizations, and study such vital topics as international law, development, the international economy, human rights, and peacekeeping.

UNIT 1: The Multipolar International System

African Union
www.africa-union.org

The official website for the African Union, accessible in multiple languages, including Arabic, English, and French.

BRICS Forum
www.bricsforum.org/

It is described as "an independent forum that works for a structured social, economic, and environmentally sustainable BRICS block." The Forum was formed in 2011.

Community of Latin American and Carribean States (CELAC)
www.celac.gov.ve/

This organization consists of 33 countries, and is aimed at reducing the hegemony of the United states in Latin America and the Carribean. The organization also excludes Canada.

Internet References

Central Europe Online

www.centraleurope.com

This site contains daily updated information, under headings such as news on the web today, economics, trade, and the economy.

The Foreign Minstry of China

www.mfa.gov.cn/eng

Contains the Chinese position on such issues as the development of multipolarization in the international system, where China states that the "trend toward world multipolarization has not changed." Contains links to activities, speeches, and communique's.

The French Foreign Ministry

www.diplomatie.gouv.fr/en

Contains information on foreign policy priorities, development and humanitarian action, disarmament and arms control, environmental and sustainable development, and the global economy.

Japan's Ministry of Foreign Policy

www.mofa.go.jp

The official site for Japan's foreign policy statements and press releases, archives, and discussions of regional and global relations.

Mercosur

www.mercosur.int

Mercosur is described as the "Southern Common Market" and consists of Argentina, Brazil, Paraguay, Uruguay, and Venezuela.

Ministry of Foreign Affairs of the Russian Federation

www.mid.ru/brp.4.nst/main_eng

Contains links to documents on foreign policy, such as the foreign concept of the Russian Federation. Also contains links to statements, speeches, and press releases on a wide variety of international relations topics.

Non-Aligned Movement(NAM)

www.nam.gov.ir

Despite the end of the Cold War, the NAM still operates in the international system. For example, its 16th summit meeting was held in Teheran, Iran from August 26–31, 2012, and was attended by the Secretary-General of the United Nations.

UNIT 2: Democratization

Al Jazeera

english.alijazeera.net

A major source of information about the revolutions in the Middle East, but also provides a Middle Eastern perspective on global news.

Arab Net

www.arab.net

An online resource from the Arab world in the Middle East and North Africa, presents links to 22 Arab countries. Each country page classifies information using a standardized system.

Freedom House

www.freedom house.org

Provides an index ranking of all states as to whether they are free, partly free, and not free. Uses charts and maps to indicate the status of democratization in countries and regions around the world. Contains reports on the progress of democratization in the Middle East.

Fund for Peace

www.for peace.org/global

Compiles failed state indices ranks countries using 12 social, economic, and political indicators dealing with economic, social, and political pressure on states. Somalia is ranked number one at the top of the list of failed states.

International Foundation for Election Systems

www.ifes.org

Tthis is an "applied" research center that operates in more than 100 countries around the world, which applies technical assistance to promote democracy. Contains surveys on democratic change and an extensive collection of data on national elections, political parties, and research on the status of women in the Middle East and North Africa.

Middle East Online

www.middle-east-online.com/english

An extensive source of critical information about developments in the Middle East.

Syrian Observatory for Human Rights

www.syriahr.com

The official website of the Syrian observatory for Human Rights. In Arabic but one can read the English version on Facebook. Contains the latest news and information about the civil war in Syria with heavy emphasis on the casualties suffered by rebel forces.

UNIT 3: Foreign Policy

Institute of Southeast Asian Studies

www.iseas.edu.sg

Analyzes and comments on critical issues from a global and regional level, especially in Asia. Recently analyzed the dispute between China and Japan in the East China Sea over the sovereignty of the Senkaku (Japanese name) islands.

The National Security Archive

www.gwu.edu/nsarchiv

This is not a government operated archive, but is operated privately by George Washington University and is an invaluable source of declassified documents.

Office of the Coordinator for Counterterrorism

www.state.gov/s/ct

This site provides links to country reports on terrorism, a list of state sponsors of terrorism, and lists of foreign terrorist organizations.

U.S. State Department

www.state.gov

This site provides information organized by categories, as well as background notes on specific countries. Also contains videos of statements and press conferences by officials.

UNIT 4: War, Arms Control, and Disarmament

The Bulletin of the Atomic Scientists

www.thebulletin.org

This site allows you to read more about the Doomsday clock and other issues, as well as topics related to nuclear weaponry, arms control, and disarmament.

Internet References

The Correlates of War Project
www.correlates of war.org

This site provides you with access to an enormous amount of data dealing with the quantitative variables of war.

The International Atomic Energy Agency
www.iaea.com

This organization was created in 1957 as part of the "Atoms for Peace" program, and was subsequently linked to the Non-Proliferation . . . Treaty? Organization? Program? The organization has the responsibility to ensure that states do not violate their obligations under the treaty, and attempt to develop nuclear weapons. In 2012, the organization was playing a critical role in investigating the nuclear weapons program in Iran.

International Crisis Group
www.crisisgroup.org

The International Crisis Group is an organization "committed to strengthening the capapcity of the international community to anticipate, understand, and act to prevent and contain conflict." Go to this site to view the latest reports and research concerning conflicts around the world."

International Security Assistance Force
www.nato.int/ISAF

This is the web page of the NATO force that is operating in Afghanistan.

National Defense University
www.ndu.edu

This site contains information on current studies. This site also provides a look at the school which many senior marine and naval officers attend prior to assuming top level positions.

Peace Research Institute at Oslo
www.prio.no

The purpose of the institute is "to conduct research on the conditions for peaceful relations between states, groups, and people." It provides data on armed conflicts and wars from around the world.

Stockholm International Peace Research institute
www.sipri.org

This institute conducts research on conflict, arms control, and disarmament. It publishes a yearbook, and provides important data dealing with military expenditures and arms transfers.

UN Conference on the Arms Trade Treaty
www.un.org/disarmament/ATT

Contains information about the UN conference which met from July 2–27, 2012, in an unsuccessful attempt to negotiate a universal, comprehensive, and binding treaty to regulate the trade in conventional weapons.

UNIT 5: International Organization, International Law, and Human Security

Amnesty International
www.amnesty.org

A nongovernmental organization that is working to promote human rights and individual liberties worldwide.

Genocide Watch Home Page
www.genocidewatch.org

Website for a nongovernmental international campaign to end genocide.

Human Security Gateway
www.humansecuritygateway.com

The Human Security gateway contains more than 30,000 entries that are free of charge on a broad range of global security issues accessible by region, country, or topic. Other linked but separately maintained web pages are the Afghanistan Conflict monitor and the Pakistan Conflict monitor.

International Court of Justice (ICJ)
www.icj-cij.org

The International Court ofJustice is the primary judicial organ of the United Nations. The ICJ acts to resolve matters of international law disputed by specific nations.

The International Criminal Court
www.icc-cpi.int/Menus/icc

The ICC is a permanent tribunal created to prosecute individuals for genocide, war crimes, and crimes against humanity.

The International Criminal Tribunal for the Former Yugoslavia
www.icty.org

Established by the UN Security Council in 1993 and as of 2012 was conducting the genocide trials of top Bosnian Serbian leaders Radovan Karadzic and Ratko Mladic.

International Criminal Tribunal for Rwanda
www.unictr.org

Established by the UN Security Council in 1994 and has convicted a number of leaders the former Hutu regime of committing genocide.

United Nations Home Page
www.un.org

Here is the gateway to information about the United Nations

U.S. Holocaust Museum
www.ushmm.org

Contains a massive amount of information, videos, and documents not only about the Holocaust, but about other genocides as well.

UNIT 6: International Political Economy

Eurobarometer
ec.europa.eu/public_opinion_index_en.hhtm

Monitors European public opinion in connection with the various issues dealing with European integration.

Europa
europa.eu/int

Europa is the major site of the European Union (EU), and will lead you to the history of the EU, the EU treaties, the EU's position on various issues, and relations with member states and candidates for membership.

International Monetary Fund
www.imf.org

This link brings you to the homepage of the International Monetary Fund.

World Bank
www.worldbank.org

Links to press releases, statements, projects, and details of relations with member states

Internet References

UNIT 7: Global Environmental Issues

The Arctic Council
www.arctic-council.org

It is described as "an intergovernmental forum for Arctic governments and peoples, includes information on the Council, member states, working groups, events, documents."

Arctic Map
geology.com/world/arctic-ocean-map-shtml

This map shows the Arctic Sea and bordering countries and also contains an international Bathymetric chart of the Arctic Ocean.

Food and Agriculture Organization
www.fao.org

the major UN affiliated organization dealing with food and agriculture. Contains links to the global food price monitor, which contains extensive graphs and data.

The International Atomic Energy Agency (IAEA)

The major UN affiliated organization, established in 1957, and dealing with the peaceful uses of atomic energy and the proliferation of nuclear weapons.

The International Data Base (IDB)
www.census.gov/population/international/data/idb/information Gateway.php.

The IDB is described on its website as providing "access to demographic data for over 25 years to governments, academics and other organizations." You can check a population clock for the United States and the world.

The International Energy Agency
www.iea.org

Consists of 28 members and focuses on energy security especially as it applies to consumers. Created during the oil crisis of 1973/74, and attempts to provide a global view of the world's energy system, for both producers and consumers.

OPEC (Organization of Petroleum Exporting Countries)
www.opec.org

Real Climate
www.realclimate.org

This site contains reports of climate scientists on recent events related to global warming and information about recent severe climate events.

World Food Program
www.wfp.org

Major organization dealing with emergency food aid to stricken areas of the world.

UNIT 1

The Multipolar International System

Unit Selections

Learning Outcomes

After reading this Unit, you will be able to:

- Explain what is meant by Grand Strategy.

- Discuss how the United States can play the role of balancer between the great powers in the East.

- Define "liberal international order."

- Explain why the emerging powers will continue to work within the current international order.

- Explain why globalization is undermining the Westphalian state system.

- Discuss the effect of globalization on the nature of power in the international system.

- Discuss the importance of Pax Americana to the international political system.

- Analyze the effect of a rising China on a strategically overextended United States.

- Analyze the factors that have contributed to a reconfiguration of regional organizations in Latin America.

- Discuss the relationship between sovereignty and the regional groupings that have emerged in Latin America.

Student Website

www.mhhe.com/cls

Internet References

African Union
www.africa-union.org
BRICS Forum
www.Bricsforum.org
Central Europe Online
www.centraleurope.com
Community of Latin American and Carribean States
www.celac.gov.ve
The Foreign Ministry of China
www.mfa.gov.cn/eng

The French Foreign Ministry
www.diplomatie.gouv.fr/en
Japan's Ministry of Foreign Policy
www.mofa.go.jp
Mercosur
www.mercosur.int
Ministry of Foreign Affairs of the Russian Federation
www.mid.ru/brp.4.nst/main_eng
Non-Aligned Movement
www.nam.gov.ir

There continues to be a general consensus among international relations specialists that a multipolar system exists, or if it has not yet solidified is in the process of emerging with perhaps six or seven centers of power. International systems don't remain the same, but change when the overall distribution of power in the system changes. As far as the position of the United States in the international system is concerned, the declinist school of thought argues that the United States is clearly losing its hegemonic position in the system, especially from an economic point of view, as it suffers from imperial overstretch. A key shift of power is occurring in the international system with the rise of China, as the Pacific region becomes more important to the vital interests of the United States than Western Europe. The Obama administration has recognized the change that has occurred in the geopolitical shift in power, as it executes a "pivot" to Asia, as it downsizes its military presence in Iraq and Afghanistan, and engages in a military buildup in the Pacific. Pivot mans a shift in the direction of U.S. policy in the aftermath of the withdrawal of the United States from Iraq and plans to withdraw from Afghanistan. The question then arises as to what role the United States can play in a multipolar system, which, as emphasized at the International Political Science Association conference in Madrid in 2012, is going through a process of reconfiguration of power. Zbigniew Brzezinski in "Balancing the East, Upgrading the West: US Grand Strategy in an Age of Upheaval," focuses on the grand strategy that the United States should pursue in Eurasia in order to maintain its influence in the international system. Brzezinski argues that the United States central challenge over the next several decades is to revitalize itself, while promoting a larger West and buttressing a complex balance in the East that accommodates China's rising status. Brzezinski concludes that the United States should try to resolve the Taiwanese problem and pursue a policy of "constructive partnership" with China.

G. John Ikenberry argues that "although the United States' position in the global system is changing, the liberal international order is alive and well" and "China and other emerging Great Powers do not want to contest the basic rules and principles of the liberal international order" because they have prospered from it, because it is "a mutual aid society." According to Ikenberry, China, India, and Brazil have benefited from a liberal international order that is based on the Westphalian concept of state sovereignty, decentralization, balance of power, and a system of open trade and free markets. Brent Scowcroft, in "A World in Transformation," also focuses on the changes that have occurred in the international system, but stresses that the fundamental changes in the world are due to the forces of globalization, which are in his view undermining the Westphalian concept of state sovereignty as globalization "erodes national boundaries." Although the conflict between the Westphalian system and globalization has resulted in chaos, Scowcroft does not anticipate any further great power wars, as the United States needs to lead and move beyond its narrow interests.

Christopher Layne, in "The Global Power Shift from West to East," draws our attention to the basic international relations principle that power transitions, when a great power that has

© Department of Defense photo by Tech. Sgt. Cherie A. Thurlby, U.S. Air Force

maintained the status quo declines and a rising power challenges the existing distribution of power, are extremely dangerous. Layne is in agreement with the declinist school of thought, best represented by Paul Kennedy's massive study of the "Rise and Fall of Great Powers," where he argues that the decline of the relative power of the United states means the end not only of U.S. hegemony, but the end of the Western world order that was established more than 500 years ago. According to Layne, the new emerging world order is marked by challenges from China as well as other emerging powers such as Brazil, India, Russia series, and Indonesia. Layne disagrees with Ikenberry's notion that China should be viewed as a responsible stakeholder in the international system, "as the international system's economic and geopolitical center of gravity migrates from the Euro-Atlantic world to Asia." Layne concludes that just as the United States replaced "Pax Britannica" with "Pax Americana," particularly after the end of World War II, and through the Cold War, China in the 21st century is replacing the "Pax Americana."

An important dimension of the structure of the emerging multipolar system consists of regional and sub-regional organizations. Regionalism therefore forms an important element of the structure of the multipolar system, which is undergoing a process of reconfiguration of power. Regional and subregional organizations represent one of the most numerous types of nonstate actors in the international system. Until recently, the best example of a successful regional organization was the European Union, although the gloss has now worn off of the European project due to the Eurozone crisis, which may have called into question the future of the organization itself. Other regions in the world have tried to emulate the European Union, but without too much success, given all of the background and process conditions that need to be met for a successful regional organization, which may have been unique in the case of Europe. The operations of regional organizations such as the OAS (Organization of American States) also can be influenced by countries in the region that could be considered as regional hegemons, such as the United States in Latin America. In "The Shifting Landscape of Latin American Regionalism," Michael Shifter concludes that the kaleidoscope of regional organizations in Latin America has been reconfigured by the decline of the United States and the rise of China, which has become a major trading partner of a number of important Latin American states, such as Brazil, and extended liberal economic aid terms to Venezuela. The regionalism in Latin America has been marked by the rise of new regional organizations such as the Union of South American nations created by Brazil in 2008. Some of the new regional organizations that exclude the United States from membership, such as CELAC (the Community of Latin American and Caribbean States), a goal that has also been pursued by Hugo Chavez, the president of Venezuela. The new regional organizations, some with a leftist orientation, represent an effort at creating a degree of independence from the United States. However, as is the case with most regional organizations, they face difficulties in promoting integration due to the continuing persistence of national sovereignty.

Balancing the East, Upgrading the West
U.S. Grand Strategy in an Age of Upheaval

ZBIGNIEW BRZEZINSKI

The United States' central challenge over the next several decades is to revitalize itself, while promoting a larger West and buttressing a complex balance in the East that can accommodate China's rising global status. A successful U.S. effort to enlarge the West, making it the world's most stable and democratic zone, would seek to combine power with principle. A cooperative larger West—extending from North America and Europe through Eurasia (by eventually embracing Russia and Turkey), all the way to Japan and South Korea—would enhance the appeal of the West's core principles for other cultures, thus encouraging the gradual emergence of a universal democratic political culture.

At the same time, the United States should continue to engage cooperatively in the economically dynamic but also potentially conflicted East. If the United States and China can accommodate each other on a broad range of issues, the prospects for stability in Asia will be greatly increased. That is especially likely if the United States can encourage a genuine reconciliation between China and Japan while mitigating the growing rivalry between China and India.

To respond effectively in both the western and eastern parts of Eurasia, the world's central and most critical continent, the United States must play a dual role. It must be the promoter and guarantor of greater and broader unity in the West, and it must be the balancer and conciliator between the major powers in the East. Both roles are essential, and each is needed to reinforce the other. But to have the credibility and the capacity to pursue both successfully, the United States must show the world that it has the will to renovate itself at home. Americans must place greater emphasis on the more subtle dimensions of national power, such as innovation, education, the balance of force and diplomacy, and the quality of political leadership.

A Larger West

For the United States to succeed as the promoter and guarantor of a renewed West, it will need to maintain close ties with Europe, continue its commitment to NATO, and manage, along with Europe, a step-by-step process of welcoming both Turkey and a truly democratizing Russia into the West. To guarantee the West's geopolitical relevance, Washington must remain active in European security. It must also encourage the deeper unification of the European Union: the close cooperation among France, Germany, and the United Kingdom—Europe's central political, economic, and military alignment—should continue and broaden.

To engage Russia while safeguarding Western unity, the French-German-Polish consultative triangle could play a constructive role in advancing the ongoing but still tenuous reconciliation between Poland and Russia. The EU's backing would help make Russian-Polish reconciliation more comprehensive, much as the German-Polish one has already become, with both reconciliations contributing to greater stability in Europe. But in order for Russian-Polish reconciliation to endure, it has to move from the governmental level to the social level, through extensive people-to-people contacts and joint educational initiatives. Expedient accommodations made by governments that are not grounded in basic changes in popular attitudes will not last. The model should be the French-German friendship after World War II, which was initiated at the highest political levels by Paris and Bonn and successfully promoted on the social and cultural level, as well.

As the United States and Europe seek to enlarge the West, Russia itself will have to evolve in order to become more closely linked with the EU. Its leadership will have to face the fact that Russia's future will be uncertain if it remains a relatively empty and underdeveloped space between the rich West and the dynamic East. This will not change even if Russia entices some Central Asian states to join Prime Minister Vladimir Putin's quaint idea of a Eurasian Union. Also, although a significant portion of the Russian public is ahead of its government in favoring EU membership, most Russians are unaware of how exacting many of the qualifying standards for membership are, especially with regard to democratic reform.

3

The process of the EU and Russia coming closer is likely to stall occasionally and then lurch forward again, progressing in stages and including transitional arrangements. To the extent possible, it should proceed simultaneously on the social, economic, political, and security levels. One can envisage more and more opportunities for social interactions, increasingly similar legal and constitutional arrangements, joint security exercises between NATO and the Russian military, and new institutions for coordinating policy within a continually expanding West, all resulting in Russia's increasing readiness for eventual membership in the EU.

It is not unrealistic to imagine a larger configuration of the West emerging after 2025. In the course of the next several decades, Russia could embark on a comprehensive law-based democratic transformation compatible with both EU and NATO standards, and Turkey could become a full member of the EU, putting both countries on their way to integration with the transatlantic community. But even before that occurs, a deepening geopolitical community of interest could arise among the United States, Europe (including Turkey), and Russia. Since any westward gravitation by Russia would likely be preceded and encouraged by closer ties between Ukraine and the EU, the institutional seat for a collective consultative organ (or perhaps initially for an expanded Council of Europe) could be located in Kiev, the ancient capital of Kievan Rus, whose location would be symbolic of the West's renewed vitality and enlarging scope.

If the United States does not promote the emergence of an enlarged West, dire consequences could follow.

If the United States does not promote the emergence of an enlarged West, dire consequences could follow: historical resentments could come back to life, new conflicts of interest could arise, and shortsighted competitive partnerships could take shape. Russia could exploit its energy assets and, emboldened by Western disunity, seek to quickly absorb Ukraine, reawakening its own imperial ambitions and contributing international disarray. With the EU passive, individual European states, in search of greater commercial opportunities, could then seek their own accommodations with Russia. One can envisage a scenario in which economic self-interest leads Germany or Italy, for example, to develop a special relationship with Russia. France and the United Kingdom could then draw closer while viewing Germany askance, with Poland and the Baltic states desperately pleading for additional United States security guarantees. The result would be not a new and more vital West but rather a progressively splintering and increasingly pessimistic West.

The Complex East

Such a disunited West would not be able to compete with China for global relevance. So far, China has not articulated an ideological dogma that would make its recent performance appear universally applicable, and the United States has been careful not to make ideology the central focus of its relations with China. Wisely, both Washington and Beijing have embraced the concept of a "constructive partnership" in global affairs, and the United States, although critical of China's violations of human rights, has been careful not to stigmatize the Chinese socioeconomic system as a whole.

But if an anxious United States and an overconfident China were to slide into increasing political hostility, it is more than likely that both countries would face off in a mutually destructive ideological conflict. Washington would argue that Beijing's success is based on tyranny and is damaging to the United States' economic well-being; Beijing, meanwhile, would interpret that United States message as an attempt to undermine and possibly even fragment the Chinese system. At the same time, China would stress its successful rejection of Western supremacy, appealing to those in the developing world who already subscribe to a historical narrative highly hostile to the West in general and to the United States in particular. Such a scenario would be damaging and counterproductive for both countries. Hence, intelligent self-interest should prompt the United States and China to exercise ideological self-restraint, resisting the temptation to universalize the distinctive features of their respective socioeconomic systems and to demonize each other.

The United States role in Asia should be that of regional balancer, replicating the role played by the United Kingdom in intra-European politics during the nineteenth and early twentieth centuries. The United States can and should help Asian states avoid a struggle for regional domination by mediating conflicts and offsetting power imbalances among potential rivals. In doing so, it should respect China's special historic and geopolitical role in maintaining stability on the Far Eastern mainland. Engaging with China in a dialogue regarding regional stability would not only help reduce the possibility of United States-Chinese conflicts but also diminish the probability of miscalculation between China and Japan, or China and India, and even at some point between China and Russia over the resources and independent status of the Central Asian states. Thus, the United States' balancing engagement in Asia is ultimately in China's interest, as well.

At the same time, the United States must recognize that stability in Asia can no longer be imposed by a non-Asian power, least of all by the direct application of United States military power. Indeed, United States efforts to buttress Asian stability could prove self-defeating, propelling Washington into a costly repeat of its recent wars, potentially even resulting in a replay of the tragic events of Europe in the twentieth century. If the United States fashioned an anti-Chinese alliance with India (or, less likely, with Vietnam) or promoted an anti-Chinese militarization in Japan, it could generate dangerous mutual resentment. In the twenty-first century, geopolitical equilibrium on the Asian mainland cannot depend on external military alliances with non-Asian powers.

The guiding principle of the United States' foreign policy in Asia should be to uphold United States obligations to Japan and South Korea while not allowing itself to be drawn into a war between Asian powers on the mainland. The United States has been entrenched in Japan and South Korea for more than 50 years, and the independence and the self-confidence of these countries would be shattered—along with the United States role in the Pacific—if any doubts were to arise regarding the durability of long-standing United States treaty commitments.

The United States-Japanese relationship is particularly vital and should be the springboard for a concerted effort to develop a United States-Japanese-Chinese cooperative triangle. Such a triangle would provide a structure that could deal with strategic concerns resulting from China's increased regional presence. Just as political stability in Europe after World War II would not have developed without the progressive expansion of French-German reconciliation to German-Polish reconciliation, so, too, the deliberate nurturing of a deepening Chinese-Japanese relationship could serve as the point of departure for greater stability in the Far East.

In the context of this triangular relationship, Chinese-Japanese reconciliation would help enhance and solidify more comprehensive United States-Chinese cooperation. China knows that the United States' commitment to Japan is steadfast, that the bond between the two countries is deep and genuine, and that Japan's security is directly dependent on the United States. And knowing that a conflict with China would be mutually destructive, Tokyo understands that United States engagement with China is indirectly a contribution to Japan's own security. In that context, China should not view United States support for Japan's security as a threat, nor should Japan view the pursuit of a closer and more extensive United States-Chinese partnership as a danger to its own interests. A deepening triangular relationship could also diminish Japanese concerns over the yuan's eventually becoming the world's third reserve currency, thereby further consolidating China's stake in the existing international system and mitigating United States anxieties over China's future role.

Given such a setting of enhanced regional accommodation and assuming the expansion of the bilateral United States-Chinese relationship, three sensitive United States-Chinese issues will have to be peacefully resolved: the first in the near future, the second over the course of the next several years, and the third probably within a decade or so. First, the United States should reassess its reconnaissance operations on the edges of Chinese territorial waters, as well as

the periodic United States naval patrols within international waters that are also part of the Chinese economic zone. They are as provocative to Beijing as the reverse situation would be to Washington. Moreover, the United States military's air reconnaissance missions pose serious risks of unintentional collisions, since the Chinese air force usually responds to such missions by sending up fighter planes for up-close inspection and sometimes harassment of the United States planes.

Second, given that the continuing modernization of China's military capabilities could eventually give rise to legitimate United States security concerns, including over United States commitments to Japan and South Korea, the United States and China should engage in regular consultations regarding their long-term military planning and seek to craft measures of reciprocal reassurance.

Third, the future status of Taiwan could become the most contentious issue between the two countries. Washington no longer recognizes Taiwan as a sovereign state and acknowledges Beijing's view that China and Taiwan are part of a single nation. But at the same time, the United States sells weapons to Taiwan. Thus, any long-term United States-Chinese accommodation will have to address the fact that a separate Taiwan, protected indefinitely by United States arms sales, will provoke intensifying Chinese hostility. An eventual resolution along the lines of former Chinese leader Deng Xiaoping's well-known formula for Hong Kong of "one country, two systems," but redefined as "one country, several systems," may provide the basis for Taipei's eventual reassociation with China, while still allowing Taiwan and China to maintain distinctive political, social, and military arrangements (in particular, excluding the deployment of People's Liberation Army troops on the island). Regardless of the exact formula, given China's growing power and the greatly expanding social links between Taiwan and the mainland, it is doubtful that Taiwan can indefinitely avoid a more formal connection with China.

Toward Reciprocal Cooperation

More than 1,500 years ago, during the first half of the first millennium, the politics of the relatively civilized parts of Europe were largely dominated by the coexistence of the two distinct western and eastern halves of the Roman Empire. The Western Empire, with its capital most of the time in Rome, was beset by conflicts with marauding barbarians. With its troops permanently stationed abroad in extensive and expensive fortifications, Rome was politically overextended and came close to bankruptcy midway through the fifth century. Meanwhile, divisive conflicts between Christians and pagans sapped Rome's social cohesion, and heavy taxation and corruption crippled its economic vitality. In 476, with the killing of Romulus Augustulus by the barbarians, the by then moribund Western Roman Empire officially collapsed.

During the same period, the Eastern Roman Empire—soon to become known as Byzantium—exhibited more dynamic urban and economic growth and proved more successful in its diplomatic and security policies. After the fall of Rome, Byzantium continued to thrive for centuries. It reconquered parts of the old Western Empire and lived on (although later through much conflict) until the rise of the Ottoman Turks in the fifteenth century.

Rome's dire travails in the middle of the fifth century did not damage Byzantium's more hopeful prospects, because in those days, the world was compartmentalized into distinct segments that were geographically isolated and politically and economically insulated from one another. The fate of one did not directly and immediately affect the prospects of the other. But that is no longer the case. Today, with distance made irrelevant by the immediacy of communications and the near-instant speed of financial transactions, the well-being of the most advanced parts of the world is becoming increasingly interdependent. In our time, unlike 1,500 years ago, the West and the East cannot keep aloof from each other: their relationship can only be either reciprocally cooperative or mutually damaging.

Critical Thinking

1. Explain the importance which Brzezinski attaches to triangular relations between states.
2. Why does Brzezinski attach so much importance to Eurasia?
3. What does Brzezinski mean by Grand Strategy?

ZBIGNIEW BRZEZINSKI was U.S. National Security Adviser from 1977 to 1981. His book *Strategic Vision: America and the Crisis of Global Power*, from which this essay is adapted, will be published this winter by Basic Books.

Brzezinski, Zbigniew. From *Foreign Affairs*, January/February 2012, pp. 97–104. Copyright © 2012 by Council on Foreign Relations, Inc. Reprinted by permission of Foreign Affairs. www.ForeignAffairs.com

The Future of the Liberal World Order
Internationalism after America

G. John Ikenberry

There is no longer any question: wealth and power are moving from the North and the West to the East and the South, and the old order dominated by the United States and Europe is giving way to one increasingly shared with non-Western rising states. But if the great wheel of power is turning, what kind of global political order will emerge in the aftermath?

Some anxious observers argue that the world will not just look less American—it will also look less liberal. Not only is the United States' preeminence passing away, they say, but so, too, is the open and rule-based international order that the country has championed since the 1940s. In this view, newly powerful states are beginning to advance their own ideas and agendas for global order, and a weakened United States will find it harder to defend the old system. The hallmarks of liberal internationalism—openness and rule-based relations enshrined in institutions such as the United Nations and norms such as multilateralism—could give way to a more contested and fragmented system of blocs, spheres of influence, mercantilist networks, and regional rivalries.

The fact that today's rising states are mostly large non-Western developing countries gives force to this narrative. The old liberal international order was designed and built in the West. Brazil, China, India, and other fast-emerging states have a different set of cultural, political, and economic experiences, and they see the world through their anti-imperial and anticolonial pasts. Still grappling with basic problems of development, they do not share the concerns of the advanced capitalist societies. The recent global economic slowdown has also bolstered this narrative of liberal international decline. Beginning in the United States, the crisis has tarnished the American model of liberal capitalism and raised new doubts about the ability of the United States to act as the global economic leader.

For all these reasons, many observers have concluded that world politics is experiencing not just a changing of the guard but also a transition in the ideas and principles that underlie the global order. The journalist Gideon Rachman, for example, says that a cluster of liberal internationalist ideas—such as faith in democratization, confidence in free markets, and the acceptability of U.S. military power—are all being called into question. According to this worldview, the future of international order will be shaped above all by China, which will use its growing power and wealth to push world politics in an illiberal direction. Pointing out that China and other non-Western states have weathered the recent financial crisis better than their Western counterparts, pessimists argue that an authoritarian capitalist alternative to Western neoliberal ideas has already emerged. According to the scholar Stefan Halper, emerging-market states "are learning to combine market economics with traditional autocratic or semiautocratic politics in a process that signals an intellectual rejection of the Western economic model."

But this panicked narrative misses a deeper reality: although the United States' position in the global system is changing, the liberal international order is alive and well. The struggle over international order today is not about fundamental principles. China and other emerging great powers do not want to contest the basic rules and principles of the liberal international order; they wish to gain more authority and leadership within it.

Indeed, today's power transition represents not the defeat of the liberal order but its ultimate ascendance. Brazil, China, and India have all become more prosperous and capable by operating inside the existing international order—benefiting from its rules, practices, and institutions, including the World Trade Organization (WTO) and the newly organized G-20. Their economic success and growing influence are tied to the liberal internationalist organization of world politics, and they have deep interests in preserving that system.

In the meantime, alternatives to an open and rule-based order have yet to crystallize. Even though the last decade has brought remarkable upheavals in the global system—the emergence of new powers, bitter disputes among Western allies over the United States' unipolar ambitions, and a global financial crisis and recession—the liberal international order has no competitors. On the contrary, the rise of non-Western powers and the growth of economic and security interdependence are creating new constituencies for it.

To be sure, as wealth and power become less concentrated in the United States' hands, the country will be less able to shape world politics. But the underlying foundations of the liberal international order will survive and thrive. Indeed, now may be the best time for the United States and its democratic partners to update the liberal order for a new era, ensuring that it continues to provide the benefits of security and prosperity that it has provided since the middle of the twentieth century.

The Liberal Ascendancy

China and the other emerging powers do not face simply an American-led order or a Western system. They face a broader international order that is the product of centuries of struggle and innovation. It is highly developed, expansive, integrated, institutionalized, and deeply rooted in the societies and economies of both advanced capitalist states and developing states. And over the last half century, this order has been unusually capable of assimilating rising powers and reconciling political and cultural diversity.

Today's international order is the product of two order-building projects that began centuries ago. One is the creation and expansion of the modern state system, a project dating back to the Peace of Westphalia in 1648. In the years since then, the project has promulgated rules and principles associated with state sovereignty and norms of great-power conduct. The other project is the construction of the liberal order, which over the last two centuries was led by the United Kingdom and the United States and which in the twentieth century was aided by the rise of liberal democratic states. The two projects have worked together. The Westphalian project has focused on solving the "realist" problems of creating stable and cooperative interstate relations under conditions of anarchy, and the liberal-order-building project has been possible only when relations between the great powers have been stabilized. The "problems of Hobbes," that is, anarchy and power insecurities, have had to be solved in order to take advantage of the "opportunities of Locke," that is, the construction of open and rule-based relations.

At the heart of the Westphalian project is the notion of state sovereignty and great-power relations. The original principles of the Westphalian system—sovereignty, territorial integrity, and nonintervention—reflected an emerging consensus that states were the rightful political units for the establishment of legitimate rule. Founded in western Europe, the Westphalian system has expanded outward to encompass the entire globe. New norms and principles—such as self-determination and mutual recognition among sovereign states—have evolved within it, further reinforcing the primacy of states and state authority. Under the banners of sovereignty and self-determination, political movements for decolonization and independence were set in motion in the non-Western developing world, coming to fruition in the decades after World War II. Westphalian norms have been violated and ignored, but they have, nonetheless, been the most salient and agreed-on parts of the international order.

A succession of postwar settlements—Vienna in 1815, Versailles in 1919, Yalta and Potsdam in 1945, and the U.S., Soviet, and European negotiations that ended the Cold War and reunified Germany in the early 1990s—allowed the great powers to update the principles and practices of their relations. Through war and settlement, the great powers learned how to operate within a multipolar balance-of-power system. Over time, the order has remained a decentralized system in which major states compete and balance against one another. But it has also evolved. The great powers have developed principles and practices of restraint and accommodation that have served their interests. The Congress of Vienna in 1815, where post-Napoleonic France was returned to the great-power club and a congress system was established to manage conflicts, and the UN Security Council today, which has provided a site for great-power consultations, are emblematic of these efforts to create rules and mechanisms that reinforce restraint and accommodation.

The project of constructing a liberal order built on this evolving system of Westphalian relations. In the nineteenth century, liberal internationalism was manifest in the United Kingdom's championing of free trade and the freedom of the seas, but it was limited and coexisted with imperialism and colonialism. In the twentieth century, the United States advanced the liberal order in several phases. After World War I, President Woodrow Wilson and other liberals pushed for an international order organized around a global collective-security body, the League of Nations, in which states would act together to uphold a system of territorial peace. Open trade, national self-determination, and a belief in progressive global change also undergirded the Wilsonian worldview—a "one world" vision of nation-states that would trade and interact in a multilateral system of laws. But in the interwar period of closed economic systems and imperial blocs, this experiment in liberal order collapsed.

After World War II, President Franklin Roosevelt's administration tried to construct a liberal order again, embracing a vision of an open trading system and a global organization in which the great powers would cooperate to keep the peace—the United Nations. Drawing lessons from Wilson's failure and incorporating ideas from the New Deal, American architects of the postwar order also advanced more ambitious ideas about economic and political cooperation, which were embodied in the Bretton Woods institutions. This vision was originally global in spirit and scope, but it evolved into a more American-led and Western-centered system as a result of the weakness of postwar Europe and rising tensions with the Soviet Union. As the Cold War unfolded, the United

States took command of the system, adopting new commitments and functional roles in both security and economics. Its own economic and political system became, in effect, the central component of the larger liberal hegemonic order.

Another development of liberal internationalism was quietly launched after World War II, although it took root more slowly and competed with aspects of the Westphalian system. This was the elaboration of the universal rights of man, enshrined in the UN and its Universal Declaration of Human Rights. A steady stream of conventions and treaties followed that together constitute an extraordinary vision of rights, individuals, sovereignty, and global order. In the decades since the end of the Cold War, notions of "the responsibility to protect" have given the international community legal rights and obligations to intervene in the affairs of sovereign states.

Seen in this light, the modern international order is not really American or Western—even if, for historical reasons, it initially appeared that way. It is something much wider. In the decades after World War II, the United States stepped forward as the hegemonic leader, taking on the privileges and responsibilities of organizing and running the system. It presided over a far-flung international order organized around multilateral institutions, alliances, special relationships, and client states—a hierarchical order with liberal characteristics.

Today's international order is not really American or Western—even if it initially appeared that way.

But now, as this hegemonic organization of the liberal international order starts to change, the hierarchical aspects are fading while the liberal aspects persist. So even as China and other rising states try to contest U.S. leadership—and there is indeed a struggle over the rights, privileges, and responsibilities of the leading states within the system—the deeper international order remains intact. Rising powers are finding incentives and opportunities to engage and integrate into this order, doing so to advance their own interests. For these states, the road to modernity runs through—not away from—the existing international order.

Joining the Club

The liberal international order is not just a collection of liberal democratic states but an international mutual-aid society— a sort of global political club that provides members with tools for economic and political advancement. Participants in the order gain trading opportunities, dispute-resolution mechanisms, frameworks for collective action, regulatory agreements, allied security guarantees, and resources in times of crisis. And just as there are a variety of reasons why rising states will embrace the liberal international order, there are powerful obstacles to opponents who would seek to overturn it.

To begin with, rising states have deep interests in an open and rule-based system. Openness gives them access to other societies—for trade, investment, and knowledge sharing. Without the unrestricted investment from the United States and Europe of the past several decades, for instance, China and the other rising states would be on a much slower developmental path. As these countries grow, they will encounter protectionist and discriminatory reactions from slower-growing countries threatened with the loss of jobs and markets. As a result, the rising states will find the rules and institutions that uphold nondiscrimination and equal access to be critical. The World Trade Organization—the most formal and developed institution of the liberal international order—enshrines these rules and norms, and rising states have been eager to join the WTO and gain the rights and protections it affords. China is already deeply enmeshed in the global trading system, with a remarkable 40 percent of its GNP composed of exports—25 percent of which go to the United States.

China could be drawn further into the liberal order through its desire to have the yuan become an international currency rivaling the U.S. dollar. Aside from conferring prestige, this feat could also stabilize China's exchange rate and grant Chinese leaders autonomy in setting macroeconomic policy. But if China wants to make the yuan a global currency, it will need to loosen its currency controls and strengthen its domestic financial rules and institutions. As Barry Eichengreen and other economic historians have noted, the U.S. dollar assumed its international role after World War II not only because the U.S. economy was large but also because the United States had highly developed financial markets and domestic institutions—economic and political—that were stable, open, and grounded in the rule of law. China will feel pressures to establish these same institutional preconditions if it wants the benefits of a global currency.

Internationalist-oriented elites in Brazil, China, India, and elsewhere are growing in influence within their societies, creating an expanding global constituency for an open and rule-based international order. These elites were not party to the grand bargains that lay behind the founding of the liberal order in the early postwar decades, and they are seeking to renegotiate their countries' positions within the system. But they are nonetheless embracing the rules and institutions of the old order. They want the protections and rights that come from the international order's Westphalian defense of sovereignty. They care about great-power authority. They want the protections and rights relating to trade and investment. And they want to use the rules and institutions of liberal internationalism as platforms to project their influence and acquire legitimacy at home and abroad. The UN

Security Council, the G-20, the governing bodies of the Bretton Woods institutions—these are all stages on which rising non-Western states can acquire great-power authority and exercise global leadership.

No Other Order

Meanwhile, there is no competing global organizing logic to liberal internationalism. An alternative, illiberal order—a "Beijing model"—would presumably be organized around exclusive blocs, spheres of influence, and mercantilist networks. It would be less open and rule-based, and it would be dominated by an array of state-to-state ties. But on a global scale, such a system would not advance the interests of any of the major states, including China. The Beijing model only works when one or a few states opportunistically exploit an open system of markets. But if everyone does, it is no longer an open system but a fragmented, mercantilist, and protectionist complex—and everyone suffers.

It is possible that China could nonetheless move in this direction. This is a future in which China is not a full-blown illiberal hegemon that reorganizes the global rules and institutions. It is simply a spoiler. It attempts to operate both inside and outside the liberal international order. In this case, China would be successful enough with its authoritarian model of development to resist the pressures to liberalize and democratize. But if the rest of the world does not gravitate toward this model, China will find itself subjected to pressure to play by the rules. This dynamic was on display in February 2011, when Brazilian President Dilma Rousseff joined U.S. Treasury Secretary Timothy Geithner in expressing concern over China's currency policy. China can free-ride on the liberal international order, but it will pay the costs of doing so—and it will still not be able to impose its illiberal vision on the world.

Democracy and the rule of law are still the hallmarks of modernity and the global standard for legitimate governance.

In the background, meanwhile, democracy and the rule of law are still the hallmarks of modernity and the global standard for legitimate governance. Although it is true that the spread of democracy has stalled in recent years and that authoritarian China has performed well in the recent economic crisis, there is little evidence that authoritarian states can become truly advanced societies without moving in a liberal democratic direction. The legitimacy of one-party rule within China rests more on the state's ability to deliver economic growth and full employment than on authoritarian—let alone communist—political principles. Kishore Mahbubani, a Singaporean intellectual who has championed China's rise, admits that "China cannot succeed

in its goal of becoming a modern developed society until it can take the leap and allow the Chinese people to choose their own rulers." No one knows how far or fast democratic reforms will unfold in China, but a growing middle class, business elites, and human rights groups will exert pressure for them. The Chinese government certainly appears to worry about the long-term preservation of one-party rule, and in the wake of the ongoing revolts against Arab authoritarian regimes, it has tried harder to prevent student gatherings and control foreign journalists.

Outside China, democracy has become a near-universal ideal. As the economist Amartya Sen has noted, "While democracy is not yet universally practiced, nor indeed universally accepted, in the general climate of world opinion democratic governance has achieved the status of being taken to be generally right." All the leading institutions of the global system enshrine democracy as the proper and just form of governance—and no competing political ideals even lurk on the sidelines.

The recent global economic downturn was the first great postwar economic upheaval that emerged from the United States, raising doubts about an American-led world economy and Washington's particular brand of economics. The doctrines of neoliberalism and market fundamentalism have been discredited, particularly among the emerging economies. But liberal internationalism is not the same as neoliberalism or market fundamentalism. The liberal internationalism that the United States articulated in the 1940s entailed a more holistic set of ideas about markets, openness, and social stability. It was an attempt to construct an open world economy and reconcile it with social welfare and employment stability. Sustained domestic support for openness, postwar leaders knew, would be possible only if countries also established social protections and regulations that safeguarded economic stability.

Indeed, the notions of national security and economic security emerged together in the 1940s, reflecting New Deal and World War II thinking about how liberal democracies would be rendered safe and stable. The Atlantic Charter, announced by Roosevelt and Winston Churchill in 1941, and the Bretton Woods agreements of 1944 were early efforts to articulate a vision of economic openness and social stability. The United States would do well to try to reach back and rearticulate this view. The world is not rejecting openness and markets; it is asking for a more expansive notion of stability and economic security.

Reason for Reassurance

Rising powers will discover another reason to embrace the existing global rules and institutions: doing so will reassure their neighbors as they grow more powerful. A stronger China will make neighboring states potentially less secure, especially if it acts aggressively and exhibits revisionist ambitions. Since this will trigger a balancing backlash,

Beijing has incentives to signal restraint. It will find ways to do so by participating in various regional and global institutions. If China hopes to convince its neighbors that it has embarked on a "peaceful rise," it will need to become more integrated into the international order.

China has already experienced a taste of such a backlash. Last year, its military made a series of provocative moves—including naval exercises—in the South China Sea, actions taken to support the government's claims to sovereign rights over contested islands and waters. Many of the countries disputing China's claims joined with the United States at the Regional Forum of the Association of Southeast Asian Nations (ASEAN) in July to reject Chinese bullying and reaffirm open access to Asia's waters and respect for international law. In September, a Chinese fishing trawler operating near islands administered by Japan in the East China Sea rammed into two Japanese coast guard ships. After Japanese authorities detained the trawler's crew, China responded with what one Japanese journalist described as a "diplomatic 'shock and awe' campaign," suspending ministerial-level contacts, demanding an apology, detaining several Japanese workers in China, and instituting a de facto ban on exports of rare-earth minerals to Japan. These actions—seen as manifestations of a more bellicose and aggressive foreign policy—pushed ASEAN, Japan, and South Korea perceptibly closer to the United States.

As China's economic and military power grow, its neighbors will only become more worried about Chinese aggressiveness, and so Beijing will have reason to allay their fears. Of course, it might be that some elites in China are not interested in practicing restraint. But to the extent that China is interested in doing so, it will find itself needing to signal peaceful intentions—redoubling its participation in existing institutions, such as the ASEAN Regional Forum and the East Asia Summit, or working with the other great powers in the region to build new ones. This is, of course, precisely what the United States did in the decades after World War II. The country operated within layers of regional and global economic, political, and security institutions and constructed new ones—thereby making itself more predictable and approachable and reducing the incentives for other states to undermine it by building countervailing coalitions.

More generally, given the emerging problems of the twenty-first century, there will be growing incentives among all the great powers to embrace an open, rule-based international system. In a world of rising economic and security interdependence, the costs of not following multilateral rules and not forging cooperative ties go up. As the global economic system becomes more interdependent, all states—even large, powerful ones—will find it harder to ensure prosperity on their own.

Growing interdependence in the realm of security is also creating a demand for multilateral rules and institutions. Both the established and the rising great powers are threatened less by mass armies marching across borders than by

transnational dangers, such as terrorism, climate change, and pandemic disease. What goes on in one country—radicalism, carbon emissions, or public health failures—can increasingly harm another country.

Intensifying economic and security interdependence are giving the United States and other powerful countries reason to seek new and more extensive forms of multilateral cooperation. Even now, as the United States engages China and other rising states, the agenda includes expanded cooperation in areas such as clean energy, environmental protection, nonproliferation, and global economic governance. The old and rising powers may disagree on how exactly this cooperation should proceed, but they all have reasons to avoid a breakdown in the multilateral order itself. So they will increasingly experiment with new and more extensive forms of liberal internationalism.

Time for Renewal

Pronouncements of American decline miss the real transformation under way today. What is occurring is not American decline but a dynamic process in which other states are catching up and growing more connected. In an open and rule-based international order, this is what happens. If the architects of the postwar liberal order were alive to see today's system, they would think that their vision had succeeded beyond their wildest dreams. Markets and democracy have spread. Societies outside the West are trading and growing. The United States has more alliance partners today than it did during the Cold War. Rival hegemonic states with revisionist and illiberal agendas have been pushed off the global stage. It is difficult to read these world-historical developments as a story of American decline and liberal unraveling.

Paradoxically, the challenges facing the liberal world order now are artifacts of its success.

In a way, however, the liberal international order has sown the seeds of its own discontent, since, paradoxically, the challenges facing it now—the rise of non-Western states and new transnational threats—are artifacts of its success. But the solutions to these problems—integrating rising powers and tackling problems cooperatively—will lead the order's old guardians and new stakeholders to an agenda of renewal. The coming divide in world politics will not be between the United States (and the West) and the non-Western rising states. Rather, the struggle will be between those who want to renew and expand today's system of multilateral governance arrangements and those who want to move to a less cooperative order built on spheres of influence. These fault lines do not map onto geography, nor do they split the

West and the non-West. There are passionate champions of the UN, the WTO, and a rule-based international order in Asia, and there are isolationist, protectionist, and anti-internationalist factions in the West.

The liberal international order has succeeded over the decades because its rules and institutions have not just enshrined open trade and free markets but also provided tools for governments to manage economic and security interdependence. The agenda for the renewal of the liberal international order should be driven by this same imperative: to reinforce the capacities of national governments to govern and achieve their economic and security goals.

As the hegemonic organization of the liberal international order slowly gives way, more states will have authority and status. But this will still be a world that the United States wants to inhabit. A wider array of states will share the burdens of global economic and political governance, and with its worldwide system of alliances, the United States will remain at the center of the global system. Rising states do not just grow more powerful on the global stage; they grow more powerful within their regions, and this creates its own set of worries and insecurities—which is why states will continue to look to Washington for security and partnership. In this new age of international order, the United States will not be able to rule. But it can still lead.

Critical Thinking

1. What is the struggle over international order all about?
2. What is the significance of the Westphalian system?
3. How can China be drawn into the liberal international order?

G. JOHN IKENBERRY is Albert G. Milbank Professor of Politics and International Affairs at Princeton University and the author of *Liberal Leviathan: The Origins, Crisis, and Transformation of the American World Order* (Princeton University Press, 2011), from which this essay is adapted.

A World in Transformation

BRENT SCOWCROFT

This special issue of *The National Interest* is particularly timely because we are living in a world that we know and that has shaped our thinking, but that world is in a process of transformation. We are struggling with institutions and practices of an Old World when that Old World is fading. This issue explores this global transformation, and I commend to you the articles contained here under the rubric of the "Crisis of the Old Order."

I would like to share some of my own thoughts on this global transformation. When the Cold War ended during the presidency of George H. W. Bush, I was serving as the president's national-security adviser. I thought at the time that the end of the Cold War marked the end of a period of history, one that began with the outbreak of World War I in 1914. The European system that had dominated the world for so long was washed away.

What followed that war was a period of instability and the rise of challenges to traditional societal organizations in the forms of fascism and communism. These ideologies took serious root in Germany, Italy and the Soviet Union. The United States soon realized it had to step up to the challenges posed by these threats to our concept of democracy. After World War II, America restored a balance of power in the early nuclear age, one that saved Western Europe from the Soviet threat and brought a measure of peace and stability to the world.

When that system crumbled with the end of the Soviet Union and its empire, we in the Bush administration may have realized the end of the Cold War marked the end of a period of history, but we did not completely visualize what the emerging new era would look like. We sought to help Europe fashion itself into a more congenial, unified system. When Saddam Hussein invaded Kuwait, we were determined to reverse that aggression, consciously seeking to do it in a way that would help establish new international rules dealing with conflict in this post-Cold War world. President Bush spoke of a "new world order." And it was true that we in the administration knew the situation called for some kind of new global vision. But we were essentially feeling our way in the dark. We sought to empower the UN Security Council's operations in the manner its founders had visualized and to organize an international coalition of forces to implement Security Council resolutions.

Then something truly fundamental became apparent, and it deeply affected the whole system. I refer to globalization, the inexorable convergence of markets, nation-states, peoples, technologies and forms of communication across national borders. It actually began during the Cold War but was slowed by that divided world. This is a significant force, working at base to undermine the old Westphalian state system that for so long dominated most of world thinking—particularly Western thinking. That venerable system was based on the concept of the sovereignty of the nation-state, territoriality and freedom of nation-states from internal interference by other nations. This concept—underpinned by industrialization, which greatly strengthened the power of the state itself—was embraced over centuries by nearly all nations, a notable exception being China. It spawned the nationalism that flowered particularly in the nineteenth and twentieth centuries.

Whereas industrialization strengthened the power of the state, globalization erodes national boundaries. More and more, things that need to be done in the world can only be done across national borders through cooperation between and among nations. The world is now operating under an uneasy mixture of the traditional Westphalian system and this new, globalized model intent on pushing things in a different direction.

Take as an example the financial crisis of 2008. The crisis demonstrated that we had a single worldwide financial system in which a crisis in one area could quickly spread throughout the world. But the world clearly had no single global way to deal with that crisis. This was far different even from the end of World War II, when a preeminent nation—the United States—could lead the free world in crafting a unified system for dealing with global economic problems. The result was the Bretton Woods agreement, establishing a system of monetary- and economic-policy management among nations so the industrial world could have rules governing commercial and financial relations. The postwar leaders set up the International Monetary Fund, the World Bank, and the General Agreement on Tariffs and Trade to develop rules of the road. The new G-20 is but a pale reflection of that once-brilliant institution building.

Those of us who studied world politics long ago in graduate school recall that nearly every textbook had a chapter entitled something like, "The Elements of National Power." And we went through those elements one at a time. But power is different now. In fact, the very nature of power is being transformed. It is not based to the same extent on how many people are under arms or the strength of the national economy but instead on more subtle attributes and levers of influence. Partly as a result, it is increasingly doubtful there will be in the foreseeable future the kinds of great-power conflicts we have seen in our lifetimes.

In many respects, we live in a messier world. Consider the impact of communications on people and institutions. Throughout much of history, most of the world's people believed they would live much like their parents and that their children would live much like they did. That was simply the inevitable order of the world. That has changed dramatically with the Internet, smartphones and social media. Politically active citizens worldwide now believe they can change things—and they do. An example is the Arab Spring.

And with globalized communications flowing rapidly around the world without checks or filters, readers may have difficulty verifying what they read. Bloggers have few restraints on what they can say or do. Discriminating between fact and opinion is more challenging.

How do we reconcile globalization and the Westphalian state system? Perhaps some refinements in the UN system—built for a world which was significantly different—could bring nation-states together in such a manner that they can cooperate in dealing with international problems such as global warming, health care, global commerce and more. But in the meantime, the world is in a state of drift, transition or even increasing chaos.

Since the end of World War II, the United States has been the country that could take the lead in moving the world from drift to transition and perhaps even to a new global order. The shining example is the immediate post-World War II period. But America is not as well positioned to do that now. The 9/11 attacks were a watershed experience for us. They were a wake-up call that jolted us from the relative calm of the 1990s, when the country basked in the notion that it did not have to think much about foreign policy. Afterward, it became clear that we had to think a great deal about foreign policy.

> **Once, we were viewed as trying to do what was best for everybody; now, we are seen as being preoccupied with our own interests. We have appeared to be seeking to dominate rather than to lead.**

That led to an anomalous decade that has changed how we think about the world and altered our image in the world. Once, we were viewed as trying to do what was best for everybody; now, we are seen as being preoccupied with our own narrow interests. We have appeared sometimes to be seeking to dominate rather than to lead. As a result, it is not as easy as it used to be to get nations to mobilize in the same direction. And that retards our ability to navigate through this time of chaos and transition.

I still believe America remains the only country that can provide this kind of leadership. My hope is we will see the emergence of a gradual understanding that groups must work in concert, not competition, for the greater good. I suspect we will see a gradual erosion of attitudes committed to the total independence of the nation-state and its responsibilities. In addition, there is a growing acceptance of the need to work together in a world in which other forces are superseding the era of nationalism to some extent. Then perhaps a true new world order will emerge. But I am loath to put this into the form of a prognostication. I just hope it isn't merely a case of wishful thinking.

Critical Thinking

1. Why does Scowcroft think that globalization is superseding nationalism?
2. Why does Scowcroft view the end of the Cold War as important?
3. Why does Scowcroft believe that another war between Great Powers will never occur?

BRENT SCOWCROFT is the president and founder of the Scowcroft Group. He served as national-security adviser to presidents Gerald Ford and George H. W. Bush. He is a member of *The National Interest's* Advisory Council.

The Global Power Shift from West to East

CHRISTOPHER LAYNE

When great powers begin to experience erosion in their global standing, their leaders inevitably strike a pose of denial. At the dawn of the twentieth century, as British leaders dimly discerned such an erosion in their country's global dominance, the great diplomat Lord Salisbury issued a gloomy rumination that captured at once both the inevitability of decline and the denial of it. "Whatever happens will be for the worse," he declared. "Therefore it is our interest that as little should happen as possible." Of course, one element of decline was the country's diminishing ability to influence how much or how little actually happened.

We are seeing a similar phenomenon today in America, where the topic of decline stirs discomfort in national leaders. In September 2010, Secretary of State Hillary Clinton proclaimed a "new American Moment" that would "lay the foundations for lasting American leadership for decades to come." A year and a half later, President Obama declared in his State of the Union speech: "Anyone who tells you that America is in decline . . . doesn't know what they're talking about." A position paper from Republican presidential candidate Mitt Romney stated flatly that he "rejects the philosophy of decline in all of its variants." And former United States ambassador to China and one-time GOP presidential candidate Jon Huntsman pronounced decline to be simply "un-American."

Such protestations, however, cannot forestall real-world developments that collectively are challenging the post-1945 international order, often called *Pax Americana,* in which the United States employed its overwhelming power to shape and direct global events. That era of American dominance is drawing to a close as the country's relative power declines, along with its ability to manage global economics and security.

This does not mean the United States will go the way of Great Britain during the first half of the twentieth century. As Harvard's Stephen Walt wrote in this magazine last year, it is more accurate to say the "American Era" is nearing its end. For now, and for some time to come, the United States will remain primus inter pares—the strongest of the major world powers—though it is uncertain whether it can maintain that position over the next twenty years. Regardless, America's power and influence over the international political system will diminish markedly from what it was at the apogee of *Pax Americana.* That was the Old Order, forged through the momentous events of World War I, the Great Depression and World War II. Now that

Old Order of nearly seven decades' duration is fading from the scene. It is natural that United States leaders would want to deny it—or feel they must finesse it when talking to the American people. But the real questions for America and its leaders are: What will replace the Old Order? How can Washington protect its interests in the new global era? And how much international disruption will attend the transition from the old to the new?

The signs of the emerging new world order are many. First, there is China's astonishingly rapid rise to great-power status, both militarily and economically. In the economic realm, the International Monetary Fund forecasts that China's share of world GDP (15 percent) will draw nearly even with the United States share (18 percent) by 2014. (The United States share at the end of World War II was nearly 50 percent.) This is particularly startling given that China's share of world GDP was only 2 percent in 1980 and 6 percent as recently as 1995. Moreover, China is on course to overtake the United States as the world's largest economy (measured by market exchange rate) sometime this decade. And, as argued by economists like Arvind Subramanian, measured by purchasing-power parity, China's GDP may already be greater than that of the United States.

Until the late 1960s, the United States was the world's dominant manufacturing power. Today, it has become essentially a rentier economy, while China is the world's leading manufacturing nation. A study recently reported in the *Financial Times* indicates that 58 percent of total income in America now comes from dividends and interest payments.

Since the Cold War's end, America's military superiority has functioned as an entry barrier designed to prevent emerging powers from challenging the United States where its interests are paramount. But the country's ability to maintain this barrier faces resistance at both ends. First, the deepening financial crisis will compel retrenchment, and the United States will be increasingly less able to invest in its military. Second, as ascending powers such as China become wealthier, their military expenditures will expand. The *Economist* recently projected that China's defense spending will equal that of the United States by 2025.

Thus, over the next decade or so a feedback loop will be at work, whereby internal constraints on United States global activity will help fuel a shift in the distribution of power, and this in turn will magnify the effects of America's fiscal and strategic overstretch. With interests throughout Asia, the Middle East, Africa, Europe and the Caucasus—not to mention the role of guarding the world's sea-lanes and protecting United States citizens from Islamist terrorists—a strategically overextended United States inevitably will need to retrench.

Further, there is a critical linkage between a great power's military and economic standing, on the one hand, and its prestige, soft power and agenda-setting capacity, on the other. As the hard-power foundations of *Pax Americana* erode, so too will the United States capacity to shape the international order through influence, example and largesse. This is particularly true of America in the wake of the 2008 financial crisis and the subsequent Great Recession. At the zenith of its military and economic power after World War II, the United States possessed the material capacity to furnish the international system with abundant financial assistance designed to maintain economic and political stability. Now, this capacity is much diminished.

All of this will unleash growing challenges to the Old Order from ambitious regional powers such as China, Brazil, India, Russia, Turkey and Indonesia. Given America's relative loss of standing, emerging powers will feel increasingly emboldened to test and probe the current order with an eye toward reshaping the international system in ways that reflect their own interests, norms and values. This is particularly true of China, which has emerged from its "century of humiliation" at the hands of the West to finally achieve great-power status. It is a leap to think that Beijing will now embrace a role as "responsible stakeholder" in an international order built by the United States and designed to privilege American interests, norms and values.

These profound developments raise big questions about where the world is headed and America's role in the transition and beyond. Managing the transition will be the paramount strategic challenge for the United States over the next two decades. In thinking about where we might be headed, it is helpful to take a look backward—not just over the past seventy years but far back into the past. That is because the transition in progress represents more than just the end of the post-1945 era of American global dominance. It also represents the end of the era of Western dominance over world events that began roughly five hundred years ago. During this half millennium of world history, the West's global position remained secure, and most big, global developments were represented by intracivilizational power shifts. Now, however, as the international system's economic and geopolitical center of gravity migrates from the Euro-Atlantic world to Asia, we are seeing the beginnings of an intercivilizational power shift. The significance of this development cannot be overemphasized.

The impending end of the Old Order—both *Pax Americana* and the period of Western ascendancy—heralds a fraught transition to a new and uncertain constellation of power in international politics. Within the ascendant West, the era of American dominance emerged out of the ashes of the previous international order, *Pax Britannica*. It signified Europe's displacement by the United States as the locus of global power. But it took the twentieth century's two world wars and the global depression to forge the transition between these international orders.

Following the end of the Napoleonic wars in 1815, at the dawn of the Industrial Revolution, Britain quickly outstripped all of its rivals in building up its industrial might and used its financial muscle to construct an open, international economic system. The cornerstones of this *Pax Britannica* were London's role as the global financial center and the Royal Navy's unchallenged supremacy around the world. Over time, however, the British-sponsored international system of free trade began to undermine London's global standing by facilitating the diffusion of capital, technology, innovation and managerial expertise to emerging new centers of power. This helped fuel the rise of economic and geopolitical rivals.

Between 1870 and 1900, the United States, Germany and Japan emerged onto the international scene more or less simultaneously, and both the European and global power balances began to change in ways that ultimately would doom *Pax Britannica*. By the beginning of the twentieth century, it had become increasingly difficult for Britain to cope with the growing number of threats to its strategic interests and to compete with the dynamic economies of the United States and Germany.

The Boer War of 1899–1902 dramatized the high cost of policing the empire and served as both harbinger and accelerant of British decline. Perceptions grew of an ever-widening gap between Britain's strategic commitments and the resources available to maintain them. Also, the rest of the world became less and less willing to submit to British influence and power. The empire's strategic isolation was captured in the plaintive words of Spenser Wilkinson, military correspondent for the *Times*: "We have no friends, and no nation loves us."

Imperially overstretched and confronting a deteriorating strategic environment, London was forced to adjust its grand strategy and jettison its nineteenth-century policy of "splendid isolation" from entanglements with other countries. Another consideration was the rising threat of Germany, growing in economic dynamism, military might and population. By 1900, Germany had passed Britain in economic power and was beginning to threaten London's naval supremacy in its home waters by building a large, modern and powerful battle fleet. To concentrate its forces against the German danger, Britain allied with Japan and employed Tokyo to contain German and Russian expansionism in East Asia. It also removed America as a potential rival by ceding to Washington supremacy over the Americas and the Caribbean. Finally, it settled its differences with France and Russia, then formed fateful de facto alliances with each against Germany.

World War I marked the end of *Pax Britannica*—and the beginning of the end of Europe's geopolitical dominance. The key event was American entry into the war. It was Woodrow Wilson who called the power of the New World "into existence to redress the balance of the Old" (in the words of the early nineteenth-century British statesman George Canning). American economic and military power was crucial in securing Germany's defeat. Wilson took the United States to war in 1917 with the intent of using American power to impose his vision of international order on *both* the Germans and the Allies. The peace treaties that ended World War I—the "Versailles system"—proved to be flawed, however. Wilson could not persuade his own countrymen to join his cherished League of Nations, and European realpolitik prevailed over his vision of the postwar order.

Although the historical wisdom is that America retreated into isolationism following Wilson's second term and Warren Harding's return to "normalcy," that is not true. The United States convened the Washington Naval Conference and helped foster the Washington naval treaties, which averted a United States naval arms race with Britain and Japan and dampened prospects for increased great-power competition over influence in China. America also played a key role in trying to restore economic, and hence political, stability in war-ravaged Europe. It promoted Germany's economic reconstruction and political reintegration into Europe through the Dawes and Young plans that addressed the troublesome issue of German reparations. The aim was to help get Europe back on its feet so it could once again become a vibrant market for American goods.

Then came the Great Depression. In both Europe and Asia, the economic cataclysm had profound geopolitical consequences. As E. H. Carr brilliantly detailed in his classic work *The Twenty Years' Crisis, 1919–1939,* the Versailles system cracked because of the growing gap between the order it represented and the actual distribution of power in Europe. Even during the 1920s, Germany's latent power raised the prospect that eventually Berlin would renew its bid for continental hegemony. When Adolf Hitler assumed the chancellorship in 1933, he unleashed Germany's military power, suppressed during the 1920s, and ultimately France and Britain lacked the material capacity to enforce the postwar settlement. The Depression also exacerbated deep social, class and ideological cleavages that roiled domestic politics throughout Europe.

In East Asia, the Depression served to discredit the liberal foreign and economic policies that Japan had pursued during the 1920s. The expansionist elements of the Japanese army gained sway in Tokyo and pushed their country into military adventurism in Manchuria. In response to the economic dislocation, all great powers, including the United States, abandoned international economic openness and free trade in favor of economic nationalism, protectionism and mercantilism.

The crisis of the 1930s culminated in what historian John Lukacs called "the last European war." But it didn't remain a European war. Germany's defeat could be secured only with American military and economic power and the heroic exertions of the Soviet Union. Meanwhile, the war quickly spread to the Pacific, where Western colonial redoubts had come under intense military pressure from Japan.

World War II reshaped international politics in three fundamental ways. First, it resulted in what historian Hajo Holborn termed "the political collapse of Europe," which brought down the final curtain on the Eurocentric epoch of international politics. Now an economically prostrate Western Europe was unable to defend itself or revive itself economically without American assistance. Second, the wartime defeats of the British, French and Dutch in Asia—particularly the humiliating 1942 British capitulation in Singapore—shattered the myth of

European invincibility and thus set in motion a rising nationalist tide that within two decades would result in the liquidation of Europe's colonies in Asia. This laid the foundation for Asia's economic rise that began gathering momentum in the 1970s. Finally, the war created the geopolitical and economic conditions that enabled the United States to construct the postwar international order and establish itself as the world's dominant power, first in the bipolar era of competition with the Soviet Union and later as the globe's sole superpower following the 1991 Soviet collapse.

Periods of global transition can be chaotic, unpredictable, long and bloody. Whether the current transitional phase will unfold with greater smoothness and calm is an open question.

Thus do we see the emergence of the new world order of 1945, which now represents the Old Order that is under its own global strains. But we also see the long, agonizing death of *Pax Britannica*, which had maintained relative global stability for a century before succumbing to the fires of the two world wars and the Great Depression. This tells us that periods of global transition can be chaotic, unpredictable, long and bloody. Whether the current transitional phase will unfold with greater smoothness and calm is an open question—and one of the great imponderables facing the world today.

As the United States emerged as the world's leading power, it sought to establish its postwar dominance in the three regions deemed most important to its interests: Western Europe, East Asia and the Middle East/Persian Gulf. It also fostered an open international-trading regime and assumed the role of the global financial system's manager, much as Britain had done in the nineteenth century. The 1944 Bretton Woods agreement established the dollar as the international reserve currency. The World Bank, International Monetary Fund, and the General Agreement on Tariffs and Trade fostered international commerce. The United Nations was created, and a network of American-led alliances established, most notably NATO.

It is tempting to look back on the Cold War years as a time of heroic American initiatives. After all, geopolitically, Washington accomplished a remarkable double play: while avoiding great-power war, containment—as George F. Kennan foresaw in 1946—helped bring about the eventual implosion of the Soviet Union from its own internal contradictions. In Europe, American power resolved the German problem, paved the way for Franco-German reconciliation and was the springboard for Western Europe's economic integration. In Asia, the United States helped rebuild a stable and democratic Japan from the ashes of its World War II defeat. For the trilateral world of *Pax Americana*—centered on the United States, Western Europe and Japan—the twenty-five years following World War II marked an era of unprecedented peace and prosperity. These were remarkable accomplishments and are justly celebrated as such. Nevertheless, it is far from clear that the reality of the Cold War era measures up to the nostalgic glow in which it has been bathed. Different policies might have brought about the Cold War's end but at a much less expensive price for the United States.

The Cold War was costly in treasure and in blood (the most obvious examples being the wars in Korea and Vietnam). America bears significant responsibility for heightening postwar tensions with the Soviet Union and transforming what ought to have been a traditional great-power rivalry based on mutual recognition of spheres of influence into the intense ideological rivalry it became. During the Cold War, United States leaders engaged in threat inflation and overhyped Soviet power. Some leading policy makers and commentators at the time—notably Kennan and prominent journalist Walter Lippmann—warned against the increasingly global and militarized nature of America's containment strategy, fearing that the United States would become overextended if it attempted to parry Soviet or communist probes everywhere. President Dwight Eisenhower also was concerned about the Cold War's costs, the burden it imposed on the United States economy and the threat it posed to the very system of government that the United States was supposed to be defending. Belief in the universality of American values and ideals was at the heart of United States containment strategy during most of the Cold War, and the determination to vindicate its model of political, economic and social development is what caused the United States to stumble into the disastrous Vietnam War.

Whatever questions could have been raised about the wisdom of America's Cold War policies faded rapidly after the Soviet Union's collapse, which triggered a wave of euphoric triumphalism in the United States. Analysts celebrated America's "unipolar moment" and perceived an "end of history" characterized by a decisive triumph of Western-style democracy as an end point in human civic development. Almost by definition, such thinking ruled out the prospect that this triumph could prove fleeting.

But even during the Cold War's last two decades, the seeds of American decline had already been sown. In a prescient—but premature—analysis, President Richard Nixon and Secretary of State Henry Kissinger believed that the bipolar Cold War system would give way to a pentagonal multipolar system composed of the United States, Soviet Union, Europe, China and Japan. Nixon also confronted America's declining international financial power in 1971 when he took the dollar off the Bretton Woods gold standard in response to currency pressures. Later, in 1987, Yale's Paul Kennedy published his brilliant *Rise and Fall of the Great Powers,* which raised questions about the structural, fiscal and economic weaknesses in America that, over time, could nibble away at the foundations of United States power. With America's subsequent Cold War triumph—and the bursting of Japan's economic bubble—Kennedy's thesis was widely dismissed.

Now, in the wake of the 2008 financial meltdown and ensuing recession, it is clear that Kennedy and other "declinists" were right all along. The same causes of decline they pointed to are at the center of today's debate about America's economic prospects: too much consumption and not enough savings; persistent trade and current-account deficits; deindustrialization; sluggish economic growth; and chronic federal-budget deficits fueling an ominously rising national debt.

Indeed, looking forward a decade, the two biggest domestic threats to United States power are the country's bleak fiscal outlook and deepening doubts about the dollar's future role as the international economy's reserve currency. Economists regard a 100 percent debt-to-GDP ratio as a flashing warning light that a country is at risk of defaulting on its financial obligations. The nonpartisan Congressional Budget Office (CBO) has warned that the United States debt-to-gdp ratio could exceed that level by 2020—and swell to 190 percent by 2035. Worse, the CBO recently warned of the possibility of a "sudden credit event" triggered by foreign investors' loss of confidence in United States fiscal probity. In such an event, foreign investors could reduce their purchases of Treasury bonds, which would force the United States to borrow at higher interest rates. This, in turn, would drive up the national debt even more. America's geopolitical preeminence hinges on the dollar's role as reserve currency. If the dollar loses that status, United States primacy would be literally unaffordable. There are reasons to be concerned about the dollar's fate over the next two decades. United States political gridlock casts doubt on the nation's ability to address its fiscal woes; China is beginning to internationalize the renminbi, thus laying the foundation for it to challenge the dollar in the future; and history suggests that the dominant international currency is that of the nation with the largest economy. (In his piece on the global financial structure in this issue, Christopher Whalen offers a contending perspective, acknowledging the dangers posed to the dollar as reserve currency but suggesting such a change in the dollar's status is remote in the current global environment.)

Leaving aside the fate of the dollar, however, it is clear the United States must address its financial challenge and restore the nation's fiscal health in order to reassure foreign lenders that their investments remain sound. This will require some combination of budget cuts, entitlement reductions, tax increases and interest-rate hikes. That, in turn, will surely curtail the amount of spending available for defense and national security—further eroding America's ability to play its traditional, post-World War II global role.

Beyond the United States financial challenge, the world is percolating with emerging nations bent on exploiting the power shift away from the West and toward states that long have been confined to subordinate status in the global power game. (Parag Khanna explores this phenomenon at length further in this issue.) By far the biggest test for the United States will be its relationship with China, which views itself as effecting a restoration of its former glory, before the First Opium War of 1839–1842 and its subsequent "century of humiliation." After all, China and India were the world's two largest economies in 1700, and as late as 1820 China's economy was larger than the combined economies of all of Europe. The question of why the West emerged as the world's most powerful civilization beginning in the sixteenth century, and thus was able to impose its will on China and India, has been widely debated. Essentially, the answer is firepower. As the late Samuel P. Huntington put it, "The West won the world not by the superiority of its ideas or values or religion . . . but rather by its superiority in applying organized violence. Westerners often forget this fact; non-Westerners never do."

Certainly, the Chinese have not forgotten. Now Beijing aims to dominate its own East and Southeast Asian backyard, just as a rising America sought to dominate the Western Hemisphere a century and a half ago. The United States and China now are competing for supremacy in East and Southeast Asia. Washington has been the incumbent hegemon there since World War II, and many in the American foreign-policy establishment view China's quest for regional hegemony as a threat that must be resisted. This contest for regional dominance is fueling escalating tensions and possibly could lead to war. In geopolitics, two great powers cannot simultaneously be hegemonic in the same region. Unless one of them abandons its aspirations, there is a high probability of hostilities. Flashpoints that could spark a Sino-American conflict include the unstable Korean Peninsula; the disputed status of Taiwan; competition for control of oil and other natural resources; and the burgeoning naval rivalry between the two powers.

These rising tensions were underscored by a recent Brookings study by Peking University's Wang Jisi and Kenneth Lieberthal, national-security director for Asia during the Clinton administration, based on their conversations with high-level officials in the American and Chinese governments. Wang found that underneath the visage of "mutual cooperation" that both countries project, the Chinese believe they are likely to replace the United States as the world's leading power but Washington is working to prevent such a rise. Similarly, Lieberthal related that many American officials believe their Chinese counterparts see the United States-Chinese relationship in terms of a zero-sum game in the struggle for global hegemony.

An instructive historical antecedent is the Anglo-German rivalry of the early twentieth century. The key lesson of that rivalry is that such great-power competition can end in one of three ways: accommodation of the rising challenger by the dominant power; retreat of the challenger; or war. The famous 1907 memo exchange between two key British Foreign Office officials—Sir Eyre Crowe and Lord Thomas Sanderson— outlined these stark choices. Crowe argued that London must uphold the *Pax Britannica* status quo at all costs. Either Germany would accept its place in a British-dominated world order, he averred, or Britain would have to contain Germany's rising power, even at the risk of war. Sanderson replied that London's refusal to accommodate the reality of Germany's rising power was both unwise and dangerous. He suggested Germany's leaders must view Britain "in the light of some huge giant sprawling over the globe, with gouty fingers and toes stretching in every direction, which cannot be approached without eliciting a scream." In Beijing's eyes today, the United States must appear as the unapproachable, globally sprawling giant.

In modern history, there have been two liberal international orders: *Pax Britannica* and *Pax Americana.* In building their respective international structures, Britain and the United States wielded their power to advance their own economic and geopolitical interests. But they also bestowed important benefits—public goods—on the international system as a whole. Militarily, the hegemon took responsibility for stabilizing key regions and safeguarding the lines of communication and trade routes upon which an open international economy depend. Economically, the public goods included rules for the international economic order, a welcome domestic market for other states' exports, liquidity for the global economy and a reserve currency.

As United States power wanes over the next decade or so, the United States will find itself increasingly challenged in discharging these hegemonic tasks. This could have profound implications for international politics. The erosion of *Pax Britannica* in the late nineteenth and early twentieth centuries was an important cause of World War I. During the interwar years, no great power exercised geopolitical or economic leadership, and this proved to be a major cause of the Great Depression and its consequences, including the fragmentation of the international economy into regional trade blocs and the beggar-thy-neighbor economic nationalism that spilled over into the geopolitical rivalries of the 1930s. This, in turn, contributed greatly to World War II. The unwinding of *Pax Americana* could have similar consequences. Since no great power, including China, is likely to supplant the United States as a true global hegemon, the world could see a serious fragmentation of power. This could spawn pockets of instability around the world and even general global instability.

The United States has a legacy commitment to global stability, and that poses a particular challenge to the waning hegemon as it seeks to fulfill its commitment with dwindling resources. The fundamental challenge for the United States as it faces the future is closing the "Lippmann gap," named for journalist Walter Lippmann. This means bringing America's commitments into balance with the resources available to support them while creating a surplus of power in reserve. To do this, the country will need to establish new strategic priorities and accept the inevitability that some commitments will need to be reduced because it no longer can afford them.

These national imperatives will force the United States to craft some kind of foreign-policy approach that falls under the rubric of "offshore balancing"—directing American power and influence toward maintaining a balance of power in key strategic regions of the world. This concept—first articulated by this writer in a 1997 article in the journal *International Security*—has gained increasing attention over the past decade or so as other prominent geopolitical scholars, including John Mearsheimer, Stephen Walt, Robert Pape, Barry Posen and Andrew Bacevich, have embraced this approach.

Although there are shades of difference among proponents of offshore balancing in terms of how they define the strategy, all of their formulations share core concepts in common. First, it assumes the United States will have to reduce its presence in some regions and develop commitment priorities. Europe and the Middle East are viewed as less important than they once were, with East Asia rising in strategic concern. Second, as the United States scales back its military presence abroad, other states need to step up to the challenge of maintaining stability in key regions. Offshore balancing, thus, is a strategy of devolving security responsibilities to others. Its goal is burden shifting, not burden sharing. Only when the United States makes clear that it will do less—in Europe, for example—will others do more to foster stability in their own regions.

Third, the concept relies on naval and air power while eschewing land power as much as possible. This is designed to maximize America's comparative strategic advantages—standoff, precision-strike weapons; command-and-control capabilities; and superiority in intelligence, reconnaissance and surveillance. After all, fighting land wars in Eurasia is not what the United States does best. Fourth, the concept avoids Wilsonian crusades in foreign policy, "nation-building" initiatives and imperial impulses. Not only does Washington have a long record of failure in such adventures, but they are also expensive. In an age of domestic austerity, the United States cannot afford the luxury of participating in overseas engagements that contribute little to its security and can actually pose added security problems. Finally, offshore balancing would reduce the heavy American geopolitical footprint caused by United States boots on the ground in the Middle East—the backlash effect of which is to fuel Islamic extremism. An over-the-horizon United States military posture in the region thus would reduce the terrorist threat while still safeguarding the flow of Persian Gulf oil.

During the next two decades, the United States will face some difficult choices between bad outcomes and worse ones. But such decisions could determine whether America will manage a graceful decline that conserves as much power and global stability as possible. A more ominous possibility is a precipitous power collapse that reduces United States global influence dramatically. In any event, Americans will have to adjust to the new order, accepting the loss of some elements of national life they had taken for granted. In an age of austerity, national resources will be limited, and competition for them will be intense. If the country wants to do more at home, it will have to do less abroad. It may have to choose between attempting to preserve American hegemony or repairing the United States economy and maintaining the country's social safety net.

The constellation of world power is changing, and United States grand strategy will have to change with it. American elites must come to grips with the fact that the West does not enjoy a predestined supremacy in international politics that is locked into the future for an indeterminate period of time. The Euro-Atlantic world had a long run of global dominance, but it is coming to an end. The future is more likely to be shaped by the East.

> **American elites must come to grips with the fact that the West does not enjoy a predestined supremacy in international politics that is locked into the future for an indeterminate period of time.**

At the same time, *Pax Americana* also is winding down. The United States can manage this relative decline effectively over the next couple of decades only if it first acknowledges the fundamental reality of decline. The problem is that many Americans, particularly among the elites, have embraced the notion of American exceptionalism with such fervor that they can't discern the world transformation occurring before their eyes.

But history moves forward with an inexorable force, and it does not stop to grant special exemptions to nations based on past good works or the restrained exercise of power during times of hegemony. So is it with the United States. The world has changed since those heady days following World War II, when the United States picked up the mantle of world leadership and fashioned a world system durable enough to last nearly seventy years. It has also changed significantly since those remarkable times from 1989 to 1991, when the Soviet Union imploded and its ashes filled the American consciousness with powerful notions of national exceptionalism and the infinite unipolar moment of everlasting United States hegemony.

But most discerning Americans know that history never ends, that change is always inevitable, that nations and civilizations rise and fall, that no era can last forever. Now it can be seen that the post-World War II era, romanticized as it has been in the minds of so many Americans, is the Old Order—and it is an Old Order in crisis, which means it is nearing its end. History, as always, is moving forward.

Critical Thinking

1. Do you agree that the great Power transition underway is dangerous? Why or why not?

2. Did the United States retreat into isolationism after the First World War? Why or why not?

3. How did World War II reshape international politics?

4. Do you agree with the Declinist school of thought as presented in Layne's article? Why or why not?

5. Is China a stakeholder in the international system? Why or why not?

CHRISTOPHER LAYNE is professor and Robert M. Gates Chair in National Security at Texas A & M University's George H. W. Bush School of Government and Public Service. His current book project, to be published by Yale University Press, is *After the Fall: International Politics, United States Grand Strategy, and the End of the Pax Americana*.

The Shifting Landscape of Latin American Regionalism

"Brazil's rise, coupled with the diminished influence of the United States and the increasingly salient global role of China, has reshuffled the kaleidoscope of regional organizations. . . ."

MICHAEL SHIFTER

Celso Amorim is understandably proud of his eight-year tenure as foreign minister during Brazil's notable ascent in regional and global arenas. Amorim, who managed foreign policy under the two highly successful administrations of Luis Inácio Lula da Silva (and currently serves as defense minister for Lula's successor, Dilma Rousseff), points less to any specific accomplishments than to Brazil's growing self-confidence and prominence in global affairs. He credits the boost to the Lula government's ability to ride a favorable wave derived largely from the country's economic dynamism, social progress, and democratic advance in recent years.

Brazil's rise, coupled with the diminished influence of the United States and the increasingly salient global role of China, has reshuffled the kaleidoscope of regional organizations in the Americas. The Organization of American States (OAS), established in 1948 in Bogotá, Colombia, is the world's oldest regional organization. Yet for a number of years it has been buffeted by profound political changes that have upset the traditional, more clear-cut asymmetrical power axis between the United States and Latin American and Caribbean nations.

Today new and competing asymmetries, shifting fault lines, and emerging counterweights in flux throughout the Americas are manifest in a dizzying array of regional groupings. Some of these groupings bear an ideological stripe, such as the leftist Latin American Bolivarian Alternative (ALBA) that Venezuela started in 2004. Most, however, are products of divergent national interests and strategic priorities and as such reflect economic agendas and geographical positions. These include the 12-member Union of South American Nations (UNASUR), created by Brazil in 2008.

It is tempting to be skeptical about the proliferation of these crosscutting and often overlapping mechanisms. So far, most have developed little institutional solidity and have even produced a measure of fatigue among regional leaders. It is hard to know whether they will be able to sustain and strengthen their efforts, or will, with time, simply fade into the background.

Even so, it would be a mistake to ignore or dismiss the rich institutional experimentation under way and the new regional architecture that is taking shape. At the least, this changing architecture offers an optic through which to view and fathom the region's political dynamics and the impact of global trends in the hemisphere. It also illuminates the changing expressions of regionalism—a serious current that enjoys a long and enduring history in the Americas.

Members Only

The founding of the Community of Latin American and Caribbean Nations, or CELAC, in Caracas, Venezuela, in December 2011, revealed how much the region's politics has changed in recent years. However vague its purposes and weak its institutional underpinnings, CELAC, which pointedly excludes the United States and Canada, encompasses all of the other countries of the Americas, including Cuba. It exemplifies the accelerated political distancing and increased independence of the region, especially from the United States. Tellingly, the December meeting was barely noticed by an otherwise preoccupied Washington.

Perhaps it was inevitable that the CELAC launching in Caracas would be widely portrayed as yet another diplomatic coup for Venezuela's president, Hugo Chávez, who has been doggedly intent on curtailing the influence of the United States in regional and global affairs since he came to power in early 1999. Not surprisingly, Chávez, whose health has been the source of much speculation since he was diagnosed with cancer in June 2011, touted the gathering as a triumphant fulfillment of the dream of regional solidarity and integration espoused by South America's independence hero—and Chávez's inspiration—Simón Bolívar nearly 200 years ago.

But Chávez's penchant for hyperbole and flair for symbolism aside, the formation of CELAC should not be interpreted as an expression of anti-Americanism or even a political move to supplant the OAS. Rather, it should be understood as an attempt to narrow political chasms and reconcile disparate actors within the region itself. The history behind the creation of CELAC in part highlights the contrasting visions and competing aims displayed by the region's two principal economic and political powerhouses: Brazil and Mexico. Indeed, one of the most significant strategic fault lines in the Americas lies between South America and North America, which extends above Panama and includes Mexico as well as the United States and Canada.

The formation of CELAC should not be interpreted as an expression of anti-Americanism.

In a number of fundamental respects—economically, demographically, and culturally—Mexico, along with the nations of Central America, is closely connected with the United States. Along these dimensions the links are, if anything, deepening. Geography, of course, also matters a great deal. More than 80 percent of Mexico's trade is with the United States. In 1993, the signing of the North American Free Trade Agreement (NAFTA) that encompassed Mexico, the United States, and Canada, helped cement commercial bonds among the three partners. And in 2005, the Central American Free Trade Agreement (or CAFTA, which also included the Dominican Republic) was adopted, reducing tariffs and helping to facilitate trade flows with the United States. Mexicans and Central Americans also constitute a disproportionate share of the dramatically increasing Latino population in the United States, thus intensifying cultural ties.

At the same time, Mexico is quite clearly a Latin American nation in all key respects and is widely viewed as such by others. Its relations with the rest of the region have been integral to its foreign policy agenda—in part to balance the traditionally overwhelming clout exercised by the United States. Mexico, for example, helped found and played an important leadership role in the Rio Group. A bloc that emerged in the context of the Central American civil wars of the 1980s, the Rio Group sought to challenge hard-line United States cold war policies and foster peace efforts. For Mexico it has also been important to have a presence in some South American regional groupings, typically led by Brazil. A prominent example is Mexico's special agreement with the Common Market of the South (Mercosur), a trading bloc established in 1991.

Brazil Steps Up

While Mexico has long been regarded as a Latin American nation, such an identity was historically more ambiguous for Brazil. The notion of "Latin America," which developed among Colombian and Argentine writers and French intellectuals in the mid-nineteenth century, had scant resonance in Brazil, which tended to be more inward-looking and separate—divided by history, culture, language, and politics from its continental neighbors.

For such a significant regional power and emerging global player—today it has the world's sixth largest economy—Brazil was notably delayed in promoting regional organizations in South America. Although Mercosur was set up in the early 1990s, it was not until 2000 that then-President Fernando Henrique Cardoso of Brazil convened the first meeting of South American leaders. But Brazil's sheer size and economic and political power made such a turn toward greater engagement with the region highly plausible.

Over the past dozen years Brazil's approach toward its neighbors has been substantially shaped by two connected objectives: the desire to keep things under control in its immediate sphere of influence, and its pursuit of global aspirations. One of Brazil's main priorities has been to secure a permanent seat on the United Nations Security Council. It was that aim—more than any regional goals—that led Brazil to play a leading role in the UN peacekeeping mission in Haiti starting in 2004. The country has also sought a significant voice in other global arenas. It has actively participated in the World Trade Organization, and has been a serious, respected player in the Group of 20 in the context of the recent economic crisis.

Moreover, Brazil has emphasized alliances with other emerging powers more than with other Latin American countries. As one of the so-called BRICS (along with Russia, India, China, and South Africa), Brazil has strengthened relationships that are aimed at enhancing its leverage with traditional powers, particularly the United States. Brazil has for the most part preferred to deal with the United States bilaterally, and has been wary of any hemisphere-wide—and presumably United States-led—arrangements, such as the Free Trade Area of the Americas (FTAA), a proposal that emerged from the first Summit of the Americas in Miami in 1994.

During the Lula era—and particularly its final years, when the country witnessed remarkable economic vitality and growing influence in global affairs—Brazil became increasingly active in social development efforts in Africa, and also tried its hand in Middle Eastern diplomacy. Its boldest move came in 2010 with a joint proposal developed with Turkey to deal with Iran's nuclear program. Brazil's accommodating approach differed sharply from Washington's more hard-line posture, reflecting mutual irritation that has been alleviated somewhat during the current Rousseff administration.

At the same time, Brazil has developed more expansive economic and political roles within the region. The Lula government devoted considerable attention to building the Union of South American Nations (UNASUR), which evolved from a fairly loose, amorphous grouping. Today UNASUR has a formally organized structure with a permanent secretariat that was initially headed by the former Argentine president Néstor Kirchner. Although other leaders responded to the Brazilian initiative with varying degrees of enthusiasm—Peruvian President Alan García showed little interest and Colombian President Álvaro Uribe was notably resistant—the exclusively South American organization appears to have taken hold.

Such a development hardly went unnoticed in Mexico, which coincidentally at that time was in charge of the Rio Group. Mexico's response was instructive. Until 2008, the Rio

Group was made up of all Latin American nations—with the exception of Cuba. But at a meeting of foreign ministers, Mexico proposed that Cuba be admitted as a member. Even though the establishment of democracy had been a condition for Rio Group membership from the outset, Mexico's proposal was adopted. (Cuba's presence has been a distinguishing feature of the Ibero-American Summit, which includes Spain and Portugal along with the rest of the region, since it began in 1991.) With Mexico's encouragement, the Rio Group then invited all of the Anglophone Caribbean nations to join as well.

Against that backdrop, in late 2008 the Lula government took advantage of an already scheduled UNASUR meeting to convene a "mega-summit" in Costa do Sauipe, Bahia. All regional governments embraced Brazil's initiative, albeit for different reasons. Mexico quickly offered to host the next such gathering of Latin American and Caribbean leaders, in Cancun, Mexico, in February 2010. It was there that the idea of CELAC was conceived, though it was essentially a renamed and more formalized Rio Group. (Regional organizations may be proliferating, but at least one, the Rio Group, has ceased to exist.)

Although Chávez and much of the media depicted the December 2011 CELAC meeting as a rejection of the United States and the realization of Bolívar's vision, it rather was a product of the rebalancing of political positions in the Americas. The series of steps that culminated in CELAC's founding can be attributed more to the dynamics in Latin American relations—particularly between Brazil and Mexico—than to any regional stance toward the United States.

Yet, unless a regional leader decides to give it a high priority and more structure, it is doubtful that CELAC will be transformed into a formal institution. There will be periodic meetings of heads of state—the next ones are scheduled to take place in Chile, followed by Cuba—but without a secretariat or any political decisions with teeth. Mexico is content to be part of the grouping, which reconnects it to South American political affairs, but at the same time enables it to focus on its NAFTA partners. Brazil's priority in the Americas is clearly centered on UNASUR, which is seen as an instrument for maintaining social peace and order in the wider region.

Ambivalent Neighbors

UNASUR proponents point to such political achievements as its role in helping to defuse tensions that flared between Colombia and Venezuela in 2008, along with responses to internal political crises in Bolivia (2008) and Ecuador (2010). Nevertheless, some observers are still dubious about the organization's efficacy. UNASUR's interventions in both national situations backed the current government, so its potential role in settling domestic disputes remains untested. There are, moreover, questions about the group's financing and its ability to establish an adequate organizational infrastructure.

After Néstor Kirchner's death, UNASUR members decided on a rotating executive secretary—first with former Colombian foreign minister María Emma Mejía, followed by Venezuela's former foreign minister Alí Rodríguez (who will assume the position in May 2012). Some projects are under way aimed

at upgrading infrastructure and communications in the continent; such projects are commensurate with Brazil's regional and global interests. In addition, the affiliated South American Defense Council seems prepared to perform a valuable function in amassing information and sharing policy ideas about security-related questions in the continent. These kinds of efforts may end up being more feasible and realistic than a genuine scheme of political integration, which remains problematic.

Indeed, relations between Brazil and its South American neighbors are complicated. To be sure, other South American nations have benefited from Brazil's role as an engine of economic growth and development. Within the continent, trade and investment flows have grown dramatically (in the context of a surge in overall trade), and Brazil has been an important driving force.

But it is not hard to discern spreading resentment among some of Brazil's South American neighbors—a natural product of increasingly marked power asymmetries in the continent. As *The New York Times* noted in a November 2011 report, some of the misgivings voiced by Brazil's neighbors have echoes of longstanding grievances leveled at the United States, including heavy-handed tactics, and dictating rather than negotiating as equal partners.

Other common complaints include Brazil's failure to consult adequately with its neighbors before it takes stands at global meetings. Also, other South American nations tend to identify more closely with "Latin America" than Brazil does, and are therefore uneasy with what they view as Brazilians' focus on South America at times to the exclusion of the rest of the region, including Spanish-speaking Mexico.

Despite its dominant role, Brazil has no discernible agenda for regional governance.

Brazil, acutely aware of such sentiments, seeks to mollify its neighbors' concerns, often resorting to multilateral instruments. Regional mechanisms like UNASUR are in part designed to smooth the rough edges that inevitably accompany the differentials in power on many crucial dimensions between Brazil and its neighbors. Despite its dominant role, however, Brazil has no discernible agenda for regional governance. And it is probably a stretch to refer to what is taking place as "integration" in any strict sense of the term. Rather, there is a move toward increased cooperation and political dialogue, which constitute the spirit and tenor of "regionalism," but without any serious attempt to cede sovereignty, which is the essence of integration.

In fact, careful examination of the performance and record of subregional groupings to date raises questions about the potential effectiveness of more far-reaching regional arrangements. Mercosur, which was to serve as a customs union involving Brazil, Argentina, Uruguay, and Paraguay, witnessed a jump in trade in the 1990s, but over time its functioning has become problematic. Protectionist practices have introduced considerable strain within the bloc.

In addition, Mercosur's inability to resolve a rancorous dispute between Argentina and Uruguay over the operation of a paper mill on their border exposed serious limitations in its effectiveness. Yet, for all of its shortcomings, Mercosur is generally regarded as less troubled than other subregional groupings in Latin America. For example, the Andean Community of Nations, which has existed since 1969, has been riven by political differences and high levels of mistrust. Other subregional arrangements face similar obstacles.

In this context, some Latin American countries have intensified bilateral ties with economic powerhouses like Brazil—but have simultaneously pursued options to offset any one nation's excessive influence. The case of Colombia is particularly telling. From the start of his presidency in August 2010, Juan Manuel Santos has assigned a high priority to reengaging with South America, from which Colombia had become relatively isolated during the Uribe administration. Uribe had concentrated on his country's battle against domestic insurgents and had, as a result, invested heavily in cultivating Washington to ensure continued support.

In seeking to rebalance and realign Colombia's foreign relations, Santos has not only reduced previously high tensions with Venezuela and Ecuador; he has also deepened economic and political ties with Brazil and has sought to play a more active role in regional affairs. For the time being, Mejía, Colombia's former foreign minister, heads UNASUR. And Colombia has happily joined and participates in CELAC.

At the same time, however, Colombia is carefully crafting its foreign policy to cultivate an alternative to Brazilian influence and to enhance its own bargaining position on the global stage. In 2011, Colombia, together with Mexico, Peru, and Chile, forged Latin America's Pacific Alliance, an incipient and potentially vital bloc that seeks to promote economic integration and free trade. For Colombia, increased commerce and investment with China in particular, but also the rest of Asia, is especially important.

The Pacific focus is also an effective way to sustain Colombia's alliance with the United States, which regards the Pacific Alliance as highly promising. The UNITED STATES-Colombia free trade agreement, finally approved in 2011, is entirely consistent with Colombia's sophisticated, multifaceted strategy.

The Anti-Empire Club

As a clear measure of how swiftly the region's institutional landscape has been transformed, just a few years ago there were signs that ALBA, a notably more defiant bloc of countries, had considerable momentum. ALBA, launched in 2004, was conceived, and has been mainly financed, by Chávez. It sought to offer a radical alternative to the United States-backed FTAA and to promote solidarity among a coalition of nations that stand up to Washington. Venezuela is the unmistakable leader; other members include Cuba, Nicaragua, Bolivia, Ecuador, and several Caribbean nations. Honduras was also an ALBA member before that country's June 2009 military coup, but has since withdrawn from the bloc.

ALBA may have reached its zenith at a Summit of the Americas gathering in Mar del Plata, Argentina, in 2005, where an acrimonious atmosphere prevailed. That United States president George W. Bush was so disliked in the region, and the Iraq War was so universally opposed, only helped fuel the Chárivez-led coalition. The organization seemed poised to expand in a region that offered fertile ground for more leftist recipes to social and economic problems.

But ALBA began losing much of its energy, chiefly because of mounting problems in Venezuela, but also in other ALBA member states (for example, Bolivia). After 13 years in office, Chávez began to confront more serious challenges, including a very bad economy, a sharply deteriorating security situation, and, finally, the cancer diagnosis. Such weaknesses have significantly undercut his ability to play a more energetic regional role. They have also made it even more difficult to undertake some of Chávez's more grandiose schemes, such as the Bank of the South, a proposed alternative to traditional multilateral lending institutions. At the same time, Brazil's rise—under Lula and now, especially, Rousseff—has mitigated Chávez's more disruptive impact, as has Colombia's rapprochement with Venezuela. In 2009 Chávez lost his favorite foil in George Bush, and in 2010, Uribe, his other main antagonist.

Although Chávez hosted the December 2011 CELAC meeting, it was striking that his proposal to replace the OAS got little traction and in the end was roundly rejected. A fiery speech by Ecuadorian President Rafael Correa attacking the OAS and, especially, its work on press freedom and human rights issues elicited virtually no support among other CELAC participants. As Santos noted, "CELAC isn't being born to be against anyone."

Still, though Chávez's regional projects seem moribund, he remains resourceful and, as the president of a major oil-producing nation, continues to have money to spend. His popular Petrocaribe scheme, which provides oil at preferential prices to some 19 member nations, is still a way Chávez can exercise "soft power." Even the current Honduran government, long the object of Chávez's wrath, is, for practical reasons, seeking to rejoin Petrocaribe.

The Regionalism Test

From Washington's standpoint, the plethora of regional groupings in its so-called "backyard" poses a test. Although the United States often deals with countries in the region bilaterally, it is most familiar with the OAS and regards it as the main hemispheric political body. The OAS, however, has a mixed record, and has recently gone through a particularly rough period, during which it has been the center of much controversy. The OAS has been criticized from both sides of the political spectrum, and both in Washington and much of Latin America, for the way it has handled challenging political situations in Honduras, Nicaragua, Venezuela, Ecuador, and Haiti.

Meanwhile, more exclusively regional organizations focused on finance and development have become increasingly relevant. These present a challenge for more traditional institutions, such as the Inter-American Development Bank, where the United States remains influential. In the region, the CAF Development Bank of Latin America has expanded and become a significant player. In addition, the Brazilian Development ment Bank is rapidly extending its reach and range of operations in the region, chiefly to support foreign investments by Brazilian companies.

The expansion of access to private capital also has had key implications for the international financial institutions. China, now the principal trading partner of Brazil, Chile, and Peru (and the second in a number of other countries) is a major source of capital and finance throughout the region. In coming years it is unlikely that such tendencies will be reversed.

Nonetheless, though Washington faces a regional configuration that bears scant resemblance to the one it faced just a few years ago, opportunities for more productive relations are emerging. In some respects, the outlook is more favorable than it has been. The confrontational politics represented by Chávez is in sharp decline across the region. And some signs of pushback against Beijing's growing influence can be discerned, in part because China's economic relationships may be putting manufacturing sectors in the region at risk. (There is also growing concern, among some South American nations especially, about excessive dependence on trade in commodities.)

More significantly, recent developments make it clear that Brazil and Mexico—which account for more than two-thirds of the region's population, territory, and economy—are interested in engaging more deeply with the United States, albeit on their own terms. For Washington, which claims a commitment to multilateralism, establishing better ties with both countries is crucial to any strategy of serious cooperation on issues ranging from security, trade, democracy, and the environment to energy, immigration, and human rights.

To its credit, Washington has not lamented its exclusion from CELAC and other regional groupings. But the United States could pursue more energetic approaches toward regional mechanisms in which it does take part. These include the Summit of the Americas, which involves all elected heads of state in the hemisphere (and will convene in Cartagena, Colombia, in April 7012), as well as the weakened OAS.

The OAS Endures

It is striking that, for all of the severe criticisms of the OAS and continuing threats from some governments to withdraw from the organization, it is unlikely to disappear any time soon. The OAS is still equipped to take on critical issues—including human rights, press freedom, and democracy—that other, newer multilateral mechanisms seem years away from being able to handle adequately. In these areas the OAS's normative frameworks, developed over time, are impressive. The inter-American human rights system, for instance, has an admirable record of shining a light on abuses committed during the period of authoritarian rule, including under Argentina's military junta.

The OAS desperately needs modernization and institutional reform.

The obstacles to greater effectiveness are fundamentally political. The OAS desperately needs modernization and thoroughgoing institutional reform. In the current regional context of redefinitions and realignments, the United States has an opportunity to marshal greater diplomatic resources and forge a more effective approach toward regional cooperation, one consonant with its own interests and rhetoric.

Critical Thinking

1. Would you consider Mexico to be North American or a Latin American state? Why?
2. What has been the impact of the rise of Brazil on Latin American regionalism and relations?
3. Is the rise of the new regionalism in Latin America a response to the power of the United States in the region?
4. What are the factors that have reduced the effectiveness of Mercosur?

MICHAEL SHIFTER, a *Current History* contributing editor, is president of the Inter-American Dialogue and an adjunct professor of Latin American studies at Georgetown University.

Shifter, Michael. From *Current History*, voll. 111, no. 742, February 2012, pp. 21–31. Copyright © 2012 by Current History, Inc. Reprinted by permission.

UNIT 2
Democratization

Unit Selections

Learning Outcomes

After reading this Unit, you will be able to:

- Explain what is meant by the process of democratization.

- Describe some of the problems associated with the transition and the consolidation of democracy in developing countries.

- Explain the factors that lay behind the Arab Spring.

- Explain why the Islamists won the elections in Egypt.

- Explain the effects of the electoral victories of the Islamist parties on the geopolitical configuration of power in the Middle East.

- Discuss the options that are available to the United States in dealing with the civil war in Syria in 2012.

- Explain why the United Nations has not been successful in resolving the conflict in Syria.

- Explain why the military junta in Burma decided to democratize the country after more than four decades of dictatorship.

- Analyze the factors that may prevent the consolidation of democracy in Burma.

- Discuss why experts believe that Nigeria is on the path toward the consolidation of democracy.

- Analyze the relationship between Islamic terrorism and democracy in Nigeria.

- Explain what is meant by Putinism.

- Analyze the forces that may bring about the collapse of the fascistoid state of Russia.

- Discuss the factors that may contribute to the legitimation of Kim Jong-un's power.

- Analyze the prospects for stability in the Korean peninsula.

Student Website

www.mhhe.com/cls

Internet References

Al Jazeera
http://engish.alijazeera.net

Arab net
www.arab.net

Freedom House
Freedomhouse.org

Fund for Peace
www.fundforpeace.org/global

International Foundation for Election Systems
www.ifes.org

Middle East Online
www.middle-east-online.com/english

Syrian Observatory for Human Rights
www.syriahr.com

Global democratization generally has proceeded in waves. The Arab Spring, in which the long-standing dictatorial regimes of Mubarak and Gadaffi were overthrown in the Middle East by uprisings based on popular revolutions, could be viewed as one of the latest examples of global democratization that were transformed into revolutions. In the case of Egypt, in 2012 the Islamists in the form of the Muslim Brotherhood were successful in winning parliamentary and presidential elections, in spite of efforts on the part of the military to block them, while former President Mubarak was sentenced to prison. Libya's Gadaffi, however, met a different fate as he was beaten and murdered when captured. Moreover, contrary to the trends in Tunisia and Egypt, the Islamists were not victorious in Libya's elections in 2012. However, a dangerous power vacuum was left behind, as evidenced by the attack on the U.S. embassy and the killing of the U.S. ambassador to Libya in August 2012. In Yemen, President Saleh was forced out as the Yemen branch of al Qaeda still operates as a deadly force, while in Bahrain the ruling royal family continued to maintain power, backed by Saudi Arabia. In "The Arab Spring at One," Fouad Ajami writes that the Arab Spring came as a surprise as "waves of democracy had swept" other regions, "but not the Middle East." The author observes that "the revolt was a settlement of accounts between the powers that be and a population determined to be done with despots." Ajami points out that "the revolution which started in Tunisia" became a pan-Arab affair, catching fire in Yemen and Bahrain, with a rebellion breaking out in Syria in 2011, while in Egypt the contest will be between the Army, the Brotherhood, and a broad liberal and secular coalition. One of the most significant results of the Arab Spring was the election of the Muslim brotherhood's Mohamed Morsi as president of Egypt in 2012, who has proceeded to assert his control over the military since his election.

Samuel Tadros, in "Egypt's Elections: Why the islamists Won," attributes the victory of the Muslim Brotherhood in the parliamentary elections to the fact that the opponents of the Islamists lacked a common ideology and a clear alternative for the Egyptian people, contrary to the world view espoused by the Islamists. The author concludes that the victory of the Muslim Brotherhood in Egypt was also based on a change in the electoral system, a better quality of candidates, and the fact that the parties competing against the Islamists were neither secular nor liberal.

The Syrian revolution, which had started peacefully in 2011, had taken a savage turn by 2012 with an estimated 20,000 people having been killed by the beginning of September, according to the Syrian Human Rights Observatory. Efforts on the part of former UN Secretary-General Kofi Annan to mediate the conflict as the special representative of the Arab League and the United Nations ended in failure as he resigned, due to lack of support for is efforts by the major powers. He was replaced by the skilled Algerian diplomat Brahimi, but a UN observer team that had been sent into the area to deal with allegations of human rights violations also was withdrawn. The UN Security Council was prevented from taking stronger action by Chinese and Russian vetoes, calling on Syrian President Assad to cease the hostilities against the loose collection of insurgents known as the Free Syrian Army.

© arabianEye/Corbis

Given that it was an election year, the Obama administration was not interested in engaging in humanitarian intervention in Syria, unlike its willingness to intervene in Libya. However, as the ferocity of the conflict intensified with growing numbers of refugees fleeing to neighboring countries such as Jordan and Turkey, the pressure increased on the Western governments to establish a safety zone inside of Syria. Jackson Diehl, in "Lines in the Sand," stresses the sectarian nature of the conflict in Syria, arguing that there is "a streak of raw sectarianism in the Syrian version of the Spring of a disgruntled Sunni majority turning on the corrupt ruling clique based on the Alawite offshoot of Shiite Islam that represents just twelve percent of Syria's population. . . ." The author concludes that " . . . the Obama administration and its NATO allies have been reluctant to intervene directly in Syria—and they have no luck persuading Russia to cease support for its traditional client."

Global democratization has also spread to Burma (Myanmar), as the country is undergoing a transition from decades of authoritarianism to a democracy. Evan Osnos in "The Burmese Spring"

27

focuses on the steps toward democratization since March 2011, undertaken by General Thein Sein, who has liberalized the regime. Leading dissident Aung San Suu Kyi has been released from house arrest, parliamentary elections have been held, censorship has been reduced, and a policy of countering Chinese influence in Myanmar by attracting Western foreign investment has been initiated. However, Osnos concludes that democracy in Burma has not been consolidated in Myanmar because not all political prisoners have been released, and the continuation of ethnic conflict threatens to undermine the transition to democracy.

Another country that is also undergoing the process of the consolidation of democracy is Nigeria. John Campbell, in "Nigeria's Battle for Stability," writes that recent events in Nigeria show that it can engage in free and fair elections. But the author concludes that democracy continues to be threatened by Islamic terrorists like Boko Hram, which has global connections.

As has also been seen in the efforts at democratization in Russia over the past 20 years, the process of democratization may depend on such factors as the method of exit from the previous regime, the political culture of the society that is undergoing the transition to democracy, and the legacy of the past. It is not that easy to graft the model of liberal democracy—a model that developed over the course of several hundred years in the United Kingdom and the United States—onto a political culture that differs from the western cultural concept of democracy. The impression gained that democracy is continuing to spread is belied by the fact that there has been some regression in some cases. Analyses by Freedom House and other think tanks such as the Bertelsmann Foundation show that there actually has been a freeze in the empirical spread of democracy and a qualitative decline in democracy as well. Democratization can also be stalled and even subject to a reversal, which seems to be the case in Putin's Russia. In "Fascistoid Russia: Whither Putin's Brittle Realm" Alexander Motyl argues that the authoritarian regime derives its authority from a commitment to "Russian greatness, hyper-nationalism, and neo-imperial rivalry." However, the author concludes that Putin's regime will collapse due to "elite in-fighting and social protest from the middle class . . . ."

The succession of Kim Jong-un to the leadership of North Korea has posed the question as to whether the regime will be more open in comparison to the autocratic and secretive nature of his father's regime. This may not happen even though Kim Jong-un has been educated in Switzerland, likes Disneyland, and has allowed himself to be photographed in public with his attractive new wife. North Korea may be just as dangerous as ever, as Kim Jong-un moves to establish his control over the military and in so doing may be tempted to take risks that could antagonize the United States and South Korea. In "Korea's Third Kim: Will Anything Change?," according to the author, Kim Jong-un's power depends on his ability to control the members of the military and his own family as he moves to consolidate his power. Aoki believes that the foreign policy of the country is characterized by the "continuity of the previous policy toward South Korea and will be marked by episodes of belligerency toward South Korea, making the Korean peninsula even more dangerous than it already is."

The Arab Spring at One

A Year of Living Dangerously.

Fouad Ajami

Throughout 2011, a rhythmic chant echoed across the Arab lands: "The people want to topple the regime." It skipped borders with ease, carried in newspapers and magazines, on Twitter and Facebook, on the airwaves of al Jazeera and al Arabiya. Arab nationalism had been written off, but here, in full bloom, was what certainly looked like a pan-Arab awakening. Young people in search of political freedom and economic opportunity, weary of waking up to the same tedium day after day, rose up against their sclerotic masters.

It came as a surprise. For almost two generations, waves of democracy had swept over other regions, from southern and eastern Europe to Latin America, from East Asia to Africa. But not the Middle East There, tyrants had closed up the political world, become owners of their countries in all but name. It was a bleak landscape: terrible rulers, sullen populations, a terrorist fringe that hurled itself in frustration at an order bereft of any legitimacy. Arabs had started to feel they were cursed, doomed to despotism. The region's exceptionalism was becoming not just a human disaster but a moral embarrassment.

Outside powers had winked at this reality, silently thinking this was the best the Arabs could do. In a sudden burst of Wilsonianism in Iraq and after, the United States had put its power behind liberty. Saddam Hussein was flushed out of a spider hole, the Syrian brigades of terror and extortion were pushed out of Lebanon, and the despotism of Hosni Mubarak, long a pillar of Pax Americana, seemed to lose some of its mastery. But post-Saddam Iraq held out mixed messages: there was democracy, but also blood in the streets and sectarianism. The autocracies hunkered down and did their best to thwart the new Iraqi project. Iraq was set ablaze, and the Arab autocrats could point to it as a cautionary tale of the folly of unseating even the worst of despots. Moreover, Iraq carried a double burden of humiliation for Sunni Arabs: the bearer of liberty there was the United States, and the war had empowered the Shiite stepchildren of the Arab world. The result was a standoff: the Arabs could not snuff out or ignore the flicker of freedom, but nor did the Iraqi example prove the subversive beacon of hope its proponents had expected.

It was said by Arabs themselves that George W. Bush had unleashed a tsunami on the region. True, but the Arabs were good at waiting out storms, and before long, the Americans themselves lost heart and abandoned the quest. An election in 2006 in the Palestinian territories went the way of Hamas, and a new disillusionment with democracy's verdict overtook the Bush administration. The "surge" in Iraq rescued the American war there just in time, but the more ambitious vision of reforming the Arab world was given up. The autocracies had survived the brief moment of American assertiveness. And soon, a new standard-bearer of American power, Barack Obama, came with a reassuring message: the United States was done with change; it would make its peace with the status quo, renewing its partnership with friendly autocrats even as it engaged the hostile regimes in Damascus and Tehran. The United States was to remain on the Kabul hook for a while longer, but the greater Middle East would be left to its Furies.

When a revolt erupted in Iran against the theocrats in the first summer of his presidency, Obama was caught flatfooted by the turmoil. Determined to conciliate the rulers, he could not find the language to speak to the rebels. Meanwhile, the Syrian regime, which had given up its dominion in Lebanon under duress, was now keen to retrieve it. A stealth campaign of terror and assassinations, the power of Hezbollah on the ground, and the subsidies of Iran all but snuffed out the "Cedar Revolution" that had been the pride of Bush's diplomacy.

Observers looking at the balance of forces in the region in late 2010 would have been smart to bet on a perpetuation of autocracy. Beholding Bashar al-Assad in Damascus, they would have been forgiven the conclusion that a similar fate awaited Libya, Tunisia, Yemen, and the large Egyptian state that had been the trendsetter in Arab political and cultural life. Yet beneath the surface stability, there was political misery and sterility. Arabs did not need a "human development report" to tell them of their desolation. Consent had drained out of public life; the only glue between ruler and ruled was suspicion and fear. There was no public project to bequeath to a generation coming into its own—and this the largest and youngest population yet.

And then it happened in December, a despairing Tunisian fruit vendor named Mohamed Bouazizi took one way out, setting himself on fire to protest the injustices of the status quo. Soon, millions of his unnamed fellows took another, pouring into the streets. Suddenly, the despots, seemingly secure in their dominion, deities in all but name, were on the run. For its part, the United States scurried to catch up with the upheaval. "In too many places, in too many ways, the region's foundations are sinking into the sand," U.S. Secretary of State Hillary Clinton proclaimed in Qatar in mid-January 2011, as the storm was breaking out. The Arab landscape lent her remarks ample confirmation; what she omitted was that generations of American diplomacy would be buried, too.

The Fire This Time

The revolt was a settlement of accounts between the powers that be and populations determined to be done with despots. It erupted in a small country on the margins of the Arab political experience, more educated and prosperous and linked to Europe than the norm. As the rebellion made its way eastward, it skipped Libya and arrived in Cairo, "the mother of the world." There, it found a stage worthy of its ambitions.

Often written off as the quintessential land of political submission, Egypt has actually known ferocious rebellions. It had been Mubarak's good fortune that the land tolerated him for three decades. The designated successor to Anwar al-Sadat, Mubarak had been a cautious man, but his reign had sprouted dynastic ambitions. For 18 magical days in January and February, Egyptians of all walks of life came together in Tahrir Square demanding to be rid of him. The senior commanders of the armed forces cast him aside, and he joined his fellow despot, Tunisia's Zine el-Abidine Ben Ali, who had fallen a month earlier.

From Cairo, the awakening became a pan-Arab affair, catching fire in Yemen and Bahrain. As a monarchy, the latter was a rare exception, since in this season it was chiefly the republics of strongmen that were seized with unrest. But where most monarchies had a fit between ruler and ruled, Bahrain was riven by a fault line between its Sunni rulers and its Shiite majority. So it was vulnerable, and it was in the nature of things that an eruption there would turn into a sectarian feud. Yemen, meanwhile, was the poorest of the Arab states, with secessionist movements raging in its north and south and a polarizing leader, Ali Abdullah Saleh, who had no skills save the art of political survival. The feuds of Yemen were obscure, the quarrels of tribes and warlords. The wider Arab tumult gave Yemenis eager to be rid of their ruler the heart to challenge him.

Then, the revolt doubled back to Libya. This was the kingdom of silence, the realm of the deranged, self-proclaimed "dean of Arab rulers," Muammar al-Qaddafi. For four tormenting decades, Libyans had been at the mercy of this prison warden, part tyrant, part buffoon. Qaddafi had eviscerated his country, the richest in Africa yet with an abysmally impoverished population. In the interwar years, Libya had known savage colonial rule under the Italians. It gained a brief respite under an ascetic ruler,

King Idris, but in the late 1960s was gripped by a revolutionary fever. *Iblis wa la Idris,* went the maxim of the time, "Better the devil than Idris." And the country got what it wanted. Oil sustained the madness; European leaders and American intellectuals alike came courting. Now, in 2011, Benghazi, at some remove from the capital, rose up, and history gave the Libyans a chance.

The Egyptian rulers had said that their country was not Tunisia. Qaddafi said that his republic was not Tunisia or Egypt. Eventually, Assad was saying that Syria was not Tunisia, Egypt, or Libya. Assad was young, not old; his regime had more legitimacy because it had confronted Israel rather than collaborated with it. He spoke too soon: in mid-March, it was Syria's turn.

Syria was where Islam had made its home after it outgrew the Arabian Peninsula and before it slipped out of the hands of the Arabs into those of the Persians and the Turks. Yet decades earlier, Bashar al-Assad's father, Hafez—a man of supreme cunning and political skill—had ridden the military and the Baath Party to absolute power, creating a regime in which power rested with the country's Alawite minority. The marriage of despotism and sectarianism begat the most fearsome state in the Arab east.

Suddenly, the despots, seemingly secure in their dominion, deities in all but name, were on the run.

When the rebellion broke out there in 2011, it had a distinct geography, as the French political scientist Fabrice Balanche has shown, based in the territories and urban quarters of the country's Sunni Arabs. It erupted in Dara'a, a remote provincial town in the south, then spread to Hamah, Horns, Jisr al-Shughour, Rastan, Idlib, and Dayr az Zawr—skipping over Kurdish and Druze areas and the mountain villages and coastal towns that make up the Alawite strongholds. The violence in the Syrian uprising has been most pronounced in Horns, the country's third-largest city, because of its explosive demographics—two-thirds Sunni, one-quarter Alawite, one-tenth Christian.

Sectarianism was not all, of course. Syria has had one of the highest birthrates in the region, with its population having almost quadrupled since Hafez seized power in 1970. The arteries of the regime had hardened, with a military-merchant complex dominating political and economic life. There was not much patronage left for the state to dispose of, since under the banner of privatization in recent years, the state had pulled off a disappearing act. The revolt fused a sense of economic disinheritance and the wrath of a Sunni majority determined to rid itself of the rule of a godless lot.

Where Things Stand

There has, of course, been no uniform script for the Arab regimes in play. Tunisia, an old state with a defined national identity, settled its affairs with relative ease. It elected a constituent assembly in which al Nahda, an Islamist party, secured a plurality. Al Nahda's leader, Rachid al-Ghannouchi, was a shrewd man; years in exile had taught him caution, and his party formed a coalition government with two secular partners.

In Libya, foreign intervention helped the rebels topple the regime. Qaddafi was pulled out of a drainage pipe and beaten and murdered, and so was one of his sons. These were the hatreds and the wrath that the ruler himself had planted; he reaped what he had sown. But wealth, a sparse population, and foreign attention should see Libya through. No history in the making there could be as deadly to Libyans, and others, as the Qaddafi years.

The shadows of Iran and Saudi Arabia hover over Bahrain. There is no mass terror, but the political order is not pretty. There is sectarian discrimination and the oddness of a ruling dynasty, the House of Khalifa, that conquered the area in the late years of the eighteenth century but has still not made peace with the population. Outsiders man the security forces, and true stability seems a long way off.

As for Yemen, it is the quintessential failed state. The footprint of the government is light, the rulers offer no redemption, but there is no draconian terror. The country is running out of water; jihadists on the run from the Hindu Kush have found a home: it is Afghanistan with a coastline. The men and women who went out into the streets of Sanaa in 2011 sought the rehabilitation of their country, a more dignified politics than they have been getting from the cynical acrobat at the helm for more than three decades. Whether they will get it is unclear.

Syria remains in chaos. Hamas left Damascus in December because it feared being left on the wrong side of the mounting Arab consensus against the Syrian regime. "No Iran, no Hezbollah; we want rulers who fear Allah," has been one of the more meaningful chants of the protesters. Alawite rule has been an anomaly, and the regime, through its brutal response to the uprising, with security forces desecrating mosques, firing at worshipers, and ordering hapless captives to proclaim, "There is no God but Bashar," has written its own regional banishment. Hafez committed cruelties of his own, but he always managed to remain within the Arab fold. Bashar is different—reckless—and has prompted even the Arab League, which has a history of overlooking the follies of its members, to suspend Damascus' membership.

The fight still rages, Aleppo and Damascus have not risen, and the embattled ruler appears convinced that he can resist the laws of gravity. Unlike in Libya, no foreign rescue mission is on the horizon. But with all the uncertainties, this much can be said: the fearsome security state that Hafez, the Baath Party, and the Alawite soldiers and intelligence barons built is gone for good. When consent and popular enthusiasm fell away, the state rested on fear, and fear was defeated. In Syria, the bonds between the holders of power and the population have been irreparably broken.

What Follows Pharaoh

Egypt, meanwhile, may have lost the luster of old, but this Arab time shall be judged by what eventually happens there. In the scenarios of catastrophe, the revolution will spawn an Islamic republic: the Copts will flee, tourism revenues be lost for good, and Egyptians will yearn for the iron grip of a pharaoh. The strong performance of the Muslim Brotherhood and of an even more extremist Salafi party in recent parliamentary elections, together with the splintering of the secular, liberal vote, appears to justify concern about the country's direction. But Egyptians have proud memories of liberal periods in their history. Six decades of military rule robbed them of the experience of open politics, and they are unlikely to give it up now without a struggle.

The elections were transparent and, clarifying Liberal and secular forces were not ready for the contest, whereas the Brotherhood had been waiting for such a historic moment for decades and seized its opportunity. No sooner had the Salafists come out of the catacombs than they began to unnerve the population, and so they pulled back somewhat from their extreme positions. The events in Tahrir Square transfixed the world, but as the young Egyptian intellectual Samuel Tadros has put it, "Egypt is not Cairo and Cairo is not Tahrir Square." When the dust settles, three forces will contest Egypt's future—the army, the Brotherhood, and a broad liberal and secular coalition of those who want a civil polity, the separation of religion and politics, and the saving graces of a normal political life.

Before the revolt, the Arab world had grown morose and menacing.

The Brotherhood brings to the struggle its time-honored mix of political cunning and an essential commitment to imposing a political order shaped by Islam. Its founder, Hasan al-Banna, was struck down by an assassin in 1949 but still stalks the politics of the Muslim world. A ceaseless plotter, he talked of God's rule, but in the shadows, he struck deals with the palace against the dominant political party of his day, the Wafd. He played the political game as he put together a formidable paramilitary force, seeking to penetrate the officer corps—something his inheritors have pined for ever since. He would doubtless look with admiration on the tactical skills of his successors as they maneuver between the liberals and the Supreme Council of the Armed Forces, partaking of the tumult of Tahrir Square but stepping back from the exuberance to underline their commitment to sobriety and public order.

The plain truth of it is that Egypt lacks the economic wherewithal to build a successful modern Islamic order, whatever that might mean. The Islamic Republic of Iran rests on oil, and even the moderate ascendancy of the Justice and Development Party, or AKP, in Turkey is secured by prosperity stemming from the "devout bourgeoisie" in the Anatolian hill towns. Egypt lies at the crossroads of the world, living off tourism, the Suez Canal, infusions of foreign aid, and remittances from Egyptians abroad. Virtue must bow to necessity: in the last year, the country's foreign reserves dwindled from $36 billion to $20 billion. Inflation hammers at the door, the price of imported wheat is high, and the bills have to be paid. Four finance ministers have come and gone since Mubarak's fall. A desire for stability now balances the heady satisfaction that a despot was brought down.

There are monumental problems staring Egypt's leaders in the face, and the reluctance of both the Brotherhood and the armed forces to assume power is telling. Good sense and pragmatism might yet prevail. A plausible division of spoils and responsibility might give the Brotherhood the domains of governance dearest to it—education, social welfare, and the judiciary—with the military getting defense, intelligence, the peace with Israel, the military ties to the United States, and a retention of the officer corps' economic prerogatives. Liberal secularists would have large numbers, a say in the rhythm of daily life in a country so hard to regiment and organize, and the chance to field a compelling potential leader in a future presidential election.

For two centuries now, Egypt has been engaged in a Sisyphean struggle for modernity and a place among the nations worthy of its ambitions. It has not fared well, yet it continues to try. Last August, a scene played out that could give Egyptians a measure of solace. The country's last pharaoh—may it be so—came to court on a gurney. "Sir, I am present," the former ruler said to the presiding judge. Mubarak was not pulled out of a drainage pipe and slaughtered, as was Qaddafi, nor did he hunker down with his family and murder his own people at will, as has Assad. The Egyptians have always had, in E. M. Forster's words, the ability to harmonize contending assertions, and they may do so once again.

The Third Great Awakening

This tumult, this awakening, is the third of its kind in modern Arab history. The first, a political-cultural renaissance born of a desire to join the modern world, came in the late 1800s. Led by scribes and lawyers, would-be parliamentarians and Christian intellectuals, it sought to reform political life, separate religion from politics, emancipate women, and move past the debris of the Ottoman Empire. Fittingly enough, that great movement, with Beirut and Cairo at the head of the pack, found its chronicler in George Antonius, a Christian writer of Lebanese birth, Alexandrian youth, a Cambridge education, and service in the British administration in Palestine. His 1938 book, *The Arab Awakening,* remains the principal manifesto of Arab nationalism.

The second awakening came in the 1950s and gathered force in the decade following. This was the era of Gamal Abdel Nasser in Egypt, Habib Bourguiba in Tunisia, and the early leaders of the Baath Party in Iraq and Syria. No democrats, the leaders of that time were intensely political men engaged in the great issues of the day. They came from the middle class or even lower and had dreams of power, of industrialization, of ridding their people of the sense of inferiority instilled by Ottoman and then colonial rule. No simple audit can do these men justice: they had monumental accomplishments, but then, explosive demographics and their own authoritarian proclivities and shortcomings undid most of their work. When they faltered, police states and political Islam filled the void.

This third awakening came in the nick of time. The Arab world had grown morose and menacing. Its populations loathed their rulers and those leaders' foreign patrons. Bands of jihadists, forged in the cruel prisons of dreadful regimes, were scattered about everywhere looking to kill and be killed. Mohamed Bouazizi summoned his fellows to a new history, and across the region, millions have heeded his call. Last June, the Algerian author Boualem Sansal wrote Bouazizi an open letter. "Dear Brother," it said,

> I write these few lines to let you know we're doing well, on the whole, though it varies from day to day: sometimes the wind changes, it rains lead, life bleeds from every pore. . . .
>
> But let's take the long view for a moment. Can he who does not know where to go find the way? Is driving the dictator out the end? From where you are, Mohamed, next to God, you can tell that not all roads lead to Rome; ousting a tyrant doesn't lead to freedom. Prisoners like trading one prison for another, for a change of scenery and the chance to gain a little something along the way.

"The best day after a bad emperor is the first," the Roman historian Tacitus once memorably observed. This third Arab awakening is in the scales of history. It has in it both peril and promise, the possibility of prison but also the possibility of freedom.

Critical Thinking

1. How does the Arab Spring fit into the pattern of global democratization?
2. Why wasn't the Obama administration more supportive of democratization in the Middle East?
3. Is Ajami optimistic about Egypt's future? Why or why not?

FOUAD AJAMI is a Senior Fellow at Stanford University's Hoover Institution and Co-Chair of the Hoover Institution's Herbert and Jane Dwight Working Group on Islamism and the International Order.

Egypt's Elections
Why the Islamists Won

SAMUEL TADROS

When asked on January 30, 2011, about the Muslim Brotherhood's role in post–Arab Spring Egypt, the man seen by the media as a leading figure in the uprising, Mohamed ElBaradei, brushed aside Western fears: "They are not a majority of the Egyptian people. They will not be more than maybe twenty percent of the Egyptian people." For ElBaradei, Western fears of the Islamists dominating the Egyptian future were "a myth that was sold by the Mubarak regime." Nor was the former IAEA chief and Egyptian presidential hopeful alone in his insistence that the Muslim Brotherhood was only a harmless minority. President Obama agreed: "I think they're one faction in Egypt. They don't have majority support in Egypt."

The nearly unanimous consensus among both the Egyptian political class and the Washington experts was that the Islamists were only a scarecrow used by Mubarak to frighten the West. The Muslim Brotherhood, according to this view, counted no more than one hundred thousand adherents out of a population of more than eighty million. And its failure to support the initial uprising in Cairo on January 25th made the group marginal to the current Arab revolt. Early warnings of a Muslim Brotherhood takeover of Egypt were dubbed "hysteria." Yes, the Islamists were in the background of Tahrir Square, but they were weaker than people assumed. This was a liberal revolution led by tech-savvy youth, and the future of Egypt was a bright one.

Ten months later, after Islamists won seventy-two percent of the seats in the Egyptian Parliament, that optimistic avoidance of reality seems hard to fathom. Those who had been blithely confident of the future admitted that they never expected this result. Some professed never to have heard of the Salafists, although the party won more than a quarter of the votes. Shock and surprise, both in Cairo and Washington, soon gave way to a desperate effort to explain why the Islamists won and why the consequences of their victory might not be as disastrous as it seemed. Unfortunately, the explanations offered have created less rather than more clarity about the present situation in Egypt.

In the aftermath of the first round of voting, some immediately argued that the Islamist victory had been heavily financed by both Qatar and Saudi Arabia. Egyptian non-Islamists, fond of blaming everyone but themselves for their failures, were the main propagators of this argument. The fact that Egypt's richest man stood behind the main non-Islamist party, and spent millions backing it, was irrelevant to them.

News stories have been published with claims that donations from the Gulf were sent to organizations devoted to Islamic teaching and preaching, and accusations have been made that some of this money might have been used in political campaigns. But while spending on Islamic teaching in general may create a favorable personality for Islamist parties, in fact, there has been no serious evidence that Gulf money flowed heavily into the Islamists' political campaign.

Another explanation was a complaint in disguise: that elections were held too soon. Because the Islamists were better organized, a short time line was in their favor. Some argued that the Muslim Brotherhood, which has been around for more than eight decades, was better positioned than the newly established parties to compete, with its extensive organization unrivaled in its efficiency. In fact, while the MB has a long history, this vaunted organization is quite new, having been reestablished from scratch in the 1970s. Furthermore, the Salafists, who were the Brotherhood's main competitor, are as new to the political scene as the non-Islamist "democrats." If superior organization explains the MB's thirty-six percent share of the vote, what explains the twenty-seven percent won by the Salafists' al-Nour party? Not only is the party new, but it does not even have a unified structure.

There were also conspiracy theories proposed mainly by some Egyptian non-Islamists, who, unable to justify their failure, resorted to accusations of election fraud. Tied to this argument was the insistence that the military was secretly backing the Islamists. (Some of these conspiracy theorists accused the ruling military council of backing the group to scare the West; others accused it of rigging the elections in favor of the Salafists to weaken the Brotherhood.) But while the elections were chaotic and disorganized, no convincing evidence was ever adduced to prove that this hectic electoral atmosphere favored one particular party over the others. Forged ballots in favor of the Salafists were discovered in a polling station, but so were others found in favor of the MB, the Wafd, the Egyptian Bloc, and numerous former National Democratic Party candidates.

Next was the argument of illiteracy. Egyptians, it was claimed by the non-Islamist elite, are ignorant and illiterate people who were led like sheep by the Islamists. But this elite has always bemoaned its fate of having to live in the same country as those ignorant Egyptians. And the elitism of this elite reflects poorly on their idea of democracy. (Edmund Burke famously reflected on their equivalent during the time of the French Revolution: "You will smile here at the consistency of those democratists who, when they are not on their guard, treat the humbler part of the community with the greatest contempt, whilst, at the same time, they pretend to make them the depositories of all power.") If it was illiterate Egyptians who carried the day for the Islamists, how to understand the fact that the Islamists won every district in the country, including cosmopolitan Cairo?

The final explanation offered by the Egyptian non-Islamists for their failure was that their votes had been spread among several competing parties. But Egypt's electoral system actually benefits smaller parties. Had the non-Islamists gathered in one unified list, they would have gained fewer seats than they did. Furthermore, whatever their own results, this amalgamation would not have affected the Islamists' percentage.

These explanations and rationalizations have little to do with the real reasons for the Islamists' victory. One of the most important of these reasons is the mundane fact of the electoral system under which the vote took place. Under Hosni Mubarak, Egypt was divided into two hundred and twenty-two electoral districts, each electing two candidates. It was a system that favored local families in small districts who were the backbone of the authoritarian National Democratic Party (originally founded by Anwar el-Sadat and since then wielding uncontested power in state elections). As a nonideological party, the NDP simply supported local candidates with a strong patron-client relationship in the various districts as their members. Even when the party's official candidate lost a seat, this outcome simply opened the door for the winners to join.

It was the non-Islamists who insisted on changing the electoral system. Obsessed with what they termed "the remnants of the regime," they sought a new system, based on party lists, to kill the chances of continued domination by the local families. In the end, the ruling military council, attempting to appease everyone, chose a mixed system whereby two-thirds of the seats are chosen through party lists and one-third in individual districts. This meant that roughly three former districts were now combined into one, diluting the influence of local families, who were now forced to compete against each other outside their strongholds. With nothing in common, and realizing that only the top names of a party list would actually win, they could not agree on a unified list. The result was that some local families decided not to compete this time around, while others battled against each other, with the Islamists reaping the fruits of the disarray.

The electoral system chosen also gave a clear advantage to the smaller rural governates at the expense of Cairo. Since the system required two candidates in each individual-seat district and double that number in each party-list district, the governates were allocated seats in multiples of six. This meant that the smallest governate received six seats. A governate like Matruh, which demographically should have received two seats, got six. A governate like Fayyoum was allocated eighteen seats instead of fourteen, while Bani Suef got eighteen instead of fifteen. All of this came at the expense of the urban centers, especially greater Cairo, which was allocated forty-one fewer seats than it should have had according to population. In total, the urban centers were deprived of fifty-eight seats.

A final significant aspect of the new system is that it required Egyptians to vote for two individual candidates as well as a party list. It is important to notice the gap between the number of votes received by the Islamists on the party lists and the votes their individual candidates received. Those who voted for the Islamists on the individual seats are their actual supporters. Outside of the cities, most Egyptian voters were going out to vote for a local candidate that they knew and that had provided services to them. Being forced to choose a party list alongside their local candidate, they chose the

Islamists. Had the elections been held according to the old electoral system with small districts, the local families would have checked the power of the Islamists.

The quality of the candidates they offered also helped the Islamists. The Muslim Brotherhood offered its most powerful candidates on the individual seats. It also put a leading MB figure on top of every party list. The rest of each list was composed of relative unknowns. Their calculation proved correct: Reserve your strong candidates, who have local support, in the districts for the individual seats where name recognition and services matter and strengthen the appeal of your list with famous figures. The results of this strategy were spectacular. Out of a total of one hundred and sixty-six individual seats, the MB won one hundred and eight and the Salafists thirty-three. The non-Islamists won only eleven of these seats, with the remaining fourteen going to former NDP members. The Salafists' weak performance in the individual seats, compared to the party lists, reflects the reality of their strength. While they have a mass appeal among voters, they are incapable of operating in small districts where local grassroots work of "retail politics" is required.

The Salafists' overall performance deserves a special look. Lacking a central party command, their electoral strength depended on two key components: Salafi organizations and sheikhs. The two major Salafi organizations are el-Gameya al-Sharia and Gameyet Ansar al-Sunna. The first was established by Sheikh Mahmoud el-Sobky in 1912, while the second was established by Sheikh Mohamed Hamed el-Fiky in 1926. Both organizations have thousands of offices around Egypt and control thousands of mosques. They have been spreading Salafi ideas and practices since the 1920s. The ultraconservative Islamist al-Nour party tapped into those two existing organizations, choosing many of its candidates from among their local branches. Besides the grassroots base, the performance of the Salafists in the different governates reflected whether a leading Salafi sheikh lives in that area. Kafr el-Sheikh and Behira, for example, were two governates where the Salafists got the most support in the list voting and defeated the Brotherhood due to the following Sheikh Abu Ishaq el-Howeini has there. The same goes for Alexandria, where their victory is due to the influence and following of the Salafist school of Alexandria founded by Sheikh Mohamed Ismail el-Mokadem. This explains why in a governate like Monofia, which should have been an ideal place for the Salafists, they won only nineteen percent of the vote. With no Salafi sheikh residing there, they could not build the level of support they had in neighboring Delta governates.

Different groups and parties, an amalgam of Christians, the business-oriented middle class, socialists, human rights activists, leftists, and Arab nationalists, had nothing in common except their hatred and fear of the Islamists. Having no common ideology, they lacked the ability to offer the Egyptian people any clear alternative.

Those parties competing against the Islamists were neither secular nor liberal. (Trotskyites and Arab nationalists, after all, can hardly be described as liberal; neither are Copts necessarily secular.) Those different groups and parties, an amalgam of Christians, the business-oriented middle class, socialists, human rights activists, leftists, and Arab nationalists, had nothing in common except their hatred and fear of the Islamists. Having no common ideology, they lacked the ability to offer the Egyptian people any clear alternative to the Islamists.

A look at the main non-Islamist list shows the consequences of the lack of an ideological common ground. The Egyptian Bloc is made up of three parties, one supposedly right-of-center, one left-of-center party, and one explicitly socialist. Outside of its anti-Islamism, the Bloc was incapable of offering any coherent program, particularly a coherent economic program. Instead of forcing the Islamists to compete on economic grounds, therefore, where they could be defeated, they played into the Islamists' hands and made this a battle of identity—whether the state would be Islamic or a "civil" one, in the non-Islamists' phrase. "Civil state" was, of course, a meaningless term, but the non-Islamists were too scared to use the word "secular." Notwithstanding their attempt to camouflage their views, the choice given to the voters was between those who are for religion and those who are against it. To further complicate the matter, the non-Islamist argument for a civil state was shallow, focusing on such trivial matters as the Islamist threat to bikinis and alcohol. This allowed the Islamists to brand the non-Islamists as nothing more than sluts and drunks. When videos of the key figure behind the Egyptian Bloc emerged in which he expressed his fears for his wife's ability to wear short clothes in an Islamist Egypt, the branding was complete.

Behind such poor judgment was a deeper failure to take Islamism seriously. The non-Islamists viewed the Islamists as clowns. Since the Islamist argument did not make sense to them, they assumed it wouldn't make sense to the average Egyptian either. For them, Salafi preachers were nothing more than crazy people still living in the sixth century, whose videos they passed around with sarcastic commentary. What they ignored was that Islamism offers a coherent worldview presenting its followers an explanation of the past, present, and future—and of the world itself. Islamism encompasses a moral structure that is the only available one for Egyptians. When an individual in Egypt might not be particularly religious, there is no alternative ethical compass to guide one's life other than Islamism. (The failure of a natural rights argument to emerge within the realm of Islam after the demise of the Mu'tazilah in the tenth century factors heavily in this predicament.)

The non-Islamists' electoral campaign was also chaotic and disorganized. While the Islamists announced their candidates' names early and reached out to voters well before the elections, non-Islamist voters were still trying to discover who the Egyptian Bloc's candidates for the individual seats were the day before the election. Outside of the Coptic Church's efforts, no voter mobilization campaigns were conducted. Non-Islamist parties did not bother with the groundwork of gathering information and data on the districts, their voters, and their specific issues and problems. The general assumption seemed to be that you can win an election campaign by bombarding television audiences with ads. Furthermore, the quality of the candidates chosen was weak. Candidates who had little support in their districts were put at the top of the lists solely due to their connections inside the party leadership. Few efforts were carried out to recruit strong local candidates who might have broadened the non-Islamists' appeal, out of fear that such people might be viewed as "remnants of the regime."

Finally, the non-Islamists allowed themselves to be drawn into the saga of the never-ending revolution. A fight near Tahrir between the police and football Ultras led the candidates to put their campaigns on hold to join the battle. Non-Islamist politicians and parties were forced to follow the mob's mood no matter how irrational or self-destructive it was. Instead of offering leadership to "the street," they chased its whims, leaving the Islamists as the only rational actor in the eyes of voters who were fed up with the idea of permanent revolution and anxious for functioning government.

> **Unless two interlinked problems are adequately addressed, the Islamists will repeat their success in any future elections. The first is the non-Islamists' failure to form clear platforms and programs; the second is their failure to provide a political, economic, and moral alternative to Islamism.**

The Islamist tsunami that washed over the Egyptian elections was overwhelming. But the mistakes the non-Islamists made can certainly be avoided in the future. Better candidates can be chosen, election campaigns can be conducted more efficiently, and the electoral system can be changed. But unless two interlinked problems are adequately addressed, the Islamists will repeat their success in any future elections. The first is the non-Islamists' failure to form clear platforms and programs; the second is their failure to provide a political, economic, and moral alternative to Islamism. You can't, after all, defeat something with nothing.

Critical Thinking

1. What explains the victory of the Muslim Brotherhood in Egypt's parliamentary elections?
2. What were some of the reasons why the Egyptian bloc did not do well in the parliamentary elections?
3. How can the non-Islamists do better in the future?

SAMUEL TADROS is a research fellow at the Hudson Institute's Center for Religious Freedom and a board member of the Egyptian Union of Liberal Youth. The article was written in Egypt while the author was observing the elections.

Lines in the Sand

Assad Plays the Sectarian Card

JACKSON DIEHL

On March 6, 2011, a group of fifteen schoolboys in the southern Syrian town of Daraa were arrested by local security forces. Aged ten to fifteen, the boys were caught spray-painting the slogan "As Shaab Yoreed Eskaat el nizam!"—"The people want to topple the regime!" They had taken the words from satellite television coverage of the uprisings in Tunisia and Egypt.

The boys' parents were members of Daraa's most prominent families: Sunni tribesmen from the Haroun plains, which run from the Golan Heights along the Jordanian border. Their captor was Atef Najib, the head of local security, a first cousin of President Bashar al-Assad and a member of his minority Alawite sect. When the families approached him with a local Sunni sheikh, seeking the release of the boys, Najeeb responded with crude insults, according to an account by an Al Jazeera reporter. He told them to forget their children, go home to their wives, have sex, and make more.

On March 18th, with their boys still in custody, the furious families and local clerics marched on the offices of Faisal Kalthoum, the local governor—another Assad intimate from Damascus. Security forces opened fire, killing at least four persons. When the boys were freed several days later, they were disfigured with marks of torture, including extracted fingernails. Another demonstration erupted; the governor's office was burned. Syria's uprising had begun.

What began as a trifling provincial conflict has since exploded into a civil war upon which the future of the Middle East may pivot.

What began as a trifling provincial conflict has since exploded into a civil war upon which the future of the Middle East may pivot. Most of Syria has been enveloped by fighting. By March 2012, more than seventy-five hundred people had been reported killed. The first confrontations came between crowds of unarmed protestors, often chanting "peaceful, peaceful," and security forces that invariably responded with gunfire. Now there are full-scale military assaults by regime tanks,

artillery, and infantry against urban neighborhoods defended by ad hoc militias equipped with rifles and rocket-propelled grenades.

One by one, Syria's neighbors, allies, and enemies have been drawn in. Iran, Russia, and Venezuela are supplying arms, fuel, and cash to the Assad regime. Turkey, Saudi Arabia, and Qatar are arming, funding, or sheltering the opposition Free Syrian Army. Militants from Iraq and Lebanon are trafficking weapons across the border. Al-Qaeda is said to have dispatched cadres to carry out suicide bombings.

The reasons all this has happened can be discerned in the story of that first episode in Daraa, which embodies the initial appeal of the Arab Spring—a yearning for political freedom and economic modernization that, spread by satellite television and the Internet, has captivated a rising generation across the Middle East. As an equal and opposite reaction, there is the vicious and brutal response of the regime to reasonable demands for justice, which has inflamed rather than squelched public anger.

But there has also been, from the very beginning, a streak of raw sectarianism in the Syrian version of the Spring: of a disgruntled Sunni majority turning on the corrupt ruling clique based in the Alawis—an offshoot of Shiite Islam that represents just twelve percent of Syria's population. It is sectarianism that has motivated much of the foreign intervention, from Shiite Iran to the Sunni Persian Gulf kingdoms and Turkey's Sunni Islamist government.

Syria, which has always defined itself as the "beating heart" of the Middle East, has become the focal point of at least four regional conflicts: between the old autocratic order and the liberal movements for modernization and democracy; between Iran and its allies and the United States, Israel, and the "moderate" Arab states; between the Western powers and Russia and China; and between the Sunni and Shiite sects. In the end, the sectarian battle—with its potential for unending, pitiless carnage—may drive all the rest.

Sectarian conflict has been part of the Middle East since the wars over the succession to the prophet Muhammad in the seventh century. For most of the twentieth century, the rivalries among various currents of Islam, Christians,

Kurds, and others were stifled by an overlay of colonialism, and later by the secular, nationalist regimes that came to power in Egypt, Iraq, and Syria in the 1950s.

The war in Lebanon from 1975 to 1989 was a horrific exception to this stability, pitting Christians against Shiites and Sunnis and prompting armed interventions by Syria, Israel, the United States, France, and Iran. Meanwhile, the inconclusive war between Sunni Iraq and Shiite Iran from 1980 to 1988 left Sunni-ruled states in the Persian Gulf—some with their own large Shiite populations—with an enduring animus against what they regard as Iran's Shiite imperialist aspirations.

The United States invasion of Iraq in 2003 had the unintended consequence of reopening the Shiite-Sunni conflict across the region. While Shiite and Sunni militias battled for power in postwar Baghdad, Iran and the Persian Gulf states lined up on opposite sides. (Curiously, the Assad regime, eager to bloody the United States, mostly abetted Sunni insurgents and al-Qaeda, allowing foreign fighters from Saudi Arabia and the Maghreb to transit its territory to western Iraq.) At enormous cost, the United States eventually managed to subdue the sectarian militants on both sides and, after the 2010 Iraqi election, broker a government led by the Shiite majority but including Sunni and Kurdish leaders.

One of the first effects of the Syrian uprising has been to blow up this fragile quasi-democratic order. Iraqi Prime Minister Nuri Kamal al-Maliki, a Shiite with close ties to Iran, seemed to be inching away from sectarian politics: He personally led an offensive against a Shiite militia in southern Iraq and seemed intent on preventing the establishment of Iranian suzerainty in Baghdad. In conversations with American interlocutors, he frequently predicted that Iraq's sectarian divisions would slowly recede with the advances of democracy and economic recovery.

Syria, however, has spooked Maliki, say those who know him. By nature a suspicious and conspiratorial politician, Maliki sees the possible downfall of Assad as a likely triumph for the Sunni Muslim Brotherhood—and therefore also for the hard-line Sunni Islamists of Iraq's majority Sunni provinces, which border on Syria. A Sunni Syria endangers what Maliki views as the central outcome of the Iraq War, which is the political preeminence of Shiites in Baghdad.

The Iraqi leader is also under growing pressure from Iran's clerical regime, for which the Syrian conflict is an existential threat. Assad is not just Tehran's closest ally in the Middle East, but its bridge to the Shiite Hezbollah movement in Lebanon and its platform for pressuring Israel. Hezbollah's arsenal of missiles, supplied by Iran through Syria, are one of Iran's principal deterrents against an Israeli strike on its nuclear program.

According to United States and Arab sources, Iran has sent advisers from the Quds Force of its Revolutionary Guard to Syria to advise Assad, supplied him and his family with bodyguards, and flown in planeloads of weapons through Iraqi airspace. Maliki has tried to resist the creation of this air corridor, with uncertain results. But he is meanwhile taking his own protective measures: The Syrian crisis, as much as the United States troop withdrawal at the end of last year, explains his sudden political offensive in December against Sunni political leaders in Baghdad, including an attempt to arrest Vice President Tariq al-Hashimi.

Maliki's rash campaign produced its own backlash. Hashimi took refuge in Iraqi Kurdistan, whose leaders also support the anti-Assad forces. Both Iraqi Sunnis and Kurds are now considering whether they should split their regions off into mini-states independent from Baghdad—a move that looks much more feasible if Syria tilts toward Sunni rule.

That brings us to Turkey, which also might provide a tacit security umbrella for Iraqi Sunnis and Kurds. Turkey, with its Islamist prime minister, Recep Tayyip Erdogan, was one of the most ambitious players in the Middle East before the Arab Spring. It remains so—but its policies have been turned upside down. Before last year, Erdogan devoted considerable effort to courting Assad, expanding economic ties and attempting to broker Israel's return of the Golan Heights. When the protests first began, the Turkish leader attempted to persuade Assad to adopt reforms. When the strongman broke his promises to do so, the mercurial Erdogan was infuriated.

Now Turkey has adopted a policy in keeping with the emerging sectarian showdown. It is tacitly backing the Free Syrian Army, which is headquartered in refugee camps on its territory, as well as the Syrian National Council, the opposition political front. In political talks, it leans toward Syria's Muslim Brotherhood. Meanwhile, Ankara is allied with the Iraqi Sunnis and Kurds against Maliki. The regime's ideologues dream of restoring Turkey's influence to the former Ottoman provinces of Syria and western Iraq, at the expense of Iran.

The most militant backers of the Syrian opposition, however, are the Gulf Arabs—particularly Saudi Arabia and Qatar. It was Qatar that pushed the Arab League to adopt sanctions against Syria, and a plan for forcing Assad's departure from power. Both countries have come out in favor of Arab military intervention on the side of the opposition. According to diplomatic sources, both have delivered cash to the Free Syrian Army for use in purchasing and smuggling weapons. In March, they were pressing Turkey and the United States to develop a plan for creating and protecting an opposition safe zone inside Syria.

United States officials argue that the motives of the Sunni kings and emirs are not entirely sectarian. "Now why is this happening," asked Assistant Secretary of State Jeffrey D. Feltman in testimony before the United States Senate Foreign Relations Committee on March 1st. "I think, in part, this is happening because of the Arab Spring."

"If you look at opinion poll after opinion poll, Bashar al-Assad is at the bottom of the list of popularity among Arab leaders. He has no credibility in the Arab world. And I think Arab leaders want to show their own populations that they get it, that they understand that they need to be in tune with their popular opinion."

The reality is that at the same moment it was arming the opposition against Assad, Saudi Arabia was putting down demonstrations by its own restless Shiite population by force.

Maybe so. Yet the reality is that at the same moment it was arming the opposition against Assad, Saudi Arabia was putting down demonstrations by its own restless Shiite population by force. On consecutive days in February, security forces opened fire on protestors in the eastern town of Qatif; at least two persons were reported killed. Saudi and United Arab Emirate troops meanwhile continue to back the embattled Sunni regime in Bahrain, where what began last year as a pro-democracy movement has turned into yet another Sunni-Shiite standoff.

American policymakers tend to argue against the importance of sectarian motivations in Syria in part because sectarianism is poison to United States interests and goals across the region. In particular, sectarian conflict undermines the prospect for democracy—in Syria, Iraq, Bahrain, Lebanon, and elsewhere. "When you put sectarianism alongside democracy and human rights, sectarianism wins," one veteran diplomat ruefully conceded in a recent conversation.

Of course, some of the products of Syria's sectarianism have been positive, from Washington's point of view. Chief among them has been the transformation of the Palestinian Hamas movement, which like the Erdogan government in Turkey has flipped its allegiances since the uprising began and now opposes the government. Based for more than a decade in Damascus, the last member of the Hamas politburo left Syria in December; not long afterward, the Sunni Islamist movement formally denounced Assad. The implications are far-reaching. Deprived of its link to Iran and Iranian weapons, Hamas may now gravitate toward Egypt, where its parent organization, the Muslim Brotherhood, now is the largest party in parliament. Over time, that could lead to a decision by Hamas to adopt the Egyptian organization's commitment to non-violence. Already the group appears to be cleaving over the issue of joining a "unity" Palestinian government with the secular Fatah movement, which has embraced both non-violence and recognition of Israel.

The Syrian conflict has served to tighten United States relations with allies with whom it has been at odds in recent years—especially Turkey and Saudi Arabia. It has given cause for collaboration between the Obama administration and the Israeli government of Benjamin Netanyahu, which have been jointly exploring how to protect against the use or dispersal of Assad's stocks of chemical and biological weapons. The harm that the turmoil in Syria is causing to Iran was one of the arguments President Obama deployed in attempting to dissuade Netanyahu from an Israeli military strike against Iran when the two leaders met in early March.

The central thrust of United States policy has nevertheless been to head off a full-scale sectarian war in Syria. The quicker Assad falls, administration officials believe, the more likely it is that he could be replaced with a liberal and democratic order. Conversely, the longer the domestic bloodshed goes on, the more likely it is that sectarian fighting will take over the country, and possibly spread to Lebanon or Iraq.

"The opposition leadership recognizes those dangers," Assistant Secretary of State Feltman said in his Senate testimony. "It's one of the reasons why I said our policy is to try to accelerate the arrival of that tipping point" at which Assad falls. "The longer this goes on, the higher the risks of long-term sectarian conflict, the higher the risk of extremism. So we want to see this happen earlier."

The Syrian opposition, too, has tried hard to avoid sectarianism. In early demonstrations, marchers chanted slogans in favor of a "Syria for all"; the Syrian National Council has issued statements offering assurances to the Alawi community, as well as to Christians (ten percent of the population) and Kurds (nine percent). Echoing the opposition position, the United States ambassador to Damascus, Robert S. Ford, testified to the Senate in March that "this is not about Alawis versus a Sunni Arab majority. This is about a family that happens to be Alawi that has dominated the country and stripped it for forty years. Alawis are suffering too."

The problem, as both administration officials and Syrian opposition leaders acknowledge, is that as the fighting goes on—and gets bloodier—democratic liberals in the opposition tend to get pushed aside by Sunni Islamists who are more willing to die for their cause. Before his untimely death from an asthma attack, *New York Times* correspondent Anthony Shadid reported that Sunni-against-Alawi fighting was in fact overtaking the city of Homs.

"Paramilitaries on both sides have burned houses and shops," he reported in a November dispatch. "Alawite residents have been forced to flee to their native villages. Kidnappings, many of them random, have accelerated. . . . Alawites wear Christian crosses to avoid being abducted or killed when passing through the most restive Sunni neighborhoods."

Shortly after Shadid's death in February, Assad's elite Army units launched an all-out assault on one of those Homs neighborhoods, Bab al-Amr. For weeks, indiscriminate artillery fire rained down on apartment buildings, destroying or damaging hundreds of them, and killing an uncounted number of civilians. Finally, tanks moved in and routed the ragtag forces of the Free Syrian Army. In the aftermath, the "inevitable collapse" of Assad repeatedly and publicly predicted by Obama appeared far from certain.

Assad, for his part, has cultivated a sectarian showdown all along. From the beginning, he has described the opposition as "jihadists" linked to al-Qaeda. In May of last year, his cousin and close collaborator, Rami Makhlouf, warned Anthony Shadid that the clan would go down fighting. "We will not go out, leave on our boat, go gambling," Shadid quoted him as saying. "We will sit here. We call it a fight to the end."

This might seem suicidal, given the regime's growing isolation in Syrian society. In fact it is a desperate but shrewd effort to divide and rule. The regime's message to the Alawi community is simple: "If we die, you will die with us." To minority Christians, Kurds, and Druse, the message is: "You will be crushed by the Islamist Sunni majority if it comes to power." Just that sort of logic kept Lebanon fighting for fourteen years, as minority Christian Maronites, with no boat to leave on, refused to concede their leading political position, while Lebanese Sunnis, Shias, Druse, and Palestinians fought them and occasionally each other.

The Obama administration's hope has been that a combination of sanctions, international pressure, and its own public jawboning would persuade Christians, Muslim merchants in

38

Aleppo and Damascus, and, eventually, Alawi colonels and generals that their best interest lay in abandoning the Assad clan. By late March, however, there was scant sign of that happening. The reality the United States and allies like Turkey appeared to face was this: Unless confronted with more military force, or the loss of its supplies from Russia and Iran, the Assad regime was unlikely to cease its bloody offensives against opposition-held ground.

Yet the Obama administration and its NATO allies have been reluctant to intervene directly in Syria—and they have had no luck persuading Russia to cease support for its traditional client. Russia, too, stands to lose from a prolonged sectarian conflict in Syria, since the likely winner, the Sunni Muslim Brotherhood, would be sure to punish Moscow. Russia's hope is that Assad can win the domestic war quickly with its support, or at least force the opposition into an accommodation that leaves his regime in power, along with Russia's arms sales and access to its Mediterranean naval base at Tarsus.

Although they agreed in March on a UN-endorsed peace mission by former Secretary General Kofi Annan, the strategies of Washington and Moscow risked cancelling each other out.

That left the field to those who stand to gain by a longer sectarian fight: Iran, the Gulf states, Iraq's Sunnis and Kurds, and, to a lesser degree, Israel.

Any regime under siege is vulnerable to fragmentation and collapse, of course, and given the rapid unraveling of the domestic economy, it would hardly be a surprise if Assad were suddenly dispatched by an internal coup. Yet as the Syrian revolt passed its first anniversary, its end appeared as likely to be far away as close. With the help of his neighbors, Assad had succeeded in releasing the ancient virus of religious hatred among his people. History shows that once loosed, that toxin is almost never quickly dispersed.

Critical Thinking

1. Explain the sectarian nature of the conflict in Syria.
2. Why won't the Obama administration intervene in Syria?
3. Why is Russia supporting the Assad regime?

JACKSON DIEHL is the deputy editorial page editor of the *Washington Post*.

Diehl, Jackson. From *World Affairs*, May/June 2012, pp. 7–15. Copyright © 2012 by ©2010 American Peace Society. Reprinted by permission of World Affairs Institute. www.WorldAffairsJournal.org

Letter from Rangoon

The Burmese Spring

A brutal regime's shift toward democracy surprised nearly everyone. How did it happen?

EVAN OSNOS

On the evening of January 12th, Chitmin Lay was in his cell, in Moulmein Prison, in the lush tropical hills of southern Burma, when guards informed him that he was a free man. He had reasons not to believe them. Burmese prisons are exceptionally isolated, and Chitmin Lay had picked up only scattered news, from a hidden radio that he shared with other inmates, about a rush of political changes that were beginning to unwind the world's longest-running military dictatorship. He was thirty-eight, and had been arrested in 1998 for taking part in a campus demonstration at Rangoon University, where he was a literature major. Under interrogation, he was beaten and starved. Put in front of a judge in a mass trial, he was convicted of making pamphlets without approval, breaking the Emergency Provisions Act and the Unlawful Associations Act, and sentenced to thirty-one years. He had expected to resume his life in 2029.

Less than twenty-four hours later, Chitmin Lay walked out of prison amid a clamorous crowd of fellow-inmates, released as part of the government's attempt to pull itself from the ranks of the world's most reviled regimes. There was nobody there to greet him. Chitmin Lay is not famous, and Burma had so many political prisoners that the inmate lists maintained by activists could not even agree on the English spelling of his name. He was healthy, though his left eye was failing after so many years of reading in half-light. He had full cheeks around a broad smile that gave him an oddly childlike aspect, as if his body had paused the year he went away. He had no money to get to his mother's house in Rangoon, a daylong trip. Finally, some local opposition activists gave him the equivalent of about twelve dollars for the bus.

On the road, Chitmin Lay noticed that the traditional thatch-roofed bamboo villages were now dotted with concrete-block houses with metal roofs. "And cell phones, those were a surprise," he told me. "And the cars. We never used to see shiny cars." He was eager to try the Internet. "I'd only heard about it, how essential the Internet was, and I decided that I must learn about it as soon I'm out." Once he had greeted his startled mother and begun to consider the tasks before him—"marriage, family, job"—he signed up for a Gmail account.

Wedged like an arrowhead between India and China, Burma has been ruled by dictators so ineptly and for so long that it can feel, these days, as if the country itself were stepping warily out of jail. Since taking office in March, 2011, the former generals who make up Burma's first civilian government in forty-nine years have released almost seven hundred activists and monks and artists, and taken more steps in the direction of democracy than Burma has seen in four decades. They have relaxed media censorship, legalized the right to unionize, and allowed members of the main opposition party to compete for office; they have also distanced themselves from Burma's longtime patron, China.

In June, Australia took the symbolic step of abandoning the name Burma, which has been the choice of exiles and of Washington, in favor of the name preferred by the government: Myanmar. The United States and other nations suspended many of the economic sanctions that, for years, had sought to cripple the regime. The sudden access to a new market on China's southern border has inspired flights of extraordinary optimism. "If I could put all my money into Myanmar, I would," Jim Rogers, the Singapore-based American investor, declared recently.

Even by the standards of authoritarian regimes, Burma lives in an epoch unto itself, a relic of the prosperous country that was once the world's largest exporter of rice. Rangoon—or Yangon, as it is now known—which was so alive with diversity and immigration that it had a Jewish mayor in the nineteen-thirties, is today a place of deprivation and haunting beauty. The banyan trees reach out from the moldering remains of villas and colonial offices. Ancient buses, cast off by Japan, and now absurdly overloaded, wheeze through canyons on the broken macadam. Outside the law courts, men in crisp white shirts and longyis, Burma's traditional ankle-length sarong, hunch over ancient typewriters, feeding the maw of the bureaucracy. Gaping sinkholes in the sidewalk reveal the sewer beneath, exhaling into the tropical air. Book vendors, not far from where Pablo Neruda lived in the nineteen-twenties, display on their blankets books with such titles as "Essentials of Selling," "Radio and Line Transmission," and the I.M.F.'s "Seventh Annual Report: Exchange Restrictions, 1956."

In the countryside, Burma lives by candlelight. Three-quarters of the population get no electricity, though the nation has abundant oil, gas, and hydropower resources. The number of cell phones per capita is the lowest in the world, behind North Korea. Less than one per cent of the population is connected to the Web. In eastern Shan state, where I chatted with a woman who had never heard the name of the sitting President, cars are vastly outnumbered by horse-drawn carts.

Burma's opening has so far defied the narrative logic we've come to associate with political transformation: there is, as yet, no crowd picking through a ruined palace, no dictator in the dock. The world has witnessed more than a hundred attempts to end authoritarianism in the past twenty-five years, but the top-down, bloodless variety is rare. More often, as Thomas Carothers, a specialist on democratization at the Carnegie Endowment for International Peace, said of dictators, "It has to be taken away from them, usually by angry citizens."

In Burma, unlike the street revolutions of Egypt and Tunisia or the civil wars in Libya or Syria, many members of the former dictatorship have retained power. When top generals retired their commissions a year ago, they removed their uniforms, but one adviser told me that they still salute one another in private. Many of the reforms can be reversed if the government declares a state of emergency, and hundreds of political prisoners remain behind bars. And in the countryside the regime is embroiled in a brutal war against ethnic rebels, which has gone on for decades. For all the transformations Burma is undergoing, its people still find themselves strangely captive to men who were, until recently, some of history's most dedicated enemies of democracy.

I arrived in Rangoon in March, on Armed Forces Day. Traditionally, this had been an opportunity for generals to speechify and goose-step their men through the city. (The opposition once renamed it Fascist Resistance Day.) The country was preparing for the first major test of the new era: a special election, on April 1st. Although less than seven percent of the parliamentary seats were being contested, it was the first time that the dissident Aung San Suu Kyi had endorsed the legitimacy of an election since 1990, when her party's victory was ignored by the government, a signal event in Burma's descent into misery. In that election, Aung San Suu Kyi had already been placed under house arrest, where she remained for fifteen of the next twenty-one years, as she was awarded the Nobel Peace Prize (in absentia) and became one of the world's most famous political prisoners. When the regime finally released her, in November, 2010, she was met at her front gate by a frenzy of admirers, who seemed to be heralding not only her long-awaited entry into politics but also the prospect of a new era in Burmese history.

When the regime finally released the Noble laureate Aung San Suu Kyi, in November, 2010, she began a long-awaited entry into politics. This spring, she was cheered by crowds of supporters as she campaigned for the parliamentary elections, which seem to herald a new era in Burmese history.

Activists abroad were dubious, but Suu Kyi declared that the country was "on the verge of a breakthrough to democracy." Suu Kyi was running for the seat in Parliament representing Kawhmu, a township with vast stretches of land that had no electricity or running water. She campaigned for weeks, waving from the open sunroof of an S.U.V., shaded from the tropical sun by a parasol, as guards kept at bay tens of thousands of her supporters who lined the roads, desperate and reaching, and shouting, "A'mae Suu"—Mother Suu.

The daughter of Aung San, the martyred national hero who negotiated independence from the British Empire, Suu Kyi left the country in 1960 as a teenager, graduated from Oxford, and worked at the United Nations. Though she talked of starting public libraries in Burma, and of helping students to go abroad, in 1972 she married Michael Aris, a Tibet scholar, and settled fitfully into British suburbia with him and their two children. She didn't return to Burma until 1988, for a visit with her sick mother. Before long, she was swept up in politics, and emerged as the leader of the opposition. "It's very different from living in academia in Oxford," she once said of the turn in her fortunes. "We called someone vicious in a review for the *Times Literary Supplement.* We didn't know what vicious was."

A couple of days before the election this spring, Suu Kyi invited reporters over to the back yard of her house. It was a two-story colonial villa, stately but threadbare, and in the darkest days she had roamed listlessly from room to room. In the garden, she looked pale. "I'm feeling a little delicate," she said. The campaign had been gruelling, and her doctor had urged her to rest during the final days. "Any tough questions, I shall faint straight away," she said, and smiled. Over the years, the regime had tried to kill her at least once (in 2003), labelled her a "genocidal prostitute," and denied her husband's desperate requests to visit her before his death, from prostate cancer, in 1999. But she was taking a chance on this race, because, she said, "this is what our people want."

For years, Suu Kyi had called for a "revolution of the spirit," but, over the years, the poetry had been leeched from the phrase and, as one writer put it despairingly, it began to smack of "obscurantism and sheer metaphysics." In the garden that day, she reclaimed the idea. It must be "a revolution that will help our people to overcome fear, to overcome poverty, to overcome indifference, and to take the fate of their country into their own hands," she said. "An election alone is not going to change our country. It's the people, the change in the spirit of the people, which will change our nation."

To foreign reporters, who recalled Burma as a nation of whispers—where you never uttered a name on a phone line and, in some cases, carried a wig to help shake off the intelligence officers in a crowd—even a simple open-air meeting with Suu Kyi was bewildering. "Was it really only five years ago that soldiers were shooting protesters and beating monks?" Andrew R. C. Marshall, of *Reuters*, wrote after watching Suu Kyi in front of a crowd. For years, the country was so inaccessible that outsiders resorted to reading the aspirations of fifty-five million people through the struggle between Suu Kyi and the generals—between "Beauty" and "the Beast," as headline writers often described it. Suddenly, the narrative seemed to have eclipsed the fable and spilled out into a raucous ensemble. At least thirty other former prisoners were running for office as well, giving themselves a crash course in politics.

The Burmese people have been subjected to the whims of despotic leaders for so long that "government" has been included in a traditional lament about the "five evils" in life, along with fire, water, thieves, and enemies. Their history has not been without glory: the first major Burmese kingdom, which flourished at Pagan, in the eleventh century, created spectacular Buddhist temples and pagodas more than a century before comparable cathedrals appeared in Europe. The Burmese went on to conquer present-day Laos and Thailand. But in 1885 a British general arrived with enough pith-helmeted troops to force the final king out of his palace on an oxcart, and declared Burma a minor province of India.

In 1942, when Japan invaded, the Burmese, including the fiercely single-minded young revolutionary Aung San, Suu Kyi's father, joined in the fight against the Allies. Three years later, Aung San turned his troops against the Japanese and helped liberate the country alongside the British, signing an agreement to guarantee Burma's independence within a year. The achievement made him a secular saint—the lone Burmese leader who had gained the trust of a range of ethnic groups. His face appeared on the currency, but he never lived to see it. On July 19, 1947, when Suu Kyi was two, he was assassinated by a disaffected Burmese politician. Suu Kyi's mother was named Ambassador to India and Nepal, and Suu Kyi joined her in Delhi, where she acquired the diction of the Indian elite and the upright posture, still visible to this day, that came from never being permitted to lean against the back of a dining chair.

For the next decade, Burma enjoyed relative peace. But in Rangoon the civilian government was failing, and, after years of invasion and war, the military stepped into the vacuum. Vowing to prevent "chaos," General Ne Win led a coup in 1962, evicting students and aid workers and banning the teaching of English, while nationalizing timber companies, newspapers, and the Boy Scouts. As the economy began its half-century implosion, the General consoled himself at European spas and at the races at Ascot, and with a string of wives, despite a capacity for violence that drove one of his companions away after he threw an ashtray at her throat.

By 1992, power had migrated to the man who ruled Burma until 2010: Senior General Than Shwe, a postal clerk turned psy-ops specialist, who was described by those around him, in a biography by Benedict Rogers, with telling consistency—"Our leader is a very uneducated man" and "There were many intelligent soldiers, but he was not one of them." The poverty of his people did nothing to curb Than Shwe's ambitions. He once considered spending a billion dollars to buy Manchester United as a gift to his grandson, a soccer fan. In 2007, Burma was tied with Somalia as the most corrupt country in the world, according to Transparency International. In July, 2010, Than Shwe had been in power for eighteen years. He had a bullfrog frown and a chest covered with medals. *Foreign Policy* named him the world's third-worst dictator, behind Kim Jong Il and Robert Mugabe.

His aides shielded him from unwanted information, and the culture of isolation permeated his government. Nay Phone Latt, a blogger who was arrested in 2008 for coördinating anti-regime protests, discovered, during his trial, that the judge and the prosecutors had a tenuous grip on twenty-first-century technology:

"They knew that I was a blogger, but they thought the word was 'blocker,' that I was creating economic 'blocks' against the country or something. I could see from their faces that they weren't joking. They had never heard the word 'blog.' " (He was sentenced to twenty years and six months in prison, but was released in January.) Self-righteous seclusion extended to the highest ranks. Hla Maung Shwe, a businessman whose brother is commandant of the National Defense University, told me, "In the Army for twenty-nine years, my brother had one chance at exposure— a trip to Thailand for three days." Describing the nation's elite, Hla Maung Shwe said, "Our mind-set is in the Stone Age."

For years, the regime was able to overlook its people's contempt, but that became impossible in September, 2007, when tens of thousands of monks streamed into Rangoon to lead protests that became known as the Saffron Revolution. The Army opened fire, killing monks and civilians and arresting thousands.

As Than Shwe aged, he and his compatriots confronted growing worries about their future. By 2010, the U.N. had escalated its accusations to the level of suspected war crimes, and Than Shwe told visitors that he had what the United States Embassy, in a cable released by WikiLeaks, called a "strong desire not to appear before an international tribunal." Moreover, it was beginning to seem likely that if a prosecution materialized the top man would not be the only target; the U.N. had concluded that state violence originated in the "executive, military and judiciary at all levels." If change was going to happen, time was running out.

In January, 2011, Than Shwe, who was seventy-seven, anointed a successor, General Thein Sein, who had all the makings of a Burmese Medvedev. Generally regarded as a nonentity, Thein Sein had been the acting Prime Minister when the government opened fire on the monks, in 2007. If he showed any evident virtue, it was that, in a kleptocratic regime, he was relatively uncorrupt. "He carried out the orders like everybody else," a prominent Burmese entrepreneur told me. "But every businessman in the country knows he's clean— and that's why he was never that powerful." The dictator may have had another reason for choosing a cipher as his successor. When Burma's last king took the throne, he ordered his advisers to kill seventy rivals and their families in three days. Once a king lost his palace, as a Burmese saying held, "he is left with nothing but his umbrella." Than Shwe was acquainted with the tradition, because he had helped insure that his predecessor died under house arrest, with three grandsons and a son-in-law on death row. Choosing the pallid heir was "the best insurance policy," the businessman said, adding, "And, sure enough, he announced, right after his inauguration, that we are not interested in pursuing the past. Translation: amnesty."

And yet, in ways that are only now becoming clear, Thein Sein was not entirely who he appeared to be. As Prime Minister to a dictator, he had few duties, and had used his trips abroad to slip out and walk around in foreign cities. In May, 2008, as Cyclone Nargis devastated the Irrawaddy Delta, where he'd grown up, he found himself in charge of the state's breathtakingly inept response. (Among other failures, the generals initially turned down foreign aid, fearing an invasion.) More than a hundred and thirty-eight thousand people died.

Thein Sein was hardly the only one in the military who was awakening to the magnitude of the nation's failure. The ferocity of the assault on the monks—an unprecedented use of violence against the country's most revered institution—had drawn lines within the military. A source close to the military told the United States Embassy that "Than Shwe and Maung Aye"—his second-in-command—"gave the orders to crack down on the monks, including shooting them if necessary," according to a November, 2007, cable. As a result, the source said, there was "growing daylight between the top two leaders and the regime's second-tier commanders." The following summer, the Embassy noted, "Some of the regional commanders are reform-minded and aware of the need for political and economic reform."

On March 31, 2011, in Thein Sein's inauguration speech, he called for workers' rights and for an end to corruption; he welcomed international expertise; and, most startling, he said that Burma's numerous ethnic groups had been subjected to a "hell of untold miseries," suggesting his intention to end the conflicts that have made Burma host to the world's longest-running civil war.

"When Burmese listened to that speech," the entrepreneur told me, "they said, 'This is so unusual, so alien to what we have been hearing for the past four decades!'" The Burmese merchant class had been pushing for political change that could boost trade, but, to many, it was impossible to imagine the old strongman allowing this. Than Shwe's imprint on government was fading faster than people had predicted, and his step back had emboldened younger generals. "They were in a position where they could start fighting for reform," Priscilla Clapp, a former Chief of Mission of the American Embassy, said. "If they had done this during the earlier years, they would have been purged." What's more, if they needed any added incentive to forge ahead on reforms, the Arab Spring was toppling dictators one after another, and as the Presidential adviser Nay Zin Latt told a reporter, "We do not want an Arab Spring here."

A group of Burmese businessmen, journalists, and academics who had developed ties to the military were eager to exploit the growing desire for a path out of Burma's isolation. They'd formed an N.G.O. called Myanmar Egress—a way out—and though it attracted considerable suspicion from activists abroad, who feared that the group was more interested in controlling reform than in unleashing it, the businessmen were pushing the younger generals to confront how little they truly understood. To provide a glimpse of a functioning executive branch, the group gave the new President DVDs of "The West Wing." Thant Myint-U, a historian and an author who advises President Thein Sein, also urged top leaders to consider reform. "Abstract moral arguments weren't going to cut much ice," he told me. "And they were deeply cynical of Western rhetoric on human rights. The argument we made that got the most traction was: 'We're falling so far behind our neighbors economically—China and India—that, unless we change, politically as well as economically, it's going to be disastrous.'" Thomas Carothers calls it the "neighborhood effect," and explained, "When Laos overtakes you in per-capita G.D.P., it's time to rethink your basic national strategy."

One of the generals the businessmen spoke to was a former intelligence officer named Aung Min. He'd been the railway minister since 2003, and though he retains the title, he now has sweeping responsibilities for brokering peace with ethnic rebels and shaping the reform agenda. When Aung Min travelled to Bangkok to deliver a talk, Egress took the opportunity to show him around a modern city. "We took him to the food court, and on the Skytrain," one of the men on the tour told me. "On the car ride, he observed how the farms worked, how the roads worked, how the tolls worked." Routine details of government responsiveness seemed to impress him. When he flew to Europe, he commented on the fact that Westerners scheduled fewer flights at night in order to reduce the noise for people who live near the airport.

When I met Aung Min this spring in Rangoon, he had about him a Brylcreem crispness that evoked an Asian Robert McNamara. He and the President had been young officers together, and I asked him why Thein Sein was making these changes. "He understands that he can't run the government the way it used to be run by the previous government, that this government is elected by the people," he said, adding, "If you don't do what the people want, you won't survive."

Talking with Aung Min was a peculiar experience, not only because approaching a Burmese minister could have got a journalist deported a year ago but also because I couldn't figure out how much of what he said was pabulum, for international consumption, or how a man who had spent eight years in the Cabinet of one of the world's most vicious dictators could think that his people had forgotten. "This is only the beginning," he said. "There will be many things to do in this country. But step by step, one at a time."

That tension—between vowing change and calling for patience—reflects the fact that, among former generals, the idea of reform remains so intensely polarizing that even some of its standard-bearers flinch at the term. When I met the industry minister, Soe Thane, a small, hyper-alert former Navy man, and one of the few members of the Cabinet who speak English, he was in a buoyant mood. "We feel good. We have to move," he said. I asked if he knew when the remaining political prisoners would be released, and a pained expression creased his face. "My duty is apart from that," he said. When an Australian reporter approached with a question that described the minister as part of the "reform group," Soe Thane let out a nervous bark of a laugh and said, "No, no, no, no, no." A moment later, he announced, "Time's up!," and marched off. When I encountered him again, he explained that he worries about inflaming his conservative peers. "We must be patient, and give favor to the other party," he said.

But no amount of rhetoric would earn the government credibility in Burma or abroad unless it could secure the blessing of Suu Kyi. Less obvious was just how much Suu Kyi stood to gain from an alliance. After more than two decades of dissent, she was internationally renowned but not yet an active participant in the proposed reforms. In boycotting the 2010 election, her party, the National League for Democracy, had frustrated young activists, and she was at risk of becoming sainted but peripheral. For the first time in decades, all sides had a reason to find a way out of the impasse. After an exchange of secret messages, the President met Suu Kyi for dinner last August, and when she returned home she told Tin Oo, the deputy leader of the N.L.D., "I have the feeling that I can work with him." Her endorsement was a turning point. The world took notice, and the President cleared the way for Suu Kyi's supporters to register as a political party and for former political prisoners to run for office.

One of the first things the new President did was hire an assortment of academics and former officers as advisers. Among those whose aid he enlisted was Nay Zin Latt, a businessman who, since retiring from the Army, had become a political commentator. "I was asked to prepare a report for the government about the next fifty years for the United States and the next fifty years for China," he told me, as he chain-smoked in his office. His conclusion? "Let's put it this way: In the long run, the United States is still strong!"

For two decades, American policy was designed to choke the regime into submission. After Burma's crackdown in 1988, the United States had reduced its presence there to a low-key embassy, with no ambassador, and in Washington, apart from a small community of activists and lawmakers, the country was ignored. Americans had been barred from investing since 1997, and, among additional measures, in 2007 and 2008 Washington moved against individuals—leaders and well-connected tycoons—by freezing assets and issuing travel bans. But by the summer of 2009 diplomats from Malaysia, Indonesia, and others in the region were funnelling signals that Burma wanted to talk.

President Obama came into office vowing to seek engagement with hostile regimes, and several people in Burma quoted to me a phrase from his Inauguration speech: "We will extend a hand if you are willing to unclench your fist." The Administration saw the prospect of growing dissatisfaction within the military as powerful leverage. An Embassy source close to the military "recommended the United States exploit the emerging differences within the top levels of the regime by tightening our sanctions against the senior generals." Leslie Hayden, the Embassy's political officer at the time, cabled Washington that "the generals despise the sanctions and want them removed because they challenge the regime's legitimacy. If we really want to see the generals make progress, we need to show them what they will get in return." What could the United States offer? Larry Dinger, another diplomat, signed a cable that laid out options, including "dangle World Bank and I.M.F. technical assistance" or "consider accepting the country name 'Myanmar.'"

The Administration decided to keep sanctions in place but also to open negotiations. Kurt Campbell, the Assistant Secretary of State for East Asian and Pacific Affairs, met U Thaung, then Burma's minister for science and technology, at the Waldorf-Astoria in Manhattan, but left largely baffled by the Burmese negotiator's long digressions about the toll of imperialism and war. "We had to figure out, How were these people communicating?" Campbell told me. "What we would tend to think of as basically killing the clock, they would interpret as an essential expression of their historical legacy and trajectory." At one point, Campbell flew to Burma to press for elections, the release of prisoners, and talks with ethnic groups. He met with Suu Kyi, but he made "absolutely no progress whatsoever" with the government, he said. A second trip was even less productive, and the Administration returned to a hostile posture, declaring support for establishing a U.N. commission of inquiry to investigate war crimes in Burma.

But last November, encouraged by Suu Kyi's meeting with Thein Sein, President Obama phoned her to discuss the next steps. "If she's supportive of this, then we're going to go," he told aides, and the following day he announced that Hillary Clinton would visit Burma—the first Secretary of State to do so since John Foster Dulles, in 1955. The visit was highly choreographed even by diplomatic standards: to underscore American support for the opposition, Clinton and Suu Kyi were photographed in matching white jackets. Over dinner, according to an Administration official, Suu Kyi told Clinton, "I don't want to be an icon, I want to be a politician," and Clinton replied, "Get ready to get attacked." As a gift to Suu Kyi, Clinton brought books on Eisenhower and George Marshall, to help her understand the mind-set of soldiers who go into politics.

Nobody was more baffled by the turn of events in Burma than the Chinese. For years, Beijing had been Burma's most ardent defender in the U.N. Security Council, the supplier of arms and loans, and a customer for timber, gold, and other resources. But last September Thein Sein, citing "the will of the people," suspended construction of the $3.6-billion Myitsone dam, which had been financed by China to provide electricity across the border in Yunnan Province. Chinese analysts hinted at a conspiracy—they noted WikiLeaks cables that indicate that the United States. Embassy had given grants to anti-dam groups—and debated whether the opposition would spread to North Korea or elsewhere.

In Burma, however, people talk about how their country had felt subsumed and taken for granted. The dam was designed to flood an area four times the size of Manhattan, but when Burma asked for a more thorough environmental-impact assessment "the Chinese completely shut them off, saying, We've already done it and see no reason to repeat the process," Yun Sun, a China analyst based in Washington, told me. On another occasion, a delegation visited Beijing to discuss debt obligations at the Export-Import Bank of China, only to discover that the debt had been sold. The representatives were shunted aside and diverted to officials at a state-owned insurance company. Perhaps most damaging, Burmese senior military leaders concluded that Chinese military hardware wasn't worth the billion or so dollars that had been spent. "Army officers are saying to me, 'The Chinese cheated us. They've given us all this crap and taken our resources,'" Maung Zarni, a visiting Burmese academic at the London School of Economics, said.

As the parliamentary election approached, it was unclear whether the old generals could stomach an honest-to-goodness vote, and whether ordinary Burmese trusted them enough to show up at the polls.

On Election Day, I rode the ferry across the brown waters of the Irrawaddy and then took a rattletrap taxi to the river-delta township of Kawhmu, to watch Suu Kyi visit polling booths in her district. The heat shimmered above a pan-flat landscape of meandering rivers and thatch-roofed homes. Farmers drove ox-drawn plows through rice paddies. A few minutes after nine, Suu Kyi arrived at a high school in the village of Nat Sin Kong, striding gingerly across the yard, "arms swinging like a soldier," as her biographer, Peter Popham, had put it in his recently published book "The Lady and the Peacock."

In a tenth-grade classroom, with "Discipline, Education, Attitude" stencilled on the wall, she surveyed a lineup of plastic boxes, waved to the crowd, and was on to the next stop, trailed by a swarm of students and reporters. I stayed behind to have tea with some of the voters, and met Khin Ma Ma Chit, a farmer and a mother of two, who was still giddy with the experience of voting for the opposition. "Our parents and grandparents waited for this, but never saw it," she said.

A former diplomat told me that, if the opposition could win half the votes, it would be "a howling success." But it swiftly became clear that something far more decisive was under way. "We had so many feelings, so much hatred, but we kept it all inside," another mother whom I spoke with said. "The government always oppressed us. Every rainy season, when we finally had a crop, they would take it for half the price on the market, and say, 'It's for the government.'"

The ruling party had held out the promise of new schools and roads to those who fell in line, and the people had smiled and handed them a humiliation. The opposition took forty-three of the forty-five contested seats, even winning neighborhoods in the capital that are home to civil servants. In Rangoon that night, thousands of supporters swarmed the ramshackle headquarters of Suu Kyi's National League for Democracy, a building that is a cross between a storefront and a garage, wallpapered in yellowed news clippings and littered with the megaphones, speakers, and other flotsam of perpetual opposition. They danced and sang and mocked the generals. For years, the dilapidated office had symbolized how long Burma's democrats toiled in vain; that night, it struck me as a symbol, as well, of how unprepared they were for the sudden arrival of success.

When I stopped by the local headquarters the next morning, Aung Thein Linn, a military man and former mayor of Rangoon with a thick black comb-over, veered between indignation and victimhood as he hailed the process that his party vowed would be fair while fulminating over the outcome. He accused his opponents of "intimidation" for sending many people to watch the counting of ballots. "There may be some kind of psychological pressure," he said, "some mistakes as a result." Despite the vitriol, Aung Thein Linn knew that he had lost. He gestured toward his torso and declared, "I have so many scars on my body from fighting for the good of my country."

Three days after the election, Secretary of State Clinton announced that the United States was suspending sanctions against Burma and would be appointing an ambassador to the country for the first time in twenty-two years. Human-rights groups urged the State Department to relax restrictions sector by sector, to prevent the military from exploiting a rush into the energy business. Suu Kyi warned

against the "reckless optimism" of allowing firms to deal with a state-owned energy company that lacks "transparency and accountability." But American oil companies, among others, said that they were losing business to international competitors, and in July the Obama Administration suspended sanctions across all sectors. Activists assailed the decision for going too far. Even though the Administration has expanded asset freezes and travel bans on individuals, and will require companies to report on their Burma investments, suspending sanctions, critics contend, "looks like it caved to industry pressure and undercut Aung San Suu Kyi," Arvind Ganesan, the director of the human-rights division of Human Rights Watch, told me.

Burma has added a new dimension to the debate about the handling of rogues: Did the sanctions work? Does Burma tell us anything about how we should approach Syria or Iran? Inside the country, the consensus has not changed. "It didn't hurt the ruling junta one iota," Serge Pun, a prominent Burmese businessman, told me. "It actually hurt all the normal people, the poor people. Thousands of factories had to close down, because their products could not be sold to the West. Honestly, when you have China and India on both sides, who did not participate in the sanctions, and you had nine other ASEAN countries who also didn't participate, the sanctions, in effect, couldn't work."

Curiously, that was also the consensus in Washington for many years. Tom Malinowksi, a Burma expert and an advocate of sanctions who worked in the Clinton White House when the first round of sanctions were imposed, said, "They imposed sanctions not because they genuinely believed that they would work but because they wanted to do *something*." As the generals endured and enriched themselves, the measures were declared a failure. "They were only strong enough to weaken the country, not strong enough to remove the leaders," Nay Zin Latt, the Burmese Presidential adviser, told me.

But that verdict may have been premature. For all the suffering they produced, sanctions and scorn did narrow the junta's options. Sanctions drove the leaders deeper into China's embrace than they could tolerate and piqued their fears of falling behind their neighbors. The generals were denied access to the World Bank and other facilities that they believed had been indispensable to the rise of China and Vietnam. "They realized they had no choice but to bring Aung San Suu Kyi on board," Maung Zarni said. "That is not a values shift, where they say we need to treat our people like human beings. It's a technical, strategic move."

The struggle to bring democracy to Burma has been so tortuous that it's easy to overlook the uncomfortable fact that the greatest challenge confronting the country's future now lies hundreds of miles from Rangoon, in borderlands where ethnic minorities are demanding their share of power. Burma is blessed with and bedevilled by diversity—home to an estimated hundred and thirty-five ethnic groups—and, in the year since reforms began, government negotiators have succeeded in striking agreements with ten out of eleven main ethnic groups. But the conflicts that persist are bitter. In a remote expanse of emerald hills and jagged ridges in Burma's northern reaches, a seventeen-year ceasefire collapsed a year ago, pitting government forces against the Kachin Independence Army, a rebel insurgency that has demanded greater political autonomy and control over the country's natural resources. The Kachin war had proved especially difficult to resolve, because the land is rich with gold and gems and other things worth fighting about. Each side blamed the other for the resumption of hostilities. In December, the President ordered the commander-in-chief to halt attacks and fire only in self-defense, but the war raged on—suggesting that the President lacked the power or the resolve to make his commanders carry out his orders.

By spring, when I reached the site of the Kachin conflict, the fighting had uprooted seventy-five thousand people, according to a report by Human Rights Watch, which accused the Burmese military, since last June, of having "threatened and tortured civilians during interrogations for information about KIA insurgents, and raped women." The Army also, according to the report, "used antipersonnel landmines and conscripted forced labor." It accused the K.I.A. of "using child soldiers and antipersonnel landmines."

I arrived a few days ahead of the monsoon, and the fighting had intensified. The rebels, who augment their supply train with the use of pack elephants, had steadily lost ground in recent months and were regrouping in the remote town of Laiza, beside the Chinese border. The town was awash in soldiers on motorbikes and in pickup trucks, and people were arriving from villages already gripped by fighting. "This is the most intense period in our revolutionary journey," Kumhtat La Nan, the Joint General Secretary of the political wing of the rebel army, told me, when I stopped by the headquarters, a small hotel that had been fortified with gun positions and adorned with a banner that read, "God Is Our Victory." China had reportedly turned refugees away at the border, but the rebel commanders expected an exodus in the event of an attack, because people had nowhere else to go.

Recently, President Thein Sein had announced a renewed commitment to negotiations, but nobody I met in Kachin expected a swift conclusion: not the father of seven, entrenched in an outpost of tunnels and foxholes, who was fighting because "the Burmese Army took everything (land, fields, prosperity)"; not the Baptist pastor who feared that violence was radicalizing a new generation of youths; and not the farmer who had been burned out of his house, and was now in a bamboo shelter for displaced persons, and told me, "The new government talks about peace, but if it doesn't give us our rights, then the war will take a long time."

The risk that withdrawing the military from Burma's politics could lead to flashes of unrest became vivid in June, when sectarian clashes exploded near the border with Bangladesh, between a Muslim ethnic group, the Rohingya, and local Buddhists. The President declared a state of emergency in the region—his first exercise of that power since taking office—and by the time calm had been restored more than two dozen people were dead and thirty thousand had been displaced. This did not bode well for ethnic harmony. On Burma's newly uncensored Internet forums, bloggers poured rage on the Rohingya—a stateless people who are persecuted in Asia, much like the Roma in Europe—calling them terrorists, bandits, and dogs.

Even at the epicenter of Burma's transformation—Rangoon, the city that stands to benefit most from the deluge of new ideas and investment—the changes have been so disorienting that the dominant sensation in the teahouses and the moldering office blocks is not so much joy as vertigo. For Khin Maung Swe, who spent sixteen years in prison, the reforms ceased to be abstract when he looked out his front door one morning in January. "The man from military intelligence who had been waiting there every day was no longer there," he told me. "I have no idea where he went."

Things are no less unsettled for the spooks and minders who have spent their lives eavesdropping on the nation. At a campaign rally, Swe Win, a local journalist, was taking notes when a young plainclothes officer from the secret police, known as the Special Branch, mistook him for a fellow-agent and sidled up to him. "He said, 'We're like fish out of water here. Who knows what we're supposed to do?' Under the old law, he should have detained anyone holding a meeting that consisted of more than five people. I told him to go and take a seat. He obeyed my order and went and took a seat, and waited for his colleagues." Telling the story, Swe Win, who spent six years in prison, shook his head and said, "I almost felt sorry for him." Clapp, the former diplomat, compares the disorder of the security apparatus to "a creature that has lost its central nervous system. The legs are flailing, and it doesn't know which way to turn," she said.

One afternoon in May, when I met Chitmin Lay, the newly released prisoner with an interest in the Internet, he'd been out of jail for four months. By then, the thrill had ebbed to reveal an acute awareness of loss. "Fourteen years," he said, and flashed a large bitter smile. We were in a booth at a candy-colored café called J'donuts, in an air-conditioned mall; a young couple were canoodling in a corner booth. Chitmin Lay wanted to be a teacher, but he was over the age limit for entry-level positions. "Right now, I'll take anything I can find," he said. Burma's prison culture had been designed to promote maximum feelings of futility—at one jail, a new arrival was given a shard of a clay pot and ordered to "polish the mud outside until it shines like a mirror."

One afternoon, I visited leaders of the '88 Generation, the activists who have been in and out of jail since the uprising that took place that year. They now work from a two-story house previously occupied by a brothel. When I arrived, they were in the back yard, in a concrete shed, crowded around a PowerPoint presentation on the environment, as they tried to make sense of SO_2 and NO_x and heavy metals. The shack held a pantheon of Burmese heroes—the charismatic poet Min Ko Naing, the strategist Ko Ko Gyi—all comically wedged into school chairs with plastic desks on the arms. Jailed as college students, they are now pushing fifty, and they pose an uncertain new political force: not in the street, and not in Parliament.

After the presentation broke up, Ko Ko Gyi said, "We're ready to cooperate with the new government." He thought for a moment, and revised his sentence: "cooperate and *compete*." Former prisoners drifted back into the house to smoke and eat in a kitchen cluttered with sacks of rice and shallots. After eighteen years of being away, Ko Ko Gyi is gaunt but healthy, with a receding wave of black curls. "I don't count the years of prison life, so I'm twenty-eight years old," he said with a smile. When he was released, on January 13th, he was in solitary confinement, in a cell that measured seven paces across, serving a sixty-five-year sentence. He left behind everything except a few books: two volumes by Barack Obama, one by Nelson Mandela, and a textbook called "Learn French in Three Months."

Ko Ko Gyi is considered one of the former prisoners who have the greatest potential in politics, but for him, and for many others in Burma, the path from dissident to politician is fraught; for every Nelson Mandela, there is a Lech Walesa, whose fiery persistence, the very quality that allowed him to survive, failed him in government. But Ko Ko Gyi thinks that the focus on individuals is precisely the problem: "People here don't know they can stand up themselves. Again and again, we must say it: Politics is your job; it's not only for the politicians." He went on, "For such a long time under dictatorship, each and every citizen lost a role in society. Trust disappeared. They tried to escape the crisis, to find their own way. They couldn't care who suffers or who loses. They had to focus only on themselves." If Burma is to recover, he said, people will need to begin to trust the system again. "The most important thing is institutionalization," he said. "We cannot depend on any one person."

By early summer, the Burmese people were becoming acclimated to radically altered roles both at home and in the world. Suu Kyi, after winning her seat in Parliament, travelled abroad for the first time in more than two decades, including a seventeen-day European tour fit for a head of state. On a stop in Thailand, she drew such frantic crowds that President Thein Sein cancelled his own visit there a few days later, apparently to avoid being upstaged—an episode that indicated how hard it may be for the regime to accommodate the freshman lawmaker from Kawhmu, who happens to be a Nobel laureate. She used her first short speech in Parliament to call for "equal rights" for ethnic minorities, beyond simply protecting their languages and culture. "The flames of war are not completely extinguished," she said.

On the street, ordinary Burmese tested their new political freedoms. In May, in the airless pre-monsoon days, a wave of power outages left people stewing without fans or water pumps for their toilets, and more than a thousand protesters took to the streets of Mandalay, raging about the shortage of electricity. It was the nation's largest demonstration in five years, and when I drove into Mandalay on the night after the protests, through a countryside as black as the sea, police officers occupied every corner downtown. It was becoming clear that the issue had far less to do with electricity than with the dawning realization that so much of the nation's wealth had been salted away over the years by so few. A man in his twenties, showing me around a darkened neighborhood in the sidecar of his bicycle, pointed to a private clinic, whose lights had been provided by a generator,

and said, bitterly, "The rich man's hospital." The streets were tense but, so far, peaceful. The police held their fire.

In the West, Burma's efforts toward openness and democratization had touched off that rare thing in diplomacy: a race to declare not who had lost a country but who had won it. In the Administration, there was a sense that Burma is a risky source of pride: a successful test of President Obama's commitment to engagement, and a vast new market for American business, but also a high-profile bet on men of immense moral flexibility. "A lot of the stuff that Thein Sein has done is smart, wise, and bold," an Administration official said. "The question is about the local official ten levels below—will he follow through? The local commander, will he follow through? And that's going to need to be a systemic change over years, not months."

For all the uncertainty about Burma's future, the facts of the present are astounding: a nation roundly described as irredeemable has stepped back from the brink. The former generals are not without vanity, and, after decades of being mocked and scorned, they are savoring the trappings of statesmanship. Moreover, the opposition is, at last, free enough to make an impact, and it is loath to squander its freedom on infighting. But the real test of the two sides' ability to forge an open society together may not come until Burma's next general election, in 2015.

The Burmese people today would not tolerate a return to the eccentric seclusion of the past, and, month by month, reforms become more difficult to undo. But if it was cynical to assume that Burma could not change, it is naïve to predict a smooth and peaceful future. Forty-nine years of brutality and suspicion have distorted the body and soul of the nation, and the greatest threat may rise from within. Freedom, circumscribed, is an unstable state of nature, and the generals may not be able to control the forces they have unleashed. That fact—the volatility of rising expectations—reminded me of a story that Swe Win, the journalist, once mentioned in connection with his six years in prison. "For a long time, they didn't let us have anything to read or write," he said. "And then, one day, they gave us religious books. After a while, we said, 'Since you gave us religious books, you must allow us to have non-religious books.' And they said no. But we persisted, and eventually they said O.K. Then we said, 'Now that we have non-religious books, you must let us read state newspapers, because you control them anyway.' And they said no. But we persisted." By the time he left prison, the inmates had nudged and negotiated their way to obtaining not only state newspapers but also local journals and, at last, foreign publications. "It took three years," Swe Win said. "But we got them."

Critical Thinking

1. Why has the dictatorship in Myanmar liberalized the regime?
2. Who is Aung San Suu Kyi, and why is she important?
3. What are the prospects for the continued democratization of Myanmar?

Nigeria's Battle for Stability

JOHN CAMPBELL

Recent events in Nigeria, including its presidential elections last April, have produced two narratives on the current state of that oil-rich West African nation with a history of civic turmoil. The first is that events there have unfolded rather favorably since its elected president, Umaru Yar'Adua, fell ill in late 2009 and the country was left leaderless. That raised fears of a military coup, but then Goodluck Jonathan emerged to fill the power vacuum, first as an extraconstitutional "acting president," then as a constitutional successor after Yar'Adua's death and finally as the elected executive following the 2011 elections. This optimistic narrative notes that those elections were praised by international observers as better than in the past—and hence they reflected the will of the national majority. An amnesty for militants in the oil-rich Niger Delta, combined with disarmament, training and reintegration, ended a long insurrection there. One serious specter, however, still haunts the country—the expansion of the Islamic "terrorist group" Boko Haram, with its global connections. Hence, Nigeria's security challenge has become internationalized, and Westerners grappling with Islamist movements need to keep a sharp eye on that situation.

This is the narrative of conventional wisdom embraced by many in President Barack Obama's administration and in Congress, the business community and the media.

The other narrative is quite different. It posits that, despite a veneer of democratic institutions, Nigeria has suffered from dysfunctional governance for decades. The 2011 elections, according to this view, generated serious violence and polarized the country. Militants in the Niger Delta are regrouping. Boko Haram, hardly an Islamist threat to the world, is an indigenous uprising spawned by persistent alienation in the largely Muslim North, which is stricken with poverty and official corruption. The country's Middle Belt is beset by ongoing ethnic and religious conflict between Christians and Muslims, with attendant ethnic cleansing. Crime is ubiquitous in the cities and on the highways. The police, a national entity, are underpaid and notoriously corrupt. They prey on ordinary Nigerians at numerous checkpoints set up to address the breakdown in security. And for many, the police are merely the face of a "secular" or "Christian" Abuja regime. Thus they have become targets themselves for groups disaffected with the federal government.

That is the narrative to which the Obama administration and others concerned about Africa should probably pay some heed.

Thus far, the Jonathan administration has been remarkably inept in addressing the challenges it faces. Its military is exercising more authority in areas formerly under civilian purview. The president's heavy-handed, even brutalizing, security forces are exacerbating Muslim alienation in the North and have failed to control the Middle Belt's ethnic and religious strife. Concerns of impoverished Niger Delta residents have not been addressed, and there is anecdotal evidence that officials in the upper reaches of the federal and state governments participate actively in oil theft. More and more Nigerians are alienated from a state they regard as inept and corrupt.

Indeed, Nigeria's fundamental problem is a system of institutionalized corruption that channels public money into the pockets of a few Nigerian "big men." The result is some of the greatest income inequality and worst social statistics in Africa. And the political class doesn't manifest any will to reform the system. Politics are intense and often violent because they are suffused with a winner-takes-all mentality. Patron-client networks control politicians and the political system, and those within the networks get access to the few available jobs and social services. Hence, the political economy favors personal relationships over institutions. Not surprisingly, national sentiment is declining in favor of religious and ethnic identity—and animosity.

Despite this bleak picture, there are reasons to consider Nigeria a potentially important United States partner in Africa. With more than 160 million people, it is the continent's most populous nation. It has demonstrated impressive leadership in the Economic Community of West African States and the African Union. Working through those organizations, it helped end wars in Liberia and Sierra Leone. And its decision to supply peacekeepers in war-torn Darfur made Nigeria an invaluable partner in an area where America had only limited leverage. Beyond that, Nigeria consistently has been the fourth- or fifth-largest foreign supplier of oil to the United States, and shipping routes from Port Harcourt and Lagos to refineries in Baltimore or Philadelphia have no Persian Gulf—like choke points. Importantly, Nigeria has often ignored production limits set by OPEC during politically motivated oil shocks tied to developments in the volatile Middle East. And the country's "Bonny Light crude" is high quality and requires minimal refining.

Beyond economics, cultural and family links between Nigeria and the United States underpin the official relationship. The Nigerian diaspora community in America is economically successful and often vocal in its criticism of the corruption and poor governance in its home country. Two million Nigerians live in the United States, and an additional million have spent time here in recent years. Thus, it isn't surprising that Nigerian influences can be seen in American culture. Fela Kuti's "Afrobeat" and other musical styles of Nigerian origin have seeped into American popular music, and popular culture from New York and Los Angeles is ubiquitous in Lagos. Nigeria's dynamic and confident Christian churches have influenced American Christianity, sometimes controversially. A retired Anglican primate of Nigeria, a bitter critic of the Episcopal Church in the United States over gay issues, encouraged a schism within that church that sharpened differences between American liberal and conservative approaches to Christianity.

Given the prevailing narrative and ongoing ties between the United States and Nigeria, it isn't surprising that the Obama administration embraced Goodluck Jonathan when he assumed office as the country's best hope for stability and reform. But managing the United States relationship with Nigeria should be based on current Nigerian realities. Otherwise, the Obama administration risks undermining its credibility among Nigerians working for meaningful democratic change. It also risks alienating Africa's largest Muslim population.

Since the beginning of the year, the country has been roiled by demonstrations against the Jonathan government's ending of the traditional fuel subsidy for Nigerian consumers. The protests appeared to crystallize widespread Nigerian anger at the country's current political leadership. It remains to be seen whether these demonstrations will morph into a "Nigerian Spring" or what their impact will be on northern alienation that provides Boko Haram with its oxygen. Events are moving rapidly and pose particularly difficult challenges for administration policy makers.

The way forward for the United States in its relations with Nigeria can become discernible through a review of that country's recent history. President Yar'Adua was evacuated to Saudi Arabia in November 2009 for treatment of kidney disease and organ dysfunction. His departure left the country leaderless and precipitated a constitutional crisis when he withheld the necessary authorization to install his vice president, Goodluck Jonathan. Amid rumors of a brewing coup, political elites working through the National Assembly installed Jonathan extraconstitutionally as "acting president." This action prompted Yar'Adua's midnight return to Nigeria and a subsequent standoff between Jonathan and Yar'Adua's wife, Turai, who continued to prevent access to the president until he died of complications from a rare autoimmune syndrome. After Yar'Adua's death, Jonathan became the constitutional president, and the standoff between the Jonathan and Turai camps ended.

Nigeria was ruled by military dictators for nearly thirty years before civilian governance was established in 1999. Since then, under an informal understanding within the ruling People's Democratic Party (PDP), the country's presidency has alternated every eight years between Christians, who dominate the southern part of the country, and Muslims, who dominate the North. Under this approach, if the president were a northern Muslim, the vice president would be a southern Christian and vice versa. Often referred to as "zoning," the arrangement was intended to keep sectarian identity out of presidential politics and promote an elite consensus in favor of a single candidate. Hence, the southern Christian Olusegun Obasanjo held the presidency from 1999 to 2007. He was succeeded by Umaru Yar'Adua, a northern Muslim, who was expected to hold the presidency until 2015.

Yar'Adua's death upset this rotation by restoring a southern Christian to the presidency before the North had completed its turn. According to the Nigerian press, it was widely understood that Jonathan would hold the presidency only until the 2011 elections if Yar'Adua were to die. Then he would step aside for a northern Muslim candidate to preserve zoning. Jonathan would then run for the presidency in 2015, when it would again be a southern Christian's turn.

Perhaps under pressure from members of his Ijaw ethnic group and other southern groups hitherto excluded from the upper reaches of government, Jonathan reversed himself and ran for the presidency in 2011. Employing the power of incumbency, he defeated the northern Muslim Atiku Abubakar for the PDP presidential nomination at the January 2011 party convention, which participants described as an "auction" for delegate support. As a result of Jonathan's decision to end zoning, the presidential election became a polarizing contest between the incumbent and northern Muslim Muhammadu Buhari.

To secure victory, Jonathan's political allies spent large sums of money to win the support of incumbent governors who control the election process in many states. In the North, they also co-opted certain traditional Muslim rulers, and the sultan of Sokoto openly supported him.

It is difficult to know how much public money was spent for political purposes during this period. The lack of transparency in official expenditures, such as from Nigeria's Excess Crude Account, creates the appearance that state resources could easily be used on behalf of incumbents. For example, the Excess Crude Account dropped from about $20 billion (in United States dollars) when Yar'Adua assumed the presidency in 2007 to $3 billion when Jonathan became "acting president," then rose to approximately $5 billion. There has been little credible explanation for the fluctuations. According to the central bank, foreign reserves fell from $34.6 billion in 2010 to $30.86 billion in 2011. They have since recovered to $32.8 billion. (Throughout this period, oil prices have been high.)

The April 2011 elections, despite being hailed by international elections observers as better than the 2007 "election-like event," appear to have been rigged strategically in certain places to ensure Goodluck Jonathan's victory. To avoid a runoff, he needed a countrywide plurality of total ballots cast and at least 25 percent of the vote in two-thirds of the country's thirty-six states. In the Christian Southeast, Jonathan's vote totals were in the range of 97–99 percent. This guaranteed that he met the first requirement. Twenty-six of the thirty-six governors were from the ruling PDP, and governors were deeply involved in the conduct of the elections. Two or three governors in the North likely ensured that Jonathan received more than 25 percent of the vote in their states, thereby meeting the second requirement. The Independent National Electoral Commission (INEC), the ostensibly independent body that conducts elections, reported Jonathan's share of the vote in Sokoto—Buhari's home state—as 35 percent; in Gombe, 38.5 percent; and in Jigawa, 38.7 percent. These numbers seem high for the sharia heartland.

While the president appoints the chair of the INEC, his authority over the state electoral commissioners is limited; they are often beholden to the governors. Jonathan appointed Attahiru Jega, an American-educated academic known for his integrity, as INEC chair. Under Jega's leadership, the registration and voting processes improved, though they remained far from perfect. In more places than in the past, polling stations opened, ballots were available and security-service intimidation declined. However, in other areas it is widely believed that registration numbers were inflated, ballot boxes were stuffed and vote tabulation was manipulated sufficiently to ensure Jonathan's victory without a runoff. If the mechanics at the polling places in 2011 were an improvement, the outcome of the elections remained elite business as usual, albeit with more sophisticated methods than in the past.

Not surprisingly, in the southern half of the country people generally believed the election was credible and accepted Jonathan's victory. But in the predominantly Muslim North, Jonathan's national victory was widely viewed as fraudulent. The announcement of his victory sparked three days of riots in northern cities in which at least one thousand people were killed, making the 2011 elections the bloodiest in Nigeria's history. The private houses of the sultan of Sokoto and the emirs of Kano and Zaria were destroyed because they had supported Jonathan. What started as protests against the largely Muslim political establishment, which was believed to have sold out to Jonathan, degenerated into ethnic and religious violence. Today, many in the North continue to see the elections as lacking legitimacy.

The Abuja government appointed a panel to investigate the causes of the violence, informally called the Lemu Panel after its chairman, Sheikh Ahmed Lemu, a prominent retired Islamic judge. The text of the report has not been made public, but Chairman Lemu's public comments on the report amount to an indirect indictment of Nigeria's current political economy. He concludes that the postelection violence resulted from widespread frustration with Nigeria's poverty, corruption, insecurity and inequality, as well as with the inability of successive governments to address these issues.

Nigeria's vast oil reserves underpin its economy and its dysfunctional political culture. Its oil comes from the Niger Delta and from offshore platforms in the Atlantic's Gulf of Guinea. Though these oil reserves constitute the source of much of Nigeria's wealth, the region is remarkably underdeveloped. Fifty years of oil exploitation have led to numerous environmental accidents, hindering the traditional aquaculture of the indigenous people. For example, some environmental NGOs estimate that the region suffers from oil spills equivalent in magnitude to the 1989 Exxon Valdez spill each year. While there is a multitude of ethnic groups, the most prominent are the Itsekiri and the Ijaw, who in certain areas compete for turf and power. Governance in the region has been particularly corrupt, fueled by oil revenue to state and local governments with little or no accountability. The line between politics and thuggery is thin.

Governance in the region has been particularly corrupt, fueled by oil revenue to state and local governments with little or no accountability. The line between politics and thuggery is thin.

The result of this witches' brew has been a low-level insurrection that has waxed and waned for years. At times, insurgents have been able to shut down significant amounts of petroleum production, which has had a serious impact on international markets. At other times, federal and state governments have bought off militants—but never for long because the fundamental grievances that fuel the insurrection are never addressed.

As an Ijaw from Bayelsa state in the Niger Delta, Jonathan was widely expected to address Delta grievances, building on President Yar'Adua's 2008 amnesty for militants. But the disarmament, education and reintegration included in the amnesty have been incomplete. Instead, the most salient characteristic of the amnesty has been payoffs to militant leaders. While the insurrection in the Delta has been relatively quiet, it will likely escalate as new militant leaders rise to replace co-opted ones. Kidnappings and piracy are increasing; oil-production facilities have been attacked; and new militant leaders have expressed dissatisfaction with the government's focus on insecurity in the North. In 2012, shadowy Delta groups are threatening the region's small Islamic community, ostensibly in revenge for Boko Haram attacks on Christians in the North.

The suicide bombing of the ON headquarters in Abuja galvanized international attention on Boko Haram, the violent radical Muslim sect centered in the Northeast that claimed responsibility. Boko Haram is often translated from Hausa, a major West African language, to mean "Western education is evil." Originally, the name referred to followers of Mohammed Yusuf, a charismatic Islamic preacher who was murdered by police during a 2009 uprising. (The group generally referred to itself as The Movement for Sunna and Jihad.) Now, the term "Boko Haram" is used mostly by the media and security services to label loosely organized groups in northern Nigeria waging war against the federal government. What appears to hold these groups together is support for sharia and, for some, a millenarian version of Islam. However, the label implies more coherence in this grassroots movement than probably exists.

Daily attacks on politicians, soldiers, police, bars and churches, particularly since Jonathan's inauguration in May 2011, have led British prime minister David Cameron and AFRICOM commanding general Carter Hamm to suggest counterterrorism assistance. They are concerned that Boko Haram may establish links with al-Qaeda in the Islamic Maghreb and al-Shabab in Somalia. Suicide is cultural anathema in West Africa. Hence, to many, a suicide bombing indicated influences from outside the region. There is also concern about Boko Haram's apparently new access to sophisticated weapons and bomb-making technology.

Waves of radical, eschatological and millenarian Islamic revival occur intermittently in northern Nigeria, especially during periods of alienation and hardship such as now. Until recently, this anger normally has been directed against the indigenous, corrupt political and religious establishment that exploits the poor and is perceived as un-Islamic. Some militants seek to establish the kingdom of God on Earth and justice as defined by sharia law. In their efforts to achieve such an outcome, uprisings can be quite bloody. The Maitatsine uprising centered in Kano during the early 1980s, which claimed five thousand lives, superficially resembles aspects of Boko Haram.

This tradition animates Boko Haram, its founder Mohammed Yusuf and his followers. Yusuf, the young, charismatic Islamic preacher, was based at the Railroad Mosque in Maiduguri and initially led a somewhat pacifist community of thousands of university graduates, high-school dropouts and political figures, as well as the impoverished and uneducated. Like many, he and his followers welcomed the imposition of sharia law in 1999 in twelve Nigerian states. But they were disappointed and disillusioned by its lackadaisical enforcement by secular authorities. In 2009, Yusuf launched an insurrection against the secular state, ostensibly prompted by the killing of some of his followers in a dispute with police. Hundreds, if not thousands, were killed on both sides before the army suppressed the insurrection, captured Yusuf and turned him over to the police. The police then murdered him and his father-in-law while they were in custody. Yusuf's surviving followers went underground and turned to field preaching.

Probably small in number, these groups appear to have won much wider public support. When they can, they murder government officials and members of those parts of the Islamic establishment that they see as allied with Abuja. They attack venues of un-Islamic behavior, especially bars and brothels, and rob banks to distribute the proceeds to the poor (doubtless keeping some for themselves).

Yusuf's disciples have repudiated the sultan of Sokoto and the emirs of Kano and Zaria because of their support for Jonathan in the 2011 elections. They have also claimed responsibility for the murder of the brother of the *shehu* of Borno, the second-ranking Islamic traditional ruler. In addition to the VN bombing, people claiming to be Boko Haram spokesmen also took credit for a June 2011 bomb attack on the Abuja headquarters of the national police. They have never attacked schools, despite their hostility toward Western education. In the past, they have attacked churches and murdered clergy, but most of their violence has been perpetrated against other Muslims. However, attacks on Christian churches appear to be escalating; a few months ago a church in an Abuja suburb was bombed on Christmas Day, and similar attacks occurred elsewhere during the Christmas–New Year holiday.

Since Mohammed Yusuf's death, his followers have had no charismatic leader. They appear to be part of a wider, highly diffuse structure composed of religious fanatics, criminals and political thugs with no politburo or other governing body. Their stated goals include punishment of Yusuf's murderers, recompense for property destroyed by the security services and establishment of Islamic law throughout Nigeria. In the aftermath of the April 2011 elections, some may have links with parts of the traditional establishment and possibly some mid-level political figures that fear marginalization. The security services' heavy-handed response to unrest in Maiduguri and elsewhere, resulting as it did in many deaths, doubtless swelled the ranks of Boko Haram groups.

Indeed, violence and unrest have become widespread enough in the North to look like something of a popular insurrection, but it does not seem to be centrally organized or tied to international terrorism. Yusuf's disciples and other radical millenarian Islamic groups in northern Nigeria are inward looking. Their concerns are local, and their hostility is toward state governments, Jonathan's secular federal government and brutish police behavior. They feed off bad government and the collapsing economy.

With its oil, ongoing peacekeeping efforts and robust population growth, Nigeria continues to be an important international player despite dangerous North-South polarization, sectarian conflict and simmering insurrections.

Given this reality, the Obama administration should continue, and perhaps even enhance, its normal diplomatic dialogue with Abuja. But the administration must recognize the reality that Nigeria is a weak state with a largely unresponsive government that faces significant domestic opposition. The result is that it has only a very limited ability to serve as a diplomatic partner.

That is why the United States must maintain good diplomatic relations with a predominately southern, Christian administration without appearing to favor one religious, regional or sectarian group over another. In Nigeria, there is the presumption that Jonathan was Washington's candidate, which he fostered with his electoral base. He displayed a campaign billboard showing him standing next to President Obama with the slogan, "Yes We Can, Sir!" The United States should work to dispel this presumption and cease seeming to court Jonathan, who has been received twice by President Obama since becoming acting president. The White House should also drop its rhetoric about the virtues of the 2011 elections, which are often overstated. They grate on Nigerians, who know better, and alienate many in the North.

In addition, the Obama administration should engage in targeted outreach to Nigerian Muslims. To begin, it should treat Muhammadu Buhari, the most credible opposition leader in Nigeria, as it does the leaders of the opposition in other friendly states. He should be publicly received in Washington at an appropriately high level. Despite the costs and risks, the United States should proceed to establish a consulate in Kano, the metropolis and cultural center of the Islamic North, where it can build a stronger relationship with a region that has received too little Western attention in the past.

Affiliation with Nigerian security agencies should be treated extremely carefully. Just as al-Qaeda has fed off the resentment of many Saudis over the United States military presence in their country, Nigerian radicals in the North likely would do the same. The administration also should be outspoken about security-service abuses against civilians and publicly raise questions about official investigations of postelectoral violence—especially if there are signs of a cover-up. Nevertheless, support for training of the army and the police, especially improving their ability to conduct investigations and interact with the communities in which they work, could, over the long term, reduce animosity between security services and Nigerian civilians.

Nigerians often identify corruption as their nation's greatest challenge. Many of the most notoriously corrupt have residences and other assets in the United States, and they value their ability to visit, often for long periods. The Obama administration should make greater use of the visa-sanction tool against those who use their official position for personal gain. Such an approach would be highly popular with Nigerians, most of whom are struggling to feed their families rather than shopping on Rodeo Drive.

For the first time since the 1967–70 civil war, Nigerians in all parts of the country are questioning whether their country can hold together. It is very much in the United States interest that it does.

For the first time since the 1967–70 civil war, Nigerians in all parts of the country—not only in the North—are questioning whether their country can hold together. It is very much in the United States interest that it does. A fragmentation of Nigeria would likely lead to ethnic and religious clashes and shifts in population that would constitute a humanitarian disaster, perhaps recalling the 1947 partition of India and Pakistan or the more recent breakup of Yugoslavia. It would be inherently destabilizing for Nigeria's small and weak neighbors. It would certainly provide a new scope for the operations of international terrorism. In the words of the supporters of the federal government during the Nigerian civil war: "It is a task that needs to be done, to keep Nigeria one." True, given commitments elsewhere, a weak economy and a divided government, the United States faces limits in its ability to influence events in Nigeria. But United States policy makers should look at the long term and cultivate close relations with those working to keep Nigeria together and on a path to democracy.

Critical Thinking

1. Is Nigeria undergoing the process of the consolidation of democracy? How?
2. What is Boko Hram and why is it important?
3. What are the two narratives that characterize the process of political stability in Nigeria?

JOHN CAMPBELL is the Ralph Bunche Senior Fellow for Africa Policy Studies at the Council on Foreign Relations. He served as U.S. ambassador to Nigeria from 2004 to 2007.

Fascistoid Russia
Whither Putin's Brittle Realm?

ALEXANDER J. MOTYL

The massive demonstrations that rocked Russia in the aftermath of the Duma elections of December 4, 2011, surprised everyone, including most Russians. But they shouldn't have. The conditions for such an upheaval have been ripening as a result of the growing power and decrepitude of Putinism. It is likely that popular mobilization will continue, and that the regime's days may be numbered.

Observers generally agree that the fraudulent elections, in which the pro-regime United Russia party won 49.3 percent of the vote, sparked the countrywide demonstrations on December 10th and December 24th, in which, respectively, an estimated thirty to fifty thousand and eighty to one hundred thousand people participated in Moscow alone. They also agree that President Dmitri Medvedev's September 24th announcement that he and Prime Minister Vladimir Putin would swap places via the March 2012 presidential elections set the outrage in motion. And finally, they agree that the leading role in the demonstrations belonged to Russia's middle class and youth.

Although this story is correct, it is incomplete. The roots of the Russian uprising are found in the nature of the regime Putin constructed and in its inherent brittleness and ineffectiveness. Too many Western and Russian observers took the regime's claims of stability at face value, causing them to miss the fact that Putin had actually built a profoundly unstable political system, one that was likely to decay, decline, and possibly even crash. As the early warnings of the December protests suggest, this may be starting to happen.

It was during Putin's first run as president in 2000 that the question of whether Russia was a "managed democracy" or a "competitive authoritarianism" first arose. For those who thought it was a flawed democracy, the modifier hinted at authoritarian imperfections. For those who considered it a flawed authoritarian state, the modifier hinted at residual democracy. Either way, Russia was supposed to be a "hybrid" political system combining elements of both democracy and authoritarianism. For a while, the emphasis on hybridity made some sense—especially after Medvedev, the ostensible liberal, replaced Putin as president in 2008. Medvedev's liberalism rapidly proved to be illusory, however, while his connivance with Putin to transform the March 2012 presidential elections into a sham put an end to notions that Putin's Russia was anything other than an authoritarian state.

Except that that designation isn't quite accurate either. Authoritarian states are typically ruled by faceless bureaucrats or dour generals. Putin, in contrast, has charisma and he *is* popular. This factor makes Russia sufficiently different from run-of-the-mill authoritarian states to qualify it as "fascistoid"—an ugly word indicating that its hybridity quickly shifted from some combination of democracy and authoritarianism in Putin's early years in power to some combination of authoritarianism and fascism today.

> **Authoritarian states are typically ruled by faceless bureaucrats or dour generals. Putin, in contrast, has charisma and he *is* popular. This factor makes Russia sufficiently different from run-of-the-mill authoritarian states to qualify it as "fascistoid."**

Like authoritarian systems, fascist systems lack meaningful parliaments, judiciaries, parties, and elections; are highly centralized; give pride of place to soldiers and policemen; have a domineering party; restrict freedom of the press, speech, and assembly; and repress the opposition. (Consider in this light the similarities between Pinochet's Chile and Mussolini's Italy.) But unlike authoritarian systems, fascist systems always have supreme leaders enjoying cult-like status, exuding vigor, youthfulness, and manliness. And unlike authoritarians, fascist leaders are charismatic individuals who promote a hyper-nationalist vision that promises the population, and especially the young, a grand and glorious future—usually echoing past national glories—in exchange for their subservience. (Consider the differences between Pinochet and Il Duce.) Unsurprisingly, full-blown fascist systems, being the instruments of charismatic one-man rule, tend to be more violent than average authoritarian states.

"Fascistoid" captures nicely the hybridity of the wretched system Putin has created, in which authoritarian institutions serve as a platform for a charismatic leader who is committed to

Russian greatness, hyper-nationalism, and neo-imperial revival and who serves as the primary source of regime legitimacy and stability. The term also suggests why the regime is intrinsically weak, and why Putin's attempt to ratchet up the system's fascistoid characteristics by manipulating both the parliamentary and presidential elections drove hundreds of thousands of Russians into the streets.

How and when will the regime end? Accurate predictions are impossible, but good bets are not. The regime could break down overnight or decay for years. Either way, Putin's Russia is a terminal case.

The obvious place to start diagnosing its sickness is the supreme leader himself. The key weakness of any leader-centered system is that cults of vigor cannot be sustained as leaders inevitably grow old or become decrepit. Sooner or later, supreme leaders lose their aura of invincibility and, when they do, their fans and followers fall away. In addition to the depredations of mortality, we know from Max Weber that charisma is hard to sustain, becoming "routinized" over time. Twelve years ago, Putin appeared to be an outstanding politician who could do no wrong. Today, he looks like a crafty politician who's trying to hang on to power by martial arts exhibitions and shirtless location pics. Even if he manages to slog through what may become two six-year terms after March 2012, his youthfulness and charisma will wither away as inexorably as did the Marxist vision of the state.

While it might seem that extreme centralization of power in the hands of a supreme leader would ensure coordination and submission among the elites, the exact opposite occurs, as elites compete for the boss's favor, pass the buck and shirk responsibility, avoid cooperating with their colleague-competitors, and amass resources as they form mini-bureaucracies of their own. Just this happened in such hyper-centralized regimes as Nazi Germany, the Soviet Union, and Communist China—not despite, but because of, hyper-centralization. Leader-centered regimes are thus brittle, and when supreme leaders falter—as they always do, especially during times of crisis—or leave the scene, their comrades usually embark on cutthroat power struggles to assume the mantle of authority. Succession crises are especially destabilizing in all such regimes because the pressures they create cannot be ventilated by institutional mechanisms such as elections.

Finally, supreme leaders are prone to making strategic mistakes—a point first noted by Aristotle and proved repeatedly ever since. They are responsible for everything, but physically and intellectually incapable of making the right decisions all the time. Subordinates become toadies unable to act on their own, solidifying their own positions by always passing the boss good (and therefore inaccurate) news—a point recognized by Karl Deutsch back in the 1950s. Forced to make critical decisions without accurate information, the big leader will make big mistakes, especially if he already has an obsessive ideological vision.

Putin's involves his deeply rooted desire to achieve an in-gathering of the former Soviet territories, as manifested in the "gas wars" with Ukraine, the real war with Georgia, and the creeping takeover of Belarus. While his integrationist "Eurasian Union" project provides him and his rule with legitimacy—and many Russians, understandably distressed by the Soviet empire's ignominious collapse and Russia's transformation into an "Ivory Coast with the bomb," support their country's return to a place in the sun—it will at best distract Russia from its problems and at worst turn its non-Russian neighbors against Russia, thereby intensifying those problems. The fact is that, while neo-imperial projects serve all authoritarian and fascist leaders well at first, they invariably get them and their countries in serious trouble, as Argentina's military leaders discovered after their ill-fated invasion of the Falkland Islands.

The global financial crisis and its impact on Russia's economy will only intensify elite infighting and competition for scarce resources and erode Putin's aura of omnipotence, especially if living standards continue to decline. The next few years will be particularly difficult for Russia, as Putin tries to remain firmly in control of a hybrid system while the mounting problems of the global economy challenge his claims to charismatic authority. Chances are that Putin will place the blame for his failure to modernize Russia on Medvedev, who, in turn, will blame Putin. Sooner or later, however, Putin will have to accept responsibility for the system's failures, thereby admitting that the emperor has even fewer clothes than he wears on his topless photo ops.

Like every dictator, Putin hopes to make the trains run on time, but introducing marginal efficiencies will not modernize Russia. As George Soros, drawing on Karl Popper, reminds us, modernity requires open societies. Since economic change undermines political systems that cannot adapt to it, modernization and authoritarianism are incompatible—unless populations are rural, uneducated, and provincial, and thus incapable of active political involvement. If populations are urban, educated, and informed, as in Russia, authoritarian states are caught in a race against time.

They may succeed in industrializing agrarian societies—Bismarck's Germany, Stalin's Russia, and Mao's China come to mind—and they may be able to promote extensive economic growth and supervise planned economies, as in Communist states, but they cannot foster entrepreneurship, risk-taking, openness, and engagement, which are at the core of any fully modern society. Worse, if and when such entrepreneurial forces do emerge, they invariably threaten the legitimacy of the regime precisely because authoritarian regimes lack the institutions to accommodate them and their participatory aspirations. The late Samuel P. Huntington had it right when he noted, "The stability of any given polity depends upon the relationship between the level of political participation and the level of political institutionalization."

In Russia, as in all modernizing societies, these participatory qualities are associated with the middle class. The rise of a social grouping committed to private property, rule of law, and greater involvement in the political process is thus an obvious challenge to the stability of the Putin state. Even if the Kremlin follows in China's footsteps and succeeds in converting affluent and educated Russians to hyper-nationalism and neo-imperialism—and thereby deflecting their attention from internal problems—a self-confident entrepreneurial class is unlikely to allow itself to be bought off for long. Putin, like today's Chinese Communists, will attempt to square the circle by trying to co-opt the middle class into existing authority structures, but that strategy will necessarily fail since authoritarian institutions are, by definition, incompatible with democratic strivings.

> **In a word, Putin's Russia is in decay. Putin's hybrid authoritarian-fascist system is intrinsically brittle, susceptible to elite fragmentation, and incapable of sustaining modernization, coexisting with the middle class, and preventing rising discontent.**

Complicating things for Putin, as for all autocrats, are students. It is at first glance remarkable that Russia's many students have been so quiescent for so long. Like Americans and Europeans in the 1950s, they may have been responding to past economic insecurity and current economic prospects by focusing on their educations and careers. But they are also like their American and European counterparts in the 1960s, in that they can now take some prosperity for granted and translate their self-assurance and sophistication into critical thinking and social protest.

Russia is tailor-made for two types of social protest—one resulting from "relative deprivation," or the disappointment, frustration, and anger that follow when hopes are suddenly, and unexpectedly, dashed; another resulting from a sense of injustice that boils over into anger and rage and spurs people to rebel against an illegitimate order, as during Ukraine's 2004 Orange Revolution.

Relative deprivation is generally the product of rapid economic growth followed by a sudden economic downturn. Russia's energy-fueled economic growth may turn out to be similar to China's and last for several decades or, rather more likely, it may—as a result of price drops, supply disruptions, regional tensions, or political crises—suddenly fall and remain low for some time. The economy is already growing less than before. If a significant downturn occurs, especially after a self-confident middle class and a vocal student body have emerged, both groups are likely to become restive.

A smoldering sense of moral outrage, at the transgressions of public trust Putin has committed in his effort to retain and expand power, is already present and was what drove the demonstrators on December 10th and 24th. Russians expected fair and free elections. Instead they got two slaps in the face: the first, when Putin and Medvedev announced that the former would be president; the second, when results of the Duma elections were falsified. They also expected Putin, whose popularity had fallen some twenty percentage points in the last few years, to act with greater self-restraint instead of greater arrogance.

Unsurprisingly, as middle-class entrepreneurs and students chafe at authoritarian controls, they insist that the state is unjustly violating their rights. Just as social science theories would lead us to expect, everyone—from entrepreneurs to students to average Russians—has become angry at the all-pervasiveness of the Russian ruling elite's corruption and cynical indifference to popular well-being. We may expect that, as younger generations begin to ask tough questions about the Soviet Union's criminal past, they will, like young Germans who fifty years ago were incensed about Nazism, want to know why their government has refused to complete the condemnation of Stalin's crimes and even subtly and subliminally sought to reinforce continuities with his rule.

What then does the future hold for Putin's Russia? As social protests mount, tensions within the elites will multiply. As the system becomes fragmented and ineffective, factions within the central elites will begin to look for alternatives and reach out to oppositions and "the people" for support. If and when the tide begins to turn and the democrats look stronger than the authoritarians, "people power" and "color revolutions" can gain critical mass as ever larger numbers join what appears to be a sure bet. Russia's situation is far more volatile than the Putinists would have us believe. Democratic opposition looked marginalized and weak in the summer of 2011. It may be premature to say that it's now on the march, but there's no denying that it has since presented its birth certificate in the streets. Prospects for the democrats look much better now than they did in the recent past, and they will improve if the authoritarian elites continue to appear confused or weak—recall how Romanian dictator Nicolae Ceausescu's momentary show of weakness on television turned the tide against him in 1989—and if popular perceptions of stability and legitimacy continue to decline.

Putin obviously believes that Russia's vast oil and gas reserves will save the authoritarianism he created. Energy resources have fueled Russia's economic development, but easy money has also transformed Russia into a "petro-state" that has become an impediment—some would say the *greatest* impediment—to further economic development and political stability. When easy money promotes corruption and outright theft and inclines elites to use the state as a source of patronage, the state itself becomes an obstacle to modernization. The worst-case scenario for Russia would be ending up like Nigeria or the Shah's Iran. It's only somewhat less alarming that at best it could end up like Saudi Arabia or Hugo Chávez's Venezuela.

In a word, Putin's Russia is in decay. Putin's hybrid authoritarian-fascist system is intrinsically brittle, susceptible to elite fragmentation, and incapable of sustaining modernization, coexisting with the middle class, and preventing rising discontent. Like a very sick person, its condition could easily become critical—especially if some catalyzing incident hastens the disintegrative process. Putin becoming ill would be one such event; another would be some overcommitment on the part of the Kremlin to a costly misadventure in the near abroad—another quick, glorious little war, for instance, along the lines of the one with Georgia. Still another catalyst could be a sudden drop in the price of oil, a secular decline in Gazprom's ability to produce gas, or a recession.

If things were to get out of hand and Russia's non-Russian regional elites began claiming power, Russia could even turn into competing, if not quite warring, principalities. Whatever the outcome, the global effects of Russian turmoil would be substantial. These could include disruptions in energy production and supplies, the revival of the "loose nukes" problem, the emergence of full-fledged guerrilla and terrorist movements in Russia's provinces, and the inability of Russia to play any kind of role in global affairs. If Russia's problems spill over into the near abroad, some of the more fragile non-Russian states could follow in its footsteps, thereby compounding all the threats emanating from Russian instability.

What can the world do to forestall such a scenario? Very little. Russia's well-wishers can reduce the risk of the worst kind of turmoil by encouraging Putin to fix his problems at home and not overextend himself with ill-advised, neo-imperial schemes. They can also minimize the likelihood that Russia's turmoil will spill over into its neighbors by propping up the non-Russian states and enabling them to deal with their own sources of instability. Seen in this light, Germany's foreign policy toward the former Soviet Union is a textbook case of what *not* to do. On the one hand, Berlin encourages Moscow to assert its regional primacy by means of the North Stream pipeline. On the other hand, Berlin has done little to help such pivotal states as Ukraine to strengthen their sovereignty.

Such shortsightedness also encourages Russia's neighbors to imitate Putin's authoritarianism. But consider this. If the scenario I have sketched out holds for Russia, then it holds no less for Lukashenko's Belarus, Yanukovich's Ukraine, Nazarbayev's Kazakhstan, and a score of other non-Russian states. Serial crashes cannot then be discounted, especially as both the Communist breakdowns of 1989 and the Arab Spring of 2011 suggest that even seemingly stable authoritarian states can, amazingly, crumble overnight.

Critical Thinking

1. What does Motyl mean by fascitoid Russia?
2. What is the basis of Vladimir Putin's authority?
3. Why does the author believe that Putin's fascitoid state will collapse?

ALEXANDER J. MOTYL is a professor of political science at Rutgers University–Newark.

Motyl, Alexander J. From *World Affairs*, March/April 2012, pp. 53–61. Copyright © 2012 by ©2010 American Peace Society. Reprinted by permission of World Affairs Institute. www.WorldAffairsJournal.org

Korea's Third Kim
Will Anything Change?

The death of Kim Jong-il and subsequent dynastic transfer of power in North Korea caused a spasm of hope in the policy community that the secretive and totalitarian nation might embark on economic and political reforms. As the new leader, Kim Jong-un, was exposed to Western affluence while receiving his education in Switzerland—so the wishful thinking goes—surely he would realize the benefits of opening up his country. In fact, the young and inexperienced scion of the Kim dynasty derives his legitimacy solely from his family heritage. He has every reason to perpetuate the oppressive system built by his grandfather and buttressed by his father. In fact, how much Kim Jong-un's ideas and beliefs matter will remain questionable, at least over the short term. It is reasonable to assume that the untested leader will be guided by guardians or perhaps regents. This means that he may not be the one calling the shots, at least for the time being. The opaqueness of the power structure, meanwhile, has important implications for the outside world. The consolidation of power is likely to be still in progress, and it would take months—possibly even longer—for outside observers to learn how policies are determined. With Kim Jong-il, the world at least knew with whom it was dealing. Under Kim Jong-un, we may not even enjoy that advantage for some time to come.

There is little that is known about Kim Jong-un, apart from the fact that he is the third son of Kim Jong-il, is in his late twenties, and spent some time at a school in Switzerland. His youth and exposure to the Western world have prompted hope in some quarters that he would be more open to reforms aimed at reviving the country's dysfunctional economy. History has shown, however, that foreign exposure does not always lead to liberal policies. Cambodia's Pol Pot, who was responsible for the murder of approximately twenty percent of his country's population, was educated partly in France. Liberian dictator Charles Taylor holds a university degree from the United States—and is accused of war crimes and human rights abuses.

Kim Jong-un was chosen over at least two older members of the family. One is Kim Jong-nam, a half brother who reportedly fell out of favor after being detained in Japan for trying to enter the country on a forged passport in 2001. The other is Kim Jong-chol, a full brother. According to a book by a former Japanese chef of the late Kim Jong-il, the North Korean leader complained about his second-oldest son, saying that he is "like a girl." Kim Jong-un had long been his father's favorite, according to the same source, who was the North Korean dictator's chef for thirteen years until leaving the country in 2001. (The Hermit Kingdom is so thoroughly closed to Western eyes that even such anecdotal information is treasured by outside observers.)

For Kim Jong-un, upholding his own legacy means maintaining the hagiography of the Kim family's greatness. He has clearly taken pointers from 1994, when his father took over from his grandfather (and founder of the country), Kim Il-sung, and fortified himself by strengthening the personality cult his father had established and portraying himself as a son consumed with the tasks of filial responsibility. Kim Jong-il not only promoted slogans about his father's immortality, such as "The Great Leader will be eternal," but also remodeled the Kumsusan Assembly Hall—his father's living and working quarters—into a mausoleum where his father's embalmed body is preserved. Additionally, he instituted a new calendar-year system based on Kim Il-sung's birth year, 1912. He used "Juche," a guiding philosophy for North Korea loosely translated as "self-reliance," as the name of the year. (Under this system, 1912 became Juche 1. According to North Korean calendars and newspapers, this year is Juche 101.) Kim Il-sung was named eternal president of the country, and out of deference to his father, Kim Jong-il allowed himself only the title of chairman of the country's powerful National Defense Commission.

Kim Jong-un has, however, added his own twist to efforts aimed at boosting his family heritage. Images of the new leader, carried by the North Korean media during his first month in power, evoke his grandfather more than his father—not just in terms of physical appearance, but also in terms of interactions with ordinary people. The third-generation Kim has been shown putting his ams around soldiers, walking arm-in-arm with them, and even putting his hand up to a person's cheek. The pictures convey a more personal and caring image than any of Kim Jong-il.

This family hagiography—the only legitimacy for the Kim regime—will continue. (Already plans are afoot to embalm Kim Jong-il's body too, which means the son will govern against the backdrop of a hall of ancestors.) And the tight control of information will continue as well. Radios that can pick up foreign broadcasts will continue to be banned. Economic reforms that open up the country to information as well as goods will have little chance of being implemented. Such policies are crucial for ongoing dynastic control. To deviate from the grandfather and father is to call one's own legitimacy into question.

North Korea has already made clear that under Kim Jong-un there will be no change in the "military-first policy," a feature of his father's ruling style that makes the military the main pillar of support for the regime. The Korean Central News Agency, the country's official media, announced on December 26th, less than a week after Kim Jong-il's death, that the policy will be given "steady continuity at all times" under the Dear Leader's heir.

The new regime has also indicated continuity in foreign policy. A day after declaring Kim Jong-un its supreme leader, it said that there would be no deviations in its policy toward Seoul as long as South Korean President Lee Myung-bak is in power. In a statement carried by the official media on December 30th, the National Defense Commission said that "the foolish politicians" in the world, including South Koreans, "should not expect any change from us."

Even if Kim Jong-un wanted to change the course of policy, there is reason to believe he may not be free to do so, particularly over the short term. The new leader is surrounded by senior members of the ruling party and the military, who are expected to act as his guardians. Important members of this inner circle include his uncle, Jang Song-taek, a vice chairman of the National Defense Commission. A political survivor who has been rehabilitated from a demotion in 2004, Jang is well versed in policy matters as well as the power dynamics of the system, and is likely to play an important role in determining the direction of the new regime.

Kim Kyong-hui, Kim Jong-il's sister, who is married to Jang, has also been promoted steadily in the run-up to the dynastic succession. In the final mourning ceremonies for Kim Jong-il, her ranking moved up from fourteenth to fifth, according to Japan's Jiji Press. In a situation where symbolism must substitute for information, such a climb up the political ladder is an indication that she will also play a significant role.

In such a heavily militarized country, the armed forces are expected to play a crucial part in the stabilization of the new regime. The most important of its members are three heavyweights—Vice Marshal Ri Yong-ho, head of the military's general staff, Vice Marshal Kim Yong-chun, minister of the People's Armed Forces, and General O Kuk-ryol, who was head of the military's general staff in the 1970s and has been a longtime associate of the Kim family.

The presence of such an independent source of power is the biggest difference between Kim Jong-un's succession and that of his father. When Kim Jong-il succeeded Kim Il-sung, he was fifty-two years old and had been groomed for the position for two decades. He had already consolidated power within the party, military, and other governmental branches. He was also already representing the state in the country's external affairs. Kim Il-sung had begun gradually transferring power to his son, with the result that by the time he died, Kim Jong-il was already carrying out much of the regime's everyday functions—and had no need for guardians overseeing his rule.

In contrast, Kim Jong-un has been in the public eye for barely one year. His grooming began only around 2009, and he officially joined the power elite in October 2010, when he became a four-star general and was appointed deputy chairman of the party's Central Military Commission.

At least outwardly, Kim Jong-un's succession appears to be proceeding smoothly. But the speed of his elevation suggests that North Korea is likely to have undergone a significant change from the regime it was under Kim Jong-il. There are more actors involved in the leadership structure, and as the country ventures into this unknown territory, questions remain as to whether the dynamics in the power structure have already been established. Have the key players agreed to their power share? Will fissures in the regime appear as the new Kim attempts to consolidate his rule and escape the control of his advisers?

The possibility of factional strife cannot be ruled out. There are historical examples from other parts of the world. In the Soviet Union, a factional power struggle followed Stalin's death in 1953, and was only resolved after Khrushchev's ouster in 1964. In China, Mao Zedong's death triggered a violent factional struggle that ended with the defeat of the Gang of Four.

Even though its recent history is a family story even more than a political one, North Korea has not been immune from court intrigue in the past. While the secretive country may appear monolithic to outside observers, both Kim Il-sung and Kim Jong-il consolidated their power through the purging of political rivals and potential contenders for power. Kim Jong-il, for example, placed his half brothers Kim Pyong-il and Kim Yong-il in foreign countries to exclude them from political power. When Kim Il-sung died in 1994, the two half brothers were not on the list of members of the national funeral committee for their father. (Kim Jong-un may have learned from this example. Neither his half brother Kim Jong-nam nor his older full brother Kim Jong-chol was on the list of members of the national committee for the December 28th funeral of Kim Jong-il.)

For regional powers, concerns over the transition period include whether the country will resort to military adventurism to establish its legitimacy. North Korea has in recent years shown belligerent behavior toward its neighbors. Pyongyang has been held responsible for the sinking of a South Korean corvette in March 2010 that killed forty-six sailors. North Korea also fired artillery shells on South Korea's Yeonpyeong Island in November of that year, killing four South Koreans and marking the first such attack since the end of the Korean War in 1953.

Japanese officials have indicated they believe it unlikely that North Korea will resort to major military provocations during the traditional Confucian one-hundred-day mourning period for Kim Jong-il, if only because the regime will likely use the time to try to establish working operations of the new leadership. On the other hand, another nuclear test or long-range missile launch remains possible over the medium term for two purposes—as a show of force and for the practical purpose of developing its nuclear and missile programs.

Despite a history of bizarre rhetoric, pronouncements by North Korea's official media continue to be a useful gauge for the country's intentions. In this regard, Pyongyang watchers note that while these state media have called the current South Korean government a "traitor group" in a statement from the National Defense Commission on December 30th and criticized Japan in a commentary on January 3rd, they have been relatively quiet on the issue of the United States. When Kim Jong-il died, the United States and North Korea had reportedly been close to a deal that would give Pyongyang food aid in exchange for the suspension of North Korea's controversial uranium enrichment program. Such straws in the wind encourage the hope that the North Koreans might reopen dialogue with Washington.

Under Kim Jong-il, negotiators knew whom they were dealing with. With the new leadership under Kim Jong-un, we may not know who is calling the shots for some time.

Dealing with the new regime, therefore, will be particularly challenging for the outside world until the dynamics of the new power structure become clearer. Under Kim Jong-il, negotiators knew whom they were dealing with. With the new leadership under Kim Jong-un, we may not know who is calling the shots for some time, which means that the Korean Peninsula will likely become an even more dangerous place than it already is.

Critical Thinking

1. What is the basis of Kim Jong-un's power?
2. What is the relationship between North and South Korea?
3. What policy should the United States follow toward North Korea?

Naoko Aoki is a journalist based in Washington. She formerly covered Japanese domestic politics and economic policy in Tokyo for Japan's Kyodo News before serving as Beijing correspondent from 2004 to 2009. She has visited North Korea eighteen times.

UNIT 3

Foreign Policy

Unit Selections

Learning Outcomes

After reading this Unit, you will be able to:

- Explain why the United States should not pursue a policy of confrontation with China.

- Analyze the basis for cooperation between China and the United States.

- Explain why U.S. policy toward the Middle East is now based on realism.

- Analyze the U.S. policy of containment in the Middle East.

- Analyze the effect that China's rise has had upon international order in East Asia.

- Discuss the relationship between China's core interests and the norms of the international system.

Student Website

www.mhhe.com/cls

Internet References

The Association of Southeast Asian Nations (ASEAN)
www.asean.sec.org
Institute of Southeast Asian Studies
www.iseas.edu.sg
The National Security Archive
www.gwu.edu/nsarchiv
Office of the Coordinator for Counterterrorism
www.state.gov/s/ct
U.S. State Department
www.state.gov/s/ct

In 2012, the foreign policy of the Obama administration remained focused on the idea of the American Century in the face of the resurgence of the Declinist school of thought, which argued that the United States was losing its hegemonic position in the international system. By 2012, U.S. forces had been withdrawn from Iraq, although post-occupation Iraq continued to be plagued by sectarian conflict and suicide bombings that took a heavy toll among civilians. In the case of Afghanistan, the Obama administration reached an agreement with the Karzai regime that called for a withdrawal of U.S. forces by 2014, but with a commitment to help maintain stability in Afghanistan. The winding down of the wars in Iraq and Afghanistan were accompanied by a major geopolitical shift in U.S. interests from Europe to the Asian–Pacific region as the Obama administration emphasized that it was also a Pacific power. As Secretary of State Hillary Clinton pointed out in an article in the November 2011 issue of *Foreign Policy*, the termination of the wars placed the United States at a pivot point in which the United States would emphasize the importance of the Asian–Pacific region. This would mean that more of the military assets of the United States would be shifted to the Pacific area partly to counter the rising naval power of China. However, a pivot toward the Asian–Pacific region enhances Chinese fear of encirclement by the United States and fits into the Chinese view that the United States is trying to block its rise. Henry Kissinger argues that the United States should not pursue a policy of confrontation with China, but rather one of cooperation. Kissinger points out that the United States fears the creation of a "Sinocentric bloc" in the Western Pacific, but also stresses that it is not surprising that Chinese economic power is being translated into military power. All realists emphasize the important relationship that exists between economic power and military power. One could compare the Chinese fear of encirclement by the United States to Kaiser Wilhelm's fear of the encirclement of Germany by the United Kingdom prior to the outbreak of the First World War. The Chinese fear U.S. encirclement that could threaten its territorial integrity and also result in interference in its internal affairs. On the other hand, the United States is concerned that Chinese naval strategy is designed to push it out of the Western Pacific. Therefore, Kissinger observes that each state should arrive at a definition of its respective spheres of influence, which would allow both states to engage in peaceful competition with one another.

The Middle East continued to be a major foreign policy problem in 2012 as the Syrian civil conflict continued to rage, raising the issue of regime change and democratization. In "The Decline of Western Realism" the authors argue that U.S. policy in the region was motivated by the need to maintain access to oil. During the Cold War, this was one of the motivating factors behind the policy, which was designed to prevent the Soviet Union from establishing itself in the area. The authors point out that the "Red Menace" has now been replaced by the "Green Crescent" as U.S. foreign policy in the area is designed to

© Pete Souza/The White House

prevent radical Islamic fundamentalism from gaining ascendancy in the region that is vital to U.S. interests. The authors also argue that the failure of U.S. efforts at democratization in Iraq as well as the victory of Hamas in the 2006 elections in the Gaza Strip had discouraged the United States from trying to push democratization in the area. Consequently, realism seems to be the dominant approach of the United States to the area, also given the opposition of Russia and China to any western military intervention aimed at promoting regime change in Syria.

The growth of Chinese naval power has also resulted in a more aggressive policy of claiming sovereignty over disputed islands in the South China Sea such as the Spratly islands as well as the East China Sea, with a number of other states in the region. The disputes, fed by nationalism, have resulted in several incidents between China and the other states claiming sovereignty over various islands and rocks. These threaten to escalate into a more serious conflict and can draw in the United States in support of its allies in the region. The United States has taken the position that a Code of Conduct should be adopted in dealing with these disputes. The conflict over the sovereignty of islands and rocks in the South China Sea and elsewhere are driven by the international law of the sea, which would allow the state whose sovereignty is recognized to exploit adjacent resources like oil out to 200 miles. In "An Asian Security Standoff," Alan Dupont stresses that the dominance of the United States in East Asia cannot be maintained in view of China's rising power. The author points out that a critical factor is China's strategy of a "far-sea defence," which is designed to push the United States away from the Chinese coast as far as possible. The United States views such a strategy as undermining its global position in the international system. The author observes that the Chinese are also concerned with maintaining control of the vital sea lanes in the region so that they can assure that they maintain access to the natural resources and the raw materials that they need.

The Future of United States-Chinese Relations

Conflict Is a Choice, Not a Necessity

Henry A. Kissinger

On January 19, 2011, United States President Barack Obama and Chinese President Hu Jintao issued a joint statement at the end of Hu's visit to Washington. It proclaimed their shared commitment to a "positive, cooperative, and comprehensive United States-China relationship." Each party reassured the other regarding his principal concern, announcing, "The United States reiterated that it welcomes a strong, prosperous, and successful China that plays a greater role in world affairs. China welcomes the United States as an Asia-Pacific nation that contributes to peace, stability and prosperity in the region."

Since then, the two governments have set about implementing the stated objectives. Top American and Chinese officials have exchanged visits and institutionalized their exchanges on major strategic and economic issues. Military-to-military contacts have been restarted, opening an important channel of communication. And at the unofficial level, so-called track-two groups have explored possible evolutions of the United States-Chinese relationship.

Yet as cooperation has increased, so has controversy. Significant groups in both countries claim that a contest for supremacy between China and the United States is inevitable and perhaps already under way. In this perspective, appeals for United States-Chinese cooperation appear outmoded and even naive.

The mutual recriminations emerge from distinct yet parallel analyses in each country. Some American strategic thinkers argue that Chinese policy pursues two long-term objectives: displacing the United States as the preeminent power in the western Pacific and consolidating Asia into an exclusionary bloc deferring to Chinese economic and foreign policy interests. In this conception, even though China's absolute military capacities are not formally equal to those of the United States, Beijing possesses the ability to pose unacceptable risks in a conflict with Washington and is developing increasingly sophisticated means to negate traditional United States advantages. Its invulnerable second-strike nuclear capability will eventually be paired with an expanding range of anti-ship ballistic missiles and asymmetric capabilities in new domains such as cyberspace and space. China could secure a dominant naval position through a series of island chains on its periphery, some fear, and once such a screen exists, China's neighbors, dependent as they are on Chinese trade and uncertain of the United States' ability to react, might adjust their policies according to Chinese preferences. Eventually, this could lead to the creation of a Sinocentric Asian bloc dominating the western Pacific. The most recent United States defense strategy report reflects, at least implicitly, some of these apprehensions.

No Chinese government officials have proclaimed such a strategy as China's actual policy. Indeed, they stress the opposite. However, enough material exists in China's quasi-official press and research institutes to lend some support to the theory that relations are heading for confrontation rather than cooperation.

United States strategic concerns are magnified by ideological predispositions to battle with the entire nondemocratic world. Authoritarian regimes, some argue, are inherently brittle, impelled to rally domestic support by nationalist and expansionist rhetoric and practice. In these theories—versions of which are embraced in segments of both the American left and the American right—tension and conflict with China grow out of China's domestic structure. Universal peace will come, it is asserted, from the global triumph of democracy rather than from appeals for cooperation. The political scientist Aaron Friedberg writes, for example, that "a liberal democratic China will have little cause to fear its democratic counterparts, still less to use force against them." Therefore, "stripped of diplomatic niceties, the ultimate aim of the American strategy [should be] to hasten a revolution, albeit a peaceful one, that will sweep away China's one-party authoritarian state and leave a liberal democracy in its place."

On the Chinese side, the confrontational interpretations follow an inverse logic. They see the United States as a wounded superpower determined to thwart the rise of any challenger, of which China is the most credible. No matter how intensely China pursues cooperation, some Chinese argue, Washington's fixed objective will be to hem in a growing China by military deployment and treaty commitments, thus preventing it from playing its historic role as the Middle Kingdom. In this perspective, any sustained cooperation with the United States is self-defeating, since it will only serve the overriding United States objective of neutralizing China. Systematic hostility is occasionally considered to inhere even in American cultural and technological influences, which are sometimes cast as a form of deliberate pressure designed to corrode China's domestic consensus and traditional values. The most assertive voices argue that China has been unduly passive in the face of hostile trends and that (for example, in the case of territorial issues in the South China Sea) China should confront those of its neighbors with which it has disputed claims and then, in the words of the strategic analyst LongTao, "reason, think ahead and strike first before things gradually run out of hand launch[ing] some tiny-scale battles that could deter provocateurs from going further."

The Past Need Not Be Prologue

Is there, then, a point in the quest for a cooperative United States-Chinese relationship and in policies designed to achieve it? To be sure, the rise of powers has historically often led to conflict with established countries. But conditions have changed. It is doubtful that the leaders who went so blithely into a world war in 1914 would have done so had they known what the world would be like at its end. Contemporary leaders can have no such illusions. A major war between developed nuclear countries must bring casualties and upheavals impossible to relate to calculable objectives. Preemption is all but excluded, especially for a pluralistic democracy such as the United States.

If challenged, the United States will do what it must to preserve its security. But it should not adopt confrontation as a strategy of choice. In China, the United States would encounter an adversary skilled over the centuries in using prolonged conflict as a strategy and whose doctrine emphasizes the psychological exhaustion of the opponent. In an actual conflict, both sides possess the capabilities and the ingenuity to inflict catastrophic damage on each other. By the time any such hypothetical conflagration drew to a close, all participants would be left exhausted and debilitated. They would then be obliged to face anew the very task that confronts them today: the construction of an international order in which both countries are significant components.

It would be unusual if the world's second-largest economy did not translate its economic power into increased military capacity.

The blueprints for containment drawn from Cold War strategies used by both sides against an expansionist Soviet Union do not apply to current conditions. The economy of the Soviet Union was weak (except for military production) and did not affect the global economy. Once China broke off ties and ejected Soviet advisers, few countries except those forcibly absorbed into the Soviet orbit had a major stake in their economic relationship with Moscow. Contemporary China, by contrast, is a dynamic factor in the world economy. It is a principal trading partner of all its neighbors and most of the Western industrial powers, including the United States. A prolonged confrontation between China and the United States would alter the world economy with unsettling consequences for all.

Nor would China find that the strategy it pursued in its own conflict with the Soviet Union fits a confrontation with the United States. Only a few countries—and no Asian ones—would treat an American presence in Asia as "fingers" to be "chopped off" (in Deng Xiaoping's graphic phrase about Soviet forward positions). Even those Asian states that are not members of alliances with the United States seek the reassurance of an American political presence in the region and of American forces in nearby seas as the guarantor of the world to which they have become accustomed. Their approach was expressed by a senior Indonesian official to an American counterpart: "Don't leave us, but don't make us choose."

China's recent military buildup is not in itself an exceptional phenomenon: the more unusual outcome would be if the world's second-largest economy and largest importer of natural resources did not translate its economic power into some increased military capacity. The issue is whether that buildup is open ended and to what purposes it is put. If the United States treats every advance in Chinese military capabilities as a hostile act, it will quickly find itself enmeshed in an endless series of disputes on behalf of esoteric aims. But China must be aware, from its own history, of the tenuous dividing line between defensive and offensive capabilities and of the consequences of an unrestrained arms race.

China's leaders will have their own powerful reasons for rejecting domestic appeals for an adversarial approach—as indeed they have publicly proclaimed. China's imperial expansion has historically been achieved by osmosis rather than conquest, or by the conversion to Chinese culture of conquerors who then added their own territories to the Chinese domain. Dominating Asia militarily would be a formidable undertaking. The Soviet Union, during the Cold War, bordered on a string of weak countries drained by war and occupation and dependent on American troop commitments for their defense. China today faces Russia in the north; Japan and South Korea, with American military alliances, to the east; Vietnam and India to the south; and Indonesia and Malaysia not far away. This is not a constellation conducive to conquest. It is more likely to raise fears of encirclement. Each of these countries has a long military tradition and would pose a formidable obstacle if its territory or its ability to conduct an independent policy were threatened. A militant Chinese foreign policy would enhance cooperation among all or at least some of these nations, evoking China's historic nightmare, as happened in the period 2009–10.

Dealing with the New China

Another reason for Chinese restraint in at least the medium term is the domestic adaptation the country faces. The gap in Chinese society between the largely developed coastal regions and the undeveloped western regions has made Hu's objective of a "harmonious society" both compelling and elusive. Cultural changes compound the challenge. The next decades will witness, for the first time, the full impact of one-child families on adult Chinese society. This is bound to modify cultural patterns in a society in which large families have traditionally taken care of the aged and the handicapped. When four grandparents compete for the attention of one child and invest him with the aspirations heretofore spread across many offspring, a new pattern of insistent achievement and vast, perhaps unfulfillable, expectations may arise.

All these developments will further complicate the challenges of China's governmental transition starting in 2012, in which the presidency; the vice-presidency; the considerable majority of the positions in China's Politburo, State Council, and Central Military Commission; and thousands of other key national and provincial posts will be staffed with new appointees. The new leadership group will consist, for the most part, of members of the first Chinese generation in a century and a half to have lived all their lives in a country at peace. Its primary challenge will be finding a way to deal with a society revolutionized by changing economic conditions, unprecedented and rapidly expanding technologies of communication, a tenuous global economy, and the migration of hundreds of millions of people from China's countryside to its cities. The model of government that emerges will likely be a synthesis of modern ideas and traditional Chinese political and cultural concepts, and the quest for that synthesis will provide the ongoing drama of China's evolution.

These social and political transformations are bound to be followed with interest and hope in the United States. Direct American intervention would be neither wise nor productive. The United States will, as it should, continue to make its views known on human rights issues and individual cases. And its day-to-day conduct will express its national preference for democratic principles. But a systematic project to transform China's institutions by diplomatic pressure and economic sanctions is likely to backfire and isolate the very liberals it is intended to assist. In China, it would be interpreted by a considerable majority through the lens of nationalism, recalling earlier eras of foreign intervention.

What this situation calls for is not an abandonment of American values but a distinction between the realizable and the absolute. The United States-Chinese relationship should not be considered as a zero-sum game, nor can the emergence of a prosperous and powerful China be assumed in itself to be an American strategic defeat.

A cooperative approach challenges preconceptions on both sides. The United States has few precedents in its national experience of relating to a country of comparable size, self-confidence, economic achievement, and international scope and yet with such a different culture and political system. Nor does history supply China with precedents for how to relate to a fellow great power with a permanent presence in Asia, a vision of universal ideals not geared toward Chinese conceptions, and alliances with several of China's neighbors. Prior to the United States, all countries establishing such a position did so as a prelude to an attempt to dominate China.

The simplest approach to strategy is to insist on overwhelming potential adversaries with superior resources and material. But in the contemporary world, this is only rarely feasible. China and the United States will inevitably continue as enduring realities for each other. Neither can entrust its security to the other—no great power does, for long—and each will continue to pursue its own interests, sometimes at the relative expense of the other. But both have the responsibility to take into account the other's nightmares, and both would do well to recognize that their rhetoric, as much as their actual policies, can feed into the other's suspicions.

China's greatest strategic fear is that an outside power or powers will establish military deployments around China's periphery capable of encroaching on China's territory or meddling in its domestic institutions. When China deemed that it faced such a threat in the past, it went to war rather than risk the outcome of what it saw as gathering trends—in Korea in 1950, against India in 1962, along the northern border with the Soviet Union in 1969, and against Vietnam in 1979.

The United States' fear, sometimes only indirectly expressed, is of being pushed out of Asia by an exclusionary bloc. The United States fought a world war against Germany and Japan to prevent such an outcome and exercised some of its most forceful Cold War diplomacy under administrations of both political parties to this end against the Soviet Union. In both enterprises, it is worth noting, substantial joint United States-Chinese efforts were directed against the perceived threat of hegemony.

Other Asian countries will insist on their prerogatives to develop their capacities for their own national reasons, not as part of a contest between outside powers. They will not willingly consign themselves to a revived tributary order. Nor do they regard themselves as elements in an American containment policy or an American project to alter China's domestic institutions. They aspire to good relations with both China and the United States and will resist any pressure to choose between the two.

Can the fear of hegemony and the nightmare of military encirclement be reconciled? Is it possible to find a space in which both sides can achieve their ultimate objectives without militarizing their strategies? For great nations with global capabilities and divergent, even partly conflicting aspirations, what is the margin between conflict and abdication?

That China will have a major influence in the regions surrounding it is inherent in its geography, values, and history. The limits of that influence, however, will be shaped by circumstance and policy decisions. These will determine whether an inevitable quest for influence turns into a drive to negate or exclude other independent sources of power.

For nearly two generations, American strategy relied on local regional defense by American ground forces—largely to avoid the catastrophic consequences of a general nuclear war. In recent decades, congressional and public opinion have impelled an end to such commitments in Vietnam, Iraq, and Afghanistan. Now, fiscal considerations further limit the range of such an approach. American strategy has been redirected from defending territory to threatening unacceptable punishment against potential aggressors. This requires forces capable of rapid intervention and global reach, but not bases ringing China's frontiers. What Washington must not do is combine a defense policy based on budgetary restraints with a diplomacy based on unlimited ideological aims.

Just as Chinese influence in surrounding countries may spur fears of dominance, so efforts to pursue traditional American national interests can be perceived as a form of military encirclement. Both sides must understand the nuances by which apparently traditional and apparently reasonable courses can evoke the deepest worries of the other. They should seek together to define the sphere in which their peaceful competition is circumscribed. If that is managed wisely, both military confrontation and domination can be avoided; if not, escalating tension is inevitable. It is the task of diplomacy to discover this space, to expand it if possible, and to prevent the relationship from being overwhelmed by tactical and domestic imperatives.

Community or Conflict

The current world order was built largely without Chinese participation, and hence China sometimes feels less bound than others by its rules. Where the order does not suit Chinese preferences, Beijing has set up alternative arrangements, such as in the separate currency channels being established with Brazil and Japan and other countries. If the pattern becomes routine and spreads into many spheres of activity, competing world orders could evolve. Absent common goals coupled with agreed rules of restraint, institutionalized rivalry is likely to escalate beyond the calculations and intentions of its advocates. In an era in which unprecedented offensive capabilities and intrusive technologies multiply, the penalties of such a course could be drastic and perhaps irrevocable.

Crisis management will not be enough to sustain a relationship so global and beset by so many differing pressures within and between both countries, which is why I have argued for the concept of a Pacific Community and expressed the hope that China and the United States can generate a sense of common purpose on at least some issues of general concern. But the goal of such a community cannot be reached if either side conceives of the enterprise as primarily a more effective way to defeat or undermine the other. Neither China nor the United States can be systematically challenged without its noticing, and if such a challenge is noted, it will be resisted. Both need to commit themselves to genuine cooperation and find a way to communicate and relate their visions to each other and to the world.

Some tentative steps in that direction have already been undertaken. For example, the United States has joined several other countries in beginning negotiations on the Trans-Pacific Partnership (TPP), a free-trade pact linking the Americas with Asia. Such an arrangement could be a step toward a Pacific Community because it would lower trade barriers among the world's most productive, dynamic, and resource-rich economies and link the two sides of the ocean in shared projects.

Obama has invited China to join the TPP. However, the terms of accession as presented by American briefers and

commentators have sometimes seemed to require fundamental changes in China's domestic structure. To the extent that is the case, the TPP could be regarded in Beijing as part of a strategy to isolate China. For its part, China has put forward comparable alternative arrangements. It has negotiated a trade pact with the Association of Southeast Asian Nations and has broached a Northeast Asian trade pact with Japan and South Korea.

> **Lecturing a country with a history of millennia about its need to "grow up" and behave "responsibly" can be needlessly grating.**

Important domestic political considerations are involved for all parties. But if China and the United States come to regard each other's trade-pact efforts as elements in a strategy of isolation, the Asia-Pacific region could devolve into competing adversarial power blocs. Ironically, this would be a particular challenge if China meets frequent American calls to shift from an export-led to a consumption-driven economy, as its most recent five-year plan contemplates. Such a development could reduce China's stake in the United States as an export market even as it encourages other Asian countries to further orient their economies toward China.

The key decision facing both Beijing and Washington is whether to move toward a genuine effort at cooperation or fall into a new version of historic patterns of international rivalry. Both countries have adopted the rhetoric of community. They have even established a high-level forum for it, the Strategic and Economic Dialogue, which meets twice a year. It has been productive on immediate issues, but it is still in the foothills of its ultimate assignment to produce a truly global economic and political order. And if a global order does not emerge in the economic field, barriers to progress on more emotional and less positive-sum issues, such as territory and security, may grow insurmountable.

The Risks of Rhetoric

As they pursue this process, both sides need to recognize the impact of rhetoric on perceptions and calculations. American leaders occasionally launch broadsides against China, including specific proposals for adversarial policies, as domestic political necessities. This occurs even—perhaps especially—when a moderate policy is the ultimate intention. The issue is not specific complaints, which should be dealt with on the merits of the issue, but attacks on the basic motivations of Chinese policy, such as declaring China a strategic adversary. The target of these attacks is bound to ask whether domestic imperatives requiring affirmations of hostility will sooner or later require hostile actions. By the same token, threatening Chinese statements, including those in the semiofficial press, are likely to be interpreted in terms of the actions they imply, whatever the domestic pressures or the intent that generated them.

The American debate, on both sides of the political divide, often describes China as a "rising power" that will need to "mature" and learn how to exercise responsibility on the world stage. China, however, sees itself not as a rising power but as a returning one, predominant in its region for two millennia and temporarily displaced by colonial exploiters taking advantage of Chinese domestic strife and decay. It views the prospect of a strong China exercising influence in economic, cultural, political, and military affairs not as an unnatural challenge to world order but rather as a return to normality. Americans need not agree with every aspect of the Chinese analysis to understand that lecturing a country with a history of millennia about its need to "grow up" and behave "responsibly" can be needlessly grating.

On the Chinese side, proclamations at the governmental and the informal level that China intends to "revive the Chinese nation" to its traditional eminence carry different implications inside China and abroad. China is rightly proud of its recent strides in restoring its sense of national purpose following what it sees as a century of humiliation. Yet few other countries in Asia are nostalgic for an era when they were subject to Chinese suzerainty. As recent veterans of anti-colonial struggles, most Asian countries are extremely sensitive to maintaining their independence and freedom of action vis-à-vis any outside power, whether Western or Asian. They seek to be involved in as many overlapping spheres of economic and political activity as possible; they invite an American role in the region but seek equilibrium, not a crusade or confrontation.

The rise of China is less the result of its increased military strength than of the United States' own declining competitive position, driven by factors such as obsolescent infrastructure, inadequate attention to research and development, and a seemingly dysfunctional governmental process. The United States should address these issues with ingenuity and determination instead of blaming a putative adversary. It must take care not to repeat in its China policy the pattern of conflicts entered with vast public support and broad goals but ended when the American political process insisted on a strategy of extrication that amounted to an abandonment, if not a complete reversal, of the country's proclaimed objectives.

China can find reassurance in its own record of endurance and in the fact that no United States administration has ever sought to alter the reality of China as one of the world's major states, economies, and civilizations. Americans would do well to remember that even when China's GDP is equal to that of the United States, it will need to be distributed over a population that is four times as large, aging, and engaged in complex domestic transformations occasioned by China's growth and urbanization. The practical consequence is that a great deal of China's energy will still be devoted to domestic needs.

Both sides should be open to conceiving of each other's activities as a normal part of international life and not in themselves as a cause for alarm. The inevitable tendency to impinge on each other should not be equated with a conscious drive to contain or dominate, so long as both can maintain the distinction and calibrate their actions accordingly. China and the United States will not necessarily transcend the ordinary operation of great-power rivalry. But they owe it to themselves, and the world, to make an effort to do so.

Critical Thinking

1. Why does China fear the United States?
2. How can China and the United States develop a more cooperative relationship?
3. Why does Kissinger contend that China is not rising, but is returning to its position of predominance in the international system?

HENRY A. KISSINGER is Chair of Kissinger Associates and a former U.S. Secretary of State and National Security Adviser. This essay is adapted from the afterword to the forthcoming paperback edition of his latest book, *On China* (Penguin, 2012).

Decline of Western Realism

Nikolas K. Gvosdev and Ray Takeyh

When Operation Odyssey Dawn commenced in the skies over Libya on March 19, 2011, it represented a major turnaround in United States policy. Only nine months earlier, United States ambassador Gene Cretz had characterized the regime as a "strategic ally" of the United States due to Libyan cooperation on counterterrorism and nonproliferation issues (and its halting, tentative steps toward greater openness). Now Libya found itself on the receiving end of conventional United States military power for repressing a civilian population agitating for governmental change. Considerations that over the past sixty years might have stayed the hand of an earlier president—fears about regime change leading to a hostile government taking power in an oil-rich and geostrategic Middle Eastern state, or concerns about the potential debilitating costs of intervention—were set aside. And while Muammar el-Qaddafi's distant past as an international renegade and sponsor of terrorism was invoked by Barack Obama, there was little effort to portray twenty-first-century Libya as a looming security threat to the United States. Indeed, given the more recent history of Libyan-American rapprochement, including Qaddafi's active cooperation with the West in the struggle against al-Qaeda, such an attempt would have rung hollow. Instead, the Obama team embraced Qaddafi's treatment of his population as the central rationale for the operation.

This marks a fundamental break with past American emphasis on serious threats to United States national security as the prime motivation for action, especially armed intervention. In making the case for war against Saddam Hussein in 2003, the Bush administration highlighted the Iraqi tyrant's abuse of his citizens and his war crimes against Iran and the Kurds. But the case for invading Iraq rested not so much on humanitarian concerns as on displacing a volatile actor who threatened core American security interests. Saddam's suspected depositories of unconventional weapons and his ties to terrorists became the central rallying cries of the proponents of coercive regime change, while humanitarian impulses to liberate an oppressed population were a secondary justification. In the case of Libya, however, no such national-security arguments were seriously proffered in support of the necessity for military action. The Obama administration never suggested that its intervention was designed to redeem any critical national interests; as a matter of fact, outgoing defense secretary Robert Gates loudly and repeatedly proclaimed that there were no vital interests at stake in Libya.

Moreover, the Libya operation took place against a backdrop of regional ferment that already had claimed the political lives of two close United States partners, Egypt's Hosni Mubarak and Tunisia's Zine el-Abidine Ben Ali, and was threatening to depose other American friends from Jordan to Yemen. Saddam Hussein had been an avowed enemy of the United States, which lent a certain geopolitical logic to George W. Bush's invasion. But now Washington was demonstrating a willingness to side "with the street" against regimes that were pro-American. Six years ago, writing in these pages, Dov Zakheim expressed the prevailing United States outlook in dealing with friendly autocrats in the region:

> Given their steps, however halting, toward creating freer societies, their willingness to countenance a Middle East peace settlement and the virulent anti-Americanism of much of their opposition, it must be asked whether it is really in America's interest to distance itself from such regimes. Constructive engagement with friends who are slow to respond but respond nonetheless is one thing; rejection is quite another.

The gap between that philosophy and recent United States actions poses some questions: Are we witnessing a subtle paradigm shift, where governments' treatment of their citizens, as opposed to their geopolitical conduct, is more important as a factor for United States policy? Does the Libya operation provide a model for low-cost, no-consequence interventions that Obama and other presidents may seek to employ elsewhere in the region and around the world? In short, has America entered a postrealist phase in its foreign policy, where it believes that it is possible to promote United States values at minimal cost to United States interests?

If these questions can be answered in the affirmative, then America could stand at the threshold of a new foreign-policy era dominated by a twenty-first-century iteration of Wilsonism—the widespread application of American power on behalf of humanitarian ideals even when it risks compromising key interests. What this would mean for America and the world remains an open question of profound dimension.

For decades, the specter of an Iran "lost" after the overthrow of the shah has hung over America's Middle East policy. Washington saw how a revolution initially defined by calls for democracy and liberalization ended up ushering in an Islamic Republic bitterly hostile to United States interests. As Jeane Kirkpatrick concluded in November 1979:

> The American effort to impose liberalization and democratization on a government confronted with violent internal opposition not only failed, but actually assisted the coming to power of new regimes in which ordinary people enjoy fewer freedoms and less personal security than under the previous autocracy—regimes, moreover, hostile to American interests and policies.

While experiments with democracy could be tolerated in some parts of the world because vital United States interests were not at stake, there was no room for error in the Middle East during the Cold War. In January 1980, Jimmy Carter made it explicit that the United States would respond, by military means if necessary, to any "grave threat to the free movement of Middle East oil" to the Western world.

In the years following the rise of Ayatollah Ruhollah Khomeini, a generation of hereditary monarchs and authoritarian presidents throughout the Middle East convinced Washington that, as much as their illiberal regimes might offend American democratic sensibilities, the alternatives would be worse—whether revolutionary regimes more inclined to side with the Soviet Union or Islamists convinced that America was indeed the Great Satan. The "Reagan Corollary" to the so-called "Carter Doctrine," announced in October 1981, more explicitly committed the United States to preserving the internal stability of Western partners in the region, beginning with Saudi Arabia and its ruling House of Saud.

The unelected, absolute monarch of a theocratic state seemed to be an unlikely partner for an American president who, in quoting Winston Churchill in 1982, had reaffirmed his commitment to establishing "conditions of freedom and democracy as rapidly as possible in all countries." But when King Fahd visited Washington in 1985, he received no lectures about the urgent necessity to democratize his realm. Instead, Reagan took the view that the best way to promote democracy in the long run was to prevent countries from going communist or Islamist in the short run.

America's experience in East Asia and Latin America during the Reagan years buttressed this approach. Over time, in places such as Chile, South Korea and Taiwan, authoritarian presidents created the frameworks for gradual transitions to democracy without undermining their security relationships with the United States. Instead of siding with protestors calling for immediate democratic reform, Washington supported existing regimes in cracking down on the opposition, provided a long-term, gradualist program for change was being implemented.

So the Middle Eastern imperatives of geology and geography conspired to disabuse American officialdom of any Wilsonian impulses to push for democracy and human rights. The region's oil was necessary for the free world's economic vitality, and its strategic outposts were needed for the containment of the Soviet and Iranian menaces. The constellation of conservative monarchies and presidential dictatorships was important in subduing the radical clients of the Soviet Union; Saudi Arabia's embrace of the mantle of the defenders of Islam was essential in negating Iran's theocratic rage, while Saddam Hussein proved indispensable in checking Iran's ambitions. And when Hussein himself sought to reorder the region's politics more to his liking with his invasion of Kuwait in 1990, the United States assembled an international coalition that ejected him from his conquest and crushed his military.

The United States strategy succeeded. After Egyptian leader Anwar Sadat expelled some twenty thousand Soviet military "advisers" from his country in 1972, the Soviet Union never made substantial inroads into the Middle East. (While Syria remained a close client of Moscow, it could never aspire to play the same role as Egypt.) The radical Arab republics failed to dislodge the conservative order and nudge the region toward neutralism or, even worse, communism. The region's oil, especially after the collapse of oil prices in the 1980s, continued to lubricate the Western economic surge. The revisionist states of Iran and Iraq were confined in their boundaries, stripped of their ambitions for regional hegemony and power, and served as regional counterweights to each other.

The collapse of the Soviet Union in 1991 did not fundamentally alter the trajectory of United States policy. Replacing the "Red Menace" was now the "Green Crescent"—fears that militantly anti-Western Islamist groups were on the march. When Algeria's Islamists seemed on the verge of taking control of a key North African state after the results of the first round of elections in 1991, the West acquiesced in the Algerian military's January 1992 decision to cancel further balloting. In Egypt, the most populous state in the Arab world, a terror campaign by Al Gamaa al-Islamiyya to bring down the government by targeting police and foreign tourists reinforced the belief that the regime of Hosni Mubarak must get America's unconditional support or Egypt could be "lost" to a hostile ideology. This was, remember, a time when Bill Clinton was hoping to expand the Middle East peace process by having more leaders—even if not democratically empowered—join Egypt in concluding peace treaties with Israel.

If preventing the Soviet Union from furthering its toehold in the region was the paramount objective of earlier administrations, the Clinton team focused on isolating the so-called "backlash states" that "seek to advance their agenda through terror, intolerance and coercion." This propelled the United States to prevent the potential resurgence of Iraq, to prolong the policy of coercing Iran, and to continue to isolate bad actors such as Libya and Yemen. All this necessitated partnerships with authoritarian monarchs and presidents and militated against any "third wave of democratization" in the Middle East to complement developments in Eastern Europe and Latin America. But the Clinton administration was also uneasy about accepting the cold dictates of realism that rated interests over values. Hence, continued support for autocrats was justified by arguments that governments in the region lacked the skills to engineer transitions to democracy. That is why the United States government, working with private-sector democracy initiatives, began to churn out programs to train judges, publish guides on voting procedures and extend financial support for NGOs that pledged their commitment to liberal values (but which commanded very little popular support). Still, one heard little sustained public criticism about Egypt's deformed politics, Saudi support for inflammatory Islam or a Persian Gulf order comfortable with its autocratic ways.

Indeed, when Sheikh Hamad bin Khalifa al-Thani removed his father and took control of Qatar in 1995, this coup d'état was quietly hailed as the possible beginning of a generational transfer of power in the Middle East that would bring younger, more liberal leaders to power. These expectations were heightened when Bashar al-Assad succeeded his father Hafez as president in Syria in 2000 and quickly dropped hints about "reform." This "Damascus Spring," when liberal-leaning discussion groups sprang up in the capital, proved short-lived. But these assumptions helped define a strategy of accepting the status quo for the foreseeable future while training a group of democracy activists and waiting for the next generation of supposedly more liberal leaders to take power.

Mubarak, Qaddafi and others assumed that close cooperation with America's security agenda would buy their regimes a certain degree of immunity from United States criticism and pressure. They were wrong.

It was perhaps inevitable that the tragedies of 9/11 would jolt the Washington establishment and call into question the value of America's long-standing relationships with regional despots. Indeed, the argument was soon advanced that the United States was being imperiled by the lack of democracy in the region, which nurtured a dysfunctional political culture serving as a feeding ground for organizations such as al-Qaeda. The approach embraced by previous administrations was explicitly rejected; the United States could not wait for generational change to "drain the swamp" through gradual reform and liberalization. Speaking in Cairo in 2005, Secretary of State Condoleezza Rice bluntly commented that "for sixty years, my country, the United States, pursued stability at the expense of democracy in this region here in the Middle East—and we achieved neither."

But the use of United States power to promote democratic change through direct intervention remained a contested proposition. In the past, concerns about costs to United States interests had always acted as a brake on American interventions unrelated to national interests. Large-scale interventions, particularly using conventional military forces to achieve forcible regime change, were expensive and risky. Reagan's Grenada operation and George H. W. Bush's Panama incursion were the exceptions, not the rule. The limitations of the Cold War also meant that large swaths of the world were effectively "off-limits" for United States action. These considerations were very much evident in the arguments marshaled by former national-security adviser Brent Scowcroft in his famous *Wall Street Journal* op-ed of August 2002, which decried the rush to war in Iraq.

But the 1999 Kosovo operation marked a critical turning point in how Washington conceptualized the risks and opportunities of intervention. In contrast to the first Gulf War, which occurred with the concurrence of Moscow and Beijing, this action lacked their support. But opposition to military intervention in the former Yugoslavia wasn't sufficient to prevent it from occurring. And the operation took place in a part of Europe that only ten years earlier would have been deemed a no-go area for NATO forces. The apparent ease of the campaign—an air war that was nearly casualty free for the allies and produced a capitulation and transition without need of ground forces—also changed the intervention calculus in Washington, displacing the failed legacy of Vietnam with a belief that a "shock and awe" campaign could produce dramatic on-the-ground transformations.

There was near unanimity in Washington that Saddam Hussein, as Scowcroft noted, was

> a menace. He terrorizes and brutalizes his own people. He has launched war on two of his neighbors. He devotes enormous effort to rebuilding his military forces and equipping them with weapons of mass destruction. We will all be better off when he is gone.

But there were very different ways to prosecute the war. An invasion designed to decapitate the regime and ensure that Iraq was disarmed would look very different from a campaign aimed at reconstructing the country in the image of postwar Germany or Japan. So the subsidiary theme of the invasion was that removing Hussein would not be enough; a prospective democratic government in Baghdad would establish an inclusive polity that would be accountable at home and align itself with United States security interests abroad, including concluding a peace treaty with Israel and aggressively containing Iran and Syria.

In some of his most eloquent speeches, George W. Bush cast aside the assertion that the Arab masses were ill equipped for self-determination and democratic accountability. But he also cautiously emphasized that America would safeguard its interests while redeeming its ideals. The assumption was that, starting in a reformed Iraq, an empowered Arab citizenry would choose leaders focused on fixing broken economies, addressing institutional decay and the consequences of the region's demographic bulge—rather than striving to thwart United States security interests. To be sure, the process would be unsteady and sometimes tumultuous, but in the end large areas of a new Middle East would be governed by popularly elected regimes that would freely choose to join a United States-led global order as opposed to plotting against its norms.

The first part of the Iraq invasion fulfilled the promise of Kosovo: Saddam Hussein was removed quickly with few coalition casualties. But securing the democratic peace in Iraq proved far more elusive, reawakening the ghost of Vietnam as more soldiers were killed and wounded and as costs kept rising (to a cumulative total of $1 trillion). And Iraqi elections have overwhelmingly empowered ethnosectarian parties whose leaders did not play out the role scripted for them by Washington. None of the grandiose expectations of American officials were fulfilled. Indeed, from an unwillingness to condemn Hezbollah or Syria to the maintenance of close ties with Iran, first the Bush and now the Obama administrations have expressed repeated frustrations with the government of Nuri al-Maliki.

Elsewhere the picture was similar. The 2005 Cedar Revolution in Lebanon initially brought to the fore a pro-Western coalition of parties but ended up strengthening Hezbollah's hold on the country. The Bush administration's flirtation with the proposition that promoting democracy advances American security in the Middle East came to a sudden end with the results of the January 2006 elections in the Palestinian territories. There was an air of unease about the entire situation, as the radical Islamist group, Hamas, seemed poised to undo the political hegemony of Fatah. In previous decades, Washington might have called for postponement of the elections or acquiesced to their rigging by Fatah to produce a more desirable government. However, the Bush administration had invested so much in its democratic advocacy that it almost had no choice but to watch the ballots being cast and hope for the best. When it was over, Hamas won seventy-four out of 132 parliamentary seats and claimed the post of premiership. In due course, Palestinian unity would fall apart, and Hamas would confine itself to Gaza, from which it would periodically launch missile attacks against Israel. Not for the first time, the Middle East escaped Washington's preferred template and confronted the United States with choices and decisions that it had hoped to avert.

In the aftermath of the Palestinian elections, the Bush administration's democratic enterprise limped along, devoid of ambition or any clear agenda. Coercive pressure for reforms in places such as Egypt or Saudi Arabia was abandoned. The administration returned to "practical" issues—stabilizing Iraq, resuming the Israeli-Palestinian peace process and attempting to restrain Iran's ambitions. The Bush team fell back on the earlier paradigm of relying on hereditary monarchs and authoritarian presidents to deliver stability in the region. The league of despots proved as useful to the Bush administration as it did to its predecessors. In a sense, realism seemed to have overwhelmed the ideological convulsions of post-9/11 Washington.

The second half of the Bush administration focused its efforts not on forcible regime change but on regime rehabilitation followed by gradual liberalizing amelioration: cultivating liberalizing autocrats who could retain control over the process and keep United States security interests intact but who would lay the groundwork for an eventual democratic transition. As Zakheim noted:

> Brandishing "democracy" like a sword over the rulers of other nations, distancing itself even from those rulers who initiate reforms, on the grounds that they are moving too slowly, and creating an atmosphere that leads them to believe that they will be destabilized if not forcefully removed, will not enable the United States to achieve its objectives in the Middle East.

The United States-Libya relationship became the incubator of this approach after Qaddafi renounced state support for terror activities, ended Libya's embryonic mass-destruction weapons program and aligned Libya with Western interests. This laid the basis for Tripoli's rapprochement with Washington, a policy that enjoyed strong bipartisan support in the United States Congress. In 2007, the late Tom Lantos, chairman of the House Foreign Affairs Committee, concluded:

> I am very proud of America's success in convincing Qadhafi to become a decent citizen of the global community. . . . Our engagement with Qadhafi and the prosperity it has brought Libya serves as a model to countries currently sponsoring terror or compiling weapons of mass destruction. They should know that they, too, can come in from the cold.

In dealing with hereditary politics in the Middle East, the United States held out hope that the Taiwan scenario (the passage of power from an autocratic father to a more liberalizing son) might be duplicated in the region—especially when it came to two sons, Seif al-Islam el-Qaddafi and Gamal Mubarak, who were seen as liberalizing "heirs-in-waiting" to take over Libya and Egypt from their elderly fathers. Having younger, Western-educated sons take control from aging parents seemed the best way to encourage democratization in the Middle East.

For its first two years, the Obama administration continued to adhere to this script. Then a university-educated fruit seller in Tunisia immolated himself, and everything changed.

The Arab Spring was bound to present the United States with stark choices. Suddenly a regional revolt in the name of democracy and accountability confronted pliable American allies who sought to cloak their repressive tendencies in the name of resisting Islamic radicalism. Mubarak, Qaddafi and others threatened by revolts from below had assumed that close cooperation with America's security agenda for the Middle East would buy their regimes a certain degree of immunity from United States criticism and pressure. They were wrong.

Initially, many expected the Obama team to embrace the two-track approach undertaken by earlier administrations in other parts of the world, particularly in East Asia during the 1980s: up-front backing for an embattled leader to take whatever steps were needed to secure his regime and restore order with a promise to initiate reforms over the long term. Indeed, the initial responses of the Obama administration to unrest in Egypt seemed to indicate that Washington might follow the script that Ronald Reagan and his team crafted to deal with Chun Doo Hwan of South Korea: getting a leader to first accept term limits for office, then slowly laying the groundwork for the transition that culminated in the 1987 elections. But when Obama's special envoy to Egypt, Frank Wisner, expressed support for the old approach, his remarks were repudiated in Washington, and Obama abruptly changed course to push for Mubarak's complete and immediate removal.

Realist voices in the administration raised all the traditional cautionary flags. But they were brushed aside. In Egypt, the notion that any post-Mubarak government would be less sensitive to core United States interests was seen as a condition that Washington would have to live with; in earlier times it was considered an eventuality to be crushed. The concerns that Libya might disintegrate as a nation-state, facilitating the rise of Islamist militants in ungoverned spaces, were set aside for the benefit of preventing a feared humanitarian crisis. Certainly, by the end of 2011, political figures and movements that the United States worked hard for decades to keep away from the levers of power— the Muslim Brotherhood in Egypt, members of the Libyan Islamic Fighting Group, Libyan Islamists, Rachid al-Ghannouchi in Tunisia—were all playing roles in the postdictator political arena.

There has been a real shift in American attitudes, a willingness to take the risks of losing short-term security advantages in favor of encouraging long-term societal change.

Undoubtedly the death of Osama bin Laden, the successful elimination of other key al-Qaeda leaders and operatives, and the belief that al-Qaeda was "losing its struggle for relevance" in the region, to quote from Obama's May 2011 address at the State Department, contributed to the assessment that backing revolutionary ferment in the Arab world would not automatically hand power over to an implacable foe of the United States. Obama has expressed his optimism that successor regimes will not seek to alter fundamentally their countries' ongoing cooperation with the United States, particularly in continuing efforts to combat terrorism and broker a lasting Middle East peace settlement. He has declared that "America's interests are not hostile to peoples' hopes; they're essential to them." But it remains a big question whether Islamists will undergo a democratic transformation and eventually create moderate governments.

Indeed, there has been a real shift in American attitudes, a willingness to take the risks of losing short-term security advantages in favor of encouraging long-term societal change. To be sure, such a paradigm shift is not categorical or complete. America's foreign policy is never without its inconsistencies and contradictions. Washington continues to cater to Saudi sensibilities, and it looked askance as Riyadh marched into Bahrain to buttress its Sunni satrap through continued repression of the majority Shia population. The fact that the Gulf monarchies demonstrated limited appetite for viable political reforms has not elicited loud American objections. The need for Gulf oil and military bases and the common cause of containing a recalcitrant Iran continue to overwhelm Washington's democratic penchants. Nonetheless, a new tendency has fractured America's long-held realism in the Middle East. How these states conduct their internal affairs and treat their citizens will be taken into account as the United States determines its alliances, shifts its loyalties and considers its interests. No country has ever conducted its policy solely on the basis of humanitarian considerations, but, given the events of the past year, they are poised to exercise more influence over decision making than ever before.

foreign-policy doctrine must be suited for its times, tailored to exploit available opportunities, and flexible enough to take advantage of sudden and subtle shifts in the international system. Many critics allege that realism is hardly suitable for the changing regional landscape confronting Washington today, that America needs a foreign policy based on values, and that embracing and encouraging rapid political change throughout the Middle East is both necessary and desirable.

But what is to be done if change must be nudged or forced? The 2003 Iraq War vindicated many realist objections, but the apparent success of the 2011 Libya operation—which ended up deposing Qaddafi from power without the loss of a single American life and without any serious rupture in United States relations with other powers—begs the question as to whether the Obama administration wants to enter a postrealist era where the old trade-offs between pursuing American ideals and securing United States interests are no longer relevant.

In the past, debates over the advisability of intervention were driven by two considerations: the potential cost of the proposed action and the likelihood that it would precipitate a clash with another major power. Obama acknowledged as much in March 2011 when he observed: "Given the costs and risks of intervention, we must always measure our interests against the need for action. But that cannot be an argument for never acting on behalf of what's right." The Arab Spring could offer the United States a template for future limited interventions that could uphold American values without exacting much cost in return.

One of the factors that may be driving the administration's confidence that a new era of interventionism is warranted comes from the reality that so-called "rogue regimes" around the world are under a new set of pressures. In the 1990s, regimes from Iran to Cuba found relief from unilateral United States sanctions and pressure by turning to European states that were willing to continue engagement. The Europeans embraced a policy of critical dialogue, which stressed that through diplomatic discussions and economic incentives rogue regimes could be persuaded to modify their behavior. The proponents of such an outlook argued that even rogue states contain factions of moderates and pragmatists that serve as potential interlocutors. From this perspective, an inclusive approach was designed to empower the pragmatists and diminish the standing of the hard-liners. Clever despots could exploit the divergence between the United States and Europe, as punitive United States measures were frequently undermined by a European policy of commerce and dialogue. Meanwhile, United States pressure on Europe, manifested primarily through the imposition of secondary sanctions on European firms doing business in places such as Tehran and Havana, often backfired.

During the first years of the Bush administration, transatlantic ties were aggravated over a whole host of issues, ranging from climate change to the Iraq invasion. In particular, the United States and several of its key allies in Europe, especially Germany and France, saw the Middle East from vastly different perspectives. Yet during the latter part of the Bush presidency, the first signs of convergence began to emerge. Once the allies put the divisive issue of Iraq behind them, they found much common ground. Washington accepted the need for international coalitions to deal with regional problems, and a new generation of European leaders such as France's Nicolas Sarkozy began to see that financial incentives and soothing words were unlikely to temper hardened ideologues.

What the Arab Spring has demonstrated is that many autocratic regimes around the world are particularly vulnerable to protest movements that originate in concerns about poor economic prospects. The despots of anemic economies cannot pay off their revolting masses if sanctions prevent them from selling their commodities or raising loans once easily available from Paris or London. Over the last several years, European governments began to place a greater emphasis on values over business interests, imposing stronger economic sanctions on illiberal regimes even when European economic interests could be negatively affected. While traditional concerns of statecraft—among them access to energy and security cooperation—remain key motives for both American and European policy in the Middle East, the question of how governments in the region treat their populations is gaining traction as a point which must be given equal consideration. The emergence of a broad transatlantic consensus makes it harder for other power centers to wholeheartedly oppose all interventions.

Thus, there is a growing perception that concerted opposition to any new humanitarian interventions will be limited. Certainly, while other great powers such as China, India or Russia may not join the effort, just as they abstained from the Security Council vote that authorized the Libya no-fly zone, it is not entirely clear that Beijing, New Delhi or Moscow would risk frayed relations with the West in order to prevent such operations from going forward in areas of the world where they do not have fundamental interests. This outlook may be summarized as: let the Western countries expend their blood and treasure if they wish. A Beijing, for instance, that still remains preoccupied with domestic economic growth and stability will not be handing out blanket security commitments to authoritarian governments around the world with any sort of guarantee that is equivalent to NATO's famed Article 5. Of course, there will be exceptions involving countries in their immediate neighborhood. Russia, for example, might assent to a NATO mission in Libya but be much more hostile to an intervention in Central Asia seeking to displace a pro-Russian government.

But what of the times when Russian and Chinese opposition in the Security Council has seemingly torpedoed calls for intervention or otherwise watered down its provisions? To some extent, this has served as a convenient excuse when the Western powers themselves have been unsure or unwilling to get involved, such as in Darfur. But as we have seen in recent years, when the United States is particularly committed to action, these countries begin to give ground, allowing for an opening wedge to emerge that could serve as justification for intervention.

In addition, China has discovered that it can retain and perhaps expand its influence even after an intervention creates a supposedly "pro-Western" government. China has much greater access to the Iraqi oil industry in the wake of the United States invasion than it did during the days of Saddam Hussein. Beijing counts on the attractiveness of its terms for economic engagement; governments unable or unwilling to meet Western criteria have found in China an alternative partner for economic development. An interesting test will be whether, despite early criticisms of Beijing for its lack of support for intervention against Qaddafi, a new Libyan government ends up turning to China for the same reason that has led so many other states in Africa and Latin America to do so in the recent past: the country's no-strings-attached aid and development policies. If this happens, it would further diminish China's appetite for trying to directly challenge United States interventions around the world.

Finally, there is the ongoing revolution in military affairs—particularly the emergence of new technologies such as unmanned drones and advances in cyberwarfare—that hold out the promise of low-cost interventions that do not require a large conventional force. The Libya operation is estimated to have cost only $1 billion, a trifle compared to what has been spent in Iraq and Afghanistan. The Obama national-security team has embraced Libya as a useful example in these times of budget austerity for facilitating United States values and interests around the world. Deputy national-security adviser Ben Rhodes commented:

> When we came to office you had a situation where there were very large United States military footprints in Iraq and Afghanistan. And what we're moving towards is a far more targeted use of force in which we apply direct power against . . . those who pose a direct threat to the United States and then galvanize collective action against global security challenges.

Instead of relying upon large concentrations of ground forces to deliver knockout blows, the belief is that a combination of air power and special-forces units allows for small, light-footprint, rapid-strike missions that take out an opposing regime.

If, in order to alleviate concerns about costs, the United States in the future will be forgoing large-scale interventions in favor of covert actions and small-scale special military operations, then it suggests that a postrealist approach will focus on taking steps that are likely to produce a satisfactory outcome rather than guarantee an optimal one.

If the current situation holds—that no durable anti-American coalition is emerging to put checks on the exercise of United States power around the globe—then the postrealist view may gain greater traction. The strictures of the Cold War imposed a certain discipline on the process of deciding whether and when to intervene militarily in a given conflict. Intervention in some states was ruled out for reasons of geography—in the case of close proximity to the Soviet Union, for instance. Security considerations governed other situations. There was a reluctance to take action against a reasonably pro-Western, authoritarian regime for fear that it might be replaced by a pro-Soviet successor. None of these considerations is weighing on the minds of policy makers today.

Instead, if an intervention can be sold to policy makers as quick and inexpensive, with little likelihood that other major powers will significantly raise the cost of action, the propensity for intervention rises. In addition, if policy makers believe that the successor government is likely to be no worse than, or even better than, the status quo, then the path to intervention is cleared. After laboring for several years to wind down the Bush legacy in international affairs, the Obama team may be prepared to start implementing this new approach.

Critical Thinking

1. Why is realism so important to U.S. foreign policy in the Middle East?

2. Why doesn't the United States support humanitarian intervention in Syria?

3. What is the relationship between Wilsonism and democratization in the Middle East?

NIKOLAS K. GVOSDEV is a senior editor at *The National Interest* and a professor of national-security studies at the United States Naval War College. **RAY TAKEYH** is a senior fellow for Middle Eastern studies at the Council on Foreign Relations. The views expressed here are entirely those of the authors.

Nikolas K. Gvosdev and Ray Takeyh. From *The National Interest*, January/February 2012. Copyright © 2012 by National Interest. Reprinted by permission.

An Asian Security Standoff

ALAN DUPONT

Pivotal moments in history are seldom anticipated. And when change is systemic, this rule is even truer. There are unmistakable signs in East Asia, however, that the old, United States-dominated order can no longer be sustained in the face of Chinas emerging challenge and the relative weakness of both the United States and Japan. A failure of American diplomacy to adjust to these new power realities, or of China to accommodate long-standing United States and Japanese interests, could jeopardize the promise of the much-heralded Asian century and return East Asia to its bloody and fractious past. What emerges in this critical region will have global consequences. As the locus of economic and military power shifts decisively from the Atlantic to the Pacific, it is clear that East Asia has never been so centrally important to the international order. Never before have the world's three preeminent states—the United States, Japan and China—all been Asia-Pacific powers. This raises the stakes for everyone should the Old Order fail precipitously.

The old, U.S.-dominated order can no longer be sustained in the face of China's emerging challenge and the relative weakness of both the U.S. and Japan.

For nearly seven decades, this order has been underpinned by United States economic and military strength, dating back to the defeat of Japan at the end of World War II and reinforced forty-five years later by the collapse of the Soviet Union. During the Cold War, American preeminence in East Asia was vitiated by both the illusion and reality of Soviet military power. Thereafter, for a brief "unipolar moment," the United States seemed able to do as it pleased without worrying about peer competitors or balancing coalitions. In retrospect, President George W. Bush's first term may be seen as the apogee of *Pax Americana*. Since then, it has been mostly downhill for a United States weakened by ten years of war, a gridlocked political system and the lingering contagion from the 2008 global financial crisis. President Obama's pivot to Asia, and his attempt to quarantine the region from defense-budget cuts, cannot disguise the sober reality that the United States capacity to shape East Asia is no longer what it was.

Once seen as the reliable northern anchor of the United States alliance system in East Asia and lauded for its dependability and dynamism, Japan's two-decade political and economic malaise is a significant cause of the weakening of the Old Order. The near meltdown of the tsunami-crippled Fukushima nuclear-power plant in 2011 can be seen as a metaphor for the corrosion of Japan's increasingly inward-looking body politic. The country lacks confidence and is beset by a host of domestic problems. Leadership stasis has made it difficult for the United States to reinvigorate the strategic partnership with Japan or to be sure where the country is heading. This is reflected in the failure to reach agreement on the relocation of the important Marine base on Okinawa. While Japan remains a major economy, its gross domestic product has not grown for twenty years, and the country suffered the indignity of being overtaken by China as the world's second-largest economy in 2011. Aging and shrinking demographically, Japan faces the prospect of being consigned to the second rank of East Asia's middle powers unless it can recapture its lost elan and purpose.

But China's rise is the main reason for the loss of Washington's once-unrivaled ability to influence the region's affairs. With a population of 1.4 billion, more than the rest of East Asia and the United States combined, China is a megastate that for millennia was the dominant polity in Asia and now makes little secret of its desire to reclaim its former status. These dreams are no longer illusory, for modern China has the strategic clout to realize them. Its population and economy dwarf those of Fascist Germany, Imperial Japan and the Soviet Union—previous and ultimately vanquished challengers of United States power. China's reemergence poses strategic challenges of a complexity and magnitude not previously experienced by the United States, or the rest of East Asia, for that matter. The principal unknown is the path China's leaders will follow, often posed in overly stark and simplistic terms as a choice between responsible stakeholder or revisionist state. In fact, China is likely to be both, conforming to the norms of the international system except when its core interests conflict with those norms.

While long anticipated—indeed, United States policy planners were warning of these strategic implications as far back as the mid-1990s—the Middle Kingdom's new prominence in East Asia has been boosted by two seminal recent events, one financial and the other geopolitical. The 2008 global financial crisis led many in China to believe that the United States was in decline, suffering from imperial overreach and living beyond its means. This belief is perhaps overstated, but owing more than a trillion dollars to China has dearly placed the United States in the distinctly uncomfortable position of being seen as a financial supplicant to its principal competitor. Perceptions of United States financial weakness have clearly emboldened Chinese leaders to seek geopolitical advantage over the United States in contested spaces, especially in East Asia. Of greatest concern is Beijing's evident determination to aggressively defend its claims to disputed islands, waters and resources in the East China and South China seas. Relations with the other major Asian powers, Japan and India, have become increasingly testy, and many Southeast Asian nations are fearful that China will pay only lip service to regional egalitarianism as it becomes more powerful, both economically and militarily. In the past two years, China has declared the eponymous South China Sea to be a "core interest" and made abundantly clear that it will continue to support the bellicose North Korean regime despite that maverick state's repeated provocations and violations of international norms.

At the heart of United States and regional anxieties about China's future military intentions is the ambitious "far-sea defense" strategy, designed to push the United States Navy as far from Chinese shores as possible. China is bent on turning its three coastal fleets into a genuine blue-water navy capable of controlling the western Pacific and eventually projecting significant maritime power into the central Pacific and the Indian Ocean. Beijing's strategic aim seems to be a Monroe Doctrine with Chinese characteristics, and it is rapidly acquiring the capabilities to realize this ambitious goal. From a Chinese perspective, this makes perfect strategic sense. After all, if a rising America could construct a Monroe Doctrine in the nineteenth century as a blunt but effective instrument for keeping other powers out of the Western Hemisphere, why should an ascendant, twenty-first-century China not seek a comparable outcome in the western Pacific? The problem is that Beijing's determination to push back the Unites States Navy threatens to destabilize the regional balance of power and escalate tensions not only with America but also with Japan.

Relations between China and Japan are already fraught with tensions. Neither side seems capable of moving beyond the historical enmities infecting its contemporary behavior and precluding any genuine rapprochement, despite Japan's booming trade with China and increasing level of economic interdependence. These underlying tensions periodically erupt, exposing the deep fault lines between the two nations and underlining the potential for miscalculation. The most serious recent example occurred on September 7, 2010, when simmering tensions over ownership of the disputed Diaoyu or Senkaku Islands in the East China Sea boiled over into a serious confrontation after a Chinese fishing trawler appeared to deliberately ram a pursuing Japanese Coast Guard vessel. This brought Sino-Japanese relations to a post–World War II low. Opinion polls showed extremely high levels of mutual disaffection, with 87 percent of Japanese and 79 percent of Chinese surveyed regarding the

other country as "untrustworthy." Fully 79 percent of Japanese considered China a military threat.

It would be wrong to infer from these actions that China is intent on military confrontation with the United States and Japan or that it is yet in a position to supplant America as the region's most influential power. But China's new assertiveness illustrates the structural tensions that inevitably occur when a rising power challenges the existing order and, by definition, the place of the previously dominant state. As Harvard's Richard Rosecrance and Peking University's Jia Qingguo have documented, over the past five hundred years, six of the seven hegemonic challenges to the existing order have led to serious conflict. We also know that strong economic and trade links between aspiring and incumbent hegemons do not, by themselves, reduce the risk of conflict, as Britain and Germany demonstrated a century ago when their deepening economic interdependence couldn't prevent their going to war in 1914. Thus, it would be an egregious mistake to conclude that strengthening ties between China and the United States make military conflict between them unthinkable.

Some liberals argue that the unique character, cultural identity and historical experience of China make it intrinsically less aggressive than other nations. According to this view, the Middle Kingdom is an exceptional state and marches to a different foreign-policy tune. However, the proposition that China has historically been less aggressive or less expansionist than its Western or Eastern counterparts does not withstand scrutiny. Like many powerful nations, and the United States in particular, China has a long tradition of territorial expansionism and subduing or coercing neighboring peoples and states. Although different in character from European colonialism, the endgame of China's tributary-state system has been the imposition of a Chinese suzerain over neighboring peoples and polities, a point not lost today on fellow Asians. While Beijing regards reunification with Taiwan and pacification of Tibet as a restoration of Chinese authority over ancestral lands lost through the perfidious interference of foreigners, it is possible to draw an altogether different conclusion: Beijing's policies toward Taiwan and Tibet reflect China's likely behavior toward the wider region. Certainly, China's revanchism has done little to build confidence that a *Pax Sinica* would be demonstrably fairer, more stable and peaceful than *Pax Americana*.

But if *Pax Sinica* lacks appeal and *Pax Americana* cannot endure in its current form, what kind of new order might emerge in East Asia that could maintain peace and accommodate the aspirations of all the region's states? One possibility is a "Concert of Asia." Drawing their inspiration from the post-Napoleonic accord of powers that controlled Europe for much of the nineteenth century, supporters of a Concert of Asia maintain that in the absence of a dominant state, a contemporary Asian version of the European concert holds out the best prospect for regional peace and stability. To be credible and enduring, however, only the strongest powers would be entitled to a seat at the table. The five obvious candidates are the United States, China, Japan, India and Indonesia.

One clear problem with this formulation is the dubious assumption that East Asia's smaller nations would readily agree to have their individual or collective interests adjudicated by the large powers. This runs counter to the whole thrust of East Asian regionalism over the past two decades, with its emphasis on the empowerment of smaller states and the collective management of the region's security problems. It also ignores the global diffusion of power that has accompanied what Fareed Zakaria calls the "rise of the rest." Robust, medium-sized states are demanding a greater say in regional and international affairs, and they are not going to accept readily any return to a past of great-power dominance. It is also difficult to see the major powers agreeing to accept a stewardship role of the kind envisaged in a Concert of Asia. Japan is too weak; China is unwilling, and its political values are too different; India is preoccupied with its own problems; Indonesia's geopolitical ambitions are confined to Southeast Asia; and the United States has neither the inclination nor the resources to take on an enhanced leadership role in Asia.

What of the argument that America should accept the inevitable and share power with China as an equal? Paralleling the G-2 would be an Asia2, allowing Beijing and Washington to divide the region into spheres of influence in much the same way as the United States and the Soviet Union managed a politically bifurcated Europe during the early part of the Cold War. While superficially appealing because it holds out the prospect of a peaceful transition to a new international order, power sharing between the United States and China is unlikely to work for two reasons. First, no United States administration, regardless of its political complexion, would voluntarily relinquish power to China, just as China wouldn't if the roles were reversed. Second, China's new great-power status is hardly untrammeled. Nor is it guaranteed to last, for the country faces formidable environmental, resource, economic and demographic challenges, not to mention a rival United States that shows no sign of lapsing into terminal decline despite its current economic travails. Sooner than it thinks, Beijing may have to confront the prospect of a resurgent Washington determined to reassert its strategic interests.

The question, then, is: How can China and the United States ensure that healthy competition does not give way to an entrenched bloody-mindedness that aggravates existing insecurities and results in serious conflict? That may be difficult, if not impossible, should Beijing maintain its current political and military strategy in the western Pacific. Like any other state, China is entitled to modernize its armed forces and protect its legitimate security interests. But Beijing's assertion of its territorial claims in the East and South China seas has been counterproductive—alienating neighbors, raising international concerns about China's strategic ambitions and provoking hedging behavior in the region. China's challenge to United States maritime power in East Asia strikes at a deeply held American conviction that continued naval dominance of the Pacific is not only critical to United States security but also to the nation's standing as the preeminent global power, something that all but guarantees a countervailing military and political response.

At issue here is Beijing's often harsh and uncompromising official rhetoric when dealing with sensitive political and sovereignty issues as well as the government's willingness to accept and even sometimes foster nationalist sentiment at home, which is aggravating and complicating disputes with the United States and Japan. A more pluralistic, globally connected China would mean that foreign policy is no longer the exclusive preserve of the Standing Committee of the Politburo and the small policy elite that supports it in the Foreign Ministry and State Council. Nationalist sentiment expressed through chat rooms, blogging and Internet sites is complicating, and making less predictable, the management of Sino-United States and Sino-Japanese relations. Of course, no country is immune from the demonization of competitors, as attested by "Japan bashing" in the United States during the 1980s. But the incubus of extreme nationalism is having a particularly destabilizing effect in China, where sensationalist and emotive reporting, more often associated with Western tabloids, is making it difficult for Chinese leaders to avoid caricaturing rather than making nuanced assessments of United States intentions and capabilities. If Beijing is not yet ready for a free press, it must accept the responsibility for the outbursts of a controlled press.

America's challenge, meanwhile, is to develop a more coherent China strategy that explicitly recognizes Beijing's resource anxieties and corollary need to take on greater responsibility for the protection of sea-lanes in the western Pacific. What has been missing from many Western explanations of China's more assertive recent behavior is recognition of the economic importance that Beijing attaches to this vital waterway, which is a major conduit for international trade and a rich repository for minerals and valuable marine life. By 2030, up to 80 percent of China's oil and 50 percent of its gas will be imported by sea, through the Malacca Strait—a classic maritime choke point due to the narrowness and shallowness of its approaches, the number of ships that pass through it daily, and the Strait's vulnerability to interdiction or environmental blockage.

The rate of growth in China's energy imports has few historical parallels, if any. In less than twenty years, the country has moved from a net exporter to importing more than 55 percent of its oil, with crude-oil imports increasing by a staggering 17.5 percent in 2010 alone. This resource vulnerability weighs heavily on the minds of Chinese decision makers who, in addition to worrying about terrorism, piracy and environmental disruptions to their energy supplies, are acutely aware that their major competitor exercises effective naval control over the Malacca Strait and most of the western Pacific. Invoking the so-called Malacca dilemma, President Hu Jintao first gave voice to these anxieties in 2005, and his officials have made it clear since that China is no longer prepared to outsource sea-lane security in the western Pacific to the United States Navy. Thus, whether the United States and Japan like it or not, Chinese naval pennants will be sighted far more frequently in the western Pacific and as far south as the Malacca Strait. This is a natural consequence of China's growing economic and strategic weight, just as the emergence of the United States Navy heralded the rise of the United States as a major power at the dawn of the twentieth century.

Another danger point lies in various inconsistencies in United States behavior and approaches to China. Over the past two decades, United States China policy has been a confusing mix of engagement, partnership, competition, hedging and lectures on China's internal political structure. With resentment and hostility toward Beijing on the rise, American administrations face the challenge of ensuring that China does not become a whipping boy for United States domestic-policy failings or replace the Soviet Union as the new strategic bogeyman. Any attempt to demonize China would be counterproductive to United States strategic interests in East Asia. It would undercut moderates in the Chinese leadership and encourage a reciprocal response that would aggravate existing tensions.

How the United States and China manage their relationship will have strategic implications extending well beyond East Asia. As competition increases, preventing conflicts from escalating will not be easy. This isn't necessarily because Beijing seeks territorial expansion, has become a revisionist power or has serious differences with Washington over values. Presumably, these can be managed. The real danger is that China's resource vulnerabilities, sense of entitlement and determination to restore its historically dominant position in East Asia will deepen regional anxieties about Chinese behavior and trigger a countervailing response from the United States and Japan. This could pose a contemporary expression of the classic security dilemma articulated a half century ago by the eminent American international-relations theorist Kenneth Waltz: in seeking to enhance their own security by building a strong military, large states often increase everyone else's insecurity because this military force is frequently regarded as a potential threat rather than as a reasonable, defensive measure.

Already, China's attempt to test Washington's resolve in the western Pacific by "periphery probing" has resulted in a predictably vigorous United States response. The United States Navy and Air Force are working on plans to suppress and blind China's potent missile capabilities by means of an emerging "air-sea battle" strategy, which is rapidly gaining political traction in Washington. It would not take much for this to turn into a full-blown arms race, drawing in other nations concerned by China's rising military might. Avoiding worst-case outcomes will require a sustained, long-term commitment to building trust and preventive diplomacy as well as the establishment of an effective system of risk management that can prevent localized disputes and incidents from escalating into major region-wide conflicts.

In short, the dissolution of the Old Order in East Asia has created a delicate power balance there, rendered intrinsically unstable by China's regional ambitions, understandable though they may be, and America's equally understandable resolve to preserve as much of its old regional dominance as possible. Whether the two nations can successfully manage this fragile transition and thus stabilize the regional power balance remains a central question facing Asia—and the world beyond—in these times of global flux.

Critical Thinking

1. How has the International Order in East Asia changed?
2. Why would China conform to the norms of the international system?
3. What is the relationship between international law and the claim to sovereignty over islands in the South China Sea?

ALAN DUPONT is professor of international security and director of the Institute for International Security and Development at the University of New South Wales in Sydney, Australia.

Dupont, Alan. From *The National Interest,* no. 119, May/June 2012. Copyright © 2012 by National Interest. Reprinted by permission.

UNIT 4

War, Arms Control, and Disarmament

Unit Selections

Learning Outcomes

After reading this Unit, you will be able to:

- Understand the relationship between neo-realism and military balance.

- Analyze the logic of deterrence as it applies to Iran.

- Explain why Pakistan is not a very good U.S. ally.

- Determine the policy that the United States should follow toward Pakistan.

- Explain why Afghan forces can secure Afghanistan's key terrain by 2014.

- Explain why the coalition forces have regained the initiative in Afghanistan.

- Describe the key myths about war.

- Explain why the world feels like a more violent place than it actually is.

- Explain why it is necessary to negotiate an Arms Trade Treaty (ATT).

- Describe some of the difficulties that are associated with the negotiation of an ATT.

- Describe the key features of the Obama Doctrine.

- Analyze why the president's secret wars are backfiring.

Student Website

www.mhhe.com/cls

Internet References

The Bulletin of the Atomic Scientists
www.the bulletin.org
The Correlates of War Project
www.correlatesofwar.org
International Atomic Energy Agency (IAEA)
www.iaea.org
International Crisis Group
www.crisisgroup.org
International Security Assistance Force
www.nato.int/ISAF

National Defense University
www.ndu.edu
Peace Research Institute at Oslo
www.prio.no
Stockholm International Peace Research Institute
www.sipri.org
Conference on the Arms Trade Treaty
www.un.org/disaramament/ATT

War is a method of conflict resolution that has been institutionalized over the centuries, according to the classical realist view of international relations. Political scientists also argue that there is a relationship between the internal regime of a state and war, so that liberal democracies do not wage war on other liberal democracies. Neorealists, such as Kenneth Waltz, argue that it is the international political structure within which states function that explains the phenomenon of war. War can also result from the miscalculations and misperceptions of the opposing sides. For example, Robert Jervis writes that "Misperception . . . includes inaccurate inferences, miscalculations of consequences, and misjudgments about how one will react to one's policies." Leaders may underestimate or overestimate the intentions and threats of their rivals. In a crisis situation, foreign policy decision-making elites may be overloaded with information, have difficulty screening it, and also may be subject to the phenomenon of cognitive dissonance. Cognitive dissonance occurs when an individual is so overloaded with information that he or she reverts to stereotypes that reinforce preexisting beliefs.

One of the major concerns of the international community is the problem of the proliferation of nuclear weapons. The acquisition of nuclear weapons by "rogue" states such as Iran and North Korea is viewed by the international community not only as a threat to regional stability, but also a threat to international stability as well. In 2012, it was clear that Iran was continuing to work on the development of the capacity to produce enriched uranium, which would bring it closer to a nuclear weapon capacity. Diplomacy, efforts at dialogue, and heavy economic sanctions, the assassination of Iranian nuclear scientists, and the sabotaging of Iranian computers working on uranium enrichment have not worked. Israel, in 2012, facing what it dubbed an existential threat, was reported to be considering launching a preemptive strike against Iran to destroy its nuclear infrastructure. However, in "Iran Should Get the Bomb," Kenneth Waltz argues that the acquisition of the bomb by Iran "would yield more stability, not less," because the Iranian regime is not irrational, and the logic of deterrence would work on a new nuclear state.

One of the major problems that the United States faces in Afghanistan is the difficult relationship with Pakistan. Some elements in the Pakistani military and intelligence services are playing a double-edged game by supporting the Afghan Taliban to the extent that they can exercise control over it, ostensibly to counter an enhancement of Indian influence in Afghanistan. At the same time, Pakistan is considered to be a U.S. ally in the war against the Taliban and al Qaeda. Relations between the United States and Pakistan have also been exacerbated by "collateral damage," which results in Pakistani civilian casualties due to the excessive use of drone strikes and commando raids in Pakistan by U.S. forces, which the Pakistani government considers to be a violation of its sovereignty. The death of about two dozen Pakistani soldiers as a result of U.S. friendly fire also resulted in a major rift in U.S.-Pakistani relations as Pakistan held up the transit of vital supplies through its territory for the coalition forces in Afghanistan until the United States

© Glow Images

apologized. Stephen Krasner, in "Talking Tough to Pakistan," argues that the United States needs to shift its strategy toward Pakistan, because the lack of cooperation by Pakistan in the war in Afghanistan will "doom U.S. counter-insurgency efforts there," Krasner recommends more economic rewards to Pakistan as an inducement for increased cooperation in Afghanistan.

President Obama has made an agreement with President Karzai to withdraw U.S. troops from Afghanistan by 2014, but with a commitment of U.S. forces to help Pakistan after 2014. The question is whether in view of the U.S. draw-down of forces, the Afghan security forces will be ready to deal with the Taliban, especially given the increase in 2012 of "insider" attacks by Afghan security forces on U.S. troops. David Rodriguez, the Commander of the U.S. Army Forces Command, focuses on the ability of Afghan security forces to perform their mission effectively once the U.S. forces leave. The author concludes that he is "confident that Afghan forces, supported by the coalition, can achieve irreversible gains and successfully secure Afghanistan's key terrain by the end of 2014."

The end of the Cold War was marked by an outbreak and an intense flare-up of regional conflicts, characterized by ethnic and tribal wars. However, as Joshua Goldstein, in "World Peace Could Be Closer Than You Think" stresses, armed conflict has actually declined since the end of the Cold War, based on data gathered by the Peace Research Institute in Oslo. The author observes that " . . . the world feels like a more violent place than it actually is . . . because there's more information about war—not more wars themselves."

While the international community has placed a great deal of emphasis on the arms control and disarmament of weapons of mass destruction, the trade in conventional weapons, which runs the gamut from revolvers to tanks to jet aircraft, continues to pose a serious problem to human security. In 2011, the global arms trade added up to more than $85 billion, with the United States as the world's leading arms supplier, according to a recent report by the Congressional Research Service. Millions of innocent civilians have been killed by conventional weapons since the end of World War II. They have perished at the hands of repressive governments, revolutionaries, criminal gangs, and paramilitaries and militias, with many of the weapons supplied by private arms dealers or "merchants of death." Although there are a number of treaties and agreements dealing with the trade in conventional weapons, there is no universal, comprehensive, and binding treaty that sets international standards to regulate the trade. An international conference met at the United Nations from July 2–27, 2012, but was unable to arrive at an agreement on an ATT. As Farrah Zughni points out in "Arms Trade Talks Set to Begin," there were a number of differences among the states participating in the negotiations, such as whether to include small arms and light weapons in the treaty, while the question of the inclusion of ammunition was especially contentious. Most importantly, an ATT was needed to bring about an agreement that would prevent conventional weapons from being used to violate human rights and humanitarian law.

In the war against the Taliban and al Qaeda, President Obama has ordered the use of far more drone strikes than President Bush, raising questions of collateral damage, the legality of the use of such weapons, and the killing of U.S. citizens. As David Rhode points out in "The Obama Doctrine," the doctrine encompasses the use of military technology such as drones, which may be counter-productive because it is antagonizing Pakistani public opinion against the United States. Rhode observes that the Obama Doctrine also includes a cutback in military spending and a shift of U.S. military units "from the Middle East to the Pacific," as the U.S. administration believes that al Qaeda is "nearly defeated" and the focus of U.S. interests is shifting to the Asia–Pacific region.

Why Iran Should Get the Bomb

Nuclear Balancing Would Mean Stability

Kenneth N. Waltz

The past several months have witnessed a heated debate over the best way for the United States and Israel to respond to Iran's nuclear activities. As the argument has raged, the United States has tightened its already robust sanctions regime against the Islamic Republic, and the European Union announced in January that it will begin an embargo on Iranian oil on July 1. Although the United States, the EU, and Iran have recently returned to the negotiating table, a palpable sense of crisis still looms.

It should not. Most United States, European, and Israeli commentators and policymakers warn that a nuclear-armed Iran would be the worst possible outcome of the current standoff. In fact, it would probably be the best possible result: the one most likely to restore stability to the Middle East.

Power Begs to Be Balanced

The crisis over Iran's nuclear program could end in three different ways. First, diplomacy coupled with serious sanctions could convince Iran to abandon its pursuit of a nuclear weapon. But this outcome is unlikely: the historical record indicates that a country bent on acquiring nuclear weapons can rarely be dissuaded from doing so. Punishing a state through economic sanctions does not inexorably derail its nuclear program. Take North Korea, which succeeded in building its weapons despite countless rounds of sanctions and UN Security Council resolutions. If Tehran determines that its security depends on possessing nuclear weapons, sanctions are unlikely to change its mind. In fact, adding still more sanctions now could make Iran feel even more vulnerable, giving it still more reason to seek the protection of the ultimate deterrent.

The second possible outcome is that Iran stops short of testing a nuclear weapon but develops a breakout capability, the capacity to build and test one quite quickly. Iran would not be the first country to acquire a sophisticated nuclear program without building an actual bomb. Japan, for instance, maintains a vast civilian nuclear infrastructure. Experts believe that it could produce a nuclear weapon on short notice.

Such a breakout capability might satisfy the domestic political needs of Iran's rulers by assuring hard-liners that they can enjoy all the benefits of having a bomb (such as greater security) without the downsides (such as international isolation and condemnation). The problem is that a breakout capability might not work as intended.

The United States and its European allies are primarily concerned with weaponization, so they might accept a scenario in which Iran stops short of a nuclear weapon. Israel, however, has made it clear that it views a significant Iranian enrichment capacity alone as an unacceptable threat. It is possible, then, that a verifiable commitment from Iran to stop short of a weapon could appease major Western powers but leave the Israelis unsatisfied. Israel would be less intimidated by a virtual nuclear weapon than it would be by an actual one and therefore would likely continue its risky efforts at subverting Iran's nuclear program through sabotage and assassination—which could lead Iran to conclude that a breakout capability is an insufficient deterrent, after all, and that only weaponization can provide it with the security it seeks.

The third possible outcome of the standoff is that Iran continues its current course and publicly goes nuclear by testing a weapon. United States and Israeli officials have declared that outcome unacceptable, arguing that a nuclear Iran is a uniquely terrifying prospect, even an existential threat. Such language is typical of major powers, which have historically gotten riled up whenever another country has begun to develop a nuclear weapon of its own. Yet so far, every time another country has managed to shoulder its way into the nuclear club, the other members have always changed tack and decided to live with it. In fact, by reducing imbalances in military power, new nuclear states generally produce more regional and international stability, not less.

Israel's regional nuclear monopoly, which has proved remarkably durable for the past four decades, has long fueled instability in the Middle East. In no other region of the world does a lone, unchecked nuclear state exist. It is Israel's nuclear arsenal, not Iran's desire for one, that has contributed most to the current crisis. Power, after all, begs to be balanced. What is surprising about the Israeli case is that it has taken so long for a potential balancer to emerge.

Of course, it is easy to understand why Israel wants to remain the sole nuclear power in the region and why it is willing to use force to secure that status. In 1981, Israel bombed Iraq to prevent a challenge to its nuclear monopoly. It did the same to Syria in 2007 and is now considering similar action against Iran. But the very acts that have allowed Israel to maintain its nuclear edge in the short term have prolonged an imbalance that is unsustainable in the long term. Israel's proven ability to strike potential nuclear rivals with impunity has inevitably made its enemies anxious to develop the means to prevent Israel from doing so again. In this way, the current tensions are best viewed not as the early stages of a relatively recent Iranian nuclear crisis but rather as the final stages of a decades-long Middle East nuclear crisis that will end only when a balance of military power is restored.

Unfounded Fears

One reason the danger of a nuclear Iran has been grossly exaggerated is that the debate surrounding it has been distorted by misplaced worries and fundamental misunderstandings of how states generally behave in the international system. The first prominent concern, which undergirds many others, is that the Iranian regime is innately irrational. Despite a widespread belief to the contrary, Iranian policy is made not by "mad mullahs" but by perfectly sane ayatollahs who want to survive just like any other leaders. Although Iran's leaders indulge in inflammatory and hateful rhetoric, they show no propensity for self-destruction. It would be a grave error for policymakers in the United States and Israel to assume otherwise.

Yet that is precisely what many United States and Israeli officials and analysts have done. Portraying Iran as irrational has allowed them to argue that the logic of nuclear deterrence does not apply to the Islamic Republic. If Iran acquired a nuclear weapon, they warn, it would not hesitate to use it in a first strike against Israel, even though doing so would invite massive retaliation and risk destroying everything the Iranian regime holds dear.

Although it is impossible to be certain of Iranian intentions, it is far more likely that if Iran desires nuclear weapons, it is for the purpose of providing for its own security, not to improve its offensive capabilities (or destroy itself). Iran may be intransigent at the negotiating table and defiant in the face of sanctions, but it still acts to secure its own preservation. Iran's leaders did not, for example, attempt to close the Strait of Hormuz despite issuing blustery warnings that they might do so after the EU announced its planned oil embargo in January. The Iranian regime clearly concluded that it did not want to provoke what would surely have been a swift and devastating American response to such a move.

Nevertheless, even some observers and policymakers who accept that the Iranian regime is rational still worry that a nuclear weapon would embolden it, providing Tehran with a shield that would allow it to act more aggressively and increase its support for terrorism. Some analysts even fear that Iran would directly provide terrorists with nuclear arms. The problem with these concerns is that they contradict the record of every other nuclear weapons state going back to 1945. History shows that when countries acquire the bomb, they feel increasingly vulnerable and become acutely aware that their nuclear weapons make them a potential target in the eyes of major powers. This awareness discourages nuclear states from bold and aggressive action. Maoist China, for example, became much less bellicose after acquiring nuclear weapons in 1964, and India and Pakistan have both become more cautious since going nuclear. There is little reason to believe Iran would break this mold.

As for the risk of a handoff to terrorists, no country could transfer nuclear weapons without running a high risk of being found out. United States surveillance capabilities would pose a serious obstacle, as would the United States' impressive and growing ability to identify the source of fissile material. Moreover, countries can never entirely control or even predict the behavior of the terrorist groups they sponsor. Once a country such as Iran acquires a nuclear capability, it will have every reason to maintain full control over its arsenal. After all, building a bomb is costly and dangerous. It would make little sense to transfer the product of that investment to parties that cannot be trusted or managed.

Another oft-touted worry is that if Iran obtains the bomb, other states in the region will follow suit, leading to a nuclear arms race in the Middle East. But the nuclear age is now almost 70 years old, and so far, fears of proliferation have proved to be unfounded. Properly defined, the term "proliferation" means a rapid and uncontrolled spread. Nothing like that has occurred; in fact, since 1970, there has been a marked slowdown in the emergence of nuclear states. There is no reason to expect that this pattern will change now. Should Iran become the second Middle Eastern nuclear power since 1945, it would hardly signal the start of a landslide. When Israel acquired the bomb in the 1960s, it was at war with many of its neighbors. Its nuclear arms were a much bigger threat to the Arab world than Iran's program is today. If an atomic Israel did not trigger an arms race then, there is no reason a nuclear Iran should now.

Rest Assured

In 1991, the historical rivals India and Pakistan signed a treaty agreeing not to target each other's nuclear facilities. They realized that far more worrisome than their adversary's nuclear deterrent was the instability produced by challenges to it. Since then, even in the face of high tensions and risky provocations, the two countries have kept the peace. Israel and Iran would do well to consider this precedent. If Iran goes nuclear, Israel and Iran will deter each other, as nuclear powers always have. There has never been a full-scale war between two nuclear-armed states. Once Iran crosses the nuclear threshold, deterrence will apply, even if the Iranian arsenal is relatively small. No other country in the region will have an incentive to acquire its own nuclear capability, and the current crisis will finally dissipate, leading to a Middle East that is more stable than it is today.

For that reason, the United States and its allies need not take such pains to prevent the Iranians from developing a nuclear weapon. Diplomacy between Iran and the major powers should continue, because open lines of communication will make the Western countries feel better able to live with a nuclear Iran. But the current sanctions on Iran can be dropped: they primarily harm ordinary Iranians, with little purpose.

Most important, policymakers and citizens in the Arab world, Europe, Israel, and the United States should take comfort from the fact that history has shown that where nuclear capabilities emerge, so, too, does stability. When it comes to nuclear weapons, now as ever, more may be better.

Critical Thinking

1. Why does Waltz believe that a nuclear armed Iran does not constitute a threat to stability in the region?

2. Should Israel engage in a preemeptive strike against Iran? Why?

3. Should the international community continue to use diplomacy and economic sanctions to prevent Iran from going nuclear? Why?

KENNETH N. WALTZ is Senior Research Scholar at the Saltzman Institute of War and Peace Studies and Adjunct Professor of Political Science at Columbia University.

Waltz, Kenneth N. From *Foreign Affairs*, vol.91, no.4, July/August 2012, pp. 2–5. Copyright © 2012 by Council on Foreign Relations, Inc. Reprinted by permission of Foreign Affairs. www.ForeignAffairs.com

Talking Tough to Pakistan

How to End Islamabad's Defiance

Stephen D. Krasner

On September 22, 2011, Admiral Mike Mullen, then chairman of the United States Joint Chiefs of Staff, made his last official appearance before the Senate Armed Services Committee. In his speech, he bluntly criticized Pakistan, telling the committee that "extremist organizations serving as proxies for the government of Pakistan are attacking Afghan troops and civilians as well as United States soldiers." The Haqqani network, he said, "is, in many ways, a strategic arm of Pakistan's Inter-Services Intelligence Agency [ISI]." In 2011 alone, Mullen continued, the network had been responsible for a June attack on the Intercontinental Hotel in Kabul, a September truck-bomb attack in Wardak Province that wounded 77 United States soldiers, and a September attack on the United States embassy in Kabul.

These observations did not, however, lead Mullen to the obvious conclusion: Pakistan should be treated as a hostile power. And within days, military officials began walking back his remarks, claiming that Mullen had meant to say only that Islamabad gives broad support to the Haqqani network, not that it gives specific direction. Meanwhile, unnamed United States government officials asserted that he had overstated the case. Mullen's testimony, for all the attention it received, did not signify a new United States strategy toward Pakistan.

Yet such a shift is badly needed. For decades, the United States has sought to buy Pakistani cooperation with aid: $20 billion worth since 9/11 alone. This money has been matched with plenty of praise. At his first press conference in Islamabad following his 2007 appointment as chairman of the Joint Chiefs, Mullen called Pakistan "a steadfast and historically." In 2008, then Secretary of State Condoleezza Rice even said that she "fully believed" that Pakistan "does not in any way want to be associated with terrorist elements and is indeed fighting to root them out wherever [Pakistani officials] find them." Meanwhile, United States leaders have spent an outsized amount of face time with their Pakistani counterparts. As secretary of state, Hillary Clinton has made four trips to Pakistan, compared with two to India and three to Japan. Mullen made more than 20 visits to Pakistan.

To be sure, Mullen was not the first United States official to publicly point the finger at Islamabad, nor will he be the last.

In 2008, the CIA blamed Pakistan's ISI for aiding the bombing of the Indian embassy in Kabul. In July 2011, two months after United States Navy SEALS raided Osama bin Laden's compound near the prestigious Pakistan Military Academy, Admiral James Winnefeld, vice chair of the Joint Chiefs, told the Senate Armed Services Committee, "Pakistan is a very, very difficult partner, and we all know that." And in an October press conference with Afghan President Hamid Karzai, Clinton noted that the Obama administration intended to "push the Pakistanis very hard," adding, "they can either be helping or hindering."

Washington's tactic—criticism coupled with continued assistance—has not been effectual. Threats and censure go unheeded in Pakistan because Islamabad's leaders do not fear the United States. This is because the United States has so often demonstrated a fear of Pakistan, believing that although Pakistan's policies have been unhelpful, they could get much worse. Washington seems to have concluded that if it actually disengaged and as a result Islamabad halted all its cooperation in Afghanistan, then United States counterinsurgency efforts there would be doomed. Even more problematic, the thinking goes, without external support, the already shaky Pakistani state would falter. A total collapse could precipitate a radical Islamist takeover, worsening Pakistani relations with the United States-backed Karzai regime in Afghanistan and escalating tensions, perhaps even precipitating a nuclear war, between Pakistan and India.

Weighing of Deeds

The United States-Pakistani relationship has produced a few modest successes. Pakistan has generally allowed NATO to transport supplies through its territory to Afghanistan. It has helped capture some senior al Qaeda officials, including Khalid Sheik Mohammed, the 9/11 mastermind. It has permitted the United States to launch drone strikes from bases in Baluchistan.

Yet these accomplishments pale in comparison to the ways in which Pakistan has proved uncooperative. The country is the world's worst nuclear proliferator, having sold technology to Iran, Libya, and North Korea through the A. Q. Khan network. Although Islamabad has attacked those terrorist groups, such as al Qaeda and the Pakistani Taliban, that target its institutions, it actively supports others, such as the Haqqani network, the Afghan Taliban, and Hezb-i-Islami, that attack coalition troops and Afghan officials or conspire against India. Pakistan also hampers United States efforts to deal with those groups; although many Pakistani officials privately support the drone program, for example, they publicly exaggerate the resulting civilian deaths. Meanwhile, they refuse to give the United States permission to conduct commando raids in Pakistan, swearing that they will defend Pakistani sovereignty at all costs.

A case in point was the raid that killed bin Laden. Rather than embrace the move, Pakistani officials reacted with fury. The police arrested a group of Pakistani citizens who were suspected of having helped the United States collect intelligence prior to the operation and delayed United States interrogations of bin Laden's three wives for more than a week. Lieutenant General Ahmed Shuja Pasha, head of the ISI, condemned the United States raid before a special session of parliament, and the government passed a resolution pledging to revisit its relationship with the United States. Of course, the operation was embarrassing for the Pakistani military, since it showed the armed forces to be either complicit in harboring bin Laden or so incompetent that they could not find him under their own noses. But Pakistan could easily have saved face by publicly depicting the operation as a cooperative venture.

The fact that Pakistan distanced itself from the raid speaks to another major problem in the relationship: despite the billions of dollars the United States has given Pakistan, public opinion there remains adamantly anti-American. In a 2010 Pew survey of 21 countries, those Pakistanis polled had among the lowest favorability ratings of the United States: 17 percent. The next year, another Pew survey found that 63 percent of the population disapproved of the raid that killed bin Laden, and 55 percent thought it was a bad thing that he had died.

Washington's current strategy toward Islamabad, in short, is not working. Any gains the United States has bought with its aid and engagement have come at an extremely high price and have been more than offset by Pakistan's nuclear proliferation and its support for the groups that attack Americans, Afghans, Indians, and others.

Rational Choice

It is tempting to believe that Pakistan's lack of cooperation results from its weakness as a state. One version of this argument is that much of Pakistan's civilian and military leadership might actually want to be more aligned with the United States but is prevented from being so by powerful hard-line Islamist factions. Its advocates point to the fact that pubic officials shrank from condemning the bodyguard who in January 2011 shot Salman Taseer, the governor of Punjab, who had spoken out against Pakistan's blasphemy law. Similar silence followed the March assassination of Shahbaz Bhatti, the minorities minister and only Christian in the cabinet, who had also urged reforming the law. Presumably, the politicians held their tongues out of fear of reprisal. Another explanation of the weakness of the Pakistani state is that the extremists in the

government and the military who support militants offer that support despite their superiors' objections. For example, the May 2011 terrorist attack on Pakistan's naval air base Mehran, which the top military brass condemned, was later suspected to have been conducted with help from someone on the inside.

Still, there is a much more straightforward explanation for Pakistan's behavior. Its policies are a fully rational response to the conception of the country's national interest held by its leaders, especially those in the military. Pakistan's fundamental goal is to defend itself against its rival, India. Islamabad deliberately uses nuclear proliferation and deterrence, terrorism, and its prickly relationship with the United States to achieve this objective.

Pakistan's nuclear strategy is to project a credible threat of first use against India. The country has a growing nuclear arsenal, a stockpile of short-range missiles to carry warheads, and plans for rapid weapons dispersion should India invade. So far, the strategy has worked; although Pakistan has supported numerous attacks on Indian soil, India has not retaliated.

Transnational terrorism, Pakistanis believe, has also served to constrain and humiliate India. As early as the 1960s, Pakistani strategists concluded that terrorism could help offset India's superior conventional military strength. They were right. Pakistani militant activity in Kashmir has led India to send hundreds of thousands of troops into the province—as many as 500,000 during a particularly tense moment with Pakistan in 2002. Better that India sends its troops to battle terrorists on its own territory, the Pakistani thinking goes, than march them across the border. Further, the 2008 Mumbai attack, which penetrated the heart of India, was a particularly embarrassing episode; the failure to prevent it, and the feeble response to it, demonstrated the ineffectuality of India's security forces.

Pakistan's double game with the United States has been effective, too. After 9/11, Pakistan's leaders could hardly resist pressure from Washington to cooperate. But they were also loath to lose influence with the insurgents in Afghanistan, which they believed gave Pakistan strategic depth against India. So Islamabad decided to have things both ways: cooperating with Washington enough to make itself useful but obstructing the coalition's plans enough to make it nearly impossible to end the Afghan insurgency. This has been an impressive accomplishment.

Caring By Neglecting

As Mullen's comments attest, United States officials do recognize the flaws in their country's current approach to Pakistan. Yet instead of making radical changes to that policy, Washington continues to muddle through, working with Pakistan where possible, attempting to convince its leaders that they should focus on internal, rather than external, threats, and hoping for the best. For their part, commentators mostly call for marginal changes, such as engaging the Pakistani military more closely on the drone program and making the program more transparent, opening United States textile markets to Pakistani trade, helping Pakistan address its energy deficit, focusing on a peaceful resolution of the Kashmir dispute, and developing closer ties to civilian officials. Many of these suggestions seem to be based on the idea that if millions of dollars in United States aid has not been enough to buy Pakistani support, perhaps extra deal sweeteners will be.

The one significant policy change since 2008 has been the retargeting of aid to civilians. Under the Obama administration, total assistance has increased by 48 percent, and a much higher percentage of it is economic rather than security related: 45 percent in 2010 as opposed to 24 percent in 2008. The Enhanced Partnership With Pakistan Act of 2009, which committed $7.5 billion to Pakistan over five years, conditioned disbursements on Pakistan's behavior, including cooperation on counterterrorism and the holding of democratic elections.

Despite Pakistan's ongoing problematic behavior, however, aid has continued to flow. Clinton even certified in March 2011 that Pakistan had made a "sustained commitment" to combating terrorist groups. Actions such as this have undermined American credibility when it comes to pressuring Pakistan to live up to its side of the bargain. The United States has shown that the sticks that come with its carrots are hollow.

The only way the United States can actually get what it wants out of Pakistan is to make credible threats to retaliate if Pakistan does not comply with United States demands and offer rewards only in return for cooperative actions taken. United States officials should tell their Pakistani counterparts in no uncertain terms that they must start playing ball or face malign neglect at best and, if necessary, active isolation. Malign neglect would mean ending all United States assistance, military and civilian; severing intelligence cooperation; continuing and possibly escalating United States drone strikes; initiating cross-border special operations raids; and strengthening United States ties with India. Active isolation would include, in addition, declaring Pakistan a state sponsor of terrorism, imposing sanctions, and pressuring China and Saudi Arabia to cut off their support, as well.

Of course, the United States' new "redlines" would be believable only if it is clear to Pakistan that the United States would be better off acting on them than backing down. (And the more believable they are, the less likely the United States will have to carry them out.) So what would make the threats credible?

First, the United States must make clear that if it ended its assistance to Pakistan, Pakistan would not be able to retaliate. The United States could continue its drone strikes, perhaps using the stealth versions of them that it is currently developing. It could suppress Pakistani air defenses, possibly with electronic jammers, so as to limit military deaths and collateral damage. And even if Pakistan shot down some drones, it could not destroy them all. The United States might even be able to conduct some Special Forces raids, which would be of such short duration and against such specific targets that Pakistan would not be able to retaliate with conventional forces. Pakistan might attempt to launch strikes against NATO and Afghan forces in Afghanistan, but its military would risk embarrassing defeat if those campaigns did not go well. Pakistan might threaten to cut off its intelligence cooperation, but that cooperation has never really extended to sharing information on the Afghan Taliban, one of the United States' main concerns in Afghanistan.

Moreover, if Pakistan started tolerating or abetting al Qaeda on its own soil, the country would be even more at risk. Al Qaeda could turn against the state and attempt to unseat the government. And the United States would surely begin striking Pakistan even more aggressively if al Qaeda found haven there.

Second, the United States must show that it can neutralize one of Pakistan's trump cards: its role in the war in Afghanistan. Washington must therefore develop a strategy for Afghanistan that works without Pakistan's help. That means a plan that does not require transporting personnel or materiel through Pakistan. Nearly 60 percent of the NATO supplies sent into Afghanistan are already routed through the north, through Russia and Central Asia. The United States military is hoping to increase that number to 75 percent. Without Pakistan, therefore, the coalition could still support a substantial force in Afghanistan, but not one as big as the current one of 131,000 troops. The basic objective of that force would necessarily be counterterrorism, not counterinsurgency. Counterterrorism is less personnel- and resource-intensive because it aims only to prevent the country from becoming a haven for Islamist extremists, not to transform it into a well-functioning democracy. Given the Obama administration's current plans to withdraw 24,000 United States troops by the summer of 2012, with many more to follow, such a strategy is already inescapable.

Finally, Washington must shed its fear that its withdrawal of aid or open antagonism could lead to the Pakistani state's collapse, a radical Islamist takeover, or nuclear war. Pakistanis, not Americans, have always determined their political future. Even substantial United States investments in the civilian state and the economy, for example, have not led to their improvement or to gains in stability. With or without United States aid to Pakistan, the Pakistani military will remain the most respected institution in the country. In a 2011 Pew poll of Pakistanis, 79 percent of respondents said that the military was having a good influence on the country's direction, compared with 20 percent who said that the national government was.

As for the possibility of an Islamist takeover, the country's current power centers have a strong interest in maintaining control and so will do whatever they can to keep it—whatever Washington's policy is. It is worth remembering that Pakistan has already proved itself able to take out the terrorist networks that threaten its own institutions, as it did in the Swat Valley and the district of Buner in 2009. Moreover, government by radical Islamists has not proved to be a popular choice among Pakistanis. In the last general election, the Muttahida Majlis-e-Amal, a coalition of Islamist parties, won only seven out of 340 seats in the National Assembly.

The possibility that nuclear weapons could wind up in the hands of terrorists is a serious risk, of course, but not one that the United States could easily mitigate whatever its policy in the region. Pakistan's nuclear posture, which involves rapid dispersion, a first-strike capability, and the use of tactical weapons, increases the chances of the central government's losing control. Even so, Pakistan will not alter that posture because it is so effective in deterring India. Meanwhile, previous United States efforts to help tighten Pakistan's command-and-control systems have been hampered by mutual distrust. Any new such efforts would be, too. Finally, since India has both a first- and a second-strike capability, Pakistan would not likely strike India first in the event of a crisis. In any case, even if things did escalate, there is not much that the United States, or anyone else, could do—good relations or not.

From a United States perspective, then, there is no reason to think that malign neglect or active isolation would make Pakistan's behavior or problems any worse.

Heads I Win, Tails You Lose

Even as the United States threatens disengagement, it should emphasize that it would still prefer a productive relationship. But it should also make clear that the choice is Pakistan's: if the country ends its support for terrorism; works in earnest with the United States to degrade al Qaeda, the Taliban, and the Haqqani network; and stops its subversion in Afghanistan, the United States will offer generous rewards. It could provide larger assistance programs, both civilian and military; open United States markets to Pakistani exports; and support political arrangements in Kabul that would reduce Islamabad's fear of India's influence. In other words, it is only after Pakistan complies with its demands that the United States should offer many of the policy proposals now on the table. And even then, these rewards should not necessarily be targeted toward changing Pakistan's regional calculus; they should be offered purely as payment for Pakistan's cooperation on the United States' most important policies in the region.

A combination of credible threats and future promises offers the best hope of convincing Islamabad that it would be better off cooperating with the United States. In essence, Pakistan would be offered a choice between the situation of Iran and that of Indonesia, two large Islamic states that have chosen very different paths. It could be either a pariah state surrounded by hostile neighbors and with dim economic prospects or a country with access to international markets, support from the United States and Europe, and some possibility of détente with its neighbors. The Indonesian path would lead to increased economic growth, an empowered middle class, strengthened civil-society groups, and a stronger economic and social foundation for a more robust democracy at some point in the future. Since it would not directly threaten the military's position, the Indonesian model should appeal to both pillars of the Pakistani state. And even if Islamabad's cooperation is not forthcoming, the United States is better off treating Pakistan as a hostile power than continuing to spend and get nothing in return.

Implicit in the remarks Mullen made to the Senate was the argument that Washington must get tough with Pakistan. He was right. A whole variety of gentle forms of persuasion have been tried and failed. The only option left is a drastic one. The irony is that this approach won't benefit just the United States: the whole region, including Pakistan, could quickly find itself better off.

Critical Thinking

1. What are the issues which have created a rift in United States-Pakistani relations?
2. Why is Pakistan supporting the Taliban?
3. What can the United States do to encourage more Pakistani cooperation in the war against the Taliban and Al Qaeda?

STEPHEN D. KRASNER is Professor of International Relations at Stanford University and a Senior Fellow at Stanford's Freeman Spogli Institute for International Studies and at the Hoover Institution. He was Director of Policy Planning at the United States State Department in 2005–07.

Leaving Afghanistan to the Afghans

A Commander's Take on Security

David M. Rodriguez

In the summer of 2011, I visited the Afghan army's Regional Military Training Center in Helmand Province. The recruits had been there for two weeks, and they looked as strong as any group of United States soldiers in basic training. The Afghan drill instructors were as competent, and had the same cocky swagger, as American ones. "Sir, look at all of our volunteers," one drill sergeant proudly said to me. "They're great. We have already won. . . . We just don't know it yet."

To comprehend the United States' progress in Afghanistan, it is important to understand how and where we have focused our resources and what work lies ahead. To be sure, the United States and its coalition partners still have plenty of challenges left to tackle in Afghanistan. However, there are indisputable gains everywhere we have focused our efforts.

In 2009, General Stanley McChrystal, then the commander of United States and International Security Assistance Force (ISAF) troops, with the help of David Petraeus, then the commander of the United States Central Command, worked hard to design a comprehensive counterinsurgency campaign for Afghanistan that would "get the inputs right," as Petraeus often said. The upshot was more resources, troops, and civilian support and better command coherence. There are now more Afghan and coalition soldiers in Helmand and Kandahar Provinces alone than there were in all of Regional Command East, the formation responsible for security in Afghanistan's 14 eastern provinces, when I commanded the latter from 2007 to 2008. As 33,000 United States troops begin the drawdown, returning to the United States by next summer, 352,000 Afghan soldiers and police will be in place to continue their work. There are clear signs of progress in Afghanistan, and coalition forces have regained the initiative.

The strategy has worked because it sought to match the coalition's goals with available resources. It involved four major concepts. First, use a bottom-up approach founded on good governance, capable security forces, and engagement with local communities. If towns had good leaders and security providers, populations would find local solutions to their local problems, with just a little help from Kabul. Insurgents could no longer exploit popular grievances about security, justice, and a lack of basic services.

Yet coalition troops did not have the resources to carry out a local, bottom-up approach everywhere simultaneously, hence the second principle: certain areas—population and commercial centers and major transportation routes—are more important to the effort than others. The coalition identified about one-third of the country's landmass and one-fourth of Afghanistan's districts as such key terrain. Since then, with much-expanded Afghan security forces, it has focused on securing those places. Meanwhile, the coalition's civilian counterparts have supported the strategy by concentrating their development programs in the key terrain that troops have cleared of insurgents.

Even in those areas, coalition forces could not let what they wanted to achieve distract them from what they needed to achieve. The third principle, then, was to do only what was required to meet the coalition's objectives. In the spring of 2011, I was traveling with General Shir Mohammed Karimi, chief of staff of the Afghan army. An Afghan soldier asked him when his unit was going to get more GPS devices. "Why do you ask me this?" Karimi responded. "We are a poor country! Get out your maps." He knew all too well that we should not try to build for Afghanistan the equivalent of the United Kingdom's security forces, or Germany's government, or try to achieve Poland's level of development. Afghanistan resides in a rough neighborhood, and the coalition must be realistic about its objectives. At a minimum, the security forces must keep Afghans safe enough to live basically normal lives. Of course, it is important to monitor trends of violent activity, but such data alone do not tell the whole story. On May 8, 2011, the day after several simultaneous attacks rocked Kandahar City, I traveled there with Bismillah Khan Mohammadi, Afghanistan's minister of the interior, to study the police response. It was apparent that the police had responded well, leaving the people feeling safe enough to resume their everyday lives almost immediately.

The fourth concept of the strategy was that the Taliban and their associates were not the Afghans' only enemy. Venal or incompetent officials alienate the population. Criminal patronage networks have thrived on poorly managed aid dollars. And some of the practices of the coalition forces, such as their early reliance on casualty-heavy air strikes and brutish warlords, created legitimate grievances among the population. Over the past year, the coalition has made preventing civilian causalities a top priority. Coalition troops are experts at the precise application of violence, and they are learning to let an insurgent live to fight another day if the collateral damage from killing him would outweigh the benefits. Casualties caused by the coalition decreased by 20 percent between 2009 and 2010 and were vastly outnumbered by those caused by insurgents.

If the combined Afghan and international civil-military team enabled good leaders, limited the freedom of action of criminal patronage networks, and reformed poor international practices, the insurgency would be much easier to deal with. As United States troops depart, and Afghans are handed control, these tasks will become even more important.

The Campaign

In 2009, the Taliban enjoyed nearly uncontested control over Afghanistan's southern Helmand and Kandahar Provinces. Drawing on the four principles, that year the coalition and its Afghan partners drafted a military campaign plan for Afghanistan called Operation Omid (*omid* means "hope" in Dari). The coalition hit the Taliban where it hurt, attacking their leaders and their control of territory and people. Soon, Afghan and coalition forces had pacified the central Helmand River valley, which bisects the province. The area around the valley is also rapidly being stabilized.

Next, Afghan and coalition forces drove the Taliban, who seemed unprepared for the forces' strength, out of key terrain in Kandahar Province: Kandahar City and its environs, other densely populated areas, and commercial routes between the two provinces. Meanwhile, troops also expanded the security zone around Kabul, in eastern Afghanistan, and continue to interdict insurgents on the border between Afghanistan and Pakistan. Parts of other central and eastern provinces—Khost, Laghman, Logar, Nangarhar, and Wardak—have also seen concrete gains in terms of stability.

In Afghanistan's north, insurgents have made headlines, assassinating General Mohammed Daud Daud, northern Afghanistan's chief of police, and General Abdul Rahman Sayedkhili, a provincial police chief. Both men were prominent Tajik leaders. But the region's key terrain—Mazar-e Sharif and the commercial route along the Baghlan-Kunduz corridor—remains secure.

Finally, in Afghanistan's west, Herat City is bustling and ready to initiate the transition to local control. The area has even become stable enough to begin construction on the road to link the western province of Badghis and the northern province of Faryab, which will connect Herat to Mazar-e Sharif.

Thanks to their successes, the Afghan security forces have garnered more popular support countrywide, cultivating people's desire to work with Afghan soldiers and police to defend themselves against the insurgency. As a result, the population is more willing to tip off Afghan and coalition troops about enemy activity. Polling in Helmand has indicated that the number of respondents who believe they are secure has risen fourfold since 2009. The increased scope and tempo of Afghan and coalition operations have helped. For example, by 2011, the combined forces were recovering four times as many weapons caches per week as they had been even the year before.

In other words, the coalition strategy has been a success, and it continues to create the conditions for expanded Afghan control over security. Insurgents face more effective Afghan security forces and a more widespread government presence. They seem to have recognized this change and shifted their strategy accordingly. Insurgents now target those things and individuals who threaten their control over the people: government officials, police stations, and elders of representative community councils. They attempt spectacular attacks, such as the recent one on the Intercontinental Hotel in Kabul, and frequently wear Afghan army or coalition uniforms, in the hopes of weakening the populations growing faith in Afghanistan's security forces. So far, they have failed.

The goal is for Afghan forces to assume lead responsibility for security by the end of 2014, and they are already on their way to meeting it. At the end of 2010, the army was almost 143,000 strong, surpassing that year's goal of 134,000 soldiers. The force has quickly become one of the country's most respected institutions, but before taking their hand off the back of the bicycle seat completely, coalition forces will still have to help the army develop better leadership, decrease its attrition rate and absences without leave, balance its tribal and ethnic representation, and improve its handling of logistics.

In 2011, 95 percent of all Afghan army units have been partnered with coalition forces, and they are showing steady improvement in providing security and in their ability to independently thwart insurgent attacks. This past year, the Afghan army doubled the number of operations it successfully led. It is gratifying to see the army taking responsibility and doing some things even better than coalition troops, such as avoiding civilian casualties. As one Canadian junior officer told me, "I never leave the forward operating base without my [Afghan] partner. If I do, I am blind, deaf, and dumb."

For many Afghans, the police are the most visible security providers and representatives of the government. By the end of 2010, the Afghan police force boasted nearly 120,000 officers, 11,000 more than its target. It is imperative that the police force continue to develop professionally. For a time, police recruiting and training focused on quantity rather than quality. Only recently has the proportion of adequately trained officers exceeded half. To remedy the force's shortcomings, the coalition has initiated programs to develop leadership qualities and improve literacy. The Afghan National Civil Order Police, Afghanistan's gendarmerie-like force, is the police force's most capable arm. Its recruitment is strong, and officer retention is improving. The force is in constant and effective use, but it should not be overburdened, lest attrition become a problem.

Meanwhile, better security has allowed civilians in the Afghan government to renew their own efforts. There are now significantly more trained civil servants in Afghanistan than there were two years ago. They have been deployed to key terrain districts that have been cleared, where they provide services to people who have never before had them. Informal representative community councils have emerged, taking the opinions, needs, and desires of the people to the local governments. Those people have begun to hold their local governments more accountable. I have witnessed courageous acts. I'll never forget one 2010 meeting of local officials in Helmand Province. A young man stood before one of the regions major power brokers and, pointing his finger in the man's direction, announced to the room, "This man does not represent me."

Indeed, there have also been notable signs of progress in governance at the district and provincial levels this past year, particularly in the Helmand River valley, which saw a hard-fought contest for control; in Kandahar City and surrounding districts; and in some cities in eastern Afghanistan. These improvements are largely the work of good government officials, professionals who are unencumbered by, or are assisted in, the task of exercising local control. Last year, hundreds of government officials were replaced at the subnational level, the vast majority because someone else was more qualified for the role, showing that the Afghan government recognizes the importance of good leadership and merit-based hiring. Kabul must now supply reliable funding to help these new government officials provide services to the people.

The example of Helmand Province is illustrative. Official assessments show that governance has improved there; almost all the critical civil servant positions there have been filled, which helps ensure that the government will keep providing basic services, including stepping in during disputes and when traditional justice mechanisms fail. This is critical. One of the things that the Taliban offered was a justice system, which, although brutal, was preferable to none.

The 2010 publication of the United States military's *Counterinsurgency (COIN) Contracting Guidance,* authored by Petraeus, was accompanied by new initiatives to make the coalition's assistance more transparent. One, Task Force 2010, focused on correcting the coalition's contracting problems. The other, Joint Task Force Shafafiyat (*shafafiyat* means "transparency" in Dari and Pashto), sought to address corruption. As a result of this guidance, coalition forces have been doing a much better job of channeling assistance and construction dollars into the right hands. All companies that compete for contracts worth more than $1 million are vetted, and large contracts are routinely broken down into smaller ones to ensure broader (and fairer) competition. Coalition contracts can also now be canceled without notice or penalty in the case of wrongdoing and generally include requirements to use local labor, structure salaries fairly, and teach the Afghans those skills that are in greatest demand. In general, the new strategy, bolstered by more resources, has proved to be successful wherever we have focused our efforts.

What's Next?

The coming reduction of United States troops in Afghanistan may mean that the coalition will have to find alternative ways to accomplish some of its lowest-priority objectives. But the logic of the campaign will not change. For now, Afghan and coalition troops will continue to concentrate on securing southern Afghanistan, with supporting efforts to expand security in other areas, such as into the northern Helmand River valley, Kandahar City, Kabul, Mazar-e Sharif, and Herat and along the Baghlan-Kunduz corridor and the "ring road." In fact, many of these areas are already quite secure, especially Kabul, which is home to one-fifth of Afghanistan's population.

As stability comes to these regions, Afghan and coalition forces will likely move the main effort eastward. There is a lot of work left to be done in the country's east, and Afghan forces, supported by the coalition, will have a tough fight ahead. It is unlikely that they will ever be able to completely deny insurgents a haven, kill all their leaders, or interdict all the routes they use to infiltrate the eastern provinces. Still, Afghanistan should be able to withstand those challenges and avoid falling into the hands of the Taliban or hosting foreign terrorists, and the United States' main interest in the region will thus be met.

In the end, Afghanistan will at least see its densely populated areas and commercial routes better connected. Improved governance will cement and accelerate the security gains and bolster the population's trust in the government's ability to provide for a better future. Short of a significant increase in terrorist activity emanating from Afghanistan's neighbors, I am confident that Afghan forces, supported by the coalition, can achieve irreversible gains and successfully secure Afghanistan's key terrain by the end of 2014.

Afghan leaders and soldiers will start to lead more operations, with the coalition providing only advisory or technical support. The Afghan security forces will be capable of fighting and managing the vast majority of the organizational, administrative, and logistical tasks related to counterinsurgency on their own. Of course, the United States will continue to assist them with intelligence support, air support, medical evacuation, and quick-reaction forces (which will be located increasingly further away) until their own programs develop. I expect that United States special operations forces will operate in Afghanistan for some time.

Meanwhile, the police will have to serve the population more effectively, in partnership with Afghanistan's own army. In major urban centers, this is already starting to take place. Afghans are fighters and bring to the security forces significant spirit and capability. Their partnership with coalition troops helps them build up their confidence to use the skills they already have and learn the ones they don't. With the drawdown approaching, the task will be to do all this faster.

To win the race against time, coalition forces will need to address four issues. First, they must figure out how to maximize partnerships with all levels of the Afghan government, so as to create a comprehensive political strategy. The coalition's and the Afghan government's public criticism of each other should stop; constructive talks based on mutual interests should be the coin of the realm. The coalition must be more understanding of the constraints and pressures on the Afghan political leadership, and both must hold each other accountable for actions that clearly run counter to shared interests.

Second, the United States must work with Pakistan to address the challenges that emanate from the Taliban's and other extremist groups' sanctuaries there. If the situation worsens in Pakistan's ungoverned spaces, the Afghan government will have to build even stronger security forces and local communities. It would take time to build them up to a point where they were resilient enough to handle an expanded threat from the other side of the border.

Third, there are several reasons to worry about ethnic tensions within the government and the security forces. Although all Afghan government and security institutions have prescriptions for the balance of ethnicities, better mechanisms are needed to enforce those rules. Stability in Afghanistan depends on the existence of sufficiently fair representation and a sense of ownership among all constituencies.

Finally, the dialogue between the United States and Afghanistan, and between NATO and Afghanistan, must advance. The West's immediate objectives can best be met if it offers Afghanistan and other states in the region predictability and assurances about its plans beyond 2014. The long-term strategic partnership must be defined in advance to minimize the relationship's volatility.

When I stepped down as commander of the ISAF Joint Command in July of this year, I was certain of having tried to make best possible use of the manpower and funding available. I know the American men and women in uniform and civilian personnel who remain in Afghanistan—and the United States' coalition partners—will continue to meet the goals of the mission. As a result, United States troops can begin to return home from Afghanistan knowing that they are drawing down from a position of strength.

We have proved that wherever Afghan and coalition forces focus their efforts, they make progress. And as we go forward, we must continue to be disciplined in allocating resources, staying true to our objectives, and combating all the enemies of the Afghan people. We must continue to support the Afghan security forces and the government, encouraging good leaders and inspiring others to join in helping create a positive future. If we maintain momentum, it is possible to achieve what we desire and what the people of Afghanistan deserve—a country

stable enough to ensure a future free of the threat of al Qaeda's return or an insurgent overthrow of the government.

In the future, new wars may emerge in other poorly governed and underdeveloped nations. It is imperative for the United States military to learn from its decade long engagement in Afghanistan, absorbing the lessons of the experience there to avoid having to relearn the same lessons again later. The army must be versatile enough to succeed in regular wars, irregular wars, and wars that combine aspects of both. Those forces that can adapt with the greatest speed will prevail. As a wealthy nation, the United States has tended to rely on technology and cutting-edge equipment to prepare for war. As Americans ponder what we have learned from Afghanistan, we would do well to heed another truism: equipment becomes obsolete, but leadership and people do not. Ultimately, the United States military will succeed by cultivating leaders who can think critically, be adaptable, and embrace uncertainty—just as it has done in Afghanistan.

Critical Thinking

1. What have been the major elements of U.S. counter-insurgency strategy in Afghanistan?

2. Is Rodriguez too optimistic about the ability of Afghan security forces to deal with the Taliban after the departure of the coalition forces? Why?

3. What should the U.S. strategy be after the withdrawal of U.S. forces in 2014?

DAVID M. RODRIGUEZ is Commander of the United States Army Forces Command. In 2009–11, he was Commander of the International Security Assistance Force Joint Command and Deputy Commander of United States Forces–Afghanistan.

Rodriguez, David M. From *Foreign Affairs*, vol. 90, no. 5, September/October 2011, pp. 45–53. Copyright © 2011 by Council on Foreign Relations, Inc. Reprinted by permission of Foreign Affairs. www.ForeignAffairs.com

World Peace Could Be Closer Than You Think

Joshua S. Goldstein

The World Is a More Violent Place Than It Used to Be—*No Way*

The early 21st century seems awash in wars: the conflicts in Afghanistan and Iraq, street battles in Somalia, Islamist insurgencies in Pakistan, massacres in the Congo, genocidal campaigns in Sudan. All in all, regular fighting is taking place in 18 wars around the globe today. Public opinion reflects this sense of an ever more dangerous world: One survey a few years ago found that 60 percent of Americans considered a third world war likely. Expectations for the new century were bleak even before the attacks of Sept. 11, 2001, and their bloody aftermath: Political scientist James G. Blight and former U.S. Defense Secretary Robert McNamara suggested earlier that year that we could look forward to an average of 3 million war deaths per year worldwide in the 21st century.

So far they haven't even been close. In fact, the last decade has seen fewer war deaths than any decade in the past 100 years, based on data compiled by researchers Bethany Lacina and Nils Petter Gleditsch of the Peace Research Institute Oslo. Worldwide, deaths caused directly by war-related violence in the new century have averaged about 55,000 per year, just over half of what they were in the 1990s (100,000 a year), a third of what they were during the Cold War (180,000 a year from 1950 to 1989), and a hundredth of what they were in World War II. If you factor in the growing global population, which has nearly quadrupled in the last century, the decrease is even sharper. Far from being an age of killer anarchy, the 20 years since the Cold War ended have been an era of rapid progress toward peace.

> **If the world feels like a more violent place than it actually is, that's because there's more information about wars—not more wars themselves.**

Armed conflict has declined in large part because armed conflict has fundamentally changed. Wars between big national

armies all but disappeared along with the Cold War, taking with them the most horrific kinds of mass destruction. Today's asymmetrical guerrilla wars may be intractable and nasty, but they will never produce anything like the siege of Leningrad. The last conflict between two great powers, the Korean War, effectively ended nearly 60 years ago. The last sustained territorial war between two regular armies, Ethiopia and Eritrea, ended a decade ago. Even civil wars, though a persistent evil, are less common than in the past; there were about a quarter fewer in 2007 than in 1990.

If the world feels like a more violent place than it actually is, that's because there's more information about wars—not more wars themselves. Once-remote battles and war crimes now regularly make it onto our TV and computer screens, and in more or less real time. Cell-phone cameras have turned citizens into reporters in many war zones. Societal norms about what to make of this information have also changed. As Harvard University psychologist Steven Pinker has noted, "The decline of violent behavior has been paralleled by a decline in attitudes that tolerate or glorify violence," so that we see today's atrocities—though mild by historical standards—as "signs of how low our behavior can sink, not of how high our standards have risen."

America Is Fighting More Wars Than Ever—*Yes and No*

Clearly, the United States has been on a war footing ever since 9/11, with a still-ongoing war in Afghanistan that has surpassed the Vietnam War as the longest conflict in American history and a pre-emptive war in Iraq that proved to be longer, bloodier, and more expensive than anyone expected. Add the current NATO intervention in Libya and drone campaigns in Pakistan, Somalia, and Yemen, and it's no wonder that U.S. military spending has grown more than 80 percent in real terms over the last decade. At $675 billion this year, it's now 30 percent higher than what it was at the end of the Cold War.

But though the conflicts of the post-9/11 era may be longer than those of past generations, they are also far smaller and less lethal. America's decade of war since 2001 has killed about 6,000 U.S. service members, compared with 58,000 in Vietnam and 300,000 in World War II. Every life lost to war is one too many, but these deaths have to be seen in context: Last year more Americans died from falling out of bed than in all U.S. wars combined.

And the fighting in Iraq and Afghanistan has taken place against a backdrop of base closures and personnel drawdowns elsewhere in the world. The temporary rise in U.S. troop numbers in South Asia and the Middle East, from 18,000 to 212,000 since 2000, contrasts with the permanent withdrawal of almost 40,000 troops from Europe, 34,000 from Japan and South Korea, and 10,000 from Latin America in that period. When U.S. forces come home from the current wars—and they will in large numbers in the near future, starting with 40,000 troops from Iraq and 33,000 from Afghanistan by 2012—there will be fewer U.S. troops deployed around the world than at any time since the 1930s. President Barack Obama was telling the truth in June when he said, "The tide of war is receding."

War Has Gotten More Brutal for Civilians—*Hardly*

In February 2010, a NATO airstrike hit a house in Afghanistan's Marja district, killing at least nine civilians inside. The tragedy drew condemnation and made the news, leading the top NATO commander in the country to apologize to Afghan President Hamid Karzai. The response underscored just how much has changed in war. During World War II, Allied bombers killed hundreds of thousands of civilians in Dresden and Tokyo not by accident, but as a matter of tactics; Germany, of course, murdered civilians by the millions. And when today's civilians do end up in harm's way, more people are looking out for them. The humanitarian dollars spent per displaced person rose in real terms from $150 in the early 1990s to $300 in 2006. Total international humanitarian assistance has grown from $2 billion in 1990 to $6 billion in 2000 and (according to donor countries' claims) $18 billion in 2008. For those caught in the crossfire, war has actually gotten more humane.

Yet many people insist that the situation is otherwise. For example, authoritative works on peacekeeping in civil wars (Roland Paris's award-winning *At War's End* and Michael Doyle and Nicholas Sambanis's *Making War and Building Peace*), as well as gold-standard reports on conflict from the World Bank and the Carnegie Commission on Preventing Deadly Conflict, tell us that 90 percent of today's war deaths are civilian while just 10 percent are military—the reverse of a century ago and "a grim indicator of the transformation of armed conflict" in the late 20th century, as political scientist Kalevi Holsti put it.

Grim indeed—but, fortunately, untrue. The myth originates with the 1994 U.N. Human Development Report, which misread work that Swedish researcher Christer Ahlström had done in 1991 and accidentally conflated war fatalities in the early

20th century with the much larger number of dead, wounded, and displaced people in the late 20th century. A more careful analysis done in 1989 by peace researcher William Eckhardt shows that the ratio of military to civilian war deaths remains about 50–50, as it has for centuries (though it varies considerably from one war to the next). If you are unlucky enough to be a civilian in a war zone, of course, these statistics are little comfort. But on a worldwide scale, we are making progress in helping civilians afflicted by war.

Wars Will Get Worse in the Future—*Probably Not*

Anything is possible, of course: A full-blown war between India and Pakistan, for instance, could potentially kill millions of people. But so could an asteroid or—perhaps the safest bet—massive storms triggered by climate change. The big forces that push civilization in the direction of cataclysmic conflict, however, are mostly ebbing.

Recent technological changes are making war less brutal, not more so. Armed drones now attack targets that in the past would have required an invasion with thousands of heavily armed troops, displacing huge numbers of civilians and destroying valuable property along the way. And improvements in battlefield medicine have made combat less lethal for participants. In the U.S. Army, the chances of dying from a combat injury fell from 30 percent in World War II to 10 percent in Iraq and Afghanistan—though this also means the United States is now seeing a higher proportion of injured veterans who need continuing support and care.

Nor do shifts in the global balance of power doom us to a future of perpetual war. While some political scientists argue that an increasingly multipolar world is an increasingly volatile one—that peace is best assured by the predominance of a single hegemonic power, namely the United States—recent geopolitical history suggests otherwise. Relative U.S. power and worldwide conflict have waned in tandem over the past decade. The exceptions to the trend, Iraq and Afghanistan, have been lopsided wars waged by the hegemon, not challenges by up-and-coming new powers. The best precedent for today's emerging world order may be the 19th-century Concert of Europe, a collaboration of great powers that largely maintained the peace for a century until its breakdown and the bloodbath of World War I.

What about China, the most ballyhooed rising military threat of the current era? Beijing is indeed modernizing its armed forces, racking up double-digit rates of growth in military spending, now about $100 billion a year. That is second only to the United States, but it is a distant second: The Pentagon spends nearly $700 billion. Not only is China a very long way from being able to go toe-to-toe with the United States; it's not clear why it would want to. A military conflict (particularly with its biggest customer and debtor) would impede China's global trading posture and endanger its prosperity. Since Chairman Mao's death, China has been hands down the most peaceful great power of its time. For all the recent concern about a newly assertive Chinese navy in disputed international waters, China's military hasn't fired a single shot in battle in 25 years.

A More Democratic World Will Be a More Peaceful One—*Not Necessarily*

The well-worn observation that real democracies almost never fight each other is historically correct, but it's also true that democracies have always been perfectly willing to fight non-democracies. In fact, democracy can heighten conflict by amplifying ethnic and nationalist forces, pushing leaders to appease belligerent sentiment in order to stay in power. Thomas Paine and Immanuel Kant both believed that selfish autocrats caused wars, whereas the common people, who bear the costs, would be loath to fight. But try telling that to the leaders of authoritarian China, who are struggling to hold in check, not inflame, a popular undercurrent of nationalism against Japanese and American historical enemies. Public opinion in tentatively democratic Egypt is far more hostile toward Israel than the authoritarian government of Hosni Mubarak ever was (though being hostile and actually going to war are quite different things).

Why then do democracies limit their wars to non-democracies rather than fight each other? Nobody really knows. As the University of Chicago's Charles Lipson once quipped about the notion of a democratic peace, "We know it works in practice. Now we have to see if it works in theory!" The best explanation is that of political scientists Bruce Russett and John Oneal, who argue that three elements—democracy, economic interdependence (especially trade), and the growth of international organizations—are mutually supportive of each other and of peace within the community of democratic countries. Democratic leaders, then, see themselves as having less to lose in going to war with autocracies.

Peacekeeping Doesn't Work—*It Does Now*

The early 1990s were boom years for the blue helmets, with 15 new U.N. peacekeeping missions launched from 1991 to 1993—as many as in the U.N.'s entire history up to that point. The period was also host to peacekeeping's most spectacular failures. In Somalia, the U.N. arrived on a mission to alleviate starvation only to become embroiled in a civil war, and it quickly pulled out after 18 American soldiers died in a 1993 raid. In Rwanda in 1994, a weak U.N. force with no support from the Security Council completely failed to stop a genocide that killed more than half a million people. In Bosnia, the U.N. declared "safe areas" for civilians, but then stood by when Serbian forces overran one such area, Srebrenica, and executed more than 7,000 men and boys. (There were peacekeeping successes, too, such as in Namibia and Mozambique, but people tend to forget about them.)

In response, the United Nations commissioned a report in 2000, overseen by veteran diplomat Lakhdar Brahimi, examining how the organization's efforts had gone wrong. By then the U.N. had scaled back peacekeeping personnel by 80 percent worldwide, but as it expanded again the U.N. adapted to lessons learned. It strengthened planning and logistics capabilities and began deploying more heavily armed forces able to wade into battle if necessary. As a result, the 15 missions and 100,000 U.N. peacekeepers deployed worldwide today are meeting with far greater success than their predecessors.

> **Overall, the presence of peacekeepers has been shown to significantly reduce the likelihood of a war's reigniting after a cease-fire agreement.**

Overall, the presence of peacekeepers has been shown to significantly reduce the likelihood of a war's reigniting after a cease-fire agreement. In the 1990s, about half of all cease-fires broke down, but in the past decade the figure has dropped to 12 percent. And though the U.N.'s status as a perennial punching bag in American politics suggests otherwise, these efforts are quite popular: In a 2007 survey, 79 percent of Americans favored strengthening the U.N. That's not to say there isn't room for improvement—there's plenty. But the U.N. has done a lot of good around the world in containing war.

Some Conflicts Will Never End—*Never Say Never*

In 2005, researchers at the U.S. Institute of Peace characterized 14 wars, from Northern Ireland to Kashmir, as "intractable," in that they "resist any kind of settlement or resolution." Six years later, however, a funny thing has happened: All but a few of these wars (Israel-Palestine, Somalia, and Sudan) have either ended or made substantial progress toward doing so. In Sri Lanka, military victory ended the war, though only after a brutal endgame in which both sides are widely believed to have committed war crimes. Kashmir has a fairly stable cease-fire. In Colombia, the war sputters on, financed by drug revenue, but with little fighting left. In the Balkans and Northern Ireland, shaky peace arrangements have become less shaky; it's hard to imagine either sliding back into full-scale hostilities. In most of the African cases—Burundi, Rwanda, Sierra Leone, Uganda, the Democratic Republic of the Congo, and Ivory Coast (notwithstanding the violent flare-up after elections there in late 2010, now resolved)—U.N. missions have brought stability and made a return to war less likely (or, in the case of Congo and Uganda, have at least limited the area of fighting).

Could we do even better? The late peace researcher Randall Forsberg in 1997 foresaw "a world largely without war," one in which "the vanishing risk of great-power war has opened the door to a previously unimaginable future—a future in which war is no longer socially-sanctioned and is rare, brief, and small in scale." Clearly, we are not there yet. But over the decades—and indeed, even since Forsberg wrote those words—norms about wars, and especially about the protection of civilians caught up in them, have evolved rapidly, far more so than anyone would have guessed even half a century ago. Similarly rapid shifts in norms preceded the ends of slavery and colonialism, two other scourges that were once also considered permanent features of civilization. So don't be surprised if the end of war, too, becomes downright thinkable.

Critical Thinking

1. Is America fighting more wars than ever?
2. Have wars gotten more brutal for civilians?
3. Will a more democratic world be a more peaceful one?

JOSHUA S. GOLDSTEIN is professor emeritus of international relations at American University and author of *Winning the War on War: The Decline of Armed Conflict Worldwide*.

Goldstein, Joshua S. Reprinted in entirety by McGraw-Hill with permission from *Foreign Policy*, September/October 2011, pp. 53–56. www.foreignpolicy.com. © 2011 Washingtonpost.Newsweek Interactive, LLC.

Arms Trade Treaty Talks Set to Begin

Farrah Zughni

Delegates gathering at the United Nations this month to negotiate a treaty regulating the international arms trade will have to resolve a number of issues concerning the pact's objectives and scope that remain unsettled since the UN General Assembly decided in 2009 to convene the conference, representatives from a broad range of countries said in June interviews and earlier statements.

The negotiations, which are scheduled to run July 2–27, are supposed to produce a global arms trade treaty (ATT) to set common standards for international transfers of conventional weapons and requirements for all states-parties to set up national control systems to regulate such transfers.

The countries will aim to reach consensus on a final treaty text largely on the basis of a working paper produced by Ambassador Roberto García Moritán of Argentina, the chair of the preparatory committee, after three years and four preparatory committee sessions involving states that supply and buy conventional arms. (**See *ACT*, January/February 2012.**)

Although García Moritán's text from July 2011 "has no formal status," it "does represent a range of issues" that have been raised since 2010, said Jo Adamson, British permanent representative to the Conference on Disarmament, in a June 20 e-mail to *Arms Control Today*. Therefore, "we aren't starting from scratch," said Adamson, who is the United Kingdom's lead ATT negotiator. "We look forward to receiving a revised paper in due course to help to guide us through this next critical stage of the negotiations," she said.

To succeed, the negotiators will need to balance a number of competing forces and political demands. Many weapons suppliers envision an ATT that will affirm trade in conventional weapons as "a legitimate commercial activity," albeit "one that states have the obligation to regulate," as Assistant Secretary of State for International Security and Nonproliferation Thomas Countryman put it in describing United States policy on the treaty in an April interview with *Arms Control Today*.

Many countries want to ensure the treaty augments their security and does not infringe on their ability to procure weapons for their defense. "The ATT should be an instrument which enhances the collective security of states, rather than detracting from it. In this respect, a mainstay of the ATT must be to uphold the right of states to acquire arms in order to defend themselves," said an Israeli delegate Feb. 13 during the final preparatory committee.

Many other states, however, argue that an ATT must provide meaningful protections against illicit arms transfers that undermine human security (the security of individuals and communities) as well as human rights.

"It is often argued that national security interests need to be duly taken into account in the negotiation of the Treaty. However, from the Austrian perspective, human security is of equal importance and must appropriately resonate in the Treaty," Alexander Kmentt, director for disarmament, arms control, and nonproliferation in the Austrian Federal Ministry for European and International Affairs, said in a June 21 e-mail to *Arms Control Today*.

An ATT, argued Kmentt, should prevent the illicit trade of arms, diversion of legal arms to the illicit market, and transfers "that contribute to serious violations of international human rights law and international humanitarian law, human suffering, armed conflict, transnational organized crime and terrorist acts."

According to a report published in May by Oxfam, more than $2.2 billion worth of arms and ammunition have been imported since 2000 by countries operating under 26 UN, regional, or multilateral arms embargoes in force during this period.

Treaty Scope

To date, states have not reached agreement on a list of arms and activities that should be covered by an ATT. Most states agree that all of the weapons covered by the categories used in the UN Register of Conventional Arms should fall under the scope of the treaty. These include tanks, armored combat vehicles, artillery, combat aircraft and helicopters, warships, and missile systems. Most states, including the United States, are also in agreement that small arms and light weapons should be included in the treaty. The United States does not currently support the inclusion of ammunition within the scope, although many states do.

Some proponents of a more comprehensive treaty have pushed for clear definitions for the categories of weapons that most member states agree should be covered by the pact. Some also have suggested that specific weapons be listed in an ATT. Others point out that a detailed list of weapons would require that an ATT be regularly updated and refined to remain abreast of technological developments and that the time it would take to agree on specific definitions for that process could encumber the four-week-long negotiating conference.

"This is an arms trade regulation document, not a disarmament document, so there is no need for an extensive framework or extensive definitions to make it work," Countryman said in an address at the Henry L. Stimson Center on April 16. "The outcome of the conference ought to be a good, short document that spells out principles of what states must do in implementing an effective [system of] arms export control."

According to a tabulation by researchers with the nongovernmental organizations Control Arms Alliance and Reaching Critical Will, all but a handful of the more than 140 countries that have made statements on the issue support expanding the treaty's scope beyond the UN register's seven categories to include small arms and light weapons, such as revolvers, machine guns, portable anti-tank guns, portable anti-tank missile launchers and rocket systems, and mortars of calibers less than 75 millimeters.

"Many African countries have suffered from conflicts perpetuated by illicit trade and proliferation on small arms and light weapons," Patrick Mugoya of Uganda said at the second preparatory committee session on March 1, 2011. "These conflicts result in loss of lives, cause untold suffering to the people, and negatively impact economic and social development."

According to the UN Office for Disarmament Affairs, most present-day conflicts are fought predominantly with this category of weapons.

Only a few countries, including China, Egypt, and Iran, have voiced reservations over the so-called 7 + 1 proposal because they say that it would be difficult to monitor trade in small arms and light weapons. A number of other states, however, have said the absence of this category of arms from the final agreement is a deal breaker.

"Small arms and light weapons will have to be in the treaty. If not, there won't be a treaty," said a delegate from a Latin American country in a June 13 interview.

A 7 + 1 + 1 formula, which would include ammunition in the treaty's scope, is also on the table for the negotiating conference. More than 100 countries strongly support the measure, according to the nongovernmental groups' tabulation.

"It is the bullet and not the weapon that kills. Marking of ammunition is technically feasible and should not serve as an excuse for exempting ammunition on allegedly practical grounds," argued Kmentt. "Given the robustness and longevity of certain types of these weapons, a continuation of unregulated trade in ammunition would further their use as the real 'weapons of mass destruction' in contradiction of the objectives of an Arms Trade Treaty."

Nevertheless, major suppliers Russia and the United States have expressed doubt that ammunition can be adequately tracked following their sale. United States officials have said that they are open to suggestions on how to address this concern.

The United Kingdom, which for years has been a strong supporter of an ATT, has worked to forge a middle ground on this issue. "On ammunition, the UK favours its inclusion in the ATT as the weapons are useless without it," said Adamson in the June 20 e-mail. "But we recognise that this is going to be a subject of negotiations. Monitoring ammunition is a difficult issue. Making ammunition subject to controls would be an important first step, without prejudice to whether it is covered in detail in Reporting under an ATT."

In addition to the criteria that should be addressed in considering a transfer, the types of transfers to be regulated are also in question. UN General Assembly Resolution 64/48, which was adopted in December 2009 and mandated the ATT negotiation this month, calls for "a legally binding instrument on the highest possible common international standards for the transfer of conventional arms." A key point of controversy in the run-up to the July meeting is what the term "transfer" encompasses.

Most delegations have argued that an ATT should cover arms brokering. The United Kingdom, for instance, says transit and transshipment, loans, and gifts as well as temporary imports and exports for demonstration and exhibition should be included under the treaty's scope. Of the world's 192 governments, only 52 have laws regulating arms brokers, and less than half of these have criminal or monetary penalties associated with illegal brokering, according to an October 2011 Oxfam briefing paper.

"These are the main types of activity where diversion into the illicit market can occur. Controlling these forms of entry into the illicit market ensures that the treaty regulates the entire arms trade process without leaving any gaps which can be exploited," Adamson said.

In the run-up to the negotiating conference, China and Iran have expressed objections to this proposal.

Criteria for Transfers

A key question in the negotiations will be whether the treaty will require states to withhold a transfer if their export control review determines there is a substantial risk that it could lead to human rights violations or whether an ATT will simply require states to "take into account" such potential risks but still allow a transfer authorization to proceed if the supplier state determines that, on balance, larger economic or security concerns merit the transfer.

Some countries favor strong language that would require states not to authorize transfers that would lead to human rights or humanitarian law violations or could circumvent internationally recognized arms embargoes.

"The ATT should establish clear, objective and nondiscriminatory norms to prevent the transfer of arms when there is a clear and reasonable ground to believe that such weapons will be used in violation of international human rights law or international humanitarian law," said delegations from nine countries, including Argentina, Chile, and Colombia, in a joint statement on July 21, 2010. Some countries also want potential sales to be considered in light of their impact on a recipient country's socioeconomic development and corruption.

Critics of this position argue that implementing such criteria is neither an objective nor straightforward process. "There are ranges of what people think are human rights," Ann Ganzer, director of the United States Department of State's Office of Conventional Arms Threat Reduction, said at the April 16 Stimson Center event. "I attended a meeting a day after someone was executed in Texas and had several Europeans accuse me of representing a country that was a human rights violator," she recalled.

Critical Thinking

1. What is the purpose of an ATT (Arms Trade Agreement)?
2. Why has it been so difficult for the international community to reach an agreement on an ATT?
3. How is it possible for private arms dealers to engage in the arms trade?

Zugni, Farrah. From *Arms Control Today*, July/August 2012, pp. 35–37. Copyright © 2012 by Arms Control Association. Reprinted by permission.

The Obama Doctrine

How the President's Secret Wars Are Backfiring

DAVID ROHDE

When Barack Obama took the oath of office three years ago, no one associated the phrase "targeted killing" with his optimistic young presidency. In his inaugural address, the 47-year-old former constitutional law professor uttered the word "terror" only once. Instead, he promised to use technology to "harness the sun and the winds and the soil to fuel our cars and run our factories."

Oddly, technology has enabled Obama to become something few expected: a president who has dramatically expanded the executive branch's ability to wage high-tech clandestine war. With a determination that has surprised many, Obama has embraced the CIA, expanded its powers, and approved more targeted killings than any modern president. Over the last three years, the Obama administration has carried out at least 239 covert drone strikes, more than five times the 44 approved under George W. Bush. And after promising to make counterterrorism operations more transparent and rein in executive power, Obama has arguably done the opposite, maintaining secrecy and expanding presidential authority.

Just as importantly, the administration's excessive use of drone attacks undercuts one of its most laudable policies: a promising new post-9/11 approach to the use of lethal American force, one of multilateralism, transparency, and narrow focus.

Obama's willingness to deploy lethal force should have come as no surprise. In a 2002 speech, Illinois state senator Obama opposed Bush's impending invasion of Iraq, but not all conflicts. "I don't oppose all wars," he said. "What I am opposed to is a dumb war." And as president, in his December 2009 Nobel Peace Prize acceptance speech, Obama warned, "There will be times when nations—acting individually or in concert—will find the use of force not only necessary but morally justified." Since then, he has not only sent United States forces into Afghanistan, Iraq, and Libya, but also repeatedly approved commando raids in Pakistan and Somalia and on the high seas, while presiding over a system that unleashed hundreds of drone strikes.

In a series of recent interviews, current and former administration officials outlined what could be called an "Obama doctrine" on the use of force. Obama's embrace of multilateralism, drone strikes, and a light United States military presence in Libya, Pakistan, and Yemen, they contend, has proved more effective than Bush's go-heavy approach in Iraq and Afghanistan. "We will use force unilaterally if necessary against direct threats to the United States," Ben Rhodes, the administration's deputy national security advisor for strategic communications, told me. "And we'll use force in a very precise way."

Crises the administration deems indirect threats to the United States—such as the uprisings in Libya and Syria—are "threats to global security," Rhodes argued, and will be responded to multilaterally and not necessarily by force. The drawdown of United States troops in Iraq and Afghanistan, as well as the creation of a smaller, more agile United States military spread across Asia, the Pacific, and the Middle East, are also part of the doctrine. So is the discreet backing of protesters in Egypt, Iran, and Syria.

The emerging strategy—which Rhodes touted as "a far more focused approach to our adversaries"—is a welcome shift from the martial policies and bellicose rhetoric of both the Bush administration and today's Republican presidential candidates. But Obama has granted the CIA far too much leeway in carrying out drone strikes in Pakistan and Yemen. In both countries, the strikes often appear to be backfiring.

Obama and other administration officials insist the drones are used rarely and kill few civilians. In a rare public comment on the program, the president defended the strikes in late January. "I want to make sure the people understand, actually, drones have not caused a huge number of civilian casualties," Obama said. "For the most part, they have been very precise precision strikes against al Qaeda and their affiliates. And we are very careful in terms of how it's been applied."

But from Pakistan to Yemen to post-American Iraq, drones often spark deep resentment where they operate. When they do attack, they kill as brutally as any weapon of war. The administration's practice of classifying the strikes as secret only exacerbates local anger and suspicion. Under

Obama, drone strikes have become too frequent, too unilateral, and too much associated with the heavy-handed use of American power.

In 2008, I saw this firsthand. Two Afghan colleagues and I were kidnapped by the Taliban and held captive in the tribal areas of Pakistan for seven months. From the ground, drones are terrifying weapons that can be heard circling overhead for hours at a time. They are a potent, unnerving symbol of unchecked American power. At the same time, they were clearly effective, killing foreign bomb-makers and preventing Taliban fighters from gathering in large groups. The experience left me convinced that drone strikes should be carried out—but very selectively.

In the January interview, Obama insisted drone strikes were used only surgically. "It is important for everybody to understand," he said, "that this thing is kept on a very tight leash."

Drones, though, are in no way surgical.

I n interviews, current and former Obama administration officials told me the president and his senior aides had been eager from the outset to differentiate their approach in Pakistan and Afghanistan from Bush's. Unlike in Iraq, where Democrats thought the Bush administration had been too aggressive, they thought the Bush White House had not been assertive enough with Afghan and Pakistani leaders. So the new administration adopted a unilateral, get-tough approach in South Asia that would eventually spread elsewhere. As candidate Obama vowed in a 2007 speech, referring to Pakistan's president at the time, "If we have actionable intelligence about high-value terrorist targets and President Musharraf won't act, we will."

In his first year in office, Obama approved two large troop surges in Afghanistan and a vast expansion of the number of CIA operatives in Pakistan. The CIA was also given more leeway in carrying out drone strikes in the country's ungoverned tribal areas, where foreign and local militants plot attacks for Afghanistan, Pakistan, and beyond.

The decision reflected both Obama's belief in the need to move aggressively in Pakistan and the influence of the CIA in the new administration. To a far greater extent than the Bush White House, Obama and his top aides relied on the CIA for its analysis of Pakistan, according to current and former senior administration officials. As a result, preserving the agency's ability to carry out counterterrorism, or "CT," operations in Pakistan became of paramount importance.

"The most important thing when it came to Pakistan was to be able to carry out drone strikes and nothing else," said a former official who spoke on condition of anonymity. "The so-called strategic focus of the bilateral relationship was there solely to serve the CT approach."

Initially, the CIA was right. Increased drone strikes in the tribal areas eliminated senior al Qaeda operatives in 2009. Then, in July 2010, Pakistanis working for the CIA pulled up behind a white Suzuki navigating the bustling streets of Peshawar. The car's driver was later tracked to a large compound in the city of Abbottabad. On May 2, 2011, United States commandos killed Osama bin Laden there.

The United States intelligence presence, though, extended far beyond the hunt for bin Laden, according to former administration officials. At one point, the CIA tried to deploy hundreds of operatives across Pakistan but backed off after suspicious Pakistani officials declined to issue them visas. At the same time, the agency aggressively used the freer hand Obama had given it to launch more drone strikes than ever before.

Established by the Bush administration and Musharraf in 2004, the covert CIA drone program initially carried out only "personality" strikes against a preapproved list of senior al Qaeda members. Pakistani officials were notified before many, but not all, attacks. Between 2004 and 2007, nine such attacks were carried out in Pakistan, according to the New America Foundation.

In 2008, the Bush administration authorized less-restrictive "signature" strikes in the tribal areas. Instead of basing attacks on intelligence regarding a specific person, CIA drone operators could carry out strikes based on the behavior of people on the ground. Operators could launch a drone strike if they saw a group, for example, crossing back and forth over the Afghanistan-Pakistan border. In 2008, the Bush administration carried out 33 strikes.

Under Obama, the drone campaign has escalated rapidly. The number of strikes nearly doubled to 53 in 2009 and then doubled again to 118 in 2010. Former administration officials said the looser rules resulted in the killing of more civilians. Current administration officials insisted that Obama, in fact, tightened the rules on the use of drone strikes after taking office. They said strikes rose under Obama because improved technology and intelligence gathering created more opportunities for attacks than existed under Bush.

But as Pakistani public anger over the spiraling strikes grew, other diplomats expressed concern as well. The United States ambassador in Pakistan at the time, Anne Patterson, opposed several attacks, but the CIA ignored her objections. When Cameron Munter replaced Patterson in October 2010, he objected even more vigorously. On at least two occasions, CIA Director Leon Panetta dismissed Munter's protests and launched strikes, the *Wall Street Journal* later reported. One strike occurred only hours after Sen. John Kerry, head of the Senate Foreign Relations Committee, had completed a visit to Islamabad.

A March 2011 strike brought the debate to the White House. A day after Pakistani officials agreed to release CIA contractor Raymond Davis, the agency—again over Munter's objections—carried out a signature drone strike that the Pakistanis say killed four Taliban fighters and 38 civilians. Already angry about the Davis case, Pakistan's Army chief, Gen. Ashfaq Parvez Kayani, issued an unusual public statement, saying a group of tribal elders had been "carelessly and callously targeted with complete disregard to human life." United States intelligence officials dismissed the Pakistani complaints and insisted 20 militants had perished. "There's every indication that this was a group of terrorists, not a charity car wash in the Pakistani hinterlands," one official told the Associated Press.

Surprised by the vehemence of the official Pakistani reaction, national security advisor Tom Donilon questioned whether signature strikes were worthwhile. Critics inside and outside the United States government contended that a program that began as a carefully focused effort to kill senior al Qaeda leaders had morphed into a bombing campaign against low-level Taliban fighters. Some outside analysts even argued that the administration had adopted a de facto "kill not capture" policy, given its inability to close Bush's Guantánamo Bay prison and create a new detention system.

In April 2011, the director of Pakistan's intelligence service, Lt. Gen. Ahmed Shuja Pasha, visited Washington in an effort to repair the relationship, according to news accounts and former administration officials. Just after his visit, two more drone strikes occurred in the tribal areas, which Pasha took as a personal affront. In a rare concession, Panetta agreed to notify Pakistan's intelligence service before the United States carried out any strike that could kill more than 20 people.

In May, after the bin Laden raid sparked further anger among Pakistani officials, Donilon launched an internal review of how drone strikes were approved, according to a former administration official. But the strikes continued. At the end of May, State Department officials were angered when three missile strikes followed Secretary of State Hillary Clinton's visit to Pakistan.

As Donilon's review progressed, an intense debate erupted inside the administration over the signature strikes, according to the *Journal*. Adm. Mike Mullen, then chairman of the Joint Chiefs of Staff, said the strikes should be more selective. Robert Gates, then the defense secretary, warned that angry Pakistani officials could cut off supplies to United States troops in Afghanistan. Clinton warned that too many civilian casualties could strengthen opposition to Pakistan's weak, pro-American president, Asif Ali Zardari.

The CIA countered that Taliban fighters were legitimate targets because they carried out cross-border attacks on United States forces, according to the former official. In June, Obama sided with the CIA. Panetta conceded that no drone strike would be carried out when Pakistani officials visited Washington and that Clinton and Munter could object to proposed strikes. But Obama allowed the CIA director to retain final say.

Last November, the worst-case scenario that Mullen, Gates, and Clinton had warned of came to pass. After NATO airstrikes mistakenly killed 24 Pakistani soldiers on the Afghanistan-Pakistan border, Kayani demanded an end to all United States drone strikes and blocked supplies to United States troops in Afghanistan. At the same time, popular

opposition to Zardari soared. After a nearly two-month lull that allowed militants to regroup, drone strikes resumed in the tribal areas this past January. But signature strikes are no longer allowed—for the time being, according to the former senior official.

Among average Pakistanis, the strikes played out disastrously. In a 2011 Pew Research Center poll, 97 percent of Pakistani respondents who knew about the attacks said American drone strikes were a "bad thing." Seventy-three percent of Pakistanis had an unfavorable view of the United States, a 10 percentage point rise from 2008. Administration officials say the strikes are popular with Pakistanis who live in the tribal areas and have tired of brutal jihadi rule. And they contend that Pakistani government officials—while publicly criticizing the attacks—agree in private that they help combat militancy. Making the strikes more transparent could reduce public anger in other parts of Pakistan, United States officials concede. But they say some elements of the Pakistani government continue to request that the strikes remain covert.

For me, the bottom line is that both governments' approaches are failing. Pakistan's economy is dismal. Its military continues to shelter Taliban fighters it sees as proxies to thwart Indian encroachment in Afghanistan. And the percentage of Pakistanis supporting the use of the Pakistani Army to fight extremists in the tribal areas—the key to eradicating militancy—dropped from a 53 percent majority in 2009 to 37 percent last year. Pakistan is more unstable today than it was when Obama took office.

A similar dynamic is creating even worse results on the southern tip of the Arabian Peninsula. Long ignored by the United States, Yemen drew sudden attention after a suicide attack on the USS Cole killed 17 American sailors in the port of Aden in 2000. In 2002, the Bush administration carried out a single drone strike in Yemen that killed Abu Ali al-Harithi, an al Qaeda operative who was a key figure in orchestrating the Cole attack. In the years that followed, the administration shifted its attentions to Iraq, and militants began to regroup.

A failed December 2009 attempt by a militant trained in Yemen to detonate a bomb on a Detroit-bound airliner focused Obama's attention on the country. Over the next two years, the United States carried out an estimated 20 airstrikes in Yemen, most in 2011. In addition to killing al Qaeda-linked militants, the strikes killed dozens of civilians, according to Yemenis. Instead of decimating the organization, the Obama strikes have increased the ranks of al Qaeda in the Arabian Peninsula from 300 fighters in 2009 to more than 1,000 today, according to Gregory Johnsen, a leading Yemen expert at Princeton University. In January, the group briefly seized control of Radda, a town only 100 miles from the capital, Sanaa. "I don't believe that the United States has a Yemen policy," Johnsen told me. "What the United States has is a counterterrorism strategy that it applies to Yemen."

The deaths of bin Laden and many of his lieutenants are a step forward, but Pakistan and Yemen are increasingly unstable. Pakistan is a nuclear-armed country of 180 million with resilient militant networks; Yemen, an impoverished, failing state that is fast becoming a new al Qaeda stronghold. "They think they've won because of this approach," the former administration official said, referring to the administration's drone-heavy strategy. "A lot of us think there is going to be a lot bigger problems in the future."

The backlash from drone strikes in the countries where they are happening is not the only worry. In the United States, civil liberties and human rights groups are increasingly concerned with the breadth of powers Obama has claimed for the executive branch as he wages a new kind of war.

In the Libya conflict, the administration invoked the drones to create a new legal precedent. Under the War Powers Resolution, the president must receive congressional authorization for military operations within 60 days. When the deadline approached in May, the administration announced that because NATO strikes and drones were carrying out the bulk of the missions, no serious threat of United States casualties existed and no congressional authorization was needed. "It's changed the way politicians talk about what should be the most important thing that a nation engages in," said Peter W. Singer, a Brookings Institution researcher. "It's changed the way we in the public deliberate war."

Last fall, a series of drone strikes in Yemen set another dangerous precedent, according to civil liberties and human rights groups. Without any public legal proceeding, the United States government executed three of its own citizens. On Sept. 30, a drone strike killed Anwar al-Awlaki, a charismatic American-born cleric of Yemeni descent credited with inspiring terrorist attacks around the world. Samir Khan, a Pakistani-American jihadist traveling with him, was killed as well. Several weeks later, another strike killed Awlaki's 16-year-old son, Abdulrahman al-Awlaki, also a United States citizen. Administration officials insisted a Justice Department review had authorized the killings but declined to release the full document.

"The administration has claimed the power to carry out extrajudicial executions of Americans on the basis of evidence that is secret and is never seen by anyone," said Jameel Jaffer, deputy legal director of the American Civil Liberties Union. "It's hard to understand how that is consistent with the Constitution."

After criticizing the Bush administration for keeping the details of its surveillance, interrogation, and detention practices secret, Obama is doing the same thing. His administration has declined to reveal the details of how it places people on kill lists, carries out eavesdropping in the United States, or decides whom to detain overseas. The administration is also prosecuting six former government officials on charges of leaking classified information to the media—more cases than all other administrations combined.

Administration officials deny being secretive and insist they have disclosed more information about their counterterrorism practices than the Bush administration, which fiercely resisted releasing details of its "war on terror" and established the covert drone program in Pakistan. Obama administration officials say they have established a more transparent and flexible approach outside Pakistan that involves military raids, drone strikes, and other efforts. They told me that every attack in Yemen was approved by Yemeni officials. Eventually, they hope to make drone strikes joint efforts carried out openly with local governments.

For now, keeping them covert prevents American courts from reviewing their constitutionality, according to Jaffer. He pointed out that if a Republican president followed such policies, the outcry on the left would be deafening. "You have to remember that this authority is going to be used by the next administration and the next administration after that," Jaffer said. "You need to make sure there are clear limits on what is really unparalleled power."

To their credit, Obama and his senior officials have successfully reframed Bush's global battle as a more narrowly focused struggle against al Qaeda. They stopped using the term "war on terror" and instead described a campaign against a single, clearly identifiable group.

Senior administration officials cite the toppling of Muammar al-Qaddafi as the prime example of the success of their more focused, multilateral approach to the use of force. At a cost of zero American lives and $1 billion in United States funding, the Libya intervention removed an autocrat from power in five months. The occupation of Iraq claimed 4,484 American lives, cost at least $700 billion, and lasted nearly nine years.

"The light United States footprint had benefits beyond less United States lives and resources," Rhodes told me. "We believe the Libyan revolution is viewed as more legitimate. The United States is more welcome. And there is less potential for an insurgency because there aren't foreign forces present."

In its most ambitious proposal, the administration is also trying to restructure the United States military, implement steep spending cuts, and "right-size" United States forces around the world. Under Obama's plan, the Army would be trimmed by 80,000 soldiers, some United States units would be shifted from the Middle East to the Pacific, and more small, covert bases would be opened. Special Forces units that have been vastly expanded in Iraq and Afghanistan would train indigenous forces and carry out counterterrorism raids. Declaring al Qaeda nearly defeated, administration officials say it is time for a new focus.

"Where does the United States have a greater interest in 2020?" Rhodes asked. "Is it Asia-Pacific or Yemen? Obviously, the Asia-Pacific region is clearly going to be more important."

Rhodes has a point, but Pakistan and its nuclear weapons—as well as Yemen and its proximity to vital oil reserves and sea lanes—are likely to haunt the United States for years.

Retired military officials warn that drones and commando raids are no substitute for the difficult process of helping local leaders marginalize militants. Missile strikes that kill members of al Qaeda and its affiliates in Pakistan and Yemen do not strengthen economies, curb corruption, or improve government services. David Barno, a retired lieutenant general who commanded United States forces in Afghanistan from 2003 to 2005, believes hunting down senior terrorists over and over again is not a long-term solution.

"How do you get beyond this attrition warfare?" he asked me. "I don't think we've answered that question yet."

Critical Thinking

1. Is it legal to engage in extra-judicial killings?
2. What are the key elements of the Obama strategy?
3. How have drones changed the nature of war against terrorists?

DAVID ROHDE, a two-time Pulitzer Prize winner and former reporter for the *New York Times,* is a foreign affairs columnist for *Reuters* and the *Atlantic*.

Rhode, David. Reprinted in entirety by McGraw-Hill with permission from *Foreign Policy,* March/April 2012, pp. 65–69. www.foreignpolicy.com. © 2012 Washingtonpost.Newsweek Interactive, LLC.

UNIT 5

International Organization, International Law, and Human Security

Unit Selections

Learning Outcomes

After reading this Unit, you will be able to:

• Explain why the United Nations (UN) is still an important actor in the international system.

• Analyze what reforms would transform the United Nations into a more effective organization.

• Explain why it is so difficult to prosecute war criminals for genocide.

• Explain why there is the feeling that the war criminals and ethnic cleansers won in Srebrenica.

• Describe the role of Turkey as a regional hegemon in the Middle East.

• Analyze the relationship between Turkey and the Syrian refugees.

• Discuss the relationship between gender equality and sustainable development.

• Discuss how women can meet their sustainable development goals more effectively.

Student Website
www.mhhe.com/cls

Internet References

Amnesty International
www.amnesty.org

Genocide Watch Home Page
www.genocidewatch.org

Human Security Gateway
www.humansecuritygateway.com

International Court of Justice (ICJ)
www.icj-cij.org

The International Criminal Court
www.icc-cpi.int/Menus/icc

The International Criminal Tribunal for the Former Yugoslavia
www.icty.org

International Criminal Tribunal for Rwanda
www.unictr.org

United Nations Home Page
www.un.org

U.S. Holocaust Museum
www.ushmm.org

The United Nations (UN) was created as the successor to the failed League of Nations. The main purpose of the UN was to prevent another world war, through the application of the principles of collective security. Collective security was based on the idea that the organized power of the international community was supposed to be sufficient to deter and punish aggression. The Charter of the United Nations, which envisaged the construction of a just world order, was based on the principle of liberal internationalism. In the second decade of the twenty-first century, the UN continues to support the promotion of important world order values, such as peace, economic security, the protection of human rights, and the protection of the environment, most of which fall under the rubric of human security. However, it has been more than six and a half decades since the United Nations was created, and very few changes have taken place within the organization to reflect the changes that have taken place in the international system. For example, the Security Council is the most important organ of the UN, because it has been entrusted with the responsibility for the maintenance of peace and international security. Most third-world members of the United Nations support the reform of the Security Council so that it could function as a more democratic and representative organization. Although the UN has increased its membership from the original 51 to 193, the number of permanent members of the Security Council has remained the same five states (the United States, Russia, China, the United Kingdom, and France) since 1945. The leading candidates for additional permanent seats on the Security Council are Germany and Japan. It has also been suggested that other permanent members should be added from the major regions of Africa, Asia, and Latin America. If new permanent members are added to the Security Council, the rationale for the veto would also have to be reviewed. This might add to the overall legitimacy of the organization and strengthen its ability to function as a systems-affecting actor. Thomas Weiss, in "A Pipe Dream? Reforming the United Nations," believes that the organization still matters in terms of its norm-setting activities and writes that the UN needs to undergo a major transformation to deal with transboundary threats that pose a major threat to human survival and dignity.

The UN itself was embedded in a realist conception of international order, based on the Westphalian system, which rested on the fundamental principle of the primacy of state sovereignty. The primacy of state sovereignty has now been challenged by the doctrine of humanitarian intervention, which states that the sovereignty of the individual should take precedence over the sovereignty of the state when gross and mass violations of human rights take place. The central question is at what point should the "international community" engage in military intervention, for example, in the case of Syria in 2012, according to the norm of the responsibility to protect. According to the London-based Syrian Human Rights Observatory, it is estimated that more than 20,000 people have been killed in the civil conflict that has taken place in Syria since 2011. Other questions associated with the issue are Who should authorize humanitarian military intervention? How can one make sure that such military intervention is not designed to serve the national interest of a single

© Comstock/Jupiterimages

state or a group of states? Who determines when a threshold has been crossed by the government of a state that has committed gross and mass violations of human rights against its own people that should trigger military intervention? How many people have to be killed before such an intervention occurs? In an effort to deal with this problem, the international community has moved in the direction of holding political leaders who commit war crimes, crimes against humanity, and genocide, accountable for their actions. For example, in 1993, the UN Security Council created the ad hoc Tribunal for the Former Yugoslavia. In 2011, after eluding capture for sixteen years, the Bosnian Serbian general Ratko Mladic, who had been indicted by the Tribunal for the commission of genocide in the Bosnian town of Srebrenica, was arrested by the Serbian government and turned over to the Tribunal for trial. Michael Dobbs, in "General Mladic in the Hague: A Report on Evil in Europe—and Justice Delayed," focuses not only on the personality of Mladic as a "charismatic murderer" but also on the fact that seventeen years later Srebrenica remains divided between Muslims and

Serbians, and there is the feeling that the "ethnic cleansers" have "actually won," as nationalists on both sides have distorted the record of what happened in the former Yugoslavia. Dobbs concludes that the international system of justice in this case has failed.

As of early September 2012, President Assad of Syria had yet to be placed in the dock of an international criminal court to be held accountable for his crimes. As the conflict in Syria continued to rage on in 2012, about 200,000 Syrian refugees fled the fighting and sought refuge in the neighboring states of Jordan and Turkey. Jenna Krajeski writes in "Taking Refuge: The Syrian Revolution in Turkey" that Turkey in 2012 had thus far taken in about 25,000 refugees. Turkish involvement in the Syrian situation has resulted in a shift in its policy from one of good relations with President Assad to the call for him to step down as leader of the country. Turkish support of the Syrian refugees is also a reflection of its growing role as a regional hegemon in the Middle East.

Since the founding of the UN in 1945, the international community has established a network of treaties, declarations on human security that are designed to protect the human rights of individuals and groups against violations by their own governments as well as aggressors. These instruments, which establish norms designed to guide the behavior of states, range from the Universal Declaration of Human Rights in 1948 to the 1966 International Covenants protecting civil and political rights as well as economic, social, and cultural rights. A number of conventions have also been adopted to protect the rights of women. Fernandes and Blomstrom write about the relationship between "Gender Equality and Sustainable Development" within the context of the Rio + 20 Conference that met in Brazil in June 2012. They focus on the work of the Women's Environment and Development Organization (WEDO), arguing that "A successful Rio + 20 will enhance women's rights and their access to and control over resources and decision-making spheres" in "mainstreaming gender equity."

A Pipe Dream?
Reforming the United Nations

THOMAS G. WEISS

The year 2011 marks the beginning of retirement for many baby-boomers. The Beatles once asked: "Will you still need me/Will you still feed me/When I'm sixty-four?" This year the United Nations turns 66 and many think it should have taken early retirement. Withholding US contributions—one-fifth of the overall UN budget and a quarter of its peacekeeping costs—is a Republican perennial. And the new chair of the House of Foreign Affairs Committee, Ileana Ros-Lehtinen, began with a battle cry on the first day of commitee work in 2011: "Reform first, pay later."

Eyes glaze over at the mention of UN reform. Before becoming a minister in the last Labor government in the United Kingdom, Mark Malloch Brown headed the UN Development Programme and was deputy secretary-general under Kofi Annan. He quipped that the United Nations is the only institution where, over coffee or around water coolers, reform is a more popular topic than sex.

To be fair, more adaptation has taken place in the UN system than critics acknowledge. Indeed, the founders would probably not recognize the system whose foundations were laid in 1945. However, while it would be unfair to describe the United Nations as in a state of stasis, it also would be false to suggest that the UN system is more than woefully slow in reforming itself. Why does so little happen? What, if anything, can be done?

The Central Challenge

Why should anyone in Washington or elsewhere care? The short answer is that dramatic transformation of the world organization, and not mere tinkering, is required if we are to address transboundary problems that threaten human survival and dignity. Former UN Secretary General Kofi Annan frequently speaks of "problems without passports." Many of the most intractable challenges facing humankind are transnational—acid rain does not require a visa to move from one side of a border to another. These problems range from climate change, migration, and pandemics, to terrorism, financial flows, and proliferation of weapons of mass destruction. Effectively addressing any of these threats requires policies and vigorous actions whose scope is not unilateral, bilateral, or even multilateral, but rather global.

Ironically, the policy authority and resources for tackling global problems remain vested individually in the 192 UN member states rather than in the collective body. The fundamental disjuncture between the natures of growing global threats and the current inadequate structures for international problem-solving and decision-making goes a long way toward explaining fitful, tactical, and short-term local responses to threats that require sustained, strategic, and long-term global thinking and action.

The United States resembles most countries in opting in and out of the United Nations when it suits Washington's short term calculations of interests. Selective "à la carte multilateralism," however, is insufficient. More fundamental reforms of multilateral institutions must be made so that they work effectively and in the common interest.

The United Nations' Main Weaknesses

The United Nations too often suffers paralysis. Before prescribing how to fix it, we must understand three underlying causes of its woes.

The first is the enduring concept of the international community as a system of sovereign states—a notion dating back to the 1648 Treaties of Westphalia. "Organized hypocrisy," as former National Security Council director Stephen Krasner reminds us, is either 360 years old or 360 years young. As a result of the grip of sovereignty, the current international system functions in the middle of a growing divide between virtually all of the life-menacing threats facing the planet and the existing structures for international decisions to do something about them. Government officials and so-called realist scholars of international relations agree that narrowly defined vital interests are the only basis on which to make commitments or avoid them.

The calculated vital interests of major powers, particularly of the United States as the most powerful, obviously create obstacles to action by the United Nations, but newer and less powerful countries are as vehemently protective of their sovereign prerogatives as are the major powers. All states are loath to accept elements of overarching central authority and the resulting inroads that would interfere with their capacities to act autonomously. As such, the United Nations remains the last and most formidable bastion of sacrosanct state sovereignty even as technological advances, globalization, and transboundary problems proliferate, leaving national borders with less and less meaning. Thus, the domestic institutions necessary for providing public goods in functioning countries do not exist for the globe—there is no power to tax, to conscript, to regulate, or to quarantine.

> ... the United Nations remains the last and most formidable bastion of ... state sovereignty even as technological advances, globalization, and transboundary problems proliferate.

The second ailment stems from the diplomatic burlesque that passes for diplomacy on First Avenue in Manhattan or in UN gatherings elsewhere. The artificial divide between the aging acting troupes from the industrialized North and from the developing countries of the global South provides the drama. Launched in the 1950s and 1960s as a means to create some diplomatic space for negotiations by countries on the margins of international politics, the once creative voices of the Non-Aligned Movement and the Group of 77 developing countries have become prisoners of their own rhetoric. These rigid and counterproductive groups—and the artificial divisions and toxic atmosphere that they create—end up constituting almost insurmountable barriers to diplomatic initiatives. Serious conversation is virtually impossible; replaced by meaningless posturing in order to score media points back home. Marquee stars include former US ambassador to the United Nations John Bolton and Venezuelan President Hugo Chávez, and while former Canadian politician and senior UN official Stephen Lewis has written that "men and women cannot live by rhetoric alone," this characterization does not apply to UN ambassadors and officials.

The third malady is structural. The Australian logistics genius who moved goods to Malta and the Middle East in World War II and subsequently oversaw a number of key UN humanitarian operations, Sir Robert Jackson, began his 1969 evaluation of the UN development system by writing: "The machine as a whole has become unmanageable . . . like some prehistoric monster." The lumbering dinosaur is now more than 40 years older but certainly not better adapted to the 21st century.

The structural problems arise not only from the overlapping jurisdictions of various UN bodies, the lack of coordination among their activities, and the absence of centralized financing for the system as a whole; they are also exacerbated by the nature of the staff and its leadership. The United Nations' various moving parts work at cross-purposes rather than in a more integrated, mutually reinforcing, and collaborative fashion. Agencies relentlessly pursue cut-throat fundraising for their expanding mandates, stake out territory, and pursue mission creep. While the UN organizational chart refers to a "system," implying coherence and cohesion, the organization in reality has more in common with feudalism than with a modern organization. Frequent use is made of the term "family"—like many such units, the United Nations is dysfunctional and divided.

A related disorder stems from the overwhelming weight of the UN bureaucracy, its low productivity, and the often underwhelming leadership within international secretariats. The stereotype of a bloated administration overlooks many talented and dedicated individuals. However, the world body's recruitment and promotion methods are certainly part of what ails it. When success occurs, it usually reflects personalities and serendipity rather than recruitment of the best persons for the right reasons and institutional structures designed to foster collaboration. Staff costs account for the lion's share of the UN budget, and the international civil service is a potential resource whose composition, productivity, and culture could change quickly. There is little hope in the short run, however, while the current lackluster leadership of Secretary General Ban Ki-moon continues this year and during a second five-year term.

In fact, Rube Goldberg would have trouble finding a better design for futile complexity than the current array of agencies, each focusing on a substantive area, often located in a different city from relevant UN partners and with separate budgets, governing boards, organizational cultures, and independent executive heads. Confronting such threats as climate change, pandemics, terrorism, and weapons of mass destruction requires multidisciplinary perspectives, efforts across sectors, firm central direction, and inspired leadership. The United Nations too rarely supplies any of this.

Some Palliatives If Not Solutions

If cures for the United Nations' ailments are politically unrealistic, are palliatives available? Is there surgery that is more than cosmetic and might mean remission? The answer is a tentative "yes" for all three weaknesses.

The first remedy requires building upon spotty yet significant progress in recasting national interests. The prescription for the Westphalian system consists of more energetic recalculations of the shared benefits of providing global public goods and respecting international commitments. Democratic member states, whether large or small, should theoretically find this pill relatively easy to swallow because they have a long-term, rational, and vital interest in, as well as a moral responsibility to promote, multilateral cooperation in the interest of their own citizens as well as those of countries farther afield.

There is a therapeutic as well as actual conceptual benefit from "good international citizenship," an expression coined by Gareth Evans, the former Australian foreign minister and one-time president of the International Crisis Group. Nothing better illustrates the relationship between the provision of basic rights and wider international security than the responsibility to protect (R2P), which redefines state sovereignty as contingent upon a modicum of respect for human rights rather than as absolute. While R2P imposes the primary responsibility for human rights on governmental authorities, it argues that if a state is manifestly unwilling or unable to honor its responsibility, or worse is the perpetrator of mass atrocities, then the responsibility to protect citizens shifts upward to the international community of states.

The history of international law demonstrates that states accept limits on the exercise of their sovereignty by ratifying treaties to constrain their margins of maneuver. The R2P doctrine illustrates how to move in the direction of redefining state sovereignty to include a modicum of responsibility, a values breakthrough after centuries of passively and mindlessly accepting the proposition that state sovereignty was a license to kill. Recalculating the benefits of global public goods and solemn international commitments is the way forward. It is not farfetched to imagine that the international community of states, including the United States, will see a gradual advance of intergovernmental agreements and powers along the lines that Europe as a whole has nurtured.

Chipping away at sovereignty is a long-term project, which explains why this palliative will undoubtedly have a "Pollyannaish" ring to American ears. But the other two weaknesses could be addressed more readily.

Moving beyond the North-South quagmire and toward issues-based and interest-based negotiations is essential. We need to have different country configurations for different problems and to stop thinking about fixed memberships, and especially universal participation, for every item on the international agenda. Fortunately, states have on occasion breached the fortifications around the North-South camps and forged creative partnerships that portend other types of coalitions that could unclog UN deliberations. Less posturing and role-playing is a prerequisite for the future health of the world organization and world politics. While they got a bad name during the Iraq War, serious international politics always involves "coalitions of the willing."

> **We need to have different country configurations for different problems and to stop thinking about fixed memberships, and especially universal participation, for every item on the international agenda.**

Examples of wide-ranging partnerships across continents and ideologies include those that negotiated the treaty to ban landmines and established the International Criminal Court (ICC). Landmines mobilized a diverse group of countries across the usual North-South divide as well as global civil society under the leadership of the World Federalist Movement and the usually reticent International Committee of the Red Cross. The idea of a permanent criminal court had been discussed since the late 1940s but received a push after the ad hoc tribunals for the former Yugoslavia and for Rwanda; however, the shortcomings (including costs and the burden of evidence) demonstrated the need for a permanent court that could also act as a deterrent for future thugs. The 60-country like-minded group gathered in Rome in 1998 represented a formidable and persuasive coalition that joined forces with the 700 members of a nongovernmental organization (NGO) coalition, and the ICC treaty moved ahead vigorously in spite of strong opposition from several permanent members of the Security Council. Another example, one from the economic arena, is the Global Compact, which brings civil society and transnational corporations into a more productive partnership with the United Nations; it moves beyond a shibboleth from the capitalist North that formerly had been rejected by the global South.

The G20 is a more recent example that, in the midst of the 2008–2009 financial and economic meltdown, shifted from being a photo-op for finance ministers to being serious. Decisions in spring 2009 not only resulted in the infusion of substantial funds into the IMF, but also gave life at the fund in Washington and at the World Bank to long-sought governance reforms that provide more representation for developing countries.

If this larger grouping were to formulate a common position on institutional reform, no international organization, including the United Nations, could easily resist. Complaints about the G20's illegitimacy are hollow if the outcome is a more stable global economic order from which all states benefit. Indeed, the one-state-one-vote interpretation is merely one way to frame the sovereign equality of states. With 70 percent of the world's population, 80 percent of world trade, and 90 percent of the world's gross domestic product, the argument that the G20 lacks legitimacy is farfetched. The G7 lacked legitimacy; the G20 does not.

A unified G20 stance on climate change or pandemics, for example, could jump-start UN negotiations. For years the global South, along with Japan and Germany, have sung in unison that the Security Council and other intergovernmental organizations represent the past and not the present. The G20 could help infuse the United Nations with the political dynamics of contemporary global power.

The third line of treatment would be to pursue the possibility of making the United Nations work with more cohesion, as advocated by "Delivering as One," one of the last sets of proposals published before Kofi Annan's departure as secretary-general. No previous reform has reduced turf struggles and unproductive competition for funds within the so-called UN system. But could one? Yes, but donors would have to stop talking out both sides of their mouths and insist upon the centralization and consolidation that they often preach before UN forums and parliamentary bodies, but upon which they never act.

A related therapy consists of taking steps to reinvigorate the personnel of the United Nations. There is an urgent need to revive the notion of an autonomous international civil service as championed by the second UN Secretary General, Dag Hammarskjöld. Competence and integrity should outweigh nationality and gender considerations as well as cronyism, which have become the principal criteria for recruitment, retention, and promotion. In fact, Hammarskjöld's ideal goes back to what the Carnegie Endowment for International Peace during World War II called the "great experiment" of the League of Nations.

Moving back to the future for the United Nations would involve recruiting people with integrity and talent. There are numerous ways to attract more mobile and younger staff members with greater turnover and fewer permanent contracts while providing better career development for the world organization of the 21st century. Regional or linguistic quotas could diminish the governmental influence resulting from national ones. In addition, as the expenditures for UN staff account for 90 percent of the organization's budget, strengthening performance and productivity should be at the top of any to-do list.

Conclusion

While revitalizing the United Nations may strike readers not only as far-fetched but also as a secondary priority in the midst of massive domestic problems, it should not be. Strobe Talbott, the president of the Brookings Institution and former deputy Secretary of State, recently wrote that mega-threats can only be avoided through multilateralism that extends beyond anything we currently have. That type of change requires US leadership like that in the aftermath of World War II, when the United States boldly led the effort to construct a second generation of international organizations on the ashes of the first, the League of Nations.

Expectations of the Barack Obama presidency were as impossibly high internationally as domestically, including reviving US leadership in multilateralism. His rhetorical contributions have been appreciable—not only his Cairo speech on tolerance, but also numerous others which indicated that the United States was rejoining the planet, prepared to reengage with both friends and foes, and considered multilateralism essential to US foreign policy. Many of his first steps were in the right direction—including repaying US arrears to the United Nations, funding programs for reproductive health, joining the Human Rights Council, moving ahead with nuclear arms reductions, and preparing to initial the Comprehensive Test Ban Treaty. Still, given the "shellacking" in November 2010 and the imperative to improve unemployment and growth, the failure to mention the United Nations in his State of the Union address was unsurprising.

Nonetheless, multilateralism must re-emerge as a priority for this administration. For example, the global financial and economic meltdown should have made clearer what previous crises had not—namely the risks, problems, and costs of a global economy without adequate international institutions, democratic decision-making, or powers to bring order and ensure compliance with collective decisions. Henry Kissinger, whose realist credentials are still intact, wrote that the financial collapse revealed the lack of global institutions to alleviate the shock and reverse the trend. To date, however, trillions of dollars, euros, and pounds have been used to paper-over the cracks. Business-as-usual remains the standard operating procedure.

But perhaps we can learn from history. In a recent book about the origins of American multilateralism, Council on Foreign Relations analyst Stewart Patrick makes a persuasive case that issues concerning US multilateralism are much the same as in the 1940s. Now as then, the United States enjoyed a semblance of global hegemony, but never has that hegemony eliminated the necessity to act multilaterally.

"Le machin" is what Charles de Gaulle famously dubbed the United Nations, thereby dismissing international cooperation as frivolous in comparison with the realpolitik. He conveniently ignored that the formal birth of "the thing" was not the signing of the UN Charter in June 1945, but rather the adoption of the "Declaration by the United Nations" in Washington, DC in January 1942. The 26 countries that defeated fascism also anticipated the formal establishment of the world organization as an essential extension of their war-time commitments. These were not pie-in-the-sky idealists. The UN system was not viewed as a liberal plaything to be tossed aside when the going got tough, but a vital necessity for post-war order and prosperity. Multilateral approaches to punishing horrific deeds and mitigating global threats, then and now, must be not only pragmatic and well-adapted to local realities but also spectacular and utopian.

Could that same far-sighted political commitment rise again under the Obama administration, certainly not in 2011, but after his reelection?

For all its warts, the United Nations still matters for its norms, legitimacy, and idealism . . . [and] urgently needs to reinvent itself . . . to be a vital force in global affairs.

Readers, and certainly classmates, will undoubtedly speculate that this author has been inhaling as well as smoking, but he is guardedly sanguine about affirmatively answering that question as well. Individuals and states can be as strong as the institutions that they create. There are plenty of things wrong, but many can be fixed. For all its warts, the United Nations still matters for its norms, legitimacy, and idealism. The world organization urgently needs to reinvent itself and to be a vital force in global affairs.

Critical Thinking

1. What limits the effectiveness of the United Nations?
2. Why should the UN Charter be revised?
3. Why is it so difficult to reform the UN Security Council?

THOMAS G. WEISS is Presidential Professor of Political Science and Director of the Ralph Bunche Institute for International Studies at the Graduate Center of the City University of New York.

From *Harvard International Review*, Spring 2011, pp. 48–53. Copyright © 2011 by the President of Harvard College. Reprinted by permission via Sheridan Reprints.

General Mladic in the Hague

A Report on Evil in Europe—and Justice Delayed

MICHAEL DOBBS

Shortly after he was first charged with crimes against humanity in July 1995, Ratko Mladic was asked what it felt like to be branded "a war criminal" by an international court. The Bosnian Serb military commander seethed with a mixture of barely controlled anger and contempt as he rejected the "idiotic accusations."

"My people or I were not the first to start that war," he insisted, veins popping from his bloated red face. "I don't recognize any trials except the trial of my own people."

Seventeen years later, the once all-powerful general finally appeared this spring before the International Criminal Tribunal for the former Yugoslavia in The Hague to answer charges of genocide, persecution, extermination, unlawful attacks on civilians, and hostage-taking. Partially paralyzed on his right side and looking older than his 70 years, he is physically much diminished, a shadow of the man who became known as the "butcher of the Balkans" for the campaign of terror he waged against Bosnia's non-Serb population. But he is recognizably the same person—proud, willful, and completely unrepentant.

Mladic flashed the thumbs-up sign as he entered the courtroom in May, nodded approvingly as he listened to some of the charges against him, and even clapped his hands when the prosecutor played audio clips of him bullying United Nations peacekeepers and ordering the shelling of civilian areas of Sarajevo. "It was as if he was saying that everything that he did was completely justified," Jasmina Mujkanovic, whose father was killed in the infamous Omarska concentration camp, told me.

Together with victim representatives like her, I was seated in the public gallery of the tribunal's high-tech courtroom. We could see everything that was going on, but we were separated from the accused by a thick pane of glass. It was probably just as well, as the mother of one of his victims found it impossible to restrain herself in the presence of their tormentor and made insulting gestures. Mladic replied with a threat, slowly drawing a finger across his throat.

Mladic's alleged crimes represent the greatest evil that has been perpetrated in Europe since World War II:

the ethnic cleansing of hundreds of thousands of Bosnian Muslims, culminating in the coldblooded execution of more than 7,000 prisoners in Srebrenica. The West may have closed its eyes to worse atrocities in the past 70 years, but none in its civilizational backyard, a mere stone's throw from where the Holocaust laid bare Europe's pretensions to enlightenment. Which is exactly why I have spent the past 10 months investigating the case and traveling through the former Yugoslavia—interviewing victims, witnesses, and perpetrators—identifying what we now know about these atrocities and trying to uncover what we still don't two decades later.

Watching Mladic finally appear in court, I couldn't help thinking about another much-anticipated war crimes case, 50 years ago. Adolf Eichmann went on trial in Jerusalem in 1961 accused of crimes against humanity for his involvement in the Nazis' murder of 6 million Jews. The most celebrated chronicler of the Eichmann trial was, of course, Hannah Arendt, who wrote a series of articles for the *New Yorker* that were eventually turned into a book, *Eichmann in Jerusalem.* The book was subtitled "A Report on the Banality of Evil," a phrase that sought to explain how the ordinary, harmless-looking bureaucrat in the dock had committed such monstrous, out-of-the-ordinary crimes.

Mladic was never a harmless-looking bureaucrat. He was a general born for command who got his hands dirty—and bloody—on the battlefield. He was not simply a cog in the machinery of genocide: He set the machinery in motion and supervised every aspect of its operation. In the words of the late Richard Holbrooke, the United States diplomat who helped bring the three-and-a-half-year Bosnian conflict to an end, Mladic was "one of those lethal combinations that history thrusts up occasionally—a charismatic murderer."

But even that does not fully explain Mladic and his motivations. When I lived in Belgrade during the final years of Tito's dictatorship in the late 1970s, I did not consciously divide my friends into Serb or Croat, Muslim or Christian. No one did. Tito's insistence on "brotherhood and unity," enforced when necessary by the army and secret police, along with collective pride in his refusal to kowtow to foreign powers, resulted in a sort of ethnic harmony. Even if it was imposed from above, that system had its true believers—Mladic among them. So as I finally had a chance to look into Mladic's piercing blue eyes, I tried to understand how a man who ritualistically swore to defend Tito's achievements could have ordered the coldblooded execution of thousands.

Indeed, however unambiguous the basic facts of Srebrenica—mass graves leave little room for moral interpretation—the hearings before the Yugoslav war crimes tribunal have already revealed significant gaps in our understanding of what happened. For example, according to Bosnian Serb military documents and testimony from key participants gathered in preparation for his trial, Mladic did not at first even intend to capture the town of Srebrenica. His initial goal was to create "an unbearable situation" for its inhabitants, forcing them to leave of their own accord. Only when he met no effective resistance from U.N. troops defending the internationally recognized "safe area" did he request approval from Bosnian Serb President Radovan Karadzic to order the final "takeover of Srebrenica." In other words, this was a mass murder born of opportunism.

Since his capture after years on the run, Mladic has appeared nearly a dozen times in public, at various pretrial hearings and then, in mid-May, at the long-awaited start of his trial. Never has he shown any remorse. Yet, revered by his supporters as a mythical, godlike figure whose image remains plastered on walls all over Serbia, he has by turns also appeared rambling, defiant, domineering, melodramatic, conciliatory, argumentative, and seemingly on the verge of tears. At one point during an appearance last October, he pleaded for an additional five minutes with his wife. Mladic seems banal only in that some of his reactions have been so predictably human.

None of this makes his case unique. It is simply the latest step in the world's attempt to bring closure to its most awful crimes. Half a century after the Eichmann trial, if the arc of history is bending at all toward justice, it is doing so not because we have finally recognized the true nature of evil and thereby exorcised it, but because we have continued the painstaking work of uncovering who did what when—and finding a way, however laborious, frustrating, or belated, of punishing them for it.

Seeking insights into Mladic's life, last November I tracked down the man who sheltered him for more than five years in an obscure village on the flat Danubian plain north of Belgrade. Known to his friends as Brane, **Branislav Mladic** is Ratko's second cousin. Their grandfathers were brothers, Serbs from the mountainous region of Bosnia known as Herzegovina.

With a thin, angular face and stubble of gray beard, Brane bears little outward resemblance to his famous relative, except for the same darting eyes and abrupt, no-nonsense

manner. A bachelor, he lives by himself in a ramshackle farmhouse, with a few chickens, sheep, and pigs roaming about the courtyard. He made clear he disliked the United States ("The Americans attacked the Serbs for no reason"), but he agreed to talk to me—his first extended interview with an American reporter—because I had been introduced by a friend of a friend. Such connections count for everything in Serbia.

As Brane told the story, through a mist of tobacco smoke and repeated shots of slivovitz, the potent plum brandy that is the Serbian national drink, in early 2006 Ratko showed up on his doorstep in the village of Lazarevo in the middle of the night. By this time, he had become a vagrant, living in a series of borrowed apartments, a wanted man with a $5 million reward on his head from the United States government. First indicted for crimes against humanity in 1995, shortly after Srebrenica, Mladic lived more or less openly in Belgrade until 2002, when the Serbian parliament adopted a law belatedly promising to cooperate with the Yugoslav war crimes tribunal.

"Do you know who I am?" he whispered to Brane, before ordering him to turn off the porch light. Brane was shocked by his cousin's appearance, but recognized his voice, which still had the timbre of a man accustomed to being instantly obeyed. Although their paths had separated, Brane had followed Ratko's exploits as the legendary general who stood up for Serbian minorities, first in Croatia in 1991 and then in Bosnia, during the brutal war that ended with the 1995 Dayton peace agreement and the de facto partition of the country into mini-states controlled by Serbs, Muslims, and Croats.

Over the next few years, Ratko and Brane settled into a fixed routine, living in separate rooms across the small farmyard. In the early morning, before Brane headed off to the fields, they would drink coffee together. Ratko spoke about his father, Nedo, a member of Tito's communist partisans killed during World War II by Croatian nationalists allied with Hitler. Ratko described how he went looking for his father's grave in the mountains of Bosnia-Herzegovina. He eventually found an old Muslim who showed him the place where his father was buried. The grave had been washed away by a mountain stream, but Ratko told Brane that he was so grateful for this information that he "spared" the Muslim village of Bradina from Serbian assault during the war.

Several of Mladic's relatives, including Brane's father, Dusan, ended up in the rich agricultural region of Vojvodina after World War II. As former partisans, they were encouraged to occupy land that had been cleansed of Swabian Germans. At school, they were taught that ethnic differences no longer mattered in the brave new Yugoslavia being forged by Tito. At home, they clung to the traditions they had brought with them from the inhospitable Herzegovinian mountains, as well as the memory of defending themselves from their enemies, whether Germans, Muslims, or Croats.

Unlike Brane, a former factory worker who turned to farming when the Yugoslav economy fell apart following the collapse of communism, Ratko rose through the ranks of the Yugoslav army, serving in Kosovo and Macedonia. As a professional military officer, he had a strong incentive to embrace the Titoist idea of loyalty to an overarching nation. He described himself as a "Yugoslav," or "South Slav," rather than as a "Serb," in official censuses. At the same time, he was always very aware of his ethnic identity. With its Serb-dominated officer corps, the Yugoslav People's Army was one of the most efficient channels of upward mobility for peasant families like the Mladices who bore the brunt of the fighting in World War II.

Born in 1942 according to official Yugoslav records—1943 according to family lore—Mladic was a child of a conflict that was a struggle for national liberation, political revolution, and civil war all rolled into one. His very name, Ratko, derives from *rat,* Serbian for "war," and he spent his entire professional life preparing for war against the enemies of Tito's Yugoslavia. The war, when it came, was against internal enemies rather than external ones, but the ideological mindset was much the same. As Mladic saw it, Croats and Bosnian Muslims became proxies for Germans and Ottoman Turks, the peoples who had inflicted so much suffering on his Serbian ancestors.

Although Brane refuses to speak ill of his celebrated relative, living alone with Ratko for five years cannot have been easy. As Mladic has shown in The Hague, he is a controlling person, given to angry outbursts when he fails to get his way. Whether he is commanding an 80,000-man army, dealing with a roomful of judges and lawyers, or living at home with his hermit cousin, he must always be the focus of attention.

According to Brane, Ratko whiled away the time watching television and reading newspapers. For exercise, he would occasionally walk around the farmhouse late at night, once he was sure that all the neighbors had gone to bed. Brane let him have the keys to his ramshackle Volkswagen Polo, but he does not think his cousin ever used it. The former general liked to reminisce about his exploits during the war in Bosnia, but steered clear of controversial topics, such as the killings in Srebrenica. Brane accepted his cousin's explanation that "everything that I did was for one purpose only—to defend the rights of the Serbian people."

One evening in January 2011, Brane returned home from the fields to find Ratko slumped over in the bath, paralyzed on the right side of his body. "For four days, he could not get up. He could not go to the toilet. He could not move," Brane told me. Afraid to summon a doctor who might report Mladic to the authorities, Brane treated his cousin with heart medicine he was able to scrounge from a pharmacy.

Recovering from a stroke without proper medical attention may have weakened Mladic's resolve to evade capture and transfer to The Hague. He yearned for contact with family, particularly his son, Darko. A few weeks after what

his lawyer said was a third stroke, in May 2011, Mladic demanded to see his grandchildren, who were visiting another relative in Lazarevo. Darko brought his 10-year-old daughter and 5-year-old son to Brane's place, on the pretext of looking at the animals. Mladic stared at the children through the curtains of his room as they petted the pigs, but did not actually greet them.

"I told him it was a big mistake, but he wouldn't listen," Brane recalled.

The Serbian police were monitoring Darko's movements, hoping that he would eventually lead them to his father. Less than a week later, on May 26, they broke through the gates of the farmyard. Mladic had a loaded pistol nearby, but made little attempt to reach it. Sick and feeble, he was psychologically ready to embark on a new stage of his never-ending war.

There could scarcely be a greater contrast between the fugitive who meekly surrendered to police a year ago and the warlord who determined with a wave of his finger whether a prisoner would live or die. "I am giving your life to you as a gift," he told a frightened young man captured by Serbian troops a week after the fall of Srebrenica. "Don't go back to the front. Next time, there won't be any forgiveness."

A former silver-mining town with a population of close to 40,000 before the war, Srebrenica was one of several Muslim-controlled enclaves in eastern Bosnia that survived the initial Serbian onslaught in 1992. Declared a "safe area" by the United Nations in 1993, it was an obstacle to Serbian control of the strategically important Drina River valley separating Bosnia from Serbia. After Muslim fighters based in Srebrenica mounted raids against nearby Serbian villages, destroying dozens of homes and killing hundreds of Serbs, Mladic swore to take revenge.

Video of Mladic's triumphant entry into Srebrenica on July 11, 1995, captures a man intent on controlling every detail of the operation. He is commanding general, platoon leader, traffic cop, political commentator, and movie producer all rolled into one. "Film that," he shouts to the cameraman. "Take down that Muslim street sign," he tells someone else, addressing his subordinates as "dumb fucks." When he comes across a U.N. vehicle stuck in a ditch, he personally supervises its recovery.

"The boss can't stop commanding for five minutes," jokes a member of his staff on another occasion, when Mladic's back is briefly turned.

"You know how he is," laments another.

Mladic's penchant for micromanagement is one reason it is impossible to imagine that the brutal executions of more than 7,000 Srebrenica men and boys between July 12 and 15 could possibly have happened without his knowledge and express instructions. Evidence presented at The Hague strongly suggests that Mladic ordered the executions, which were then supervised by a trusted aide, Col. Ljubisa Beara.

Mladic personally oversaw the separation of Muslim male refugees from women and children outside the gates of the U.N. military compound in Srebrenica. He was also present when thousands of Muslim men attempting to flee across the mountains to government-held territory were captured by Bosnian Serb forces. Mladic promised the refugees they would be exchanged for Serbian prisoners. Instead, they were loaded into buses and taken to execution sites, where they were mowed down by firing squad.

In the fall of 1995, when the outside world began to learn the horror of what had happened at Srebrenica, Mladic mobilized the resources of the Bosnian Serb army to cover up the crime. His subordinates used bulldozers and dump trucks to dig up at least four mass graves containing the bones of Srebrenica victims and scatter the remains in dozens of secondary graves in remote valleys of eastern Bosnia. Unfortunately for Mladic, United States spy satellites recorded the attempted deception in detail, enabling investigators to locate the secondary graves and use DNA samples to identify victims.

The biggest remaining mystery is not whether Mladic ordered the massacre or how it was carried out, but why.

The biggest remaining mystery is not whether Mladic ordered the massacre or how it was carried out, but why. Plenty of evidence shows that he always had a ruthless, hands-on streak. Intercepted phone calls show that he stood on the hills above Sarajevo in May 1992 personally directing Serbian artillery fire. "Don't let them sleep. . . . Drive them crazy," he ordered at the beginning of the siege. "Shoot at Pofalici [a predominantly Muslim neighborhood]. There is not much Serb population there. . . . Fire one more salvo at the Presidency [headquarters of the Muslim-led Bosnian government]." His willfulness and determination to win at all costs caused him to commit acts that most of us would consider war crimes.

There is, however, an important distinction between shelling a city, even indiscriminately, and murdering 7,000 prisoners in the space of three days. Unlike Karadzic, his nominal superior, Mladic was not a Serbian nationalist, at least not initially. He disapproved of the Chetnik paramilitaries who ran riot in Bosnia at the beginning of the war, and he attempted to build a professional army. Bosnian Serb records show that Mladic urged his comrades to restrain their territorial ambitions and avoid a strategy of ethnic cleansing, which would be impossible to justify to international public opinion. Speaking to a session of the Bosnian Serb assembly on May 12, 1992, Mladic chillingly warned that such a policy "would be genocide."

So what happened? A study of the trial record of top Mladic associates shows that Mladic's thinking changed in several important ways between 1992 and 1995. First, he blamed the Muslims and the Croats for breaking up his beloved Yugoslavia in the dramatic years of 1991 and 1992, with the assistance of Western countries, notably Germany, which had been quick to recognize the new republics of Slovenia and Croatia. "We were a happy country with happy peoples, and we had a good life," he told Dutch peacekeepers in Srebrenica, "until Muslims began listening to what [European leaders] and the Western mafia were telling them."

As Mladic sees it, Yugoslavia was destroyed by the same forces that tore the country apart during World War II, when many Croat and Muslim politicians allied themselves with Nazi Germany. Yugoslavia's breakup left nearly 2 million Serbs stranded in the newly independent states of Croatia and Bosnia, easy prey for politicians intent on stirring up memories of World War II atrocities.

Then there was the logic of the war itself. Serbian atrocities against Muslims led to Muslim atrocities against Serbs (though on nowhere near the same scale). Before U.N. peacekeepers arrived in 1993, the Muslim defenders of Srebrenica had raided nearby Serbian villages in search of food, destroying property and killing civilians. And Mladic lived by a very simple code, the same code that had guided so many of his ancestors: kill or be killed. He justified the mass killing of Srebrenica Muslims by pointing to the crimes allegedly committed against Serbs.

Finally, as the international community failed to intervene, Mladic became ever more contemptuous of the West and ever more convinced of his own invincibility. In 1992, he was still concerned about how the world would react to mass killings and expulsions of non-Serbs. By 1995, he had lost all sense of restraint. A pile of U.N. resolutions that were never implemented, along with the fecklessness of Western leaders, convinced him that he could get away with anything. He was fully in control of the situation in his own country, and nobody could challenge him. NATO had become a joke.

"Are they going to bomb us?" he asked rhetorically shortly after Srebrenica fell. "No way!" (In fact, a massive NATO bombing campaign began a few days later, laying the groundwork for the Dayton peace negotiations.)

I've come to conclude that Mladic is a prime example of Lord Acton's dictum that "Power tends to corrupt, and absolute power corrupts absolutely." By the summer of 1995, he had become the master of his little universe, cut off from political reality. Surrounded by sycophants who dared not contradict him, he became a victim of his own propaganda, comparing himself to heroes in Serbian history who had gained immortality by "fighting the Turks"—a term he used to disparage Bosnian Muslims, who, to Mladic, had committed the unforgivable historical sin of aiding the Ottomans who ruled over Bosnia for more than four centuries and crushed a series of rebellions by Orthodox Serbs. "We present this city to the Serbian people as a gift," he announced grandly the day Srebrenica fell. "Finally, the time has come to take revenge on the Turks."

Like Bosnia itself, Srebrenica today is a town divided. Several thousand Muslim refugees have returned to their homes, but they have little contact with their Serbian neighbors. "We nod at each other, but we don't drink coffee together," said Samedin Malkic. Out of the 27 boys in his high school class, only three survived, and only Malkic came back to Srebrenica. "It is a ghost town," he told me sadly. "You don't see a single person you know."

Two decades after the start of the Bosnian war, it is hard to escape the feeling that the war criminals and ethnic cleansers won. There is a painful sense on both sides of the ethnic divide that Srebrenica's former comity will never be restored. "It was like a little America here before the war," said Zejneba Ustic, another Muslim returnee. "We had everything we needed. Today, there is no work. The factories are nearly all closed. The economy has collapsed."

Two decades after the start of the Bosnian war, it is hard to escape the feeling that the war criminals and ethnic cleansers won.

It is sobering to think that a communist dictator did a better job—at least in the short term—of reconciling ethnic groups and building a functioning economy than the Western democracies that took responsibility for Bosnia after the Dayton peace agreement. Tito promoted his "brotherhood and unity" ideology by throwing dissenters into prison and forcibly suppressing any real debate about the ethnic bloodletting triggered by World War II. He forced Bosnians to forget their hatreds—or at least pretend to forget. The West, by contrast, is encouraging them to remember, even if this complicates the process of reconciliation.

The Yugoslav war crimes tribunal set itself the goal of creating an objective historical record on which all reasonable people should be able to agree, based on impartial experts' meticulous documentation of the Srebrenica massacre and other atrocities. Unfortunately, this has not prevented nationalists on all sides from challenging the evidence the court has assembled and promoting alternative, ethnic-centered versions of history. For a taste of these often-outlandish conspiracy theories, you need look no further than the comments section of my blog about the Mladic trial on FOREIGN POLICY'S website, where, for example, "experts" funded by the Bosnian Serb statelet REPUB-LIKA Srpska explain away the mass graves of Srebrenica victims by insisting that they contain the remains of Muslims "killed in combat" rather than executed prisoners.

The start of Mladic's trial was supposed to represent both a crowning moment and a decisive test for the system of international justice that, we should remember, grew out of a humiliating failure to act. Formed in May 1993 as a half-measure by the United States and other Western governments that were unwilling to intervene militarily to stop the bloodshed in the former Yugoslavia, the court was widely viewed as an empty gesture toward the victims of a terrible war, the product of one more meaningless U.N. resolution. Indeed, in its early phase, the tribunal was noteworthy primarily for its powerlessness. Indicted war criminals continued to lead almost normal lives, seemingly immune from justice. Mladic attended weddings and soccer games, and he even went skiing at an Olympic resort near Sarajevo frequented by NATO peacekeepers. Even after he was stripped of official protection in 2002, he was still able to benefit from a support network of retired army officers as he moved from one hiding place to another.

Meanwhile, the Yugoslav war crimes tribunal spawned a network of special courts for Rwanda, Sierra Leone, Cambodia, and East Timor, in addition to the International Criminal Court, which has been hearing Darfur-related cases. The tribunal's first big breakthrough came in 2001 with the transfer to The Hague of former Serbian leader Slobodan Milosevic to face charges of crimes against humanity in Croatia, Bosnia, and Kosovo. Milosevic's trial ended inconclusively in March 2006 when the defendant was found dead in his cell following a massive heart attack.

In an attempt to avoid a repetition of the unsatisfactory ending of the Milosevic case, prosecutors have eliminated 90 incidents from the list of accusations against Mladic. The slimmed-down indictment still includes 106 separate charges, however, including two counts of genocide, revolving around the 1995 Srebrenica massacre and a massive campaign of ethnic cleansing elsewhere in Bosnia. The trial is likely to take at least two years—once, that is, it actually gets going. On only its second day, the presiding judge announced an indefinite suspension, possibly for months, because of "significant disclosure errors" by prosecutors, who had failed to share tens of thousands of documents with Mladic's defense team. It was not a reassuring sign. It took the Yugoslav war crimes tribunal the better part of two decades to bring its most high-profile target to justice, only to bungle the grand opening.

To this point, the tribunal's greatest service has been the promotion of the notion of individual responsibility over the pernicious doctrine of collective guilt. The Bosnian atrocities were made possible in the first place because men like Mladic sought revenge against entire communities for crimes committed "against the Serbian people" by Muslims and Croats. Similarly, Mladic has sought to depict the criminal case against him as a conspiracy by the United States and other NATO countries to discredit the entire "Serbian nation."

"I am not defending myself," he told the court in one of his pretrial hearings. "I am still defending both the Republika Srpska and Serbia and the whole people there."

The presiding judge was quick to set the record straight. "You are charged before this tribunal . . . no one else, not a republic, not a people," he told the old man in the dock. "I would urge you to defend yourself as an accused, rather than to defend persons, entities, organizations which are not accused before this tribunal."

Mladic is right that the trial is about more than just him. But for Bosnia to escape the vicious cycle of hatred begetting more hatred, the judge's approach to history must triumph over Mladic's. As much as we may want to divine the nature of evil, it is more important that we first resolve this one case.

Critical Thinking

1. Do you agree that the international system of justice has failed in dealing with genocide in Srebrenica in the former Yugoslavia?

2. What factors limit the ability of international criminal tribunals to apprehend war criminals?

3. Is the norm of the Responsibility to Protect a viable option to the failure of states to punish genocide?

Michael Dobbs, who covered the former Yugoslavia for the *Washington Post*, is a research fellow at the United States Holocaust Memorial Museum and author of the blog *Mladic in The Hague* at ForeignPolicy.com.

Dobbs, Michael. Reprinted in entirety by McGraw-Hill with permission from *Foreign Policy,* July/August 2012, pp. 100–105. www.foreignpolicy.com. © 2012 Washingtonpost.Newsweek Interactive, LLC.

Taking Refuge

The Syrian Revolution in Turkey

JENNA KRAJESKI

Reyhanli, turkey—On a Friday in early April, for the first time since opening almost one year earlier, Turkey's Reyhanli refugee camp is quiet. Its tight security—barbed wire, guards, and a large swath of farmland isolating it from the next town—has been loosened ever so slightly by the constant movement of Syrian refugees north from Reyhanli along the Syria-Turkey border to a new camp, 90 miles away, in Kilis. Guards lounge at Reyhanli's half-open gates, letting journalists and refugees pass with a nonchalance compounded by exhaustion. Collapsed canvas tents lie in mounds beside their swept-clean concrete beds. Near the gendarme station, children swarm around a custard cake, a present from Turkey's Anatolia News Agency, the agency's logo decorating the top in blue frosting. But in the background of the isolated, half-empty camp, the acrid black plumes coming off nearby mounds of burning garbage are like smoke signals.

Most of the hundreds of remaining refugees had just arrived the night before from northern Syria, where escalating battles between rebels and the Syrian Army had pushed Syrian civilians into Turkey. They wear expressions of the newly displaced, numbed by shock or animated by anger. One woman is furious about the lack of international intervention. "You are giving Bashar more time to kill his people," she yells, invoking the Syrian dictator Bashar al-Assad, whose attempts to suppress the rebellion in his own country have sent thousands of opposition fighters across the border.

A man, worried for a friend who had left his three children alone in Taftanaz, which the Syrian Army had recently torn through, begs, "We need to find them." Just outside a tent surrounded by fragrant crisscrossed lines of hanging laundry, a woman offers meek, staccato answers to the difficult questions she has not yet grown used to hearing. "Yes," her parents are dead. "Yes," it was the Army that killed them. "Yes," she escaped on foot. She is dazed, wearing a pristine black hijab. As she talks, a crowd of refugees gathers silently around her. "Yes," here, in the camp just across the border from where her home was destroyed, she feels secure, and "yes," she is grateful to Turkey for taking her.

For Turkey, it has been a year of complicated political maneuvers, humanitarian struggles, bureaucratic hassles, and the impromptu redefining of both its policy toward refugees and its foreign policy. Turkey's role as a burgeoning regional power, as a potential member of the EU, and as a model for the transforming governments of the Arab Spring, is being viewed through the lens of its reception of those refugees. As Syrians continue to cross the border—1,000 one night, 500 another—and a fragile ceasefire shows signs of collapsing completely, Turkey is being tested not only on its humanitarian principles but also on its political savvy.

Turkey's treatment of its Syrian refugees and its tacit support of the Syrian rebels are early trials of Turkey's growing clout in the region. The country's response to a neighbor in crisis displays its growing solidarity with the Arab world—fueled by politics and religion—and its use of that solidarity to gain authority in international politics. Turkey's tenuous geographical position could also be its good fortune, so long as it stays cool militarily, keeps its border open, continues to pressure the international community to take action in Syria, and remains patient.

The country is now host to 25,000 displaced Syrians, and the number continues to rise. Among them are members of the main opposition, the Syrian National Council (SNC), and the armed rebels, the Free Syrian Army (FSA). Still, there are potential kinks in Turkey's humanitarian pledge. So far the Turkish government has preferred to act alone, which alienates human rights organizations and limits aid. It resists offering full legal rights to Syrians. The refugees could wind up staying for the long term, needing jobs, education, and real homes. Along with the majority Sunni Arabs could come significant minority populations, like Christians and, most troubling for Turkey, Kurds. Turkey has long struggled with its Kurdish population, which makes up some 20 percent of the country. Citing ties to Kurdish terrorism, Turkey has deported Iranian and Iraqi Kurds seeking refuge in the past. The influx of Syrians could be Turkey's atonement for those past deportations, as well as its chance to play a significant, not merely symbolic, role in the Arab Spring. Perhaps most important is Turkey's support of the exiled Syrian opposition—a now mostly passive helping hand that could be a first step toward Turkish military intervention.

Repositioning

In recent years, a growing economy and the ruling Justice and Development Party (AKP), led loudly by Prime Minister Recep Tayyip Erdogan, have pushed Turkey into an ever-widening and more intense spotlight. Turkey has positioned itself as a model for the changing democracies of the Arab Spring and as a defender of Palestinians. A more careful balance has replaced an almost single-minded focus on EU membership. Today, there is a keen awareness that on its own eastern flank are powerful, if often turbulent, governments in a region where Turkey could assume a key leadership position. Turkey's "zero problems with neighbors" policy, spearheaded by the AKP, was an attempt to improve relations with Iran, Iraq, and Syria. A long feud between Ankara and Damascus subsided when the Syrian government finally expelled Abdullah Ocalan, the leader of the Kurdistan Workers' Party (PKK), which Turkey, the United States, and the EU classify as a terrorist organization. But when the Syrian uprising began, Turkey found itself in the unenviable position of having a neighbor with a great many problems—serious ones that would inevitably cross borders.

Turkey has positioned itself as a model for the changing democracies of the Arab Spring.

"The Turkish government made misjudgments early on, first thinking that Assad could be persuaded to reform and then taking serious offense that he wouldn't," says Yezid Sayigh, a senior associate at the Carnegie Middle East Center in Beirut. "They're paying the price right now." Once Turkey began siding with the protesters, it became Assad's harshest critic, favoring the tumult of a changing democracy over a tyrant's status quo and banking on Assad's swift removal and a strong relationship with Syria's new government. While the international community continued to try to negotiate with Syria, Turkey realized it had already burned that bridge. "This situation forces their hand," says Sayigh. "The options for Turkey are not comfortable ones."

An open border remains a central component of its pledge to pair political hardball with humanitarian aid. Turkey has spent $150 million on aid to the refugees, building nine camps and still scrambling to accommodate more new arrivals without significant help from international aid organizations or the UN. The refugees who remained in the Reyhanli camp in April, battle-scarred and grasping at a new life, are evidence that while governments deliberate over the country's future, the Syrian people are left waiting for the long crisis to be over, even as it gives no signs of ending.

A Syrian Revolt in Turkey

On April 1, while delegates from across the Arab world, including the Syrian National Council, and much of the West mulled the political future of the Assad regime at a "Friends of Syria" conference in Istanbul, demonstrations formed outside the gates of the conference center. First the pro-Assad protesters came out, carrying photos of Bashar and chanting inside a tight circle of Turkish riot police. Later, a larger group of anti-regime protesters clustered together wearing camouflage vests embroidered with the logo of the FSA. The two groups shouted at one another across a sidewalk border, but, while the pro-Assad demonstrators were eventually dispersed with tear gas, the FSA protesters were held by a loose line of Turkish police. They remained for hours.

Inside the conference hall, the Syrian National Council was given the podium. Assad was denounced and world leaders pledged monetary assistance to the burgeoning FSA. Turkish authorities, whether the government or riot police, appeared to be throwing their support behind the expatriated Syrian revolution, giving them time to organize and grow stronger in Turkey while Syrian forces continued to pummel their homeland.

Mohammad Bassam Imadi used to be Syria's ambassador to Sweden, but since November he has been living in an Istanbul hotel and working as a member of the Syrian National Council's foreign relations committee. Politicians with the SNC are allowed to stay for a year in Turkey, but it's a "passive assistance," Imadi says. In return, he hesitates to criticize Turkey's handling of refugees. "We are sitting in Turkey. It's not polite to criticize people who are hosting us. The burden is very big. It's not easy to harbor so many refugees." Imadi, like most of his colleagues, wants Turkey to go a step further in its assistance to the opposition. "The best alternative to military intervention would be a buffer zone," he says. "The defections will help to disintegrate the Army and the regime will fall."

Whereas Imadi and the SNC are largely based in Istanbul, the FSA is based in Antakya, the largest city in the border region of Hatay. The original camps for Syrian refugees were built along this frontier. Magid, a 26-year-old member of the FSA, is himself a defector from the Syrian Army. Like many FSA members, Magid stays in Turkey only when recovering from wounds sustained while fighting in Syria. Crossing the border, he says, is simple. "We pay smugglers. We walk up the mountains and through rivers, trying to avoid mines. I go every two weeks. In our group, only the wounded go back to Turkey. The border guards don't know we are FSA. It's a humanitarian issue, letting us cross the border."

The Antakya office of the Higher Commission for Syrian Relief, an Istanbul-based organization that works to mobilize and deliver aid to Syrian opposition, is both a dorm and a clinic for FSA soldiers. A sweet stew warms the air of the small kitchen and men gather around a television, smoking cigarettes and talking about home. On basement cots, soldiers are treated then redeployed to Syria. They are given first aid training, food, and beds below red, black, and green curtains—the colors of the Syrian flag. Among them are defectors like Magid from the Syrian Army and veteran FSA fighters, as well as young male refugees who seem to have bought medical care with a vow to join ranks. One patient counts the days until he can fight again. "Since the first day they called for freedom, we carried weapons," he says.

The FSA flatters its host country, as though it wants, not fears, a visit from Turkish authorities. Samir, a young man from Latakia with a thick beard, shows off Turkish flags emblazoned with photos of Ataturk, saying, "It's the least we can do." The wounded men appreciate Turkish relief but, as soldiers, they are also quick to disavow it. "I would rather defend Syria than be safe in Turkey," says one man, a defector recovering from bullet wounds. Another says, "I think Turkey is doing its best. But if we had to go to the camps, we would put our wives and children there and we would return to Syria permanently."

Samir is used to journalists, and the clinic feels a little like a made-for-media set. Stacks of medicine are nearing their expiration, and during an interview Samir instructs a patient in Arabic to credit the FSA with his escape from Syria. But the wounds are real, and so is the strong loyalty to the Syrian opposition, the hatred of Assad, and the gratitude to Turkey, although that comes with some caveats. The patients in the FSA clinic criticize the medical care in the camps where, according to Samir, "patients are barely looked at, just prescribed medication immediately." Local hospitals are good, they say, but the doctors are overworked. "Turks go into the hospital when they are hurt, but Syrians arrive and this guy lost his leg, this guy has lost his hand," Samir says. "Turkish doctors are tired of the Syrian cases."

A short visit to a local hospital confirms the rushed, though well-meaning, care—an effective recruiting method of the FSA. Ahmed Mustafa, a day laborer from Taftanaz, lies on a cot by the window struggling to talk through a cheek swollen with embedded shrapnel. The battle in his hometown was the first time Mustafa had behaved like a soldier, he says, but now he's committed to fighting, returning to Syria rather than seeking the safety of the Turkish refugee camps. "I will work hard to topple the regime. All those people are being killed. Wouldn't you go back?"

This cross-border flow is not without serious challenges. The Turkish government has so far failed to unite the Syrian opposition in Turkey, and there are concerns about the effectiveness of that opposition in exile. The refugees have brought with them scrutiny from both the international community and the Syrians living in Turkey. There is the worry that at some near point, the passive assistance of harboring soldiers—what FSA forces referred to as the Turkish authorities "closing one eye"—will become tantamount to Turkish military intervention in Syria.

"This is a unique case in Turkish history," says Gokhan Bacik, a professor of international relations at Gaziantep's Zirve University. "For the first time, Turkey is officially struggling for regime change in another country. The Arab Spring is a great opportunity for Turkey to realize its new power, but it is finding its limits. There is a fine tuning between idealism and reality." Bacik worries that because of its humanitarian goals, Turkey is in over its head. "Eighty countries attended 'Friends of Syria,'" he says. "But Turkey is the only one still here. In practice it is only Turkey."

The Camps

Almost as soon as the first Syrians gathered at the border, the Turkish government was ready with tent cities, preparing, as President Abdullah Gül was quoted as saying, "for the worst,"

meaning a tsunami of refugees. Basic necessities—food, shelter, and security—were the priorities. But mobility for the refugees, transparency, and cooperation with nongovernmental entities were in short supply.

"In the early days, we called the camps humanitarian detention," says Oktay Durukan, director of the refugee program at the Istanbul office of the Helsinki Citizens Assembly, a human rights group. The Assembly and other organizations focused on refugees, including the UNHCR, were essentially frozen out by the Turkish government, which preferred to collaborate exclusively with the Turkish Red Crescent, a semi-governmental aid organization. Other aid workers and journalists were banned from entering the camps. Refugees, who would have provided the most crucial testimony on the conditions inside, were not allowed to leave.

Rumors began circulating. There weren't enough tents, and, come winter, the Syrians could expect the same freezing conditions as victims of last October's catastrophic earthquake in the southeast city of Van. With its heavily Kurdish population, Van had been cruelly neglected by the Turkish government. Ethnic discrimination—between Muslims and Christians, Alawites and Sunnis—intensified the stress within the camps. Turkish authorities were deporting high-ranking opposition members. Gender dynamics boiled over, leading to harassment and the segregation of young men from families—"segregation" really being an excuse to separate potential troublemakers into a more prison-like camp. Without reliable information passing the camp gates, it was impossible to distinguish truth from worry.

"For the first four months in Reyhanli I couldn't leave," recalls Mahmoud Musa, a former headmaster who lived in Reyhanli for nine months before being moved to the new camp in Kilis in April. Musa worried about his children's stalled education in the camp. He complained about the lack of privacy, the cold tents during winter, the overcrowding. "In Reyhanli, you had to walk 300 feet to the toilet. You had to walk 300 feet to the bath in the cold." Moreover, they were all but out of touch with the world. Moreover, the refugees felt oppressed by their disconnection from the outside world, particularly as violence escalated and politics roiled at home.

But in Reyhanli, Musa made friends with the Syrian smugglers he had once blamed for making the revolution violent by seeking "revenge" against security forces. "As a teacher, I would tell my students not to become smugglers. Now I am a smuggler. I smuggle journalists into Syria." Musa is quick to forgive Turkey for mishaps in its handling of the crisis. "The Turkish people, I believe, want to help us," he says now. A smart and thoughtful man, and a fluent English speaker, Musa quickly established himself as a liaison between refugees and the Turkish authorities. In April, the Ministry of Education contacted him about establishing a school for Syrian children in Antakya.

As the violence in Syria moved north and the number of refugees increased, Turkey began work on three new camps. In April, one month ahead of schedule, they opened a camp in Kilis, a border town north of Hatay. In Kilis, tents were replaced by pre-fabricated container homes, suitable for six. Schools, mosques, and a hospital awaited the refugees. In exchange for their temporary Turkish ID cards, and after undergoing biometric fingerprinting and an X-ray of belongings, the refugees would receive a credit card that they could use to buy goods in an in-camp store. A tall concrete and barbed wire fence replaced the chain-link fence of Reyhanli. There is constant surveillance.

As the violence in Syria moved north and the number of refugees increased, Turkey began work on three new camps.

"Kilis is like paradise, if you don't think about leaving," Musa says. In spite of his communication with the Turkish government, in order to get to Antakya, Musa had to sneak out of the camp with the help of a foreign journalist. "If I had come by public bus, the gendarmes would have checked."

Eventually, authorities allowed media and inspectors into the camps, but only a privileged few. To the refugees, such visits are merely an opportunity for Turkey to flatter itself. Wasim Sabagh was living in Bohsin camp for two months by the time the UN's top humanitarian official, Valerie Amos, visited. "The Turkish authorities wouldn't let her walk around," he says. "They picked people to greet her who would blindly praise Turkey." But these shows were also for high-ranking Turkish officials, according to Sabagh, who blames corrupt camp workers and middle management. He recalls preparations for a visit from Turkey's Prime Minister Recep Tayyip Erdogan. "They cleaned the whole camp," he says. "And then Erdogan's mother got sick, and he didn't even come."

Ironically, what protects Syrians in Turkey from losing their mobility altogether is their host country's seemingly indeterminate policy. Just as Turkey passively encourages the FSA, it passively affords the ability to crisscross the border to the tens of thousands according to the ebb and flow of violence in Syria. Because in Turkey, Syrians are not technically refugees.

Temporary Protection

In 2010, before the Syrian crisis began, there were 17,000 non-European asylum-seekers in Turkey. Most were from Iraq, Iran, and Afghanistan, with Somalis making up a significant minority. These refugees would register with the UNHCR, then be sent to one of 30 satellite cities around Turkey with an asylum-seeker ID card and residency permit, but little else. "You are expected to survive on your own," Durukan says. "There is no housing, no help. In some ways the Syrians in the camps are better off."

Syrians who entered Turkey because of the 2011 uprising are frequently referred to as "refugees," but the more than 25,000 Syrians residing in Hatay and later in Kilis and the surrounding area have been given "temporary protection status." They do not need a visa to enter Turkey and will not be deported back to Syria. While they are in Turkey, they can seek amenities and security in the camps. There are other benefits. The Syrians are not subject to the stresses of Turkish satellite towns, and they avoid consulting the UNHCR when they want to return to Syria—a process that depends on judgment of the UNHCR rather than the refugee. "UNHCR standards are not the same as the refugees'," says Dawn Chatty, director of the Refugee Studies Center at Oxford University. "When you enter walls and have formalized refugee status, it becomes very hard to leave. The refugees are infantilized."

But temporary protection is a term that irks many displaced Syrians. To them, it is a way for Turkey to withhold legal rights and also serves as a display of their host country's xenophobia. "The Syrian regime looks at us as terrorists. The Turkish regime looks at us as numbers," Sabagh says. "We are human beings. We must be considered refugees." Their own status denies Syrians the right to settle and work in Turkey and the chance to emigrate from there to Europe. It makes it seem that Turkey's motivation is political rather than humanitarian. "They are keeping us like a card to play," Sabagh says. Turkey's refugee camps are platforms where the regional power can showcase its humanitarianism while hosting Assad's opposition—a chance to start on good terms with a post-Assad government. But by denying status to the refugees, Sabagh believes, the Turkish state shows it cares little for the individual.

Such denial may be interpreted as a personal slight—a continuation of Arab discrimination in Turkey—but there are arguments for its practicality. "The most important thing is protection," says Metin Corabatir, the spokesperson for the Turkey branch of the UNHCR. "Temporary protection status is designed for mass influx of people." Registering each individual as a refugee is time-consuming, costly, and, in the case of Syrians living so close to their homes, confining.

While some refugees enter the limbo of camps or exploit the open border to continue fighting, some do sneak deeper into Turkey in search of a more permanent life. The children attending the all-Syrian Al-Bashayer school in Hatay find it easy to blend in. There is a distinctive cultural overlap between Hatay and Syria. Until the 1930s, the region was part of Syria. Arabic, as well as Turkish, is widely spoken. Many refugees have chosen to sidestep the camps, some living legitimately with relatives, but most illegally. Reliable numbers are difficult to come by, but if the school's attendance is any indication—rising from 15 to 190 students in nine months—the population is growing rapidly. The school also looks ahead to the longer-term. The children's education in their new country, which includes Turkish language classes and a revised history that glorifies the Ottoman Empire, is the first of the refugee community's potential new roots.

At school, students rehearse songs from a play about Syria they are set to perform in one month. "They sing songs for the revolution," says Mustafa Shakir, the principal and founder of Al-Bashayer. "There is a song for each city in Syria." But the revised curriculum withholds the worst details of the bloodshed just miles away. "We don't tell them how many people have died," Shakir says. "They come with that. We want them to be able to escape the suffering."

The school depends on the light restrictions placed on Syrians leaving the camps. But this is not a policy that Suphi Atan, from the Ministry of Foreign Affairs, thinks will last if the number of refugees continues to rise dramatically.

Atan oversees the transfer of refugees from Hatay to the new camps—"dream cities," he calls them—and he anticipates more scrutiny on the avenues and in the apartment buildings where undocumented Syrians roam freely. "We don't want to have people on the streets. In Kilis, we are forcing them to live a more comfortable life," he says.

Moreover, Antakya is 40 percent Alawite, so most support Syria's Alawi dictator, Bashar al-Assad. They are uneasy about hosting these new refugees—many of whom had until just recently engaged in pitched street battles against Assad's security forces. There is widespread speculation here that this tension is what led Turkey to move the camps north. Like the vast majority of the refugees, Turkey's government is Sunni Muslim. If the end goal, or part of it, is to secure goodwill with a post-Assad government, Turkey needs to make sure it keeps its Syrian population happy. But containing the refugees in new camps, particularly those in the opposition or who, like the students at Al-Bashayer, seek out lives in town, seems doomed to have the opposite effect.

A Death at Kilis

On April 9, fighting erupted in Syria just across the border from Kilis, and shells killed a refugee inside the container city. "The bullets were able to pierce the container houses," Musa, the headmaster, says. "At the funeral, one guy screamed, 'We are in Turkey and they killed us inside Turkey.'" Kilis's vulnerability concerns aid agencies, says Corabatir, from the UNHCR. "A principle of international refugee practice is that camps should be far from the borders when there are conflicts. We continue to provide our guidelines, but the Turkish authorities have their own expertise."

"We know that refugee camps in the south are considered the base of the FSA," adds Durukan, from the Helsinki Citizens Assembly. "This is part of Turkey's ambiguous policy." Imadi, from the SNC, hopes that the shelling of Kilis would "cause Turkey to take a stronger stance. But we can only speak and make meetings. We cannot demand anything."

Turkey, which has the second-largest military in NATO, began moving its own troops to the border to protect the camps. "I think Turkey came very close to mounting a military intervention when there were shots fired that targeted refugees," says Kemal Karisci, a professor of political science at Istanbul's Bogazici University. Turkey has been able to avoid military intervention, perhaps because of the unwitting calculations of the international community to encourage a ceasefire at a critical moment and give Turkey a chance to take stock. "The foreign minister has promised that Turkey will not do anything

unilaterally," Karisci says. "But whether Turkey will be able to stand behind this position, only time will tell."

> **When Assad falls, as he must, Turkey will have a chance to play a central role in the economic and political restructuring of its neighbor.**

When Assad falls, as he must, Turkey will have a chance to play a central role in the economic and political restructuring of its neighbor. Turkey's policy now depends on two major events—that Assad will leave soon and that the tens of thousands of displaced Syrians on Turkish soil will be able to go home. It's at this point in the near future, according to Durukan, when Turkey will face a real refugee crisis. "When things stabilize in Syria, the question of Turkey as a host country becomes extra relevant. That's when the new regime could persecute members of the Alawite or Christian or Kurdish minorities, and they would seek asylum in Turkey," Durukan says. What's happening now—the 25,000 refugees, the faltering but growing opposition, the political uncertainty—this, Durukan continues, is only "a period of transition."

For now, despite the threat of violence and Turkey's fluctuating policy, the container homes, school, mosques, and hospitals of Kilis—along with the 12,000 refugees—aren't going anywhere. A resident in the Kilis camp, Ammar, describes the funeral after the early-morning shelling. "I could hear the gunfire. When I got into the square, people were holding the martyr. They were so angry. They took down the Turkish flag and started stepping on it. A Turkish official approached us. He was also angry. He asked us, 'Why are you stepping on the flag? That flag is protecting you.'"

Critical Thinking

1. Why is Turkey aiding the Syrian refugees?
2. Should President Assad of Syria be indicted by the International Criminal Court for genocide?
3. Should Turkey engage in a humanitarian intervention in Syria?

JENNA KRAJESKI is an Istanbul-based writer, whose last contribution to *World Policy Journal*, "Beyond Tahrir Square," appeared last summer.

Gender Equality and Sustainable Development

MONIQUE ESSED FERNANDES AND ELEANOR BLOMSTROM

Championed by a wide range of stakeholders from civil society and the Women's Major Group, to Governments and United Nations agencies, the Rio + 20 Conference in June will no doubt include gender equality in several places of its outcome document. What will this mean for the achievement of true gender equality and sustainable development? The two are inextricably linked, but the discourse on gender equality and sustainable development within the context of Rio + 20 cannot be fully understood without looking back at some remarkable events which shaped the first Rio Conference 20 years ago.

History: A Look Back over Two Decades

A glaring lack of reference to women in the preparatory drafts of the United Nations Conference on Environment and Development in 1992 motivated Bella Abzug and Mim Kelber, founders of the Women's Environment and Development Organization (WEDO), to address the issue. To this end, the 1991 World Women's Congress brought some 1,500 women together who hammered out the Women's Action Agenda for the twenty-first century, an important part of the preparatory process to the Conference, at the national and regional level, and ultimately in Rio at the 1992 Earth Summit itself. It is worthy to recall that the only text that went to Rio without a single bracket was Chapter 24 of Agenda 21: Global Action for Women Towards Sustainable and Equitable Development.

Principle 20 of the Rio Declaration, Chapter 24 of Agenda 21, and the formation of the Women's Major Group and Caucus are all worthy legacies of this historic encounter that brought women from all walks of life and from all parts of the globe to inform each other, including those attending the negotiations process, about the realities of women's lives. Perhaps the most profound result was the network of activists who have continued to fight to ensure that women's voices and experiences impact policy in all fora, not just at the United Nations.

WEDO co-founder, Thais Corral, together with the Brazilian non-governmental organization Rede De Desenvolvimento Humano, spearheaded a new round of consultations before and during the 2002 World Summit on Sustainable Development in Johannesburg to assess not only the progress of Governments, but also of civil society itself during the 10 years following the Earth Summit. The Women's Action Agenda for a Healthy and Peaceful Planet defined the new and emerging issues of the twenty-first century. It recognized the growing evidence of climate change and the threat of increased militarism as perhaps two of the greatest challenges of the planet, as well as the need for women to add a new set of instruments to traditional advocacy and action in order to avoid rolling back even the most modest gains that had been achieved since Rio in 1992.

Looking back on these 20 years, WEDO has tried to draw on the lessons learned since those visionary women transformed negotiations at the United Nations in addition to, as it turned out, many other places. Following the path of environmental activists, such as the late Wangari Maathai, a Nobel Peace Prize laureate and WEDO board member, Vandana Shiva, a leading advocate at WEDO who positively impacted many poor farmers through the fight she helped wage in her native India, and the many other dedicated women who made a difference—big or small—in their own communities and worldwide, WEDO feels obliged to confront the Rio + 20 preparations with no less determination.

Today: Challenges in the Run-up to Rio + 20

In 2012, funding for spectacular meetings like the 1991 Conference is scarce. WEDO and women all over the world have embraced new technologies, working virtually to spread information quickly. Today they are able to organize, agree on and take action with speed. Stopping there, however, does not do justice to the intent and spirit of Principle 20 of the Rio Declaration: "Women have a vital role in environmental management and development. Their full participation is therefore essential to achieve sustainable development."

The space readily available for women to make their realities and experiences, much less their aspirations, a part of policy making is still limited in most countries—even within the very same international organizations that helped birth the Rio commitments. In 1991, a tribunal of women judges gathered evidence on the hazardous work and environmentally threatening conditions they endured. Have these conditions changed sufficiently?

Women identify numerous areas in which they have not seen progress, or in which progress is being reversed. Women continue to hold the vast majority of non-professional jobs; are in the lower income bracket; live in homes and areas vulnerable to climate change threats; sacrifice education in order to provide food, water and fuel for their families; face violence in the home as well as in society; encounter discrimination when trying to access productive and financial resources; encounter roadblocks to their sexual and reproductive health and rights; contract illnesses from burning biomass in their homes; lose access to communal and traditional land, as both local and international interests take over; and face environmental hazards such as chemical spills and poor sanitation that have long-term health effects. Yet, women are not helpless victims. Women are leaders and organizers; they raise awareness and fight for change and for strong roles in planning and decision making.

The Task: What Must We Do at Rio + 20?

The house of sustainable development cannot stand on an uneven foundation. Not only do the three pillars—the social, the environmental and the economic—have to bear equal weight, they have to intertwine to further strengthen the foundation for a more sustainable world. The groundwork has already been put in place in 1992 and 2002: the precautionary principle, common but differentiated responsibilities, and free, prior, and informed consent—especially in indigenous and women's communities and spaces—must be upheld. Voluntary commitments need to be strengthened with legislative teeth, accountability and financial mechanisms. Political will is a key ingredient.

As evidenced by the many men and women affected by the food, fuel, and financial crises, we have seen that economic viability cannot be gained at the expense of humanity, nor at the expense of sustainable ecosystems. Any new financial frontiers must be embedded in a rights based approach.

Social equity and environmental justice must remain at the heart of sustainable development, as should the outcomes of the Rio + 20 Conference. As countries confront the challenges of providing food, fuel, shelter, healthcare, and employment for growing and shifting populations, their Governments must find ways to preserve and protect vital ecosystems to support life and human livelihoods in an equitable manner, with an emphasis on human rights, gender equality, and environmental justice. They must find ways to limit climate change and its destructive impact that disproportionately affect the poor and women. Addressing gender equality in tandem with environmental and economic issues presents an opportunity to meet sustainable development goals more effectively.

Rio + 20 places strong emphasis on a green economy, which must be sustainable and equitable in all its aspects, with an aim to transform economies and not simply rename them. A green economy for sustainable development and poverty eradication will improve equitable distribution of wealth and will respect planetary boundaries, some of which have already been surpassed, but a green economy alone will not achieve sustainable development.

Women are making their voices heard and are fighting to ensure that Rio + 20 marks real progress for all people. A successful Rio + 20 will enhance women's rights and their access to and control over resources and decision making spheres. It must go beyond the gross domestic product to include indicators that measure women's contributions and consider externalities; ensure that gender budgeting is used for sustainable development implementation; initiate financial mechanisms that target women: include them in the design of and promotion for innovative initiatives; provide social protection measures (for example, basic services such as education and health); address access to safe, sustainable energy technologies; include women in food and agriculture priorities (related to land rights, speculation, extension services); provide for capacity building and appropriate technologies that have undergone assessment for health and environmental impacts; recognize and protect indigenous and women's traditional knowledge; and protect water rights.

Sustainable development governance systems will have to be exemplary in fostering and requiring participatory decision making and inclusion, mainstreaming gender equality and providing adequately for the many, instead of protecting the mighty few. Green governance is empty of meaning while women continue to be at the sidelines of decision making processes in too many governments and most boardrooms.

As we approach Rio + 20, we must take a closer look at what sustainable development and a green economy really mean. We must do so with the same drive and energy with which we confronted the overarching paradigm of development 20 years ago when honing the Women's Action Agenda 21 at the World Women's Congress. We must, once again, listen to those who are experiencing the ravages of the current development paradigm, we must be guided by the science that informs the climate change debates, and we must disaggregate the economic data through the eyes of poor women who are unable to participate in person.

Above all, we must show through rigorous analysis what the new jargon, the new environmental lexicon, really means: What is a green economy? What does carbon neutral mean? Who is trading greenhouse gas emissions credits and why? What does this economy offer to indigenous and traditional women who continue to bear the brunt of so-called development strategies? What are we doing when we protect areas? Finally, we must also assess our own progress and leadership and be transparent in our plans to ensure that those mechanisms we have established, including the entity UN Women, are funded and empowered by women's realities to bring about the paradigm shift that is necessary to usher in sustainable development.

WEDO has sought to focus its work over the past decade since the World Summit on Social Development on two areas: building global alliances and addressing climate change through a gender perspective. In spite of the fact that natural disasters have plagued the lives of many across the globe (particularly in those countries that can least afford it), nations are approaching the end of the Kyoto Protocol with a giddy nonchalance that is difficult to understand, given the frightening effect on the long-term outlook. Rio + 20 will need to outline the responsibilities of all in order to reach true sustainable development.

Rio + 20 will lay out the process for numerous actions that will shape development in the coming decades. Women, especially poor women, have a right to demand that those of us (women and men) privileged enough to be at the table, do not shirk our duty to ensure justice, nor pass them only the crumbs of a new economy.

Critical Thinking

1. What is the relationship between gender equality and sustainable development?
2. Should sustainable development be considered a civil and political right, or an economic and social right? Why?
3. Did WEDO achieve any of its objectives at Rio + 20?

UNIT 6

International Political Economy

Unit Selections

Learning Outcomes

After reading this Unit, you will be able to:

- Explain the difference in the economic recovery between the advanced states and the emerging markets.

- Analyze the factors that can stall the economic recovery of the global economy.

- Explain the critical role that Germany plays in the Eurozone crisis.

- Explain why China's economic growth will be limited in the future.

- Explain why China's economic growth only marks a return to its position in 1870 in the world economy.

Student Website
www.mhhe.com/cls

Internet References

Eurobarometer
   http://ec.europa.eu/public_opinion/index_en.htm
Europa
   http://europa.eu/int
International Monetary Fund
   www.imf.org
World Bank
   www.worldbank.org

International political economy is an important component of study in the field of international relations, especially in the highly globalized and interdependent world of the 21st century. Consequently, the collapse of the U.S. credit and housing market in 2009 upended a number of major U.S. banks and financial houses, with far-reaching global implications for advanced economies as well as emerging markets in the multipolar international system. The central question revolves around the extent and nature of the global recovery from the recession of 2009 and whether developments such as the crisis in the Eurozone can threaten what some view as a rather fragile recovery. In 2012, the global economy has experienced a slowdown, affecting even the emerging markets of Brazil, China, and India. Rose, Loungani, and Terrones, in the article "Tracking the Global Recovery," argue that in the case of some issues as unemployment, the recovery has been better in the emerging markets than in the advanced economies. For example, unemployment rates have fallen more slowly in the advanced economies than in the emerging markets, although some advanced economies such as Germany have continued to experience a lower unemployment rate. However, given the problems within the Eurozone, Germany could face a recession as well at some point in the near future. The authors conclude that the "world economy has recovered and the world has avoided another Great Depression," but any future oil shocks and the ongoing crisis in the Eurozone could pose a problem for the recovery. In 2012, the Eurozone crisis has now roiled the area since 2010, jeopardizing not only the future of the Eurozone, but perhaps even the future of the European Union itself. Critical to the recovery of the global economy is a successful resolution of the crisis in the Eurozone, which began in 2010, and continued to threaten the future not just of the Eurozone, but the European union itself. By the fall of 2012, the Eurozone crisis still posed a threat to the viability of the European organization that had kept the peace in Western Europe since the end of the World War II. For example, despite the infusion of bailout funds from the troika—the European Commission, the European Central Bank, and the International Monetary Fund, Greece continued to teeter on the edge of financial disaster. It was quite possible that Greece itself would either leave the Eurozone, or be forced out of it, by the more fiscally prudent members of the organization, which did not wish to support the profligacy of its peripheral members, most of whom were located in the southern part of Europe. If Greece were to leave the Eurozone, it would have to replace the Euro with the drachma, at a significantly lower value. The pages of the respectable British magazine *The Economist*, at times were characterized by a sense of panic as to what would happen to the European Union if Greece left the Eurozone. Over the past several years, other peripheral members of the Eurozone—Portugal, Ireland, and Spain—also had needed external financial aid in order to avoid defaulting on their sovereign debts. In 2012, there was also a great deal of concern expressed as to what might happen if Spain followed Greece's path and could not pay its sovereign debt either. The Spanish financial meltdown was caused by the bursting of the bubble of its housing market and the indebtedness of its regional governments. There was a great deal of concern expressed about

© Comstock Images/Getty Images

Spain, because its economy was significantly larger than that of Greeces. There was also the possibility that the Eurocrisis, which threatened the fragile world recovery from the recession of 2009, could spread from the peripheral to the core members of the European Union, such as Italy. The crisis of the Euro could also be seen as a political crisis rather than just a financial crisis. The European Union may have expanded too quickly after the end of the Cold War by admitting the former communist states of Eastern Europe. The European Union could have focused more on deeper integration, rather than a broadening of its membership. The Euro was designed as a common currency to serve as the basis of the further monetary integration of the organization, but without a sufficient institutional structure to follow up on the next steps toward economic integration. Moreover, nationalism still was an important factor preventing all of the members of the European from adopting the common currency. For example, the United Kingdom and several other members of the European Union opted not to join the Eurozone. In the final analysis, the Eurozone crisis boiled down to a question of the extent to which the members of the European Union had developed a sense of European identity. A critical role in dealing with the Euro crisis is being played by Germany and the approach that the German Chancellor Angela Merkel and her advisors have taken to the problem. Generally, the Chancellor of Germany had taken the approach that strict fiscal measures of austerity should be implemented by countries such as Greece rather than relying on a bailout by the richer members of the European Union such as Germany, given obsessive German fears about inflation. In connection with this, Germany had been opposed to the idea of Eurobonds being bought by the European Central Bank, because this would replace the concept of national fiscal responsibility with the idea of the mutual fiscal responsibility of all of the members of the organization. However, Germany did not want to see Greece default on its sovereign debt, or the Euro fail, because this would also have serious negative consequences for the German economy. Therefore, although the German Bundesbank was critical of the idea, the European Central Bank announced on September 6, 2012, that it would buy short-term bonds in the secondary market. Sebastian Mallaby, in "Europe's Optional Catastrophe:The Fate of the Monetary Union Lies in Germany's Hands," believes that the European Bank has "saved the euro system from breaking up" and concludes that "the most plausible route to debt reduction is to create a Eurozone bond, so that part of the debt can be replaced by the debt issued by the whole region," along with strengthening Europe's banking system.

The economic slowdown that the world economy has experienced in 2012 also has affected the Chinese economic miracle and taken some of the gloss off it as a member of the BRICS. Salvatore Barbones, in "The Middling Kingdom:The Hype and the Reality of China's Rise," is more critical of the economic models that predict the continuation of China's growth to become the world's richest country. The author argues that the two factors that contributed to China's economic growth were a low fertility rate and urbanization, processes that are finite. Barbones concludes that "the overall size of China's economy is thus likely to remain roughly equal to that of the United States for the remainder of the twenty-first century."

Tracking the Global Recovery

Most emerging markets are doing fine, but most advanced economies are not and things seem unlikely to change

M. AYHAN KOSE, PRAKASH LOUNGANI, AND MARCO E. TERRONES

The world has experienced four global recessions since World War II—1975, 1982, 1991, and 2009. These were years in which the global citizen's average income fell—in the jargon of economists, world per capita gross domestic product (GDP) declined—and there was a broad decline in various other measures of global economic activity. Each recession led to fears of economic apocalypse, but each time the global economy recovered in a year or two.

The global recession of 2009, which followed a financial market crisis caused by the failure of the investment banking firm Lehman Brothers the year before, was the deepest of the four recessions and the most synchronized across countries. Some worried that the world would relive the Great Depression of the 1930s. Luckily, and through often aggressive and unconventional policy actions, that did not come to pass. Since 2010, the global economy has been on a path of recovery, albeit a fragile one.

How different is the current global recovery from the earlier ones in the post–World War II period? How do prospects differ between advanced and emerging economies? And what are the risks to the global recovery?

On a Slow Track

While arriving at a definition of a global recession takes some work (see box), defining a global recovery is easier. It is simply the period of increasing economic activity that follows a global recession.

The slow path of economic recovery since 2010 has been quite similar to the path, on average, in the aftermath of the three other global recessions (see Chart 1). In fact, if the projections of average global income—world per capita real GDP—are realized, recovery from the Great Recession, as it is often called, will have been faster than after the three previous global recessions.

But the path of global income masks a very critical difference between advanced economies and emerging economies. The recovery in advanced economies has been very sluggish compared with past recoveries (see Chart 2, left panel). Average income in some of these economies has not yet rebounded to its pre-recession level and is not forecast to do so even by 2014.

The weakness in income growth is reflected, on the spending side, in both consumption and investment. Consumption has been held back as households return to safer debt-to-income levels ("deleverage"), and investment in structures has been weak in the aftermath of the housing boom in many advanced economies.

Global Recessions and Recoveries

"We live in a global world" is one of the clichés of our time—the phrase gets more than 700,000 hits in a Google search. Surprisingly, though, there is no commonly accepted definition of a global recession to tell us when our economic world as a whole is off track. The definition of a global recession used here is as follows: a period of decline in world real per capita real GDP, accompanied by a broad decline in various other measures of global activity (such as industrial production, trade, capital flows, oil consumption, unemployment). These criteria pick out four global recessions in the post–World War II period: 1975, 1982, 1991, and 2009 (Kose, Loungani, and Terrones, 2009). Once these dates are established, the definition of a global recovery is easy: it is simply the period of increasing global activity following a global recession.

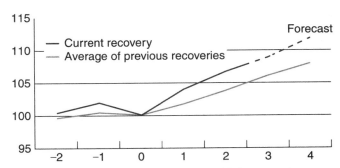

Chart 1   On track In terms of global GDP per capita, recovery from the most recent downturn is proceeding faster than after the three previous recessions.

(real GDP per capita indexed to 100 at the trough, weighted by purchasing power parity)

Source: IMF staff estimates.

Note: Measured yearly, with zero denoting the trough of the recession.

A Faster Pace

In sharp contrast to developments in advanced economies, average incomes in emerging economies are generally back on the fast track they were on before the Great Recession (see Chart 2, right panel). Income growth in these economies has already outpaced the growth seen during previous global recoveries, and is projected to continue to do so in coming years. The robust growth is widely shared among emerging economies. Notable exceptions are the emerging European economies, which are on a recovery track similar to that in advanced economies.

World trade collapsed dramatically during the global recession of 2009 and was one of the reasons the recession evoked fears of another Great Depression and a resort to protectionist measures by governments seeking to shield domestic industries from foreign competition. But world trade has rebounded, and again the pace is quicker in the emerging economies than in advanced ones (see Chart 3). Vertical specialization, in which a number of countries are involved in the production process of individual goods, may have restricted the use of traditional protectionist measures (see "Trade Policy: So Far So Good?" in this issue).

Equity markets have performed better on average during this recovery than in previous ones. This may be because corporations are increasingly operating globally. And global activity as a whole—thanks to emerging market economies—has recovered better than after previous recessions.

Waiting for the Jobs Train

Changes in unemployment generally lag changes in income. At the onset of a recession, as demand falls, companies cut back on overtime and make other adjustments before they let go of workers. As the recovery begins, companies generally wait to see whether it is durable before hiring workers again.

Despite this lag, over the course of a year, changes in incomes and unemployment tend to move together very closely. This relationship—known as Okun's Law after it was described in an article written 50 years ago by the economist Arthur Okun (1962)—held up well during the global recession of 2009.

Over the course of the recession, the unemployment rate increased in advanced economies by about 2 percentage points between 2006 and 2009. Consistent with the weak income growth in these economies, unemployment has fallen very slowly during the recovery. Even by 2014, the unemployment rate in advanced economies is forecast to fall by less than 0.5 percentage points, that is, by less than a quarter of the increase during the recession (see Chart 4). In emerging economies, in contrast, unemployment rates on average barely budged during the recession and are forecast to fall by 2014.

Among the advanced economies, the increase in unemployment varied a lot country by country during the recession. Three factors account for this variation: the extent of growth (or lack thereof) in incomes, structural bottlenecks, and the impact of macroeconomic and labor market policies. Structural factors may have played a supporting role in some countries, particularly where the collapse of the housing sector was a major reason for the drop in output. And the role of policies, particularly labor market policies such as worksharing, could be important in some specific cases, such as in explaining why Germany had a decline in unemployment. In Germany, employers receive subsidies to encourage them to retain workers but reduce their working hours and wages.

However, it was the growth factor that was by far the most important. Chart 5 shows that Spain, Ireland, Portugal, and the United States experienced the largest increases in the unemployment rate between 2007 and 2011. In Australia, Switzerland, Austria, Belgium, and Germany, however, unemployment barely increased—or even fell—over those years. These differences across countries in their unemployment experience can be explained almost perfectly by the changes in income growth in those countries. In other words, Okun's Law holds quite well (Ball, Leigh, and Loungani, forthcoming). This predominant role of income growth in driving the labor market explains why unemployment declines are expected to be rather slow in advanced economies.

Is It '92 All Over Again?

Although the world economy has recovered and another Great Depression has been staved off, the recovery remains subject to risks. Financial turmoil in Europe is an obvious risk.

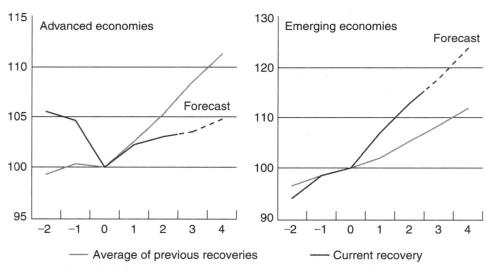

Chart 2 Two-speed rebound The recovery in advanced economies has been far more sluggish (left panel) than in emerging economies (right panel).

(real GDP per capita indexed to 100 at the trough, weighted by purchasing power parity)

Source: IMF staff estimates.

Note: Measured yearly, with zero denoting the trough of the recession.

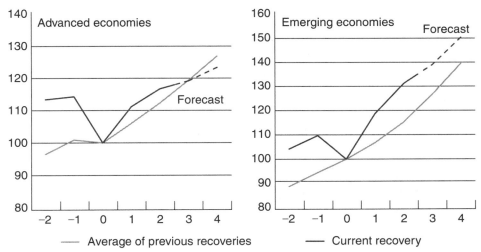

Chart 3 Trade returns International trade volume, which plummeted at the height of the recession, has rebounded—more in emerging economies (right panel) than in advanced economies (left panel).

(trade volume indexed to 100 at the trough, trade weighted)

Source: IMF staff estimates.

Note: Measured yearly, with zero denoting the trough of the recession.

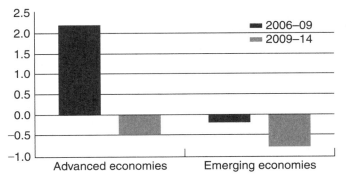

Chart 4 In search of jobs The unemployment rate rose dramatically in advanced economies and recovery is likely to continue to be slow. The rate fell in emerging economies

(change in unemployment rate, 2006–14)

Sources: IMF, *World Economic Outlook*, April 2012; and IMF staff estimates. Note: Data for 2012–14 are forecasts.

In this respect, the current recession and recovery in advanced economies share some features with the recession and recovery in 1991–92. Both recessions are associated with a bust in credit and housing markets in key advanced economies. In 1991, there were busts in credit and asset markets in the United States, the United Kingdom, Japan, and the Scandinavian countries. The recent recession was associated with severe problems in credit and housing markets in the United States and a number of other advanced economies, including Ireland, Spain, and the United Kingdom.

The path of income growth in advanced economies since 2010 is remarkably similar to that of the 1992 recovery. Both recoveries were slowed partly by challenges in Europe. The earlier recovery episode was shaped by downturns in many European economies during the 1992–93 crisis in the European Exchange Rate Mechanism, a precursor to the euro. Interest rates had to be raised during that period to defend the exchange rate arrangement, and several advanced European economies were forced to reduce their large fiscal deficits.

This suppressed economic activity and further depressed credit and housing markets in the region.

Currently, high risk premiums on sovereign debt are inflicting similar or even worse damage to fiscal balances and growth. In both cases, the lack of a timely, credible, and coordinated policy strategy heightened the financial turmoil. There has been slow growth in domestic consumption and investment driven by the legacy of the financial crisis—households and companies with high levels of debt have scaled back their activities to reach safer levels of debt (see "Shedding Debt" in this issue).

Will Oil Shocks Derail the Recovery?

Another risk to the global recovery comes from oil shocks—possible disruptions in oil supplies and the associated spikes in oil prices. These developments played a role in the global recession of 1975.

Since that time, oil-importing countries have taken numerous steps to reduce their vulnerability to oil shocks. They have increased the number of sources from which they import oil, making them less vulnerable to disruptions from any one source, and have used other sources such as natural gas and renewables—for example, solar and wind—to substitute for oil. In both advanced and emerging economies, there have been increases in energy efficiency; the amount of energy needed to generate a dollar of income has fallen steadily. And central banks have become much better at establishing an anchor for inflation expectations by communicating that oil price increases do not alter longer-run inflation prospects. Hence the public in many countries is much less fearful that oil prices will have inflationary consequences than was the case in the past. Increased oil prices no longer feed a wage-price spiral, as they did in the 1970s.

Nevertheless, while countries have built up some ability to withstand oil shocks, they remain vulnerable to severe supply disruptions or to the uncertainty induced by extreme oil price volatility. Estimates suggest that a 60 percent increase in the price of oil could reduce U.S. incomes by nearly 2 percent over a two-year period, with somewhat larger effects in Europe, Japan, and emerging economies in Asia (see Chart 6).

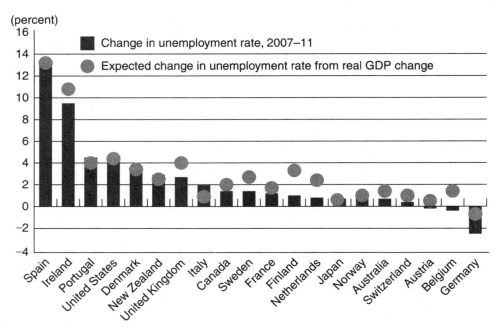

Chart 5 Joined at the hip The change in real (after inflation) GDP explains nearly all of the change in the unemployment rate in advanced economies between 2007 and 2011.

Source: Ball, Leigh, and Loungani (forthcoming).

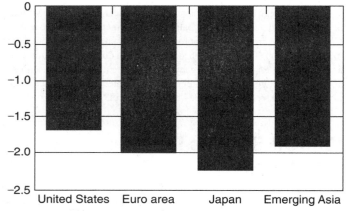

Chart 6 Oil threatens recovery A 60 percent increase in oil prices will seriously hurt economic output across the globe.

(percent change in real GDP two years after price increase)

Source: IMF staff estimates.

Fear of Stalling

The ongoing global recovery is similar in various dimensions to previous episodes, but it also exhibits some significant differences. The divergence of fortunes of advanced and emerging market economies has been one of the most surprising outcomes of the current global recovery. Emerging markets have enjoyed their strongest rebound in activity and become the engine of world growth during this recovery. In contrast, the current recovery is predicted to be the weakest one of the postwar era for the advanced economies. The trajectory of recovery in advanced economies has exhibited some parallels with that of the recovery in 1992: both the current and 1992 recoveries were hampered by the financial market problems in advanced European economies.

Failure to resolve these problems can stall the recovery and make already tepid job prospects in advanced economies worse. The threat of oil shocks looms as another risk factor for global economic prospects.

References

Ball, Laurence, Daniel Leigh, and Prakash Loungani, forthcoming, "Okun's Law: Fit at 50?" IMF Working Paper (Washington: International Monetary Fund).

Kose, M. Ayhan, Prakash Loungani, and Marco E. Terrones, 2009, "Out of the Ballpark," *Finance & Development,* vol. 46, no. 2, pp. 25–28.

Okun, Arthur M., 1962, "Potential GNP: Its Measurement and Significance," *Proceedings of the Business and Economic Statistics Section of the American Statistical Association,* pp. 89–104.

Critical Thinking

1. What are the factors that can affect the recovery of the world economy from the Great Recession of 2009?

2. Are there any differences in the economic recovery of the advanced economies as compared to the emerging economies?

3. Do you think that the authors are accurate in their analysis of the economic recovery of the advanced economies compared to the emerging economies? Why or why not?

M. AYHAN KOSE is Assistant to the Director, **PRAKASH LOUNGANI** is an Advisor, and **MARCO E. TERRONES** is Assistant to the Director, all in the IMF's Research Department.

Europe's Optional Catastrophe

The Fate of the Monetary Union Lies in Germany's Hands

Sebastian Mallaby

T
wo decades ago, when the European currency system was last on the brink of collapse, the ultimate question was how much Germany, the continent's economic powerhouse, would do to save it. The peripheral economies were hurting, weighed down by a monetary policy that was appropriate for Germany but too austere for weaker European countries. Germany's central bank, the Bundesbank, had to make a choice. It could continue to set high interest rates, thus upholding its commitment to stable prices. Or it could cut rates and accept modest inflation—and so save the rest of Europe from a prolonged recession.

We know which option Germany chose then. The Bundesbank brushed off suggestions that it should risk inflation for the sake of European solidarity; speculators correctly concluded that this made a common monetary policy intolerable for the weaker economies of Europe; and in September 1992, the continent's Exchange Rate Mechanism, a precursor of today's euro, shattered under the pressure of attacks from hedge funds. Almost 20 years later, the world is waiting for a new answer to the same question. How far will Germany go to keep Europe together?

The economist Rudiger Dornbusch observed that in economics, crises take longer to come to a head than you think they will, and then they happen faster than you thought they could. By the time you read this, the eurozone may have splintered. But whether or not that has happened, or soon will, one thing is certain. Since the beginning of the crisis, Germany has had the power to save the monetary union if it wanted to. The union's disintegration would be an optional catastrophe.

Superman Central Bankers

To see why the euro's failure could be averted, one must first grasp the awesome power of today's central banks. Until World War I, the advanced economies were tethered to the gold standard, meaning that central banks could not print money in unlimited quantities. Likewise, for almost all the years since World War II, the power of the printing press has been checked, first by a diluted version of the gold standard and then by the fear of inflation. But the combination of fiat currencies and economies

that are in a slump changes the game. Money, no longer tied to gold or any other firm anchor, can be created instantly, in infinite quantities, on the technocrats' say so. And so long as factories have spare capacity and unemployment keeps wages in check, there is unlikely to be any significant penalty from inflation.

Of course, central banks had this same power in the 1930s, when the world was in a depression and the gold standard had been abandoned. But they hesitated to use it, a decision documented and lamented by monetary historians from Milton Friedman to Ben Bernanke (the current chair of the United States Federal Reserve). Since 2008, by contrast, central bankers have been determined to prove that they understand history's lessons. Appearing on Capitol Hill shortly after the investment bank Lehman Brothers filed for bankruptcy in 2008, Bernanke himself informed Barney Frank, then chair of the House Financial Services Committee, that the Federal Reserve would stabilize the insurer AIG at a cost of more than $80 billion. "Do you have $80 billion?" Frank asked. "We have $800 billion," Bernanke responded. In fact, by December 2008, the Fed had extended fully $1.5 trillion in emergency financing to markets, dwarfing the $700 billion bailout fund authorized by Congress through the Troubled Asset Relief Program (TARP).

Central banks on the other side of the Atlantic have acted with equal resolve. For much of 2011, Europe's political leadership bickered about the details of the European Financial Stability Facility (EFSF), a TARP-like bailout fund with an intended firepower of 440 billion euros. Then, one day last December, the European Central Bank provided 489 billion euros to the continent's ailing banks, and in February 2012, it repeated this stunt, effectively conjuring the equivalent of two EFSFS out of thin air through the magic of the printing press. Since the start of 2007, the ECB has purchased financial assets totaling 1.7 trillion euros, expanding its portfolio from 13 percent to over 30 percent of the euro-zone's GDP. That means that the ECB has printed enough money to increase its paper wealth by an amount exceeding the value of eight years of Greek output.

This superman act has, at least as of this writing, saved the euro system from breaking up. Without the central bank's extraordinary support, private banks across the eurozone would have struggled to raise money and would have collapsed. Private firms, unable to take out bank loans, would also have gone under. The debtor countries would not have been able to rely on banks to purchase their government bonds and thus would have defaulted, in turn devastating the private banks that already held their bonds. The ECB's printing of money duly improved sentiment in the market. The interest rate on Italy's ten-year bonds, for example, tumbled, from around seven percent to about 5.5 percent, although it has since risen.

The ECB will eventually use up its room for maneuver. Some observers fear that the sheer volume of freshly minted euros is bound to lead to serious inflation, either when money begins to circulate faster or when the mere prospect of that event creates self-fulfilling inflationary expectations. But the best bet is that, with growth flat and unemployment over ten percent, the threat of inflation spiking across the continent is remote: with plenty of spare capacity on hand, any rise in demand will be met with increases in supply rather than with higher prices. For the foreseeable future, therefore, the ECB can keep on printing money to prop up banks. It can expand its modest direct purchases of government securities to ensure that finance ministries can raise money at less than punitive interest rates. It could even extend its support to nonfinancial firms, for example, by announcing that it stands ready to hold loans to small businesses on its own balance sheet. Most obviously, the ECB can help manage the crisis by keeping short-term interest rates low.

Increasing the money supply is sometimes dismissed as a mere palliative. But in addition to propping up banks, businesses, and governments, easy money can facilitate structural adjustment. If the ECB prints enough money to hit its target of two percent inflation across the continent, this is likely to mean zero inflation in the crisis countries, where unemployment is high, and three to four percent inflation in Europe's strong economies, where workers are confident enough to demand wage increases. By delivering on its inflation target, in other words, the ECB can help Italy and Spain compete against Germany and the Netherlands, gradually eroding the gap in labor costs that lies at the heart of Europe's troubles. At the same time, a determined and sustained period of monetary easing would probably weaker the euro. That would boost the competitiveness of the crisis economies against the rest of the world, further increasing the odds of an export-led recovery.

In short, the ECB has real power. It can avert a market meltdown and at the same time gradually make the periphery more competitive. But for the ECB to deliver on its potential, Germany must resolve not to get in the way. It must allow for an expansion of the ECB's innovative rescue measures and accept German inflation of three to four percent. Over the past year, unfortunately, German financial leaders have sent mixed signals. The big question of 1992—how far would Germany go for the sake of European solidarity?—has not been clearly answered. And so Europe's future remains cloudy.

The Path Out

Germany's leaders are correct that the countries in crisis must earn their own recoveries; the ECB cannot save them on its own. In particular, they must improve the administration of public finances, cracking down on tax evasion and wasteful spending, and remove product and labor-market regulations that undermine competitiveness. But these reforms tend to pay off in the long term. In the short term, slashing budgets will shrink demand and quell growth, while some labor-market reforms that make it easier to fire workers may initially drive up unemployment, undermine consumer confidence, and reduce growth further. The most urgent complements to the ECB's response therefore lie elsewhere—and they demand initiative from Germany.

Germany first needs to recalibrate its attitude toward public finances in the periphery. Thus far, the German strategy has emphasized deficit reduction, on the theory that countries that borrow less will accumulate less debt in the long run. But because deficit reduction keeps an economy from growing, it may defeat its own purpose. Over the past year, the eurozone has indeed cut deficits sharply, but the debt-to-GDP ratio has worsened. Germany needs to accept that aggressive austerity programs are neither politically sustainable nor economically wise. To get its debt under control, a country must attack its debt stock directly.

If Europe's leaders had mounted a forceful response earlier in the crisis, they could have imposed a meaningful debt reduction on private creditors across the continent. But by now, most private creditors have sold out, transferring their debt to the International Monetary Fund, the ECB, and other official creditors. (To be sure, private European banks hold large portfolios of European government bonds. But since the public sector stands ready to bail out these banks, they are not true private creditors.) Last year's restructuring of Greece's debt illustrated the problem. Almost two years into the Greek crisis, the country's private creditors were forced to accept a reduction of about 65 percent in the value of their claims. But at that point, most private creditors had already shed their government debt, so the resulting debt relief for Greece was far short of what the country needed to fix its finances.

Given that governments in the surplus countries and multilateral lenders have become significant creditors to the crisis countries, debt relief has to involve leniency on their part. This is unlikely to take the form of an explicit reduction in debt claims: the credibility of the International Monetary Fund and the ECB would suffer too much from an admission that their loans can be defaulted on. Nor is it likely to involve taxpayers in Europe's core explicitly paying off debts owed by the periphery: that would be politically explosive. The most plausible route to debt reduction is to create a eurozone bond, so that part of the debt of the crisis countries can be replaced by debt issued by the whole region. The German government's economic advisers have put forward a plan that would achieve this goal; now, the government needs to embrace it.

In addition to tackling governments' debt overhangs, Europe's leaders need to shore up the continent's banking system, which has been plagued by a surfeit of bad loans and, until recently at least, a deficit of honesty about them. Until the banks confess that loans to unemployed homeowners or ailing businesses won't be repaid on time, and until they set aside capital to cover their losses, their unacknowledged frailty will inhibit their lending: too few individuals and businesses will be able to borrow money, and growth will remain anemic. Moreover, the banks' return to health is a precondition for restoring confidence in the market, since the possibility of costly bank failures casts a shadow over the crisis countries. For the moment, the ECB's generous financing has guaranteed the banks' liquidity, inoculating them against the lending strike they have suffered in the private bond markets. But if millions of depositors begin to desert the banks at once, the ECB's liquidity may not be enough, and no amount of liquidity can address the banks' solvency. Unless banks keep more capital on hand, they risk collapse. Private investors are unlikely to provide these funds, and the governments of the crisis countries are too stretched to do the job alone. Some of the money will therefore have to come from stronger European governments.

Germany's Choice

In 1992, Germany prioritized managing its own economy over supporting European integration. It then seemed to show remorse and came around to supporting the creation of a common European currency. Despite the clear risks in binding disparate economies to a single monetary policy, the political drive to unite Europe won out. "The history of the European monetary unification is characterized by slow, but steady, progress in the face of constant skepticism and predictions of catastrophes," Otmar Issing, a German member of the ECB's executive board, proclaimed in 2001. "The launch of the single monetary policy was a resounding success."

Yet despite Issing's triumphalism, Germany today seems confused about which way it wants to go. The weight of blood and history argues in favor of keeping Europe together, and Germany's industrial captains understand that their success as exporters would be choked off by a return to a strong national currency. At the same time, however, Germany's leaders resist even modest inflation and are understandably wary of backing up other countries' debt or rescuing their banking systems. Germany is of course free to choose whichever path it wants. But if it replays 1992, the "resounding success" of the euro will go down in history as a resounding failure.

Critical Thinking

1. What are some of the difficulties associated with persuading members of the European Union to accept a common currency?

2. Is the Eurocrisis at bottom a crisis of political institutions? Why?

3. How will the issuance of Eurobonds solve the Eurocrisis?

Sebastian Mallaby is Paul A. Volcker Senior Fellow for International Economics at the Council on Foreign Relations and the author, most recently, of *More Money Than God: Hedge Funds and the Making of a New Elite*.

The Middling Kingdom

The Hype and the Reality of China's Rise

SALVATORE BABONES

By any measure, China's economic growth has been unprecedented, even miraculous. According to the International Monetary Fund, the Chinese economy grew by an average of 9.6 percent per year between 1990 and 2010. At the beginning of the recent global financial crisis, many feared that the Chinese growth engine would grind to a halt. In late 2008, Chinese exports collapsed, triggering fears of political instability and popular revolt in the country. In the end, however, the global economic crisis turned out to be little more than a pothole on the road of China's economic growth. Inflationary pressures may now be building up in China, and China's property bubble may be threatening to burst, but most economists continue to predict rapid growth for the country well into the future. Although their forecasts vary widely, they seem to share the view that China's growth will be fast—if not as fast as it has been—and that this rate of growth will continue for decades. These predictions are at once cautious about the near future (China's performance will not be as extraordinary as it has been) and optimistic about the distant future (they see no end to China's upward trajectory). By coincidence or design, they are moderated extrapolations of current trends.

For example, the Nobel Prize–winning economist Robert Fogel believes that China will grow at an average annual rate of eight percent until 2040, by which time it will be twice as rich as Europe (in per capita terms) and its share of global GDP will be 40 percent (compared with 14 percent for the United States and five percent for the European Union). Other economists are slightly more cautious: Uri Dadush and Bennett Stancil of the Carnegie Endowment for International Peace predict that China will grow by 5.6 percent per year through 2050.

Like many other forecasts of China's continued rise, these projections are based on careful formal economic modeling. But are they convincing? Extrapolating from current trends may make sense when predicting growth in the next year and the year after that, but once the years turn into decades, such assumptions seem more questionable. If my ancestors had invested a penny in my name in 1800 at a real compound interest rate of six percent per year above inflation, that penny would now be worth about $280,000. That does not mean, however, that reliably high-yielding 211-year investments are easy to find. Things change; things go wrong. Past returns are no guarantee of future performance.

When it comes to gauging China's future growth, economic modeling can offer only so much guidance. The models predict future economic outputs on the basis of projected future levels of economic inputs, but future economic inputs are impossible to predict. In the end, there is little to do but extrapolate from current inputs. But inputs, as well as other key features of any economy, change over time. China's economy is evolving rapidly: from subsistence agriculture to smokestack industries to the latest electronics to consumer services. And at some point in the future, perhaps in the not-too-distant future, China's excess growth rates will level out and its economic growth will slow down, returning to rates more like those experienced by comparable countries.

When the Growing Gets Tough

It may seem foolish in 2011 to even talk about calling a top to the Chinese market. Judging by the Fogel and Dadush-Stancil models, there seem to be no medium-term barriers to China's growth. So long as the country's urban labor force continues to expand, its educational levels continue to rise, and capital continues to move into China, the Chinese economy should continue to grow.

But are things as simple as that? For one thing, economic models tend to downplay the fact that as countries grow, growth gets harder. When economies move up global value chains, graduating from the production of simple manufactured goods to a reliance on the creativity of their citizens to develop new industries, they rise less and less rapidly. It took South Korea 30 years, from 1960 to 1990, to raise its GDP per capita from one-thirtieth of U.S. GDP per capita to one-third—but then it took another 20 years to nudge its way up from one-third to one-half. And South Korea today is still a long way from catching up with the United States. Japan caught up with the West (and by some accounts exceeded it) in the 1980s, but then the bubble burst, and since 1990 its economy has grown by an average of just one percent per year.

What is more, these two states have been vastly more successful than most others. No other medium-sized or large country with a diversified economy has even come close to Japan's accomplishments. Of the four "Asian tigers," the richest two (Hong Kong and Singapore) are cities, and the other two (South Korea and Taiwan) are basically cities-plus and are much farther behind economically. Other poor countries that have become rich are either offshore financial centers or small petro-sheikdoms. None of them is a full-sized country with multiple cities and regions, a large rural population, and competing political constituencies. Even Japan represents a questionable model of a state recently and rapidly catching up to the West, if only because it had already achieved much of its progress before World War II. Like the leading Western countries, it industrialized in the late nineteenth century and early twentieth century, partly through ruthless colonial exploitation. Its economy was then bombed into oblivion during World War II; thus, its rapid postwar growth was to some extent a return to prewar levels. In other words, there is no example to date of a state taking a very rapid growth trajectory to the top of the world economy, raising doubts about whether China can be the unlikely exception.

China's recent growth is often characterized as the country's natural, deserved return to its historical place in the global economy, but this argument is more clever than correct. According to the late economic historian Angus Maddison, China last reached parity with the West around the time of Marco Polo. China's subsequent decline relative to the West long predates the Industrial Revolution, Western colonialism, and even China's sixteenth-century inward turn. The overarching story of the past five centuries is not about China's absolute decline so much as about the West's relative advance. European economies grew substantially between 1500 and 1800. According to Maddison, by 1820—before the advent of the railroad, the telegraph, and the modern steel industry, and before the Opium Wars, the colonization of Hong Kong, and the Boxer Rebellion—China's national income per capita was less than half that of the average for European countries. By 1870, it had dropped to 25 percent, and by 1970, to just seven percent. Moreover, considering that Maddison's figures are all estimates based on purchasing power parity, China's position in hard-currency terms looks far worse. According to hard-currency statistics from the World Bank, between 1976 and 1994, Chinese GDP per capita was less than two percent of United States GDP per capita, and today it is still under ten percent.

In other words, China's massive economic growth over the past two decades has done nothing more—and perhaps much less—than return the country to its 1870 position (in terms of purchasing power parity). Optimists will see this as further evidence of China's potential: if China is at only 1870 levels, there is still plenty of room for further growth. But pessimists might note that if China could fall from this position in 1870, it might well fall from it again. There is no reason, on the face of it, to expect one outcome or the other; a conservative bet would be that China stays right where it is.

One-Time Benefits

Another reason that economic models forecasting China's continuing rise are too simplistic is that they tend to ignore both the one-time boosts that helped propel the country in the past and the political, environmental, and structural obstacles that will limit its growth in the future. China is now in a much stronger political and military position vis-à-vis the West than it was in 1870 and seems very unlikely to descend into another century-long ordeal of repeated human and economic catastrophes. But does that necessarily mean it will grow to become the world's richest country?

Forecasts of China's continued fast growth downplay the fact that as countries grow, growth gets harder.

China's dramatic rise over the past 20 years was propelled by two one-time bonuses: the population's declining fertility rate and its increasing urbanization. Both factors have led to massive increases in economic productivity, but they are finite processes and cannot be counted on in the future. China's fertility rate was already falling well before the first implementation of its draconian one-child policy in 1979. The decline in fertility in the 1970s meant that throughout the 1980s and 1990s, both families and the state could focus their limited resources on a relatively small number of children. Now, these children are in their mid-30s and are actively contributing to the development of the country's human capital and to its GDP. Future generations may be even better educated, but the major gains have already been made. More important, low fertility rates over the past few decades freed up adults, particularly women, to enter the formal labor market. Hundreds of millions of women who would have worked in the home or on the farm are now working in the money economy, boosting the county's GDP figures. This has given China a one-time boost—sustained higher output—but it will not help GDP continue to grow. There is little room for further fertility decline; China cannot move to a zero-child policy.

Moreover, there are today comparatively large numbers of workers born in the high-fertility 1950s, 1960s, and early 1970s making their way through their careers. Because their parents' generation is dying relatively young and because they have few children, these workers are largely unencumbered by either caregiving or child-rearing duties. Of all the generations of Chinese throughout history, this one is uniquely positioned to pursue work and create wealth. Future generations of Chinese workers will be smaller and will be saddled with the care of ever more elderly relatives. Moreover, fertility rates can only rise going forward, meaning that these workers may have more children to care for as well.

Increasing urbanization is the other one-time bonus that boosted China's economic growth during the past 20 years. Urbanization increases GDP because urban populations are generally more productive than rural ones and because

137

city dwellers typically work outside the home in paid employment, whereas many people in the countryside engage in unpaid subsistence farming. But like fertility reduction, urbanization is a process with natural limits. China's level of urbanization is still well below that of the West, and urban expansion in China shows no signs of slowing down. (At current growth rates, urbanization in China will not catch up to urbanization in the West or Latin America until the 2040s.) But what form will this expansion take? Huge shantytowns are already forming on the edges of Beijing, Shanghai, and other Chinese megacities. The Chinese government bulldozes shanties by the hundreds of thousands every year, but it is unclear whether their residents are being relocated or just being made homeless. Whether or not the government wins its war against slum development, the days when urbanization was a boost to economic growth are gone.

Structural Strictures

In addition, China is facing political, environmental, and structural barriers that will limit its economic growth in the future. For example, many analysts believe that China will not be able to move up the global value-added chain unless its politics open up. The argument is that high-value-added activities, such as branding, design, and invention, require a kind of free thinking possible only in democratic societies. China may educate hundreds of thousands of engineers, but if it continues to stifle their creativity, they will never succeed at the highest levels of the global economy. China will not reach the top ranks of the global economy (in terms of GDP per capita) until its schools, companies, and people learn to innovate more than they have in the past. This is happening, but China's stifling political culture is hindering the process. It is difficult to imagine a dynamic knowledge economy emerging in a politically repressive one-party state; none ever has before.

The environmental barriers to China's continued growth are better documented. The World Health Organization estimates that air pollution in China kills 656,000 people annually and water pollution another 95,600; China's own Ministry of Water Resources estimates that about 300 million people, two-thirds of them in rural areas, rely on water that contains "harmful substances." According to *The New York Times,* officials from China's State Council have said that the massive Three Gorges Dam is plagued by "urgent problems" that "must be resolved regarding the smooth relocation of residents, ecological protection, and geological disaster prevention." China is also now the world's largest emitter of greenhouse gases. The great drought and floods that have hit China so far this year may or may not be related to its environmental record, but it is clear that China's ability to monetize its environment to promote economic growth without regard for ecological devastation is coming to an end. China's future growth will have to be cleaner than its past growth; thus, it will be more expensive. Long a densely populated country, China has always had one of the most intensively exploited environments in the world. Today, it has little environment left to exploit.

Still, the greatest barriers to China's continuing rapid economic growth are structural. Until 1980, the country was effectively closed to the world; by 1992, nearly all of urban China had been incorporated into special economic zones open to private enterprise and foreign investment. The incredibly inefficient Maoist economy is gone and has been replaced by some of the most competitive firms in the world. Creating more value than did state industries during the Cultural Revolution was not very difficult. But creating more value than today's efficient Chinese firms do will be much harder.

This difficulty will be exacerbated by major structural changes in the economy. Since 1960, life expectancy in China has risen from 47 years to 74 years, but the number of children per family has declined from more than five to fewer than two. Today's little emperors will spend their most productive years taking care of their parents. And as they do, China's economic activity will have to move away from high-productivity manufacturing and toward low-productivity health services. This shift will further limit China's future growth prospects because productivity is harder to increase in service industries than in manufacturing, mining, or agriculture. In the past, to make the most of their comparative advantage, Chinese producers focused on manufacturing for the world's industrial market. In the future, Chinese service providers will have no choice but to focus on the domestic health-care market, without regard for getting an edge.

Can-Do or Has-Done?

Many commentators, most notably the political scientists George Gilboy and Eric Heginbotham, have warned recently of the "Latin Americanization" of China, specifically its rising income inequality. In 2003, China had just one billionaire (as measured in United States dollars); by 2011, according to *Forbes* magazine, it had 115. Yet China is still a poor country: GDP per capita in hard-currency terms is substantially lower in China (under $5,000) than in Brazil, Mexico, and Russia ($9,000–$10,000), the world's three big middle-income countries. But as China catches up to them, its inequality levels are also rising to levels close to theirs.

China shares many features with Brazil, Mexico, and Russia. Sociologists have identified these four countries as belonging to the "semi-periphery" of the world economy, a group of states that are not as rich and powerful as the developed democracies but not as poor as the small countries of Africa, Central America, and Southeast Asia. (Other examples include Indonesia and Turkey.) These countries are characterized by strong states with weak institutions, governments highly influenced by the richest citizens, and mass poverty.

At its current growth rates, China will likely catch up to Brazil, Mexico, and Russia around the year 2020 in terms of per capita GDP. At that point, all four states will have per capita national income levels between $10,000 and $15,000 (in today's dollars). All will also have similar levels of economic inequality—levels far higher than those in the developed countries. Their people will not experience serious hunger or malnutrition, but they will know mass squalor. About 40 percent of these countries' populations will live in large cities, and about 20 percent will live in rural areas, with the rest in small cities and towns. Their fertility rates will have fallen somewhat under replacement levels, and about two-thirds of their populations will be between the ages of 16 and 65. In the face of rapid aging, these countries will need to shift their economies away from growth industries and toward slow-growth health-care services.

All of which raises this question: If in 2020, China will almost certainly face structural conditions nearly identical to those in Brazil, Mexico, and Russia, why should anyone expect it to grow any faster than them? Brazil and Mexico have belonged to the middle-income league for generations. Russia was in that bracket in the early twentieth century and returned to it immediately after the collapse of communism. China was there in 1870, and it is back there again. Granted, China is bigger than those countries, but there is no reason to think that being big makes it different. Historical statistics show no correlation between a country's size and its economic growth.

The relative position of China in 2020 will look an awful lot like that of China in 1870 and of Brazil, Mexico, and Russia today. There is no particular reason to believe that the China of 2020 will be any more successful than these other states have been. Perhaps China's proactive attitude toward development will allow it to power through the middle ranks of the global income distribution despite a weak civil society, an aging population, and a devastated environment. And having already returned to its nineteenth-century position relative to the West, perhaps China might eventually regain its thirteenth-century superiority over the West. Structure is not destiny. And if China does overcome its limitations, it could provoke a complete realignment of the international system.

But it is more reasonable to see China's famous can-do attitude as more of a has-done attitude: a legitimate pride in recent accomplishments rather than a harbinger of future success. Like other middle-income countries, China will likely continue to grow slightly faster than Western countries, although not as fast as it did between 1990 and 2010 and with much more volatility. But its population will start to fall soon after 2020, whereas the United States population will keep rising. The overall size of China's economy is thus likely to remain roughly equal to that of the United States for the remainder of the twenty-first century. This is not to say that China will not become a major world player. Even if it reaches only parity

with the United States in terms of overall GDP and attains only about one-quarter of United States GDP per capita, it will still be a power to be reckoned with. It will become the second indispensable country.

But given the United States' far greater alliance network and geo-strategic position, United States hegemony is not threatened by the rise of China. The United States is encircled by long-standing allies (Canada and the countries of western Europe) or stable but weak noncompetitors (Latin America). China's neighbors are a rich and powerful Japan, rising South Korea and Vietnam, giant India and Russia, and a host of failed or failing states in Central and Southeast Asia. The United States reigns supreme over the oceans, the skies, and outer space; China struggles to maintain order within its own territory. China will, and legitimately should, play an increasing role in Asian and world politics, but it is in no position to dominate even Asia, never mind the world.

Pundits may relish the opportunity to speculate about a post-American future in which the world has to learn Mandarin, but the facts say not in this century. It is time to start treating China like a large but ordinary country. The rest of the world should neither relish nor fear the prospect of Chinese domination. Putting aside the hype and the panic, one should see in China a country that suffered terrible tragedy for 200 years and is finally returning to normal. This is a good thing—for China, for the United States, and for the world. If the international system comes to see China, and China comes to see itself, as an important but not all-powerful participant in the global system, irrational fears will diminish on all sides, and rightly so. Tomorrow's China is more likely to focus on meeting the needs of its own people than on establishing itself as the new global hegemon.

Critical Thinking

1. Will China's "economic miracle" continue into the 21st century? Why or why not?

2. What are the international political implications of a slowdown in China's economic growth?

3. Do you agree with the author that China has simply returned to the position it occupied in the international economy in 1870? Why or why not?

Salvatore Babones is Senior Lecturer in Sociology and Social Policy at the University of Sydney, in Australia.

Babones, Salvatore. From *Foreign Affairs*, vol. 90, no. 5, September/October 2012, pp. 79–88. Copyright © 2012 by Council on Foreign Relations, Inc. Reprinted by permission of Foreign Affairs. www.ForeignAffairs.com

UNIT 7

Global Environmental Issues

Unit Selections

Learning Outcomes

After reading this Unit, you will be able to:

- Explain why the prediction of conflict over the resources of the Arctic Sea is exaggerated.

- Discuss the important role that the Arctic Council plays in promoting the cooperation of the Arctic Sea states.

- Explain how the United States can protect itself from oil shocks.

- Explain why the United States is not dependent on oil imports from the Persian Gulf.

- Understand the relationship between population growth and the planet's resources.

- Explain some of the earlier misconceptions about population growth.

Student Website
www.mhhe.com/cls

Internet References

The Arctic Council
www.arctic-council.org
Arctic Map
http://geology.com/world/arctic-ocean-map-shtml
Food and Agriculture Organization
www.fao.org
International Data Base
www.census.gov/population/international/data/idb/informationGateway.php
The International Energy Agency
www.iea.org
The Organization of Petroleum Exporting Countries (OPEC)
www.opec.org
Real Climate
www.realclimate.org
World Food Program
www.wfp.org

Climate change is certainly the most important global environmental problem the international community faces and one that the global environmental governance mechanisms have not yet been able to resolve. The scientific community has developed different models that attempt to predict the effects of the warming climate, which is caused by the release of greenhouse gases into the atmosphere. This has had the effect of melting glaciers and ice sheets in Greenland and Antarctica. The melting of the Arctic Ocean has geopolitical implications and will have effects on the exploitation of oil in the Arctic. Arctic states such as Russia are staking out claims to adjacent continental shelves and seabeds, such as the Lomonosov ridge, in order to exploit the large amounts of energy that are available there. Besides Russia, some of the other important Arctic states are the United States, Canada, Denmark, and Norway. It is estimated that the energy reserves in the Arctic may amount to about 25 percent of the world's total reserves. A vast amount of scientific data, such as oceanographic data and satellite photos, show the melting of the Arctic sea ice.

The melting of the ice in Canada's fabled Northwest Passage will allow goods to be shipped from Europe to Asia and Asia to Europe, subtracting thousands of miles from the traditional sea routes. States and multinationals have expressed an interest in using the shorter routes, when they open up, perhaps by 2050 or earlier, to ship goods such as oil between East and West, as there would obviously be significant savings of shipping costs. For example, supertankers that cannot use the Panama Canal because they are too big would be interested in using the Northwest Passage, if feasible. The melting of the ice in the Northwest Passage has also opened up security issues, because it means that vessels of states other than Canada that do not accept Canadian claims to sovereignty over the waterway might be tempted to test Canada's ability to assert its sovereignty over the area. For example, the main difference between Canada and the United States about the Northwest Passage is that Canada views the Northwest Passage as lying within its internal waters, whereas the United States views the Northwest Passage as an international strait. The Canadian position on the Northwest Passage means that those states wishing to use it must seek the permission of the Canadian government. According to this line of reasoning, Canada, then, should have the capacity to control the Northwest Passage, if it wants its claim to sovereignty upheld. On the other hand, the U.S. position is that the Northwest Passage is an international waterway, and therefore can be used for the purposes of innocent passage.

In the final analysis, however, the potential of the vast energy resources opening up in the Arctic because of the melting of the Arctic sea ice is also resulting in the increasing militarization of the Arctic Ocean states, especially Canada. James Astill, in "Too Much to Fight Over" points out that the prize of oil in the Arctic is huge as the Arctic nations strengthen their military capabilities to enforce their claims to the energy that is supposed to be there. But the author stresses that the "risks of Arctic conflict have been exaggerated," and for example, Russian leader Vladimir Putin is much more cooperative so that ". . . the development of the Arctic is to be uncommonly

© StockTrek/Getty Images

harmonious." Furthermore, the author concludes that the Arctic Council is playing a key role in promoting the cooperation of the Arctic Sea states.

The economic development of emerging markets such as China and India has resulted in an intensified competition with the United States around the globe for energy and mineral resources, especially as China scours the globe for oil. The catastrophic effects of a lack of an adequate energy infrastructure were seen in India in the summer of 2012, when more than 600 million people were hit by a massive blackout. According to Niall Ferguson, the growing urbanization of India as its population increases will result in the emergence of more megacities there with an insatiable appetite for energy but with inadequate energy infrastructures.

Furthermore, energy security is a critical issue for the United States, as the rise in the price of oil due to the turmoil in the Middle East in 2012 could upset the efforts on the part of a country like the United States to recover from the recession of 2009. Most of the world's oil is located in the Middle East and is controlled by a cartel known as the Organization of Petroleum Exporting Countries (OPEC), which was formed in the 1960s. The United States, in an effort to reduce its dependency on foreign oil from regions such as the Middle East, has diversified the sources from which it imports this commodity. The United States is also taking advantage of new developments in energy technology, for example, to extract gas from shale, as well as to exploit oil from wells that have been thought to have been depleted as the United States focuses more on the development of domestic sources of energy. However, in "The Folly of Energy Independence," Luft and Korin argue that "the idea that energy independence is mostly about the security of supply is completely wrong," because the problem that the United States faces is about price. For example, Luft and Korin take the position that the United States, in terms of its energy security, is not dependent on oil imports from the Persian Gulf. But, as mentioned earlier, the recovery of the world economy from the recession of 2009 is also dependent on the price of a barrel of oil, which in 2012 has risen in anticipation of a potential Israeli military attack against Iran. However, the authors conclude that the United States can defend itself from oil shocks by "ensuring that new cars are open to fuel competition."

The growth of the world's population is also placing an enormous strain on the earth's resources and the carrying capacity of the planet to sustain the increased numbers, raising the spectre of a Malthusian nightmare. In 2012, the world's population reached 7 billion, and a population of 9 billion is projected by some experts by 2050. Experts estimate that the maximum carrying capacity of the planet is about 10 billion. Currently, in 2012, the world's population is increasing by 80 million a year. The greatest increase in global population is taking place in the developing or southern part of the world, therefore increasing the economic gaps and disparities that exist between the rich, industrialized, northern states located in regions such as North America, Western and Eastern Europe, and Russia and the states located in the southern part of the globe. This means that in the age of globalization, a significant number of the world's population will continue to exist on the periphery of the industrialized core of world society, eking out an existence of abject poverty. Robert Kunzig, in "Population 7 Billion," observes that "with the population still growing by about 80 million each year, it's hard not to be alarmed because . . . water tables are falling, soil is eroding, glaciers are melting, and fish stocks are vanishing " as "close to a billion people go hungry each day."

Too Much to Fight Over

Arctic countries have decided to join hands and gorge on Arctic resources.

J<small>AMES</small> A<small>STILL</small>

The Geopolitics of the new Arctic entered the mainstream on August 2nd 2007. Descending by *Mir* submersible to a depth of over 4km, a Russian-led expedition planted a titanium Russian flag beneath the North Pole. The news shocked the world.

The Lomonosov ridge under the pole, which is probably rich in minerals, is claimed by Russia, Canada and Denmark. The Russians, it was assumed, were asserting their claim, perhaps even launching a scramble for Arctic resources. One of their leaders, Artur Chilingarov, Russia's leading polar explorer and a Putin loyalist, fanned the flames. "The Arctic has always been Russian," he declared. Yet the expedition turned out to have been somewhat international, initiated by an Australian entrepreneur and a retired American submarine captain, and paid for by a Swedish pharmaceuticals tycoon.

Even so, fears of Arctic conflict have not gone away. In 2010 NATO's top officer in Europe, James Stavridis, an American admiral, gave warning that "for now, the disputes in the north have been dealt with peacefully, but climate change could alter the equilibrium". Russia's ambassador to NATO, Dmitry Rogozin, has hinted at similar concerns. "NATO", he said, "has sensed where the wind comes from. It comes from the north." The development of the Arctic will involve a rebalancing of large interests. The Lomonosov ridge could contain several billion barrels of oil equivalent, a substantial prize. For Greenland, currently semi-autonomous from Denmark, Arctic development contains an even richer promise: full independence. That would have strategic implications not only for Denmark but also for the United States, which has an airbase in northern Greenland.

There are also a few Arctic quirks that turn the mind to confrontation. Most countries in the region (the United States being the main exception) have powerful frontier myths around their northern parts. This is truest of the biggest: Russia, for which the Arctic has been a source of minerals and pride in the feats of Russian explorers, scientists and engineers since the late 19th century; and Canada, which often harps on Arctic security, perhaps as a means of differentiating itself from the United States.

During the cold war the Arctic bristled with Soviet submarines and American bombers operating from airbases in Iceland and Greenland. The talk of Arctic security risks sometimes betrays a certain nostalgia for that period. Some people also worry about Arctic countries militarising the north. Canada conducted its biggest-ever military exercise in the north, involving 1,200 troops, in the Arctic last year.

The risks of Arctic conflict have been exaggerated. Far from violent, the development of the Arctic is likely to be uncommonly harmonious.

Yet the risks of Arctic conflict have been exaggerated. Most of the Arctic is clearly assigned to individual countries. According to a Danish estimate, 95 percent of Arctic mineral resources are within agreed national boundaries. The biggest of the half-dozen remaining territorial disputes is between the United States and Canada, over whether the north-west passage is in international or Canadian waters, hardly a *casus belli*.

Far from violent, the development of the Arctic is likely to be uncommonly harmonious, for three related reasons. One is the profit motive. The five Arctic littoral countries, Russia, the United States, Canada, Denmark and Norway, would sooner develop the resources they have than argue over those they do not have. A sign of this was an agreement between Russia and Norway last year to fix their maritime border in the Barents Sea, ending a decades-long dispute. The border area is probably rich in oil; both countries are now racing to get exploration started.

Another spur to Arctic co-operation is the high cost of operating in the region. This is behind the Arctic Council's first binding agreement, signed last year, to co-ordinate search-and-rescue efforts. Rival oil companies are also working together, on scientific research and mapping as well as on formal joint ventures.

The third reason for peace is equally important: a strong reluctance among Arctic countries to give outsiders any excuse to intervene in the region's affairs. An illustration is the stated willingness of all concerned to settle their biggest potential dispute, over their maritime frontiers, according to the international Law of the Sea (LOS). Even the United States accepts this, despite its dislike for treaties—though it has still not ratified the United Nations Convention on the Law of the Sea, an anomaly many of its leaders are keen to end.

The LOS entitles countries to an area of seabed beyond the usual 200 nautical miles, with certain provisos, if it can be shown to be an extension of their continental shelf. Whichever of Russia, Canada and Denmark can prove that the Lomonosov ridge is an extension of its continental shelf will therefore have it. It will be up to the countries themselves to decide this: the UN does not rule on disputed territories. The losers will not do too badly, though: given the Arctic's wide continental shelves, the LOS guarantees each a vast amount of resource-rich seabed.

The 2007 furore over the Russian flag led to an important statement of Arctic solidarity, the Ilulissat Declaration, issued by the foreign ministers of the five countries adjoining the Arctic Ocean (to the chagrin of the Arctic Council's other members, Sweden, Iceland and Finland). This expressed their commitment to developing the Arctic peacefully and without outside interference. Possible defence co-operation between Arctic countries points in the same direction. Their defence chiefs met for the first time in Canada in April in what is to become an annual event.

A Warm Atmosphere

The Arctic Council, founded in 1996, was not designed as a regional decision-making forum, though outsiders often see it that way. Its mission was to promote conservation, research and sustainable development in the Arctic. The fact that six NGOS representing indigenous peoples were admitted to the club as non-voting members was evidence of both this ambition and the countries' rather flaky commitment to it. But since 2007, under Danish, Norwegian and now Swedish chairmanship, the council has become more ambitious. Next year it will open a permanent secretariat, paid for by Norway, in the Norwegian city of Tromso. A second binding pact, on responding to Arctic oil spills, is being negotiated; others have been mooted.

Russia, which has at least half of the Arctic in terms of area, coastline, population and probably mineral wealth, is in the thick of the new chumminess. It has a reputation for thinking more deeply about Arctic strategy—in which Mr Putin and his prime minister, Dmitry Medvedev, are both considered well-versed—than any other power, and appears to have concluded that it will benefit more from collaboration than from discord. Indeed its plans for the Northern Sea Route may depend upon international co-operation: Norway and Iceland both have ambitions to provide shipping services in the region.

Russia's ambassador for Arctic affairs, Anton Vasiliev, is one of the council's most fluent proponents of such collaborations. At a recent conference in Singapore, convened by *The Economist,* he surprised many by declaring Russia eager to standardise safety procedures for Arctic oil and gas production. "The Arctic is a bit special for civility," he says, "You cannot survive alone in the Arctic: this is perhaps true for countries as well as individuals."

The United States is less prominent in Arctic affairs, reflecting its lesser interest in the region and lukewarm enthusiasm for international decision-making. Although its scientists lead many of the council's working groups on subjects such as atmospheric pollution and biodiversity, it only hesitantly supports the council's burgeoning remit.

Frustrated advocates of a more forthright American policy for the Arctic, mostly from Alaska, lament that the United States hardly sees itself as an Arctic country, a status it owes to its cut-price $7.2m purchase of Alaska (Russian America as was) in 1867. A common complaint is the United States' meagre ice-breaking capability, highlighted last winter when an ice-capable Russian tanker had to be brought in to deliver fuel to the icebound Alaskan town of Nome.

The African Arctic

As governments wake up to the changing Arctic, global interest in the region is booming. A veteran Scandinavian diplomat recalls holding a high-level European meeting on the Arctic in the early 1990s to which only her own minister turned up. "Now we're beating countries away," she says. "I've had a couple of African countries tell me they're Arctic players."

Asia's big trading countries, including strong exporters like China and Japan, shipbuilders like South Korea and those with shipping hubs, like Singapore, make a more convincing case for themselves. All have applied to join the council as observers, as have Italy and the EU. Half a dozen European countries with traditions of Arctic exploration, including Britain and Poland, are observers already.

Some council members are reluctant to expand their club. Canada is especially wary of admitting the EU because the Europeans make a fuss about slaughtering seals; Russia has a neurotic fear of China. Even the relaxed Scandinavians are in no hurry to expand the council. Yet the disagreement has been overblown. If the EU, China and others were to be denied entry to the council, they would no doubt try to raise Arctic issues elsewhere, probably at the UN, which is a far more dreadful prospect for Arctic countries. So by the end of Sweden's chairmanship, in May 2013, these national applicants are likely to be admitted.

But Greenpeace, which also wants to be an observer, may not be, even though another green NGO, the World Wildlife Fund (WWF), already is. Several Arctic governments have been put off by Greenpeace's aggressive methods. Greens against governments, not country against country, looks likely to be the most serious sort of Arctic conflict. That is progress of a sort.

Critical Thinking

1. What is the relationship between the Law of the Sea and rival claims by Arctic Sea states to the energy resources of the Arctic Ocean?

2. Can Canada successfully uphold its claim to sovereignty over the Northwest passage? How?

3. How can the Arctic Council promote cooperation between the Arctic Sea states?

The Folly of Energy Independence

The only way to achieve true energy security is to end petroleum's monopoly on transportation fuel.

GAL LUFT AND ANNE KORIN

The United States stands on the cusp of a global strategic advantage of huge significance. It is now within our grasp to cut the Gordian knot of energy policy, transforming our economic prospects in a fairly short period. Seizing this advantage does not require or depend on an esoteric technological breakthrough. It does not require allied assistance. It does not require a great deal of citizen sacrifice, discipline or patience. It does not require new taxes or convoluted cap-and-trade schemes. It merely requires that the Administration and the U.S. Congress get their collective head straight for once about a policy area in which politically ecumenical futility has been the norm for nearly forty years.

It has been an article of faith at least since the Nixon Administration that, in order to strengthen its energy security and, through that, its international position generally, the United States should reduce its dependence on imported oil, particularly from the Middle East. The only significant difference between Republicans and Democrats on this point has been their choice of methods: Republicans have generally preferred supply-side solutions ("Drill, baby, drill!"), while Democrats have generally preferred demand-side responses such as greater conservation and efficiency, and higher energy taxes to encourage both. Withal, imports grew by leaps and bounds both in relative and absolute terms from 36 percent of consumption in 1973 to 60 percent in 2005.

Leaving aside for the moment the actual reasons that successive United States Administrations failed to achieve what all professed to be a critical national security goal, the fact of the matter is that the goal of import reduction was misguided. Typical Americans throughout the years have labored under a series of misconceptions about how the international oil business works, the most common of which is that exporters have the ability to fine-tune the destination of their oil exports for political or commercial purposes. This is simply not true. Think of the oil market as a swimming pool: Producers pour oil in, consumers take oil out. The oil itself is totally fungible, and everybody faces essentially the same price. While individual producing countries may have contracts with consuming countries, most oil is purchased on the spot market for an international price. This arrangement is enabled by the fact that the international oil companies determine what happens to the oil once it enters the global market. With rare exceptions, the governments of oil-exporting countries are simply unable to control where their oil goes.

Thus, the Arab oil-producing countries declared an embargo of the United States and certain selected European countries in the context of the October 1973 Middle Eastern war, but whatever modest shortage resulted from these actions was distributed evenly by the companies. There was no special, acute shortage in the United States; the long gas lines and price hikes had much more to do with panicked consumer behavior and the outright bungling of the Federal energy bureaucracy. But to this day most Americans believe otherwise.

During the Cold War American statesmen and strategists worried that the Soviet Union or its allies might be able to interdict or otherwise disrupt the flow of oil, particularly from the Middle East, to America's European and Asian allies. They worried that war or revolution in the countries of the region might have a similar effect, as seemed to be borne out in 1978–79, during the throes of the Iranian Revolution. These were not unreasonable concerns at the time. More recently we have worried about the direct and indirect flow of oil revenues to anti-American actors, be they states or non-state actors, and the physical disruption of supply by major attacks on Persian Gulf oil facilities. Again, these are not unreasonable concerns. But what has never made any sense is the argument that reducing oil imports—or even achieving oil self-sufficiency—would have shielded the United States from the consequences of such events. Yet the idea that energy independence is mainly about the security of supply is still the one stuck in the heads of most Americans and even most policymakers. Not to put too fine a point on it, this assumption is *completely wrong,* and our inability to rid ourselves of this generic misunderstanding is still leading us to overlook a readily available remedy for our problems.

The idea that energy independence is mainly about the security of supply is still the one stuck in the heads of most Americans and even most policymakers. Not to put too fine a point on it, this assumption is *completely wrong*.

The problem we face is not about supply but about price. In recent years America's volume of imported oil has dropped significantly even as the price we have paid and are still paying for it has sharply increased. It follows, then, that the policy options we ought to consider differ significantly from those of the past half century. Yet there seems to be something seriously the matter with our mental clutch. We're stuck in the wrong gear, and we're not getting anywhere. That needs to change, now.

Up to Speed

To understand more fully what the problem is and what we need to do about it, consider that in recent years America's energy landscape has turned a corner—not thanks to, but largely despite, the actions of the U.S. government. United States net imports of petroleum declined from 12.5 million barrels per day (mbd) in 2005 to 8.6 mbd in 2011. U.S. import dependence dropped from its 60 percent peak in 2005 to 46 percent, the level it was back in 1995. This 30 percent reduction in just seven years in the level of imports is equivalent to three times the number of barrels nominally imported from Saudi Arabia.

Some of the reduction is due to a recession-induced drop in consumption; some has to do with increased vehicle fuel efficiency standards; some with a ramp up in ethanol blending; and some with a ramp up in domestic oil production. Since 2008, technologies like deep-water drilling, hydraulic fracturing and horizontal drilling have increased United States crude oil output by 18 percent. In the past year alone, the United States onshore rig count has grown by 30 percent. About a million barrels per day emerged from a new source, tight oil, which is extracted from dense rocks. North Dakota, the center of the tight oil transformation, has become the fourth largest oil-producing state behind Texas, Alaska and California. For the first time in decades, the United States is experiencing an oil boom—or at least a boomlet.

But while America's oil imports dropped, its foreign oil expenditures climbed by almost 50 percent, from $247 billion in 2005 to $367 billion in 2011. The share of oil imports in the overall trade deficit grew from 32 percent in 2005 to 58 percent in 2011. The price of a gallon of regular gasoline nearly doubled. Despite lower demand, United States drivers spent more last year on gasoline than in any prior year.

Clearly, and surprisingly to those trapped in old ways of thinking, the volume of United States imports and the cost of those imports have moved in opposite directions. While America became more self-sufficient and more fuel-efficient, it became poorer and got deeper in debt. If one accepts the traditional mantra of energy security as "availability of sufficient supply at affordable prices", then whatever points we gained on the availability front were offset by those lost on the affordability side of the ledger. The latter matters more—especially in a time of economic adversity.

All but two of the post-World War II recessions were preceded by a sharp spike in oil prices; there is no question that the fivefold increase in oil prices since 2003 has contributed to the current economic dislocation. For perspective, forty years ago, at the zenith of the Cold War, the United States spent $4 billion on oil imports, an amount that equaled 1.2 percent of the defense budget. In 2006, the United States paid $296 billion, equal to half of the defense budget. By 2008, United States foreign oil expenditures grew so much they almost equaled the *entire* defense budget.

The energy security paradox of the 21st century, then, is that a country can reduce oil imports but end up paying a much higher oil import bill. What this means is that, given the current state of the global economy, a new oil shock—whether caused by war in the Persian Gulf, instability in North Africa or Nigeria, or even anxious investors rushing to buy oil futures to hedge against falling currencies—would sink Western economies. As it is, the rising cost of oil is hollowing out the United States economy, and no fuel economy standards or new oil discovery will stop this tide. What is needed is a new energy paradigm.

Cost, Not Volume

As we have already noted, dreams of autarky in oil still dominate United States energy policy discourse. The pledge to cut a third of oil imports by 2020 is at the core of President Obama's energy policy, and talk about reducing imports from the Middle East continues to be one of the best applause lines of all presidential and congressional candidates across the political spectrum.

This rhetoric relies on two false premises. First, America is not dependent on the Persian Gulf for its oil supply. Imports from the Persian Gulf never exceeded 15 percent of total United States petroleum consumption; currently, the figure stands at 9 percent. And again, these numbers are really nominal, since oil is fungible and swap arrangements the oil companies employ to reduce transportation costs make it impossible to know where any given barrel of oil really came from. Most United States oil imports originate in North America.

Second, even if all United States oil imports originated from Canada and Mexico, America would be just as vulnerable to the impact of oil price spikes due to volatility in the Persian Gulf and other unstable regions as it is today. Self-sufficiency in oil would not, indeed cannot, shield United States consumers from oil price shocks. In 2008, when oil prices reached an historic high, the United Kingdom produced most of the oil it needed, yet the price spike affected its citizens just as much as it did Americans. When the price of oil spikes, it spikes for everyone. The United States imports hardly any oil from Libya, but when the 2011 Libyan upheavals caused a supply disruption, American motorists were as affected by the resulting $25 per barrel price hike as the motorists of Libya's major oil purchasers.

The inability to keep the price of oil at bay, not the volume of imports, is the crux of America's vulnerability. But—and this is the critical yet still generally unrecognized key to the solving the energy puzzle—the price is what it is because virtually all the cars and trucks in the world are unable to run on anything but petroleum-based fuels. Oil faces no competition from other energy commodities in the sector from which its strategic importance stems, namely transportation. Since consumers are unable to choose between different commodities, suppliers do not need to compete for market share by increasing production capacity and supplying lower prices. And that, in turn, leads us to OPEC.

One can argue (and many have) that OPEC isn't particularly adept at managing its response to fluctuations in the oil market month to month or week to week. But this is simply indisputable: OPEC controls 79 percent of the world's conventional oil reserves, but its members account for only 36 percent of global production. If investor-owned oil companies such as Exxon, BP, Shell and Chevron were sitting on top of 79 percent of the world's conventional oil reserves, they wouldn't account for but a third of global supply. They'd probably account for 68 percent, or 82 percent, or something in that range. And if not, they'd be slapped with an anti-trust lawsuit. Anti-trust lawsuits, however, don't work against sovereign regimes such as those that comprise OPEC. It shouldn't be surprising that OPEC's production capacity is so low since OPEC is a cartel, and a cartel aims to maximize profit by constricting supply. Thus, in the past three decades, global GDP grew sixfold, yet OPEC's crude production increased by barely 15 percent. This is despite the fact that in 2007 the cartel inducted two new members, Angola and Ecuador, with combined daily production capacity equivalent to Norway's. (Ecuador actually rejoined OPEC in 2007; it had left the organization in 1992.) In other words, OPEC keeps production capacity well below what its reserves allow, creating a supply level designed to keep prices at a certain level.

Perhaps the best way to understand this is through the metaphor of a homeostat or, even better because more specific, a Watt's steam governor. OPEC decides on an ideal price level—one that covers expenditures but does not induce excessive conservation in its customers—and then adjusts supply accordingly. So when major consumers reduce net demand for whatever reasons, OPEC responds by throttling down supply to drive prices back up to its ideal

price level, what it calls a "fair" price, or just sitting on its hands while developing world demand picks up the slack. The thing is, this "fair" price keeps rising. In 2004, OPEC's "fair" price was $25 per barrel. Two years later it was $50. In 2010, OPEC's secretary general, Abdalla Salem El-Badri, argued for $90, and by the end of 2011, with OPEC's oil revenues topping $1 trillion, he adjusted the price to $100.

OPEC's "fair" price has increased significantly since the onset of the so-called Arab Spring. Hoping to avoid the fate of leaderships in Egypt and Tunisia, Persian Gulf regimes have showered their people with gifts and subsidies.

OPEC's "fair" price is based ultimately on the budgetary needs of the cartel's members, whose appetite for petrodollars has increased significantly since the onset of the so-called Arab Spring. Hoping to avoid the fate of leaderships in Egypt and Tunisia, Persian Gulf regimes have showered their people with gifts and subsidies. Saudi Arabia alone almost doubled its budget, committing $129 billion to entitlement programs. Despite a petrodollar-induced budget surplus in 2011, this expensive response to the protests will likely increase the break-even price the Saudis need in order to balance their budget in the coming years to at least $110 in 2015. Other OPEC members, especially Iran, Iraq, Venezuela and Nigeria, will also seek higher oil prices. OPEC's modus operandi of keeping the money coming is based on upward adjustment in the "fair" price of oil rather than on selling more oil.

Another reason for OPEC's rising break-even price is the cartel members' own oil consumption habits. Saudi Arabia is the world's largest oil producer, but due to its rapid population growth and heavy subsidization of fuels, the Kingdom is also the world's sixth largest oil consumer. With an internal demand growth rate of 7–9 percent per year, Saudi Arabia, currently using 2.8 mbd, is projected to consume roughly six mbd by 2030. Oil analysts counting on Saudi Arabia's production capacity reaching 12 mbd tend to forget that half of Saudi Arabia's oil will be burned within the Kingdom instead of reaching the world market.

Natural Gas Against Oil

In light of this dynamic, competing on the same playing field with the current set of major oil exporting countries is playing a game America can never win. The cartel's financial needs will drive it to respond to defensive behavior by its clients to the degree that any slack isn't taken up by increased developing world demand. This is easy for a cartel to do: Drill for more oil at home, and the cartel can simply reduce production to return to a tight supply-demand relationship; increase fuel efficiency, same response; mandate a specific small volume of non-petroleum fuels in the market over an extended period, same response. So it doesn't matter how well we follow the Republicans' "drill baby, drill" or the Democrats' conservation and efficiency; we'll still be on the same treadmill we've been on for decades.

In order to get leverage against manufactured increases in the price of oil, consumers must be able to respond to price changes as they occur. Drivers cannot rapidly change the fuel economy of their vehicles, but, with vehicles that enable fuel competition, they could choose to purchase a less costly substitute fuel as an immediate response to changes in oil price. In other words, they could fuel switch. That's the only way oil's monopoly over transportation fuel can be broken. Luckily for us, the current glut of cheap natural gas provides a unique opportunity to do just that.

Historically, natural gas prices tracked oil prices. But the emergence of shale gas, projected to reach 43 percent of United States natural gas production in 2015, has disconnected the prices of the two energy commodities. Since the collapse of financial markets in 2008, oil prices have rebounded more or less to their pre-2009 level, whereas natural gas prices remained suppressed and have even fallen. The utility and chemical industries, the two primary natural gas users, are limited in their ability to absorb more gas. If prices remain low, the natural gas industry will have little incentive to invest in further growth, and shale gas development will slow significantly. If, however, more vehicles could handle fuels made from natural gas, the industry would have the certainty it needs to continue to expand this job-creating sector.

There are several ways to take advantage of the low cost of natural gas. One way to use natural gas in automobiles is by employing it to generate electricity for plug-in hybrids and electric vehicles. Such vehicles are gradually entering the market. They are clean, cheap to operate, and in many respects outperform gasoline-powered cars. Furthermore, vehicle electrification offers great flexibility. If natural gas prices spike, there is always coal, nuclear or renewable power to rely upon for power generation. (Contrary to popular belief, oil is essentially no longer used to generate electricity: Only 1 percent of United States electricity generation is petroleum based, and only 1 percent of United States oil demand is due to electricity generation.)

However, due to the high cost of automotive batteries, mass-market penetration of battery-operated vehicles will take a long time. Such cars are projected to account for only 5 percent of vehicle sales in 2020. Not until 2040 will market penetration be deep enough to make a dent in the price of oil.

There is another way to run cars on natural gas via compressed natural gas (CNG) vehicles, which have a dedicated fuel line and a large gas canister in the trunk. But the cost of converting a light-duty vehicle to CNG is more than $10,000—a bad investment for most drivers given that it would take more years than most cars and light trucks are owned by the average person to recoup that in savings.

This leaves only one near term and affordable way of opening cars to natural gas *en masse:* converting the gas into liquid fuel. A recent MIT study on the future of natural gas determined that the most economical liquid fuel pathway for natural gas is methanol (wood alcohol). Other gas-to-liquids technologies can yield drop-in fuels like gasoline and diesel that can be used in the current automotive infrastructure, but on a per-mile basis these end products are 30 percent costlier than natural-gas-based methanol.

Methanol is a globally traded commodity, and its spot price averages $1.10 per gallon. Add taxes, distribution and retail markup, and on a per-mile basis methanol is substantially less expensive than gasoline. (Different fuels have different energy contents, so the proper price comparison is not per gallon but per mile.) China is already blending 15 percent methanol (made primarily from coal in China) into its automotive fuel, and in recent years 26 of its thirty mainland provinces have carried out testing and demonstrations of methanol fuel and methanol fuel vehicles. The economics of methanol are so favorable compared to gasoline that in China illegal methanol blending has become rampant.

In the United States, methanol blending will not occur without warranty guarantees for the vehicles into which this fuel is poured. In order for vehicles to run on methanol (and other alcohol fuels such as ethanol) in addition to gasoline, they must be tweaked to manage its greater corrosiveness. Essentially, all the tweaks needed are a fuel sensor and a corrosion-resistant fuel line. The cost? About $100 for a car or light truck. No, that's not a typo: just one hundred dollars.

Such flex-fuel vehicles provide a platform on which liquid fuels can compete, thus placing a variety of commodities (methanol can also be made from coal, biomass and, in the future, recycled carbon dioxide) in competition at the pump and letting the market determine the winning fuels and feedstocks based on economics: comparative per-mile cost. The proliferation of flex-fuel vehicles in Brazil has already driven fuel competition at the pump to the point that in 2008, when oil prices were at record highs, gasoline became the alternative rather than the primary fuel.

Nothing like what happened in Brazil can happen in the United States as long as vehicles are warrantied to run exclusively on petroleum fuels, with non-petroleum liquids confined to a protected and limited market as additives. Over the past seven years, as United States import dependence dropped, nearly 100 million new petroleum-only vehicles rolled onto America's roads, each with an average lifespan of 15 years. This has effectively extended the stranglehold of oil (and its possessors) on our economy by two decades. This is a needless tragedy.

We are solidly on track to continue this needless tragedy. At no point so far in the 2012 presidential elections cycle has any major candidate demonstrated even a rudimentary understanding of the actual problem of foreign oil, let alone articulated a solution for it. Clearly, our objective should not be to reduce the magnitude of United States oil imports but rather to diminish the strategic importance of oil altogether. The policy needs to be not about learning to endure the impact that price spikes have on the economy, but about banishing those spikes by placing petroleum in competition with other forms of transportation fuel.

Clinging to old mantras and new supply developments may bring America closer to self-sufficiency, but that will not help forestall economic decline. The most immediate and effective step the United States government can take to insulate our economy from oil shocks is to enact an open fuel standard, ensuring that new cars are open to fuel competition. This one act would signal that the United States transportation fuel market is no longer captive to oil. The capacity

expansion among various fuels that flex-fuel vehicles would stimulate will eventually lead to competition over fuel market share and thus drag down the price of oil. The sooner we adjust our thinking and focus on this game-changing, transformational solution instead of inconsequential, time-buying policies, the sooner we will attain true and lasting energy security.

Critical Thinking

1. What is the relationship between energy and population?
2. How important is OPEC in controlling the global supply of oil?
3. Has the United States been able to effectively reduce its dependence on Middle Eastern oil supplies? How?

Luft, Gal and Korin, Anne. From *The American Interest*, vol. VII, no. 6, July/August 2012, pp. 32+. Copyright © 2012 by American Interest. Reprinted by permission.

Lights Out in India

India's Massive Blackout Is Just the Beginning

Niall Ferguson

The British—slightly less than a thousand of them—used to govern India. Without air-conditioning.

Conan O'Brien was not the only one who watched the London Olympic opening ceremonies with amazement. "Hard to believe my ancestors were conquered by theirs," he tweeted. Every Indian watching must have been thinking the very same.

Until Their TVs Went Dark

The recent power outage in India interested me more than the Olympics. (I had a very British reaction to the opening ceremonies: I found them excruciatingly embarrassing.) The Indian blackout was surely the biggest electricity failure in history, affecting a staggering 640 million people. If you have ever visited Delhi in the summer, you will have some idea what it must have felt like.

"Every door and window was shut," Rudyard Kipling recalled of summer in the scorched Indian plains, "for the outside air was that of an oven. The atmosphere within was only 104 degrees, as the thermometer bore witness, and heavy with the foul smell of badly-trimmed kerosene lamps; and this stench, combined with that of native tobacco, baked brick, and dried earth, sends the heart of many a strong man down to his boots, for it is the smell of the Great Indian Empire when she turns herself for six months into a house of torment."

There was a reason the British moved their capital to the cool Himalayan hill station of Simla every summer. Maybe today's Indian government should consider following their example. Because power failures like this are not about to get less frequent. On the contrary, the outage has exposed the single greatest vulnerability of the Asian economic miracle: it is fundamentally underpowered.

In the past 10 years, according to the energy giant BP, India's coal consumption has more than doubled, its oil consumption has increased by 52 percent, and its natural-gas consumption has jumped by 131 percent. For China the figures are, respectively, 155 percent, 101 percent, and 376 percent. Asia as a whole is insatiably guzzling fossil fuels. And this is not about to stop. The McKinsey Global Institute expects India's economy to grow at an average rate of between 7 percent and 8 percent from now until 2030.

The good news is that all this growth will do something (though not enough) to compensate for the depressed state of indebted developed economies like the United States and Europe. The bad news—apart, of course, from the soaring CO2 emissions—is that Asia's creaking institutions may not be able to cope with the staggering social consequences.

According to McKinsey, India's urban population will increase from 340 million in 2008 to around 590 million in 2030. By then, India will have 68 cities with populations of more than 1 million, including six megacities with populations of 10 million or more, of which two—Mumbai and Delhi—will be among the five biggest cities in the world.

To cope with this breakneck urbanization, India needs to invest $1.2 trillion over the next 20 years to upgrade the infrastructure of its cities. Mumbai alone needs $220 billion. Will it happen? In India, there is a sideways movement of the head that means neither "Yes" nor "No," but "Please don't ask that."

India's electricity grid has missed every capacity addition target since 1951. The system is so dilapidated that 27 percent of the power it carries is lost as a result of leakage and theft. Even today, 300 million people—a quarter of the population—don't have access to the grid. That's one reason the blackout didn't spark more public ire.

The root of the problem is one of many leftovers of India's post-independence experiment with socialism. Half of India's power stations are coal-fired. Indian coal is produced by a state monopoly (Coal India). The price is controlled by the state, as is the price of electricity itself. The private firms running power stations are trapped between a lump of coal and a hard place. They cannot even trust the regional distributors to order the right amount of power.

In effect, Indians have a National Power Service similar in many ways to the National Health Service their former rulers in Britain are so proud of. Which brings me back to the Olympics. Surely the most embarrassing thing about Danny Boyle's opening extravaganza was the surreal dance routine involving

1950s-era hospital beds and nurses. Considering just how bad the NHS is in any meaningful international comparison, you have to wonder what the Indian equivalent would be. How about a stadium full of coal-fired power stations, all dancing in the dark?

Something to look forward to at the 2028 Mumbai Olympics.

Critical Thinking

1. What effect has India's consumption of fossil fuels had on the overall market for these products?

2. Would a move away from coal-fired power plants improve the lives of India's population?

Population 7 Billion

There will soon be seven billion people on the planet. By 2045 global population is projected to reach nine billion. Can the planet take the strain?

ROBERT KUNZIG

One day in Delft in the fall of 1677, Antoni van Leeuwenhoek, a cloth merchant who is said to have been the long-haired model for two paintings by Johannes Vermeer—"The Astronomer" and "The Geographer"—abruptly stopped what he was doing with his wife and rushed to his worktable. Cloth was Leeuwenhoek's business but microscopy his passion. He'd had five children already by his first wife (though four had died in infancy), and fatherhood was not on his mind. "Before six beats of the pulse had intervened," as he later wrote to the Royal Society of London, Leeuwenhoek was examining his perishable sample through a tiny magnifying glass. Its lens, no bigger than a small raindrop, magnified objects hundreds of times. Leeuwenhoek had made it himself; nobody else had one so powerful. The learned men in London were still trying to verify Leeuwenhoek's earlier claims that unseen "animalcules" lived by the millions in a single drop of lake water and even in French wine. Now he had something more delicate to report: Human semen contained animalcules too. "Sometimes more than a thousand," he wrote, "in an amount of material the size of a grain of sand." Pressing the glass to his eye like a jeweler, Leeuwenhoek watched his own animalcules swim about, lashing their long tails. One imagines sunlight falling through leaded windows on a face lost in contemplation, as in the Vermeers. One feels for his wife.

Leeuwenhoek became a bit obsessed after that. Though his tiny peephole gave him privileged access to a never-before-seen microscopic universe, he spent an enormous amount of time looking at spermatozoa, as they're now called. Oddly enough, it was the milt he squeezed from a cod one day that inspired him to estimate, almost casually, just how many people might live on Earth.

Nobody then really had any idea; there were few censuses. Leeuwenhoek started with an estimate that around a million people lived in Holland. Using maps and a little spherical geometry, he calculated that the inhabited land area of the planet was 13,385 times as large as Holland. It was hard to imagine the whole planet being as densely peopled as Holland, which seemed crowded even then. Thus, Leeuwenhoek concluded triumphantly, there couldn't be more than 13.385 billion

people on Earth—a small number indeed compared with the 150 billion sperm cells of a single codfish! This cheerful little calculation, writes population biologist Joel Cohen in his book *How Many People Can the Earth Support?*, may have been the first attempt to give a quantitative answer to a question that has become far more pressing now than it was in the 17th century. Most answers these days are far from cheerful.

Historians now estimate that in Leeuwenhoek's day there were only half a billion or so humans on Earth. After rising very slowly for millennia, the number was just starting to take off. A century and a half later, when another scientist reported the discovery of human egg cells, the world's population had doubled to more than a billion. A century after that, around 1930, it had doubled again to two billion. The acceleration since then has been astounding. Before the 20th century, no human had lived through a doubling of the human population, but there are people alive today who have seen it triple. Sometime in late 2011, according to the UN Population Division, there will be seven billion of us.

And the explosion, though it is slowing, is far from over. Not only are people living longer, but so many women across the world are now in their childbearing years—1.8 billion—that the global population will keep growing for another few decades at least, even though each woman is having fewer children than she would have had a generation ago. By 2050 the total number could reach 10.5 billion, or it could stop at eight billion—the difference is about one child per woman. UN demographers consider the middle road their best estimate: They now project that the population may reach nine billion before 2050—in 2045. The eventual tally will depend on the choices individual couples make when they engage in that most intimate of human acts, the one Leeuwenhoek interrupted so carelessly for the sake of science.

With the population still growing by about 80 million each year, it's hard not to be alarmed. Right now on Earth, water tables are falling, soil is eroding, glaciers are melting, and fish stocks are vanishing. Close to a billion people go hungry each day. Decades from now, there will likely be two billion more mouths to feed, mostly in poor countries. There will be billions more people wanting and deserving to boost themselves out of poverty. If they follow the path blazed by wealthy countries—clearing forests, burning coal and oil, freely scattering fertilizers and pesticides—they too will be stepping hard on the planet's natural resources. How exactly is this going to work?

There may be some comfort in knowing that people have long been alarmed about population. From the beginning, says French demographer Hervé Le Bras, demography has been steeped in talk of the apocalypse. Some of the field's founding papers were written just a few years after Leeuwenhoek's discovery by Sir William Petty, a founder of the Royal Society. He estimated that world population would double six times by the Last Judgment, which was expected in about 2,000 years. At that point it would exceed 20 billion people—more, Petty thought, than the planet could feed. "And then, according to the prediction of the Scriptures, there must be wars, and great slaughter, &c.," he wrote.

As religious forecasts of the world's end receded, Le Bras argues, population growth itself provided an ersatz mechanism of apocalypse. "It crystallized the ancient fear, and perhaps the ancient hope, of the end of days," he writes. In 1798 Thomas Malthus, an English priest and economist, enunciated his general law of population: that it necessarily grows faster than the food supply, until war, disease, and famine arrive to reduce the number of people. As it turned out, the last plagues great enough to put a dent in global population had already happened when Malthus wrote. World population hasn't fallen, historians think, since the Black Death of the 14th century.

In the two centuries after Malthus declared that population couldn't continue to soar, that's exactly what it did. The process started in what we now call the developed countries, which were then still developing. The spread of New World crops like corn and the potato, along with the discovery of chemical fertilizers, helped banish starvation in Europe. Growing cities remained cesspools of disease at first, but from the mid-19th century on, sewers began to channel human waste away from drinking water, which was then filtered and chlorinated; that dramatically reduced the spread of cholera and typhus.

Moreover in 1798, the same year that Malthus published his dyspeptic tract, his compatriot Edward Jenner described a vaccine for smallpox—the first and most important in a series of vaccines and antibiotics that, along with better nutrition and sanitation, would double life expectancy in the industrializing countries, from 35 years to 77 today. It would take a cranky person to see that trend as gloomy: "The development of medical science was the straw that broke the camel's back," wrote Stanford population biologist Paul Ehrlich in 1968.

Ehrlich's book, *The Population Bomb,* made him the most famous of modern Malthusians. In the 1970s, Ehrlich predicted, "hundreds of millions of people are going to starve to death," and it was too late to do anything about it. "The cancer of population growth . . . must be cut out," Ehrlich wrote, "by compulsion if voluntary methods fail." The very future of the United States was at risk. In spite or perhaps because of such language, the book was a best seller, as Malthus's had been. And this time too the bomb proved a dud. The green revolution—a combination of high-yield seeds, irrigation, pesticides, and fertilizers

that enabled grain production to double—was already under way. Today many people are undernourished, but mass starvation is rare.

Ehrlich was right, though, that population would surge as medical science spared many lives. After World War II the developing countries got a sudden transfusion of preventive care, with the help of institutions like the World Health Organization and UNICEF. Penicillin, the smallpox vaccine, DDT (which, though later controversial, saved millions from dying of malaria)—all arrived at once. In India life expectancy went from 38 years in 1952 to 64 today; in China, from 41 to 73. Millions of people in developing countries who would have died in childhood survived to have children themselves. That's why the population explosion spread around the planet: because a great many people were saved from dying.

And because, for a time, women kept giving birth at a high rate. In 18th-century Europe or early 20th-century Asia, when the average woman had six children, she was doing what it took to replace herself and her mate, because most of those children never reached adulthood. When child mortality declines, couples eventually have fewer children—but that transition usually takes a generation at the very least. Today in developed countries, an average of 2.1 births per woman would maintain a steady population; in the developing world, "replacement fertility" is somewhat higher. In the time it takes for the birthrate to settle into that new balance with the death rate, population explodes.

Demographers call this evolution the demographic transition. All countries go through it in their own time. It's a hallmark of human progress: In a country that has completed the transition, people have wrested from nature at least some control over death and birth. The global population explosion is an inevitable side effect, a huge one that some people are not sure our civilization can survive. But the growth rate was actually at its peak just as Ehrlich was sounding his alarm. By the early 1970s, fertility rates around the world had begun dropping faster than anyone had anticipated. Since then, the population growth rate has fallen by more than 40 percent.

The fertility decline that is now sweeping the planet started at different times in different countries. France was one of the first. By the early 18th century, noblewomen at the French court were knowing carnal pleasures without bearing more than two children. They often relied on the same method Leeuwenhoek used for his studies: withdrawal, or coitus interruptus. Village parish records show the trend had spread to the peasantry by the late 18th century; by the end of the 19th, fertility in France had fallen to three children per woman—without the help of modern contraceptives. The key innovation was conceptual, not contraceptive, says Gilles Pison of the National Institute for Demographic Studies in Paris. Until the Enlightenment, "the number of children you had, it was God who decided. People couldn't fathom that it might be up to them."

Other countries in the West eventually followed France's lead. By the onset of World War II, fertility had fallen close to the replacement level in parts of Europe and the United States. Then, after the surprising blip known as the baby boom, came the bust, again catching demographers off guard. They assumed some instinct would lead women to keep having enough children to ensure the survival of the species. Instead, in country after developed country, the fertility rate fell below replacement level. In the late 1990s in Europe it fell to 1.4. "The evidence I'm familiar with, which is anecdotal, is that women couldn't care less about replacing the species," Joel Cohen says.

The end of a baby boom can have two big economic effects on a country. The first is the "demographic dividend"—a blissful few decades when the boomers swell the labor force and the number of young and old dependents is relatively small, and there is thus a lot of money for other things. Then the second effect kicks in: The boomers start to retire. What had been considered the enduring demographic order is revealed to be a party that has to end. The sharpening American debate over Social Security and last year's strikes in France over increasing the retirement age are responses to a problem that exists throughout the developed world: how to support an aging population. "In 2050 will there be enough people working to pay for pensions?" asks Frans Willekens, director of the Netherlands Interdisciplinary Demographic Institute in The Hague. "The answer is no."

In industrialized countries it took generations for fertility to fall to the replacement level or below. As that same transition takes place in the rest of the world, what has astonished demographers is how much faster it is happening there. Though its population continues to grow, China, home to a fifth of the world's people, is already below replacement fertility and has been for nearly 20 years, thanks in part to the coercive one-child policy implemented in 1979; Chinese women, who were bearing an average of six children each as recently as 1965, are now having around 1.5. In Iran, with the support of the Islamic regime, fertility has fallen more than 70 percent since the early '80s. In Catholic and democratic Brazil, women have reduced their fertility rate by half over the same quarter century. "We still don't understand why fertility has gone down so fast in so many societies, so many cultures and religions. It's just mind-boggling," says Hania Zlotnik, director of the UN Population Division.

"At this moment, much as I want to say there's still a problem of high fertility rates, it's only about 16 percent of the world population, mostly in Africa," says Zlotnik. South of the Sahara, fertility is still five children per woman; in Niger it is seven. But then, 17 of the countries in the region still have life expectancies of 50 or less; they have just begun the demographic transition. In most of the world, however, family size has shrunk dramatically. The UN projects that the world will reach replacement fertility by 2030. "The population as a whole is on a path toward nonexplosion—which is good news," Zlotnik says.

The bad news is that 2030 is two decades away and that the largest generation of adolescents in history will then be entering their childbearing years. Even if each of those women has only two children, population will coast upward under its own momentum for another quarter century. Is a train wreck in the offing, or will people then be able to live humanely and in a way that doesn't destroy their environment? One thing is certain: Close to one in six of them will live in India.

> I have understood the population explosion intellectually for a long time. I came to understand it emotionally one stinking hot night in Delhi a couple of years ago. . . . The temperature was well over 100, and the air was a haze of dust and smoke. The streets seemed alive with people. People eating, people washing, people sleeping. People visiting, arguing, and screaming. People thrusting their hands through the taxi window, begging. People defecating and urinating. People clinging to buses. People herding animals. People, people, people, people.
>
> —Paul Ehrlich

In 1966, when Ehrlich took that taxi ride, there were around half a billion Indians. There are 1.2 billion now. Delhi's population has increased even faster, to around 22 million, as people have flooded in from small towns and villages and crowded into sprawling shantytowns. Early last June in the stinking hot city, the summer monsoon had not yet arrived to wash the dust from the innumerable construction sites, which only added to the dust that blows in from the deserts of Rajasthan. On the new divided highways that funnel people into the unplanned city, oxcarts were heading the wrong way in the fast lane. Families of four cruised on motorbikes, the women's scarves flapping like vivid pennants, toddlers dangling from their arms. Families of a dozen or more sardined themselves into buzzing, bumblebee-colored auto rickshaws designed for two passengers. In the stalled traffic, amputees and wasted little children cried for alms. Delhi today is boomingly different from the city Ehrlich visited, and it is also very much the same.

At Lok Nayak Hospital, on the edge of the chaotic and densely peopled nest of lanes that is Old Delhi, a human tide flows through the entrance gate every morning and crowds inside on the lobby floor. "Who could see this and not be worried about the population of India?" a surgeon named Chandan Bortamuly asked one afternoon as he made his way toward his vasectomy clinic. "Population is our biggest problem." Removing the padlock from the clinic door, Bortamuly stepped into a small operating room. Inside, two men lay stretched out on examination tables, their testicles poking up through holes in the green sheets. A ceiling fan pushed cool air from two window units around the room.

Bortamuly is on the front lines of a battle that has been going on in India for nearly 60 years. In 1952, just five years after it gained independence from Britain, India became the first country to establish a policy for population control. Since then the government has repeatedly set ambitious goals—and repeatedly missed them by a mile. A national policy adopted in 2000 called for the country to reach the replacement fertility of 2.1 by 2010. That won't happen for at least another decade. In the

UN's medium projection, India's population will rise to just over 1.6 billion people by 2050. "What's inevitable is that India is going to exceed the population of China by 2030," says A. R. Nanda, former head of the Population Foundation of India, an advocacy group. "Nothing less than a huge catastrophe, nuclear or otherwise, can change that."

Sterilization is the dominant form of birth control in India today, and the vast majority of the procedures are performed on women. The government is trying to change that; a no-scalpel vasectomy costs far less and is easier on a man than a tubal ligation is on a woman. In the operating theater Bortamuly worked quickly. "They say the needle pricks like an ant bite," he explained, when the first patient flinched at the local anesthetic. "After that it's basically painless, bloodless surgery." Using the pointed tip of a forceps, Bortamuly made a tiny hole in the skin of the scrotum and pulled out an oxbow of white, stringy vas deferens—the sperm conduit from the patient's right testicle. He tied off both ends of the oxbow with fine black thread, snipped them, and pushed them back under the skin. In less than seven minutes—a nurse timed him—the patient was walking out without so much as a Band-Aid. The government will pay him an incentive fee of 1,100 rupees (around $25), a week's wages for a laborer.

The Indian government tried once before to push vasectomies, in the 1970s, when anxiety about the population bomb was at its height. Prime Minister Indira Gandhi and her son Sanjay used state-of-emergency powers to force a dramatic increase in sterilizations. From 1976 to 1977 the number of operations tripled, to more than eight million. Over six million of those were vasectomies. Family planning workers were pressured to meet quotas; in a few states, sterilization became a condition for receiving new housing or other government benefits. In some cases the police simply rounded up poor people and hauled them to sterilization camps.

The excesses gave the whole concept of family planning a bad name. "Successive governments refused to touch the subject," says Shailaja Chandra, former head of the National Population Stabilisation Fund (NPSF). Yet fertility in India has dropped anyway, though not as fast as in China, where it was nose-diving even before the draconian one-child policy took effect. The national average in India is now 2.6 children per woman, less than half what it was when Ehrlich visited. The southern half of the country and a few states in the northern half are already at replacement fertility or below.

In Kerala, on the southwest coast, investments in health and education helped fertility fall to 1.7. The key, demographers there say, is the female literacy rate: At around 90 percent, it's easily the highest in India. Girls who go to school start having children later than ones who don't. They are more open to contraception and more likely to understand their options.

So far this approach, held up as a model internationally, has not caught on in the poor states of northern India—in the "Hindi belt" that stretches across the country just south of Delhi. Nearly half of India's population growth is occurring in Rajasthan, Madhya Pradesh, Bihar, and Uttar Pradesh, where fertility rates still hover between three and four children per woman. More than half the women in the Hindi belt are illiterate, and many marry well before reaching the legal age of 18. They gain social status by bearing children—and usually don't stop until they have at least one son.

As an alternative to the Kerala model, some point to the southern state of Andhra Pradesh, where sterilization "camps"—temporary operating rooms often set up in schools—were introduced during the '70s and where sterilization rates have remained high as improved hospitals have replaced the camps. In a single decade beginning in the early 1990s, the fertility rate fell from around three to less than two. Unlike in Kerala, half of all women in Andhra Pradesh remain illiterate.

Amarjit Singh, the current executive director of the NPSF, calculates that if the four biggest states of the Hindi belt had followed the Andhra Pradesh model, they would have avoided 40 million births—and considerable suffering. "Because 40 million were born, 2.5 million children died," Singh says. He thinks if all India were to adopt high-quality programs to encourage sterilizations, in hospitals rather than camps, it could have 1.4 billion people in 2050 instead of 1.6 billion.

Critics of the Andhra Pradesh model, such as the Population Foundation's Nanda, say Indians need better health care, particularly in rural areas. They are against numerical targets that pressure government workers to sterilize people or cash incentives that distort a couple's choice of family size. "It's a private decision," Nanda says.

In Indian cities today, many couples are making the same choice as their counterparts in Europe or America. Sonalde Desai, a senior fellow at New Delhi's National Council of Applied Economic Research, introduced me to five working women in Delhi who were spending most of their salaries on private-school fees and after-school tutors; each had one or two children and was not planning to have more. In a nationwide survey of 41,554 households, Desai's team identified a small but growing vanguard of urban one-child families. "We were totally blown away at the emphasis parents were placing on their children," she says. "It suddenly makes you understand—that is why fertility is going down." Indian children on average are much better educated than their parents.

That's less true in the countryside. With Desai's team I went to Palanpur, a village in Uttar Pradesh—a Hindi-belt state with as many people as Brazil. Walking into the village we passed a cell phone tower but also rivulets of raw sewage running along the lanes of small brick houses. Under a mango tree, the keeper of the grove said he saw no reason to educate his three daughters. Under a neem tree in the center of the village, I asked a dozen farmers what would improve their lives most. "If we could get a little money, that would be wonderful," one joked.

The goal in India should not be reducing fertility or population, Almas Ali of the Population Foundation told me when I spoke to him a few days later. "The goal should be to make the villages livable," he said. "Whenever we talk of population in India, even today, what comes to our mind is the increasing numbers. And the numbers are looked at with fright. This phobia has penetrated the mind-set so much that all the focus is on reducing the number. The focus on people has been pushed to the background."

It was a four-hour drive back to Delhi from Palanpur, through the gathering night of a Sunday. We sat in traffic in one market town after another, each one hopping with activity that sometimes engulfed the car. As we came down a viaduct into Moradabad, I saw a man pushing a cart up the steep hill, piled with a load so large it blocked his view. I thought of Ehrlich's epiphany on his cab ride all those decades ago. People, people, people, people—yes. But also an overwhelming sense of energy, of striving, of aspiration.

The annual meeting of the Population Association of America (PAA) is one of the premier gatherings of the world's demographers. Last April the global population explosion was not on the agenda. "The problem has become a bit passé," Hervé Le Bras says. Demographers are generally confident that by the second half of this century we will be ending one unique era in history—the population explosion—and entering another, in which population will level out or even fall.

But will there be too many of us? At the PAA meeting, in the Dallas Hyatt Regency, I learned that the current population of the planet could fit into the state of Texas, if Texas were settled as densely as New York City. The comparison made me start thinking like Leeuwenhoek. If in 2045 there are nine billion people living on the six habitable continents, the world population density will be a little more than half that of France today. France is not usually considered a hellish place. Will the world be hellish then?

Some parts of it may well be; some parts of it are hellish today. There are now 21 cities with populations larger than ten million, and by 2050 there will be many more. Delhi adds hundreds of thousands of migrants each year, and those people arrive to find that "no plans have been made for water, sewage, or habitation," says Shailaja Chandra. Dhaka in Bangladesh and Kinshasa in the Democratic Republic of the Congo are 40 times larger today than they were in 1950. Their slums are filled with desperately poor people who have fled worse poverty in the countryside.

Whole countries today face population pressures that seem as insurmountable to us as India's did to Ehrlich in 1966. Bangladesh is among the most densely populated countries in the world and one of the most immediately threatened by climate change; rising seas could displace tens of millions of Bangladeshis. Rwanda is an equally alarming case. In his book *Collapse,* Jared Diamond argued that the genocidal massacre of some 800,000 Rwandans in 1994 was the result of several factors, not only ethnic hatred but also overpopulation—too many farmers dividing the same amount of land into increasingly small pieces that became inadequate to support a farmer's family. "Malthus's worst-case scenario may sometimes be realized," Diamond concluded.

Many people are justifiably worried that Malthus will finally be proved right on a global scale—that the planet won't be able to feed nine billion people. Lester Brown, founder of Worldwatch Institute and now head of the Earth Policy Institute in Washington, believes food shortages could cause a collapse of global civilization. Human beings are living off natural capital, Brown argues, eroding soil and depleting groundwater faster than they can be replenished. All of that will soon be cramping food production. Brown's Plan B to save civilization would put the whole world on a wartime footing, like the United States after Pearl Harbor, to stabilize climate and repair the ecological damage. "Filling the family planning gap may be the most urgent item on the global agenda," he writes, so if we don't hold the world's population to eight billion by reducing fertility, the death rate may increase instead.

Eight billion corresponds to the UN's lowest projection for 2050. In that optimistic scenario, Bangladesh has a fertility rate of 1.35 in 2050, but it still has 25 million more people than it does today. Rwanda's fertility rate also falls below the replacement level, but its population still rises to well over twice what it was before the genocide. If that's the optimistic scenario, one might argue, the future is indeed bleak.

But one can also draw a different conclusion—that fixating on population numbers is not the best way to confront the future. People packed into slums need help, but the problem that needs solving is poverty and lack of infrastructure, not overpopulation. Giving every woman access to family planning services is a good idea—"the one strategy that can make the biggest difference to women's lives," Chandra calls it. But the most aggressive population control program imaginable will not save Bangladesh from sea level rise, Rwanda from another genocide, or all of us from our enormous environmental problems.

Global warming is a good example. Carbon emissions from fossil fuels are growing fastest in China, thanks to its prolonged economic boom, but fertility there is already below replacement; not much more can be done to control population. Where population is growing fastest, in sub-Saharan Africa, emissions per person are only a few percent of what they are in the United States—so population control would have little effect on climate. Brian O'Neill of the National Center for Atmospheric Research has calculated that if the population were to reach 7.4 billion in 2050 instead of 8.9 billion, it would reduce emissions by 15 percent. "Those who say the whole problem is population are wrong," Joel Cohen says. "It's not even the dominant factor." To stop global warming we'll have to switch from fossil fuels to alternative energy—regardless of how big the population gets.

The number of people does matter, of course. But how people consume resources matters a lot more. Some of us leave much bigger footprints than others. The central challenge for the future of people and the planet is how to raise more of us out of poverty—the slum dwellers in Delhi, the subsistence farmers in Rwanda—while reducing the impact each of us has on the planet.

The World Bank has predicted that by 2030 more than a billion people in the developing world will belong to the "global middle class," up from just 400 million in 2005. That's a good thing. But it will be a hard thing for the planet if those people are eating meat and driving gasoline-powered cars at the same rate as Americans now do. It's too late to keep the new middle class of 2030 from being born; it's not too late to change how they and the rest of us will produce and consume food and energy. "Eating less meat seems more reasonable to me than saying, 'Have fewer children!'" Le Bras says.

How many people can the Earth support? Cohen spent years reviewing all the research, from Leeuwenhoek on. "I wrote the book thinking I would answer the question," he says. "I found out it's unanswerable in the present state of knowledge." What he found instead was an enormous range of "political numbers, intended to persuade people" one way or the other.

For centuries population pessimists have hurled apocalyptic warnings at the congenital optimists, who believe in their bones that humanity will find ways to cope and even improve its lot. History, on the whole, has so far favored the optimists, but history is no certain guide to the future. Neither is science. It cannot predict the outcome of *People* v. *Planet,* because all the facts of the case—how many of us there will be and how we will live—depend on choices we have yet to make and ideas we have yet to have. We may, for example, says Cohen, "see to it that all children are nourished well enough to learn in school and are educated well enough to solve the problems they will face as adults." That would change the future significantly.

The debate was present at the creation of population alarmism, in the person of Rev. Thomas Malthus himself. Toward the end of the book in which he formulated the iron law by which unchecked population growth leads to famine, he declared that law a good thing: It gets us off our duffs. It leads us to conquer the world. Man, Malthus wrote, and he must have meant woman too, is "inert, sluggish, and averse from labour, unless compelled by necessity." But necessity, he added, gives hope:

"The exertions that men find it necessary to make, in order to support themselves or families, frequently awaken faculties that might otherwise have lain for ever dormant, and it has been commonly remarked that new and extraordinary situations generally create minds adequate to grapple with the difficulties in which they are involved."

Seven billion of us soon, nine billion in 2045. Let's hope that Malthus was right about our ingenuity.

Critical Thinking

1. What is the demographic transition?

2. What is the relationship between Malthusian theory and the growth of the world's population? Is Malthus correct?

3. Why is the population in the Northern part of the globe more prosperous than the population in the Southern part of the globe?

Test-Your-Knowledge Form

We encourage you to photocopy and use this page as a tool to assess how the articles in *Annual Editions* expand on the information in your textbook. By reflecting on the articles you will gain enhanced text information. You can also access this useful form on a product's book support website at www.mhhe.com/cls

NAME: DATE:

_____

TITLE AND NUMBER OF ARTICLE:

_____

BRIEFLY STATE THE MAIN IDEA OF THIS ARTICLE:

_____

LIST THREE IMPORTANT FACTS THAT THE AUTHOR USES TO SUPPORT THE MAIN IDEA:

_____

WHAT INFORMATION OR IDEAS DISCUSSED IN THIS ARTICLE ARE ALSO DISCUSSED IN YOUR TEXTBOOK OR OTHER READINGS THAT YOU HAVE DONE? LIST THE TEXTBOOK CHAPTERS AND PAGE NUMBERS:

_____

LIST ANY EXAMPLES OF BIAS OR FAULTY REASONING THAT YOU FOUND IN THE ARTICLE:

_____

LIST ANY NEW TERMS/CONCEPTS THAT WERE DISCUSSED IN THE ARTICLE, AND WRITE A SHORT DEFINITION: